# SHARED BEGINNINGS,
# DIVERGENT LIVES

# SHARED BEGINNINGS, DIVERGENT LIVES

## DELINQUENT BOYS TO AGE 70

JOHN H. LAUB

ROBERT J. SAMPSON

HARVARD UNIVERSITY PRESS

Cambridge, Massachusetts, and London, England   2003

*Library of Congress Cataloging-in-Publication Data*

Laub, John H.
Shared beginnings, divergent lives : delinquent boys to age 70 /
John H. Laub, Robert J. Sampson.
   p.   cm.
Includes bibliographical references and index.
ISBN 0-674-01191-0 (alk. paper)
1. Juvenile delinquency. 2. Juvenile delinquency—United States—Longitudinal studies.
3. Criminal behavior—United States—Longitudinal studies. I. Sampson, Robert J.
II. Title.

HV9069.L28  2003
364.36'0973—dc21      2003050944

# CONTENTS

Acknowledgments    *vii*

**1**  Diverging Pathways of Troubled Boys    *1*

**2**  Persistence or Desistance?    *13*

**3**  Explaining the Life Course of Crime    *36*

**4**  Finding the Men    *61*

**5**  Long-Term Trajectories of Crime    *81*

**6**  Why Some Offenders Stop    *114*

**7**  Why Some Offenders Persist    *150*

**8**  Zigzag Criminal Careers    *196*

**9**  Modeling Change in Crime    *250*

**10**  Rethinking Lives in and out of Crime    *275*

Notes    *297*

References    *313*

Index    *333*

# ACKNOWLEDGMENTS

The making of a book often takes longer than planned, and this one has been no exception. It is a pleasure to acknowledge those who have helped us over the years from the time of the book's conception to its actual birth.

First, and without any doubt, we dedicate this book to the subjects of our follow-up inquiry. The "Glueck men," as we came to call them, spent long hours talking to us, listening, and opening up their homes to visits. Even the men whose cooperation was not easily obtained or whose behavior repelled us were fundamental to our enterprise. Quite simply, as a whole the Glueck men are the centerpiece of this book, and we thank them for their participation. It is our hope that the insights offered here will matter to them and perhaps even, in some small way, help make sense of their lives—both the struggles and the victories alike.

Several students assisted us with data collection, coding, data management, and other aspects of the large-scale follow-up study in Boston. Special thanks go to Suzanne Armfield-Anderson, Curtis Gannon, Chris Kenaszchuk, Roni Mayzer, Jessica Miller, Jinney Smith, and Lara Suziedialis. It is hard to imagine where we would have been without the help of these individuals. With the data in hand, Sandra Gauvreau at the University of Chicago and Elaine Eggleston, Andrew Ditchfield, and Melissa Reimer at the University of Maryland deserve kudos for their painstaking work. Elaine, in particular, has worked hard on the project for the last five years and deserves special recognition for performing a myriad of tasks with care, thoughtfulness, and good humor.

Over the course of this project, we taught seminars on crime and the life course at the University of Maryland and the University of Chicago, respectively. We wish to thank all of the graduate students who took these courses and provided challenges to our thinking.

Barbara Mawn merits a huge thank you for her wonderful transcription of interviews that often contained background noise, crude remarks, and tales of despair.

In addition, several state and local institutions provided invaluable assistance in our efforts to follow up the Glueck men. We wish to thank the Boston Police Department, especially Timothy Murray; the Office of the Commissioner of Probation, especially Don Cochran and Ron Corbett; the Massachusetts Department of Corrections, especially Mike Shively and Jen Dolan; and the Massachusetts Department of Parole, especially Tina Hurley and Richard Lunden.

We also received an unusual amount of institutional support from Northeastern University, especially from Jamie Fox, Bob Croatti, and Jack McDevitt; the Murray Research Center, especially from Anne Colby, Jackie James, Erin Phelps, and Mette Sorenson; the Harvard Medical School, specifically from George Vaillant, Robin Western, and Tim Davis; the University of Chicago; the University of Maryland, especially from Larry Sherman and Charles Wellford; and the Center for Advanced Study in the Behavioral Sciences, especially from Kathleen Much.

Of course, all of this would not be possible without some cold, hard cash. A hearty thanks to our funders, the Harry Frank Guggenheim Foundation, the Russell Sage Foundation, the Murray Research Center, and the National Institute of Justice. Without Winnie Reed's help at the National Institute of Justice, the Glueck project as we know it would not exist.

Over the last decade, a number of colleagues gave us good advice and made this work better and stronger in the process. Although we did not always agree with them, we want to warmly thank the following individuals: Avshalom Caspi, Glen Elder, Michael Gottfredson, John Hagan, Travis Hirschi, Terrie Moffitt, Daniel Nagin, Raymond Paternoster, Stephen Raudenbush, and George Vaillant.

From *Crime in the Making* to the present, Michael Aronson at Harvard University Press has been a huge believer in our long-term project. We thank him for his continuing support, along with others at the Press, especially our manuscript editor, Elizabeth Gilbert, who helped make the final product as good as it is.

Finally, we thank our families for supporting our efforts and putting up with interminable dialogue over the issues raised in this book. No matter how obsessed we seemed, they believed strongly in the project, often with a large dose of needed humor.

We are grateful to the following journals and publishers for allowing us to use, in part and in revised form, materials published elsewhere: John H. Laub and Robert J. Sampson, "Understanding Desistance from Crime," in *Crime and Justice: A Review of Research,* vol. 28, edited by Michael Tonry (Chicago: University of Chicago Press, 2001; © 2001 by The University of Chicago, all rights reserved), pp. 1–69; and Robert J. Sampson and John H. Laub, "Life-Course Desisters? Trajectories of Crime among Delinquent Boys Followed to Age 70," *Criminology* 41, no. 3 (August 2003).

## A Note on Confidentiality

For all of the life-history narratives we present here, identifying dates (for example, birthdays and marriages) and other potentially revealing information (for example, addresses) have been altered in order to protect the confidentiality of the research subjects. All names are pseudonyms.

# SHARED BEGINNINGS,
# DIVERGENT LIVES

# CHAPTER ONE

# Diverging Pathways
# of Troubled Boys

When asked to assess his life at age 65, Arthur answered, "What am I? What do you look at? Nothing. A piece of shit."

Michael at age 63 was asked the same question. He responded, "What I done here is a success story. I have no education whatsoever. I have no grammar school. No high school. No nothing. In plain English I done all the shit jobs, because I had no education . . . My life now is beautiful. Raised five kids. No education. Worked every day in my life. Whenever I lost one job, I got another. No, I think I done pretty goddamn good."

Such divergent life outcomes are not considered surprising in our culture, because they are commonly thought to evolve from divergent childhood backgrounds. As it turns out, this belief is unwarranted. When the lives of Arthur and Michael are examined in more depth, we find that both men had remarkably similar beginnings. For example, both men grew up in Boston, Massachusetts, during the Great Depression, both lived in disadvantaged neighborhoods, both had difficult family and school experiences, and perhaps most important, both were early juvenile delinquents and incarcerated for their crimes in state reform schools. What accounts for their different adult trajectories? A consideration of these men's lives only deepens the mystery.

Arthur grew up in an Italian neighborhood in a poor section of East Boston. This neighborhood was overcrowded, with more than its fair share of barrooms and street gangs. Arthur was one of thirteen children. His father died when he was four years old, and his mother was unable to manage the children. Furthermore, Arthur did not do well in school and was frequently truant. He was eventually placed in a "special class." Arthur scored 72 on the full-scale Wechsler-Bellevue Intelligence test, with scores of 63 and 87 for the verbal and performance portions, respectively. With this kind of background, perhaps it is no surprise to learn that Arthur was extensively involved in delinquency during his childhood and adolescence. His first arrest came at age 9 for setting off false fire alarms. He was arrested a total of twelve times as a juvenile (up to age 17 in Massachusetts) and spent close to two years in reform schools. Most of his arrests were for larceny. In addition, reports from his mother indicate that he began keeping late hours at age 8, smoking at age 10, and running away at age 11. As Arthur's experience makes clear, the early onset of delinquency is nothing new.

Like Arthur, Michael grew up in a poor section of Boston, an Irish neighborhood in Dorchester south of downtown. Coming from a family much smaller than Arthur's, Michael had one brother and two sisters. His father was a "heavy drinker" and Michael recalled that his father would "take his pay every week and blow it at the track." During Michael's childhood and early adolescence, his family moved excessively (he moved twelve times prior to age 12). Like Arthur, Michael had a particularly difficult time with school. His mother reported that "he hated school from the first day." Michael repeated second grade several times, and eventually he too was placed in a "special class." He scored an 89 on the full-scale Wechsler-Bellevue Intelligence test, a 74 on the verbal test, and a 106 on the performance test. Like Arthur, Michael's involvement in delinquent activities began at a young age, 6 and 7 years old. In his early years he was involved in smoking, truancy, running away, petty theft, and setting off false alarms. The most serious offense consisted of performing sexual favors for small sums of money. Michael and his friends would hang out in bus stations, train stations, and movie theaters and solicit customers. He was arrested five times as a juvenile and was incarcerated for the first time at age 10. As a juvenile, he served more than two years in reform school.

We interviewed Arthur in his apartment in East Boston. He was 65 years old at the time. Since age 55, Arthur has lived alone in a public housing building for low-income residents in a seedy area. The neighborhood is well known for drug dealing and prostitution. During his adult life, Arthur worked on and off—"cabbing"—for about forty years. On some days Arthur made out pretty well. Much of the income he obtained, moreover, was under the table and never claimed for purposes of income tax. But Arthur also experienced several bouts of unemployment. When we interviewed him, he was living on welfare and his current source of income was social security (SSI). Arthur never served in the military. He told us that he was rejected because he had "flat feet." Independent information, however, indicates that he was rejected for Selective Service because of his criminal record. Arthur was married twice with both marriages ending in divorce. At the age of 57, Arthur became a father for the fifth time when his girlfriend gave birth. When we interviewed Arthur he was not in good physical or mental health. Arthur reported that he had had three-quarters of his stomach removed at age 50 because of ulcers. At the time of our interview, he was taking Paxil for stress. He also smoked four to five packs of cigarettes a day.

As an adult, Arthur had an extensive criminal record, including an astonishing forty-five arrests. He was incarcerated in prison or jail on average thirty-nine days per year over his lifetime. Included in his criminal record were arrests for robbery, assault and battery, including threats on his wife, and indecent assault and battery on a child under the age of 14. At the time of our interview, Arthur was in the midst of a five-year custody dispute involving his son and his girlfriend, a case involving charges and countercharges of physical abuse.

Michael's adult experience could not be more different. We interviewed Michael in his home in Lawrence, Massachusetts, a small city about thirty miles north of Boston. He and his wife plus one of their five children have lived in this house for seven years. Michael has been married forty years to the same woman. During his early adult years, Michael served a seven-year stint in the U.S. Army. Michael enlisted in the Army without either the knowledge or the permission of his parole officer. Apparently he did well in the service, and by the time of his discharge he had obtained the rank of corporal. Michael was also awarded a Purple Heart. Although it was not until much later, Michael used the G.I. Bill to help purchase the house he was living in when we interviewed him. Michael worked virtually all of his adult life at a variety of jobs, mainly in factories. For the last twenty-five years, Michael had worked in security, fifteen of those years as a supervisor. Although he had retired about nine months before our interview, he was moonlighting as a security guard at a local hospital. A year before our interview, Michael had undergone surgery to relieve a blockage in an artery. About three to four years earlier, he had been diagnosed with diabetes. In response to this diagnosis, Michael stopped drinking, but he continues to smoke about a pack and a half of cigarettes a day.

To be sure, there are some differences between Arthur and Michael despite their generally similar backgrounds. Arthur was raised in a large family (thirteen children) by a single parent, while Michael was one of four children raised by two parents. Moreover, Arthur's overall IQ score was lower than Michael's. But while large family size, being raised by single parents, and low IQ scores are related to adolescent delinquency, we have found that these factors do not account for later differences in *adult* outcomes (see, for example, Laub, Nagin, and Sampson 1998). We are left with the question: what accounts for the radically different adult lives of these two men?

### Making Sense of Lives

Our aim in this book is to understand the lives of Arthur and Michael and many others like them. More specifically, we try to account for patterns of criminal offending and many other behaviors over the full life course of high-risk children. The question of behavioral change and stability within individuals over the life span is virtually uncharted territory in criminology and the social sciences at large. In addressing this topic, we reject several popular notions. For one, we reject the idea that childhood experiences such as early involvement in antisocial behavior, growing up in poverty, and woeful school performance are sturdy markers for predicting long-term patterns of offending. In a similar vein, we reject the notion that individual "traits" such as poor verbal skills, low self-control, and difficult temperament can explain long-term patterns of juvenile delinquents. From our perspective, in order to explain longitudinal patterns of offending, data are needed on childhood, adolescence, *and* adulthood experiences.

We also reject the popular idea that offenders can be neatly grouped into distinct categories, each displaying a unique trajectory and etiology of offending. We believe such approaches reify the idea of offender groups and ignore the instability of categorizations over time.

Consistent with this belief, our aim is to examine criminal and deviant offending as a general process, with the goal of using both quantitative and qualitative data to explicate the pathways to persistent offending and desistance over the full life course.[1]

### *Crime in the Making* and the Origins of Life-Course Criminology

This book builds directly upon our earlier work, *Crime in the Making: Pathways and Turning Points through Life* (1993), where we developed and tested a theory of crime over the life course. In this section we provide a brief description of that work, discuss several challenges to it, and outline its major unanswered questions. We believe that distinguishing this book from our earlier work is crucial, and we want to make clear to those who have already read our previous work why they should continue here. To be candid, while we think *Crime in the Making* was a great start, several significant questions remain unanswered.

Since 1987 we have been involved in a long-term research project using a unique data archive—the *Unraveling Juvenile Delinquency* study and subsequent follow-ups conducted by Sheldon and Eleanor Glueck of the Harvard Law School. This study is considered to be one of the most influential in the history of criminological research. The Gluecks' data were derived from a three-wave prospective study of juvenile and adult criminal behavior that originated with *Unraveling Juvenile Delinquency* (1950; see also Glueck and Glueck, *Delinquents and Nondelinquents in Perspective*, 1968). The research design involved a sample of 500 male delinquents aged 10–17 and 500 male nondelinquents aged 10–17 matched case by case on age, race/ethnicity, IQ, and low-income residence in Boston. Extensive data were collected on the 1,000 boys at three points in time—ages 14, 25, and 32. Over a period of six years (1987–1993), we reconstructed and analyzed the full longitudinal data set, currently housed in the Murray Research Center archive at the Radcliffe Institute of Advanced Study at Harvard University.

In *Crime in the Making,* we developed an age-graded theory of informal social control to explain childhood antisocial behavior, adolescent delinquency, and crime in early adulthood. Our theory emphasized the importance of social ties at all ages across the life course. The organizing principle was that crime and deviance are more likely to occur when an individual's bond to society is weak or broken. We highlighted the role of informal social controls that emerge from the social exchanges and structure of interpersonal bonds that link members of society to one another and to wider institutions such as work, family, school, and community.

The first building block in our life-course theory focused on the mediating role of informal family and school social bonds in explaining child and adolescent delinquency (Sampson and Laub 1993, chaps. 4–5). The second building block incorporated the role of continuity in childhood and adolescent problem behavior that extends into adulthood across a variety of life's domains, such as crime, alcohol abuse, divorce, and unemployment (Sampson and Laub 1993, chap. 6). The third building block examined change in antisocial behavior over time. A fundamental theme of our age-graded theory of informal social control and crime was that while individual traits and childhood experiences are important for understanding behavioral stability, experiences in adolescence and adulthood can redirect criminal trajectories in either a more positive or a more negative manner. Our theory thus incorporated both stability and change in criminal behavior over the life course.

The logical question for us, then, was what factors explain stability and change over the life course? In *Crime in the Making,* we examined the predictors of desistance and persistence in adult crime and violence and found that despite differences in early childhood experiences, adult social bonds to work and family had similar consequences for the life-course trajectories of the 500 delinquents and 500 nondelinquent controls we studied. More precisely, job stability and marital attachment in adulthood were significantly related to changes in adult crime—the stronger the adult ties to work and family, the less crime and deviance among both delinquents and nondelinquent controls (Sampson and Laub 1993, chaps. 7–9). We concluded that "turning points" related to work, marriage, and military service were crucial for understanding processes of continuity and change across the adult life course (see Sampson and Laub 1993, 1996; Laub and Sampson, 1993).

### Challenges and Unresolved Questions

Three major challenges to our work on behavioral change and stability over the life span have appeared.[2] The first challenge comes from developmental theorists such as Terrie Moffitt. Moffitt argues that there are two types of offenders—what she calls the "Life-Course-Persistent" and the "Adolescence-Limiteds," with each offender type displaying a distinct causal pathway to criminal behavior (Moffitt 1993, 1994). A variation of this theme can be found in the work of Gerald Patterson, who identifies two groups of offenders—early and late starters (see Patterson and Yoerger 1993). To a certain degree Rolf Loeber and his colleagues, who offer the idea of three distinct and different pathways to specific types of criminal behavior, use this approach as well (see, for example, Loeber and Hay 1997).[3] When addressing the issue of continuity and change in offending over time, Moffitt contends that the answer lies primarily in the background of the offender. Namely, those with a more severe past are less likely to change. Moffitt writes, "Contemporary continuity arises if the Life-Course-Persistent person continues to carry into adulthood the same underlying constellation of traits that got him in trouble as a child" (1994, 25). So while Moffitt claims that change occurs for adolescence-limited offenders, meaningful within-individual change is evidently not possible for the smaller number of life-course-persistent offenders. Arthur and Michael's lives notwithstanding, persistent childhood troublemakers therefore make for persistent adult criminals according to her theory.

The second major challenge relates to the analytical strategy used in *Crime in the Making*. Daniel Nagin (1999) in particular has argued that focusing on stability and change in behavioral trajectories over the life course requires a dynamic methodological approach. Longitudinal models like those employed in *Crime in the Making* may establish causal order, but they do not necessarily capture the progression of change. Moreover, if researchers like Moffitt are correct, different offenders will display different patterns of stability and change over the life course. Nagin and his colleagues have thus developed an analytical strategy for identifying distinctive offending trajectories—a semi-parametric, group-based approach. This "grouping" technique allows one to group offenders not only by their level of offending, but also by their rate of change in offending over time. We apply these and other dynamic approaches in this book (for example, hierarchical change models), testing their ability to identify meaningful patterns of change in crime.

The third and most important challenge to our work was well articulated by John Modell. Despite our claims to integrate a person-based and a variable-based analysis in *Crime in the Making,* Modell's review concluded that we did not fully meet our objective, that our person-based analysis was "not entirely satisfying." Modell elaborated: "The authors cannot divorce themselves from a variables focus, and they virtually treat their small intensive sample as a microscopic quantitative test of their hypotheses. Nor are they adept at discerning (or portraying) the inner logic of lives as revealed in data such as these" (1994, 1391). Reflecting on this critique, we are compelled by the evidence to agree.

## Analytic Focus

This book is an attempt to address these and other challenges. We do so by presenting and analyzing newly collected data on crime and development up to age 70 for the 500 men who were the original subjects of the classic *Unraveling Juvenile Delinquency* study by the Gluecks (1950). These combined data represent what is arguably the longest longitudinal study of crime in the world. As noted earlier, the boys in the *Unraveling* study were remanded to reform schools in Massachusetts during their adolescence, followed to age 32 by the Gluecks (see Glueck and Glueck 1968), and studied in our previous work (see, for example, Sampson and Laub 1993). This book updates these men's lives at the close of the twentieth century, and connects them to life experiences all the way back to early childhood.

Why should one care about juvenile delinquents who were born during the Great Depression era and were turning 70 at the end of the twentieth century? Because our theoretical focus is on within-individual patterns of stability and change, we turn to a longitudinal study begun many years ago that permits the updating and empirical investigation of various life adaptations over the long term (see also Vaillant 2002). Put differently, to study crime from childhood until age 70 requires the long-term strategy we have employed. Moreover, our results will show that the processes of persistent offending and desistance from crime are surprisingly robust across place and historical time. In the present case the "old" data critique is thus scientifically without merit. We return to these important issues in Chapter 10.

Our goal for this book, then, is to understand and explain the lives of formerly delinquent boys as they progress from childhood to later adulthood, especially patterns of criminal offending and behaviors in other key domains of adult life (for example, work, family, military). In trying to explain continuity and change in crime over the full life span, we assess competing explanations of persistent offending and criminal desistance to discover whether there are in fact unique developmental trajectories as argued by Moffitt and others. We also present a revised conceptualization and integrated life-course theory of persistence in and desistance from crime. We specifically revise our age-graded theory of informal social control by bringing into account the interplay of human agency and choice, situational influences, routine activities, local culture, and historical context.

Our data are original in two ways. One is that we conducted national death record and criminal history searches for all 500 men in the delinquent sample up to age 70. The second and more innovative feature of our study is that we tracked, located, and conducted detailed life-history interviews with 52 men from the original juvenile-delinquent group as they approached age 70. These men had not been contacted in over thirty-five years. Cases were selected on the basis of their trajectories of juvenile and adult offending (for example, "persisters," "desisters," and "intermittent" offenders) as derived from official criminal records.[4] Overall, we interviewed 52 men across the persistent offender, desister, and intermittent offender categories. These 52 life-history interviews were combined with our collection of criminal histories and death records for all 500 former delinquents to age 70. Integrating these diverse data over seven decades and emphasizing within-individual patterns of variability, we illuminate age, crime, and human development using both quantitative and qualitative methods. For example, we use state-of-the-art dynamic techniques, including linear hierarchical change models and semiparametric, group-based approaches, to analyze data on crime, incarceration, and mortality over the full life course.

On the other hand, the bulk of the book rests on life-history narratives that we collected in part to respond to Modell's (1994) critique. We contend that life-history narratives are especially valuable in uncovering issues overlooked in more traditional quantitative approaches in criminology. By using life histories, we move away from a strict variable-based approach—a study of the relations among variables across individuals—and shift to a person-based approach—a study of several constructs that, taken as a whole, represent the person. In our view, life-history narratives combined with quantitative approaches can be used to develop a richer and more comprehensive picture of why some men persist in offending and why others stop. Narratives help us unpack mechanisms that connect salient life events across the life course, especially regarding personal choice and situational context. Life histories that are contrary to one's theory or quantitative data—"negative cases"—can also be exploited to reassess theory and probe new ideas and directions.

### Organization of the Book

Explaining crime over the full life course presents both empirical and theoretical challenges, and we have structured the book as follows. Chapters 1 to 4 outline the major theoretical and methodological strategies for studying criminal and deviant lives through time. Chapter 2 highlights the literature on persistent offending and desistance from crime. To make sense of this literature, we develop a theoretical taxonomy of competing explanations of persistent offending and desistance from criminal behavior. Chapter 3 describes the life-course framework and the main conceptual tenets of our original theoretical model of age-graded informal social control and crime. There we offer important extensions of our previous work by incorporating human agency and situational influences, especially routine activities, into a life-course explanation of crime. We also emphasize the importance of collecting long-term data to unveil the patterning of crime and deviance over time. Finally, we make the case that narrative data are essential for understanding the processes of persistent offending and desistance from crime over multiple phases of the life course.

In Chapter 4 we present our research methods. In many respects these take the form of a detective story in which we seek out criminal and deviant men. Finding the men and carrying out in-depth personal interviews (all of which we conducted ourselves) turned out to be one of the most interesting and satisfying experiences of our careers. There is evidence that many of the men themselves were also affected, as reflected in their continuing contact well after the close of our initial interviews. We thus take special pains to highlight our data collection strategies and the key methodological issues that we were forced to confront in finding the men and interviewing them.

Chapter 5 examines the life course of crime from a quantitative standpoint. We present trajectories of criminal offending from the first recorded arrest at age 7 to the last recorded arrest at age 69. The quantitative data for this chapter come from state and national criminal records and death records covering the period from childhood to later adulthood for the original 500 delinquents from the Gluecks' study. Our major goal is to assess trajectories of crime in the light of prospectively and theoretically defined taxonomies based on early risk factors. We also take the opposite tack by defining offending trajectories retrospectively, or ex-post, on the basis of patterns of observed offending over the full life course, and then assessing individuals' criminal predictability from childhood and adolescent risk factors. This dual analytic approach allows us to shed new light on prevailing theories that rest fundamentally on the idea of distinct and predictable groups of offenders.

Chapters 6 to 8 explore stability and change in crime over the life course using the life-history narratives that we collected. Our analysis centers on an examination of persistence and desistance for the 52 men we selected for detailed study. These 52 men were selected to maximize variation in patterns of offending over the life course—a goal we believe has been achieved quite well. We begin in Chapter 6 with an examination of desistance from crime. In Chapter 7 we explore persistence in criminal offending over the life course. Chapter 8 then examines the life-history narratives for those men who did not fit neatly in the expected patterns of offending. Some of these men were persistent offenders who were arrested for violence for the first time in middle age, while others experienced what could be called "delayed desistance," and still others displayed an erratic or intermittent pattern of offending over the life course. In all three sets of analyses we rely mainly on our follow-up study of the 52 former delinquents at age 70, but the narratives and life histories we collected are also linked to the extensive quantitative and qualitative data collected by the Gluecks' research team for the same men up to age 32.

In Chapter 9 we revisit long-term trajectories of offending and within-individual patterns of change. We present the results of an analysis of our quantitative data using hierarchical linear modeling that simultaneously examines variations within individuals over time and propensity differences between individuals. We specifically investigate how changes in adult transitions to marriage, work, and military service are linked to changes in offending. We do this for the full sample of 500 men up to age 32 and for the 52 men we interviewed up to age 70. This quantitative focus on turning points complements our qualitative focus in Chapters 6–8 and integrates these diverse data sources in a unique fashion.

In Chapter 10 we conclude with a synthesis of our major findings and discussion of the implications of our study for understanding the life course. In particular, we articulate how our work challenges a number of current conceptions in criminological theory, research, and policy, along with human development more generally. As Block (1971) has shown so well, studying lives through time is a messy affair fraught with methodological and theoretical challenges. Nevertheless, we believe our end result is ultimately rewarding both for the individuals involved as participants and for a better appreciation of the human complexity of crime and of growing old.

# CHAPTER TWO

# Persistence or Desistance?

There is no shortage of explanations in the field of criminology for the onset of criminal behavior, typically assumed to occur in childhood or early adolescence. What is not known with much certainty is why some offenders stop committing crimes when they do, while others continue over large portions of the life course. What accounts for stability and change in patterns of criminal offending over time? The longitudinal studies needed to answer this central question are virtually nonexistent. Most criminological research consists of cross-sectional snapshots or relatively short-term panel studies of offending, whereas long-term studies that follow the same individuals over time are as rare as they are difficult to carry out.

In this chapter we address these issues by examining a theoretical taxonomy of explanations for persistent offending and desistance from crime.[1] We organize our discussion by presenting and critiquing four conceptual accounts that have been prominently advanced to explain desistance from crime—maturation, development, rational choice, and social learning. We then present an integrated approach based on the core principles of life-course inquiry, building from our previous research (Sampson and Laub 1993). We believe that a life-course perspective offers the most compelling and unifying framework for understanding the processes underlying continuity (persistence) and change (desistance) in criminal behavior over the life span. Before addressing specific theoretical accounts, however, we briefly review the literature on long-term studies of offending and confront the relevant findings about persistent offending and desistance from crime. In addition, we highlight key conceptual and definitional issues surrounding the study of persistent offending and desistance.

### Long-Term Studies of Criminal Careers

Few longitudinal studies contain data on criminal behavior during childhood, adolescence, young adulthood, and middle to older age for the same people. Among the first researchers to examine the relationship between age and criminal behavior, including age at termination of offending, were Sheldon and Eleanor Glueck. In their fifteen-year follow-up of 510 male reformatory inmates, the Gluecks found that the proportion of subjects arrested decreased from 71 percent in the first five-year follow-up period to 57 percent in the third five-year follow-up period (1943, 109). However, over the same follow-up period, the average number of arrests among those arrested increased from 3.3 to 3.6. It appeared that while arrests for property crimes declined, they were replaced by arrests for drunkenness. The average age of the subjects at the end of the fifteen-year follow-up was 40 (Glueck and Glueck 1943, 3). Similar patterns can be found in the Gluecks' fifteen-year follow-up of 1,000 juvenile delinquents referred to the Judge Baker Clinic (1940) and their follow-up of 500 juvenile delinquents from the *Unraveling Juvenile Delinquency* study (1950, 1968).

The Gluecks did not systematically investigate the causes of the decrease in offending over time, although they did compare the reformed and unreformed as well as those who remained serious offenders compared with those who de-escalated to minor offending. The Gluecks concluded that those who reformed "were better circumstanced than those who continued to recidivate over the long-term follow-up span" (Glueck and Glueck 1974, 141). Many of these differences were due to varying experiences, personal traits, and circumstances *before* the onset of offending. From these findings, the Gluecks developed the hypothesis of "delayed maturation" to explain desistance from crime, which we discuss in more detail below.

In another research project on continuity and change, Joan McCord has followed subjects from the Cambridge-Somerville Youth Study into their forties (median age 47). McCord (1980) found that while the vast majority of juvenile delinquents committed a crime as an adult, the majority of the adult offenders had no history of offending as juveniles. McCord reported that the earlier the age of onset, the greater the likelihood of recidivism in adulthood.

Lee Robins's (1966) follow-up study of child guidance clinic patients is also pertinent to the topic of continuity and change in offending over time. Robins found that 72 percent of the male children referred to the clinic for antisocial behavior were subsequently arrested between the ages of 18 and 30. Of those arrested between age 18 and 30, 59 percent were arrested after age 30. Conversely, of those not arrested between age 18 and 30, 18 percent were arrested after age 30 (Robins 1966, 47). Thus while these data show continuity of offending well into middle age, they also suggest that "the effect of the early experience begins to diminish after age 30 and recent experiences become more significant" (Cline 1980, 666).

Wolfgang and his colleagues (1987) followed a sample from the 1945 Philadelphia birth-cohort study (Wolfgang, Figlio, and Sellin 1972) to age 30. They reported strong continuity in offending across the juvenile and adult years. The peak age of offending was 16, and declined thereafter into adulthood. Yet Wolfgang and colleagues also found that the average number of crimes committed among active offenders was relatively constant from ages 10 to 30 (1987, 41). Continuing the Philadelphia birth-cohort tradition, Tracy and Kempf-Leonard (1996) collected criminal records up to age 26 for 27,160 males and females from the 1958 Philadelphia birth-cohort study (Tracy, Wolfgang, and Figlio, 1985). They found that the vast majority of cohort subjects had no record of delinquency or adult crime (71 percent). Six percent committed crimes only as adults and 8 percent committed criminal acts in both the juvenile and the adult period. Sixteen percent of the cohort had a record of delinquency, but no official police record in adulthood. It is noteworthy that about two-thirds (68 percent) of the cohort delinquents did not continue their offending in adulthood (1996, 80–81).

There is empirical evidence that similar criminal career patterns exist in countries outside the United States as well. For example, in the Cambridge Study in Delinquent Development, Farrington (2002) reported considerable continuity in offending from adolescence to adulthood (defined as age 40). As in the U.S. studies, age of onset predicted persistence in offending. Farrington (2002) also reported that the prevalence of offending increased up to age 17 and then declined.

Interestingly, the prevalence of certain offenses (for example, theft from work, assault, drug use, and fraud) did not decline with age. (For similar results from Sweden, see Stattin and Magnusson 1991).

These findings can now be considered against the backdrop of the age-crime controversy that has roiled the field of criminology. After the publication of Hirschi and Gottfredson's seminal paper (1983) on age and crime, the field of criminology witnessed a series of heated debates about age, crime, and criminal careers (for a sampling of these debates, see Gottfredson and Hirschi 1986; Blumstein, Cohen, and Farrington 1988a,b; Gottfredson and Hirschi 1988). The controversy has had the salutary effect of clarifying the facts about crime that need to be explained. Any reasonable theory of persistent offending and desistance from crime must address the following fundamentals.

- The prevalence of criminal participation in the population declines with age, although there appears to be more variability in the age distribution across offense types than is commonly believed (Steffensmeier et al. 1989). Typically, criminal offending begins in pre-adolescence, peaks sharply during adolescence, and rapidly declines in the transition to young adulthood.

- The incidence of crime does not necessarily decline with age, and may, in fact, increase with age for certain types of crime and subgroups of offenders (Blumstein et al. 1986; Farrington 1986; but see Hirschi and Gottfredson 1983).

- There appears to be substantial continuity in offending from childhood to adolescence and from adolescence into adulthood, with the earlier the onset of criminal activity, the longer the criminal career (Robins 1966; Wolfgang, Figlio, and Sellin 1972; Blumstein et al. 1986, 86–88).

- Despite this continuity, there is a great deal of variability in criminal behavior over the life span. While it is clear that juvenile delinquency is linked to adult crime, it must be recognized that "40 to 50 percent of adult offenders do *not* have records of juvenile police contacts" (Blumstein et al. 1986, 88). Cline argues that although there is "more constancy than change . . . there is sufficient change in all the data to preclude simple conclusions concerning criminal career progressions" (1980, 665). Cline rightly concludes that there is far more variation in criminal behavior than previous work has suggested, and that many juvenile offenders do not become career offenders (Cline 1980, 669–670; see also Loeber and LeBlanc 1990, 390).

In short, despite some promising leads and an accumulation of important facts on age, crime, and criminal careers, there are many unanswered questions. It is remarkable, for example, how little agreement there is regarding the variability of the age-crime relationship for individual offenders. Moreover, little is known about the age-crime relationship over the full life course. Even more important is the fact that much remains to be discovered about the processes that explain persistent offending and desistance from criminal behavior across various stages of the life course. A focus on onset, participation, incidence, career length, and desistance is the essence of a criminal career approach to the study of crime and criminals. But though the criminal career model takes it as given that the causal factors that explain participation in crime, the frequency of offending, and the termination of a criminal career are all different, the empirical support for this notion is at best mixed (for a review, see Piquero, Farrington, and Blumstein 2003). A key idea stemming from this approach that we investigate in this book is whether high-rate offenders are really a distinctive group. In other words, is there a group of offenders that have a stable rate of offending over the full life course and hence do not desist from crime? This question goes to the heart of the typological thinking about crime that has come to dominate the recent criminological literature.

Although desistance from crime is seemingly the conceptual reverse of persistence and hence another major component of the criminal career model, desistance is the least-studied process (Loeber and LeBlanc 1990, 407; Farrington 1986, 221–223), especially compared with the voluminous research in criminology on the onset of delinquency. The limited literature focusing directly on desistance from crime indicates that there are multiple pathways, including attachment to a conventional person such as a spouse, stable employment, transformation of personal identity, and the aging process (see Laub and Sampson 2001 for a complete review); however, no clear consensus has emerged on the causes and correlates of desistance.

To illustrate, Rutter (1988, 3) asks whether the predictors of desistance are unique or simply the opposite of predictors leading to offending and notes that this fundamental question remains unanswered. One school of thought argues that the predictors of desistance are simply the reverse of risk factors predicting offending (LeBlanc and Loeber 1993, 247; Gottfredson and Hirschi 1990). Farrington (1992), for example, contends that the onset of delinquency is due to changes in social influence from parents to peers and that desistance is due to changes in social influence from peers to spouses. The implication is that the predictors of desistance may be distinguished from the predictors of the onset of crime. Although there is some evidence for this "desistance" position going back to the Gluecks' (1943) research on criminal careers conducted in the 1930s and 1940s, we investigate the idea of "asymmetrical causation" (Uggen and Piliavin 1998) for understanding the desistance process over the full life course.

To understand the processes of persistence and desistance requires a theory of crime and the criminal "offender." Crime is typically defined as a violation of societal rules of behavior that are embodied in law. When officially recognized, such violations may evoke sanctions by the state. Deviance is typically defined as violations of social norms or generally accepted standards of society (that is, institutionalized expectations). Even with these definitions, the operational definition of an "offender" remains ambiguous, as does the point at which persistent offending or desistance occurs. Therefore, before we begin our review of explanations for persistence and desistance from crime, we take a closer look at the terms themselves.

### Are Persistence and Desistance Meaningful Terms?

Defining terms like persistent criminal activity or identifying a group called "persistent offenders" is fraught with difficulty. Indeed, discerning readers are likely to wonder whether these are arbitrary designations or, alternatively, valid groupings that serve a scientific function. This debate is especially relevant because terms like "super-predators," "chronic offenders," "career criminals," and "life-course persisters" are used frequently in the criminological literature and in the popular culture (see, for example, Bennett, DiIulio, and Walters 1996; Loeber and Farrington 1998; Moffitt 1993). These offenders represent challenges for both criminological theory and criminal justice policy, yet it is remarkable how little we know about them.

The issue is both conceptual and methodological. What should be counted? How many offenses, arrests, or convictions does one need to be called a persistent offender? How long a time frame should be considered? For example, does a person who was arrested once every decade of his life up to age 60, for a total of six arrests, deserve a "persistent offender" label? What do we call a person who was arrested fifteen times before the age of 30, but desisted from crime thereafter? A related problem concerns incarceration. Should time spent in prison and jail be considered in the definition of persistent offenders? Is time served in prison perhaps a better indicator of a career criminal than arrest history? Consider the homicide offender who serves a long prison term, but would not necessarily display the frequency of offending that the term *persistent* implies. Perhaps, then, both arrests and incarcerations should be taken into account.

Our point is that persistent offenders can be defined by an assortment of relatively objective indicators such as arrest frequency, variety of offending, incarceration time, arrests in each decade, arrests in each phase of the life course, and so on. Alternatively, one can examine the life record and make a clinical (subjective?) assessment about whether someone is truly a persistent offender. It may be that some combination of objective and clinical assessment could be reliably accomplished. In the end, though, it is not obvious that either approach is beneficial in establishing a clear-cut definition of persistent offending.

Even thornier problems arise when examining desistance from criminal activity. Defined as ceasing to do something, desistance from crime is commonly acknowledged in the research literature. Most offenders, after all, eventually stop offending. Yet there is relatively little conceptualization about crime cessation (see also Bushway et al. 2001). As Maruna (2001, 17) notes, "Desistance from crime is an unusual dependent variable for criminologists because it is not an event that happens, rather it is the sustained *absence* of a certain type of event (in this case, crime)." Compounding this lack of conceptual clarity is the confounding of desistance with aging. It is well known that crime declines with age in the aggregate population (Gottfredson and Hirschi 1990). The decline of recidivism with age led Hoffman and Beck (1984, 621) to argue for the existence of an age-related "burnout" phenomenon. These authors found that rates of recidivism decline with increased age and that this relationship was maintained when controlling for other factors linked to recidivism (for example, prior criminal record). Moreover, there is evidence that even among offenders perceptions and attitudes change with aging (Shover 1985, 1996). As one former delinquent we interviewed remarked, "Every year I get more mellow and more mellow." Another told us that he "grew out of being fresh" and "resentful of authority." It also appears that fear of doing time in prison becomes especially acute with age (Shover 1996).

Several additional questions remain unanswered. For example, can desistance occur after one act of crime? If so, are the processes of desistance from a single act of crime different from desistance after several acts of crime? Is there such a thing as "spontaneous remission" and if so can the term be precisely defined? Stall and Biernacki (1986) define spontaneous remission as desistance that occurs absent any external intervention. How can "genuine desistance" be distinguished from "false desistance"? How long a follow-up period is needed to establish desistance? Baskin and Sommers (1998, 143) argue that a two-year hiatus indicates temporary cessation and is a long enough period to consider the processes that initiate and sustain desistance. Yet how does one distinguish intermittency in offending from true desistance? For instance, Elliott, Huizinga, and Menard (1989, 118) employ the term "suspension," because suspension can imply either temporary or permanent cessation. Farrington has stated that "even a five-year or ten-year crime-free period is no guarantee that offending has terminated" (1986, 201). And in fact Barnett, Blumstein, and Farrington (1989) found a small group of offenders who stopped offending and then restarted after a long period of time.

Moreover, we underscore the role of death or physical incapacitation in the study of desistance. Reiss (1989, 229–239) has emphasized that criminologists tend to mistakenly assume that desistance is always a voluntary decision. The fact is, however, that high-rate offenders are disproportionately likely to exit the risk pool involuntarily through death (see, for example, Lattimore, Linster, and MacDonald 1997), injury, and incarceration. Incarceration and mortality thus need to be taken into account in any study of persistent offending or desistance.

Another question turns on whether de-escalation to less serious offending is an indication of desistance. For example, if serious offending ceases, but problem behavior remains or increases, what does that say about desistance? Weitekamp and Kerner make the point that "desistance of crime could . . . be considered as a process which may lead to other forms of socially deviant, unwanted or personally dreadful problems" (1994, 448). Some offenders, even though they desist from criminal activity, continue to engage in a variety of acts that are considered deviant or the functional equivalents of crime (Gottfredson and Hirschi 1990). They may drink alcohol excessively, have children out of wedlock, "loaf" instead of work, gamble, and congregate in bars. Can such "offenders" accurately be called desisters? Perhaps from the narrow confines of the criminal justice system they are, but from a theoretical vantage point, they display traits that imply little change in their antisocial trajectory.

So the critical questions pile up: How much offending must ensue before one is defined as an "offender"—one, five, ten, twenty acts? What distinguishes a persistent offender from a nonpersistent offender? And over what period of time must a former offender be free of crime before we say that he or she has desisted—one year, five years, ten years? Although answers to these questions are difficult, we believe that some ground rules are possible and in fact necessary before meaningful research can proceed.

## Conceptual Ground Rules and Approach

To develop a theory of crime that focuses on within-individual change over the long haul, it is first important to distinguish termination of offending from the concept of desistance. Termination is the point at which one stops criminal activity, whereas desistance is the causal process that supports the termination of offending. Although it is difficult to ascertain when the process of desistance actually begins, it is apparent that it continues after the termination of offending. That is, the process of desistance maintains the continued state of nonoffending. Thus both termination and the process of desistance need to be considered in understanding cessation from offending. By using different terms for these distinct phenomena, we separate termination (the outcome) from the dynamics underlying the process of desistance (the cause), which have been confounded in the literature to date.

The termination of offending is characterized by the absence of continued offending (a nonevent). Unlike, say, stopping smoking, where setting a specific quit date is so important, criminal offenders typically do not set a date to quit offending. The actual period of time necessary to establish that termination has occurred is a sticky issue, but one that is possible to overcome. For example, in the criminal career literature, the end of the criminal career is defined as the age at which the last crime is committed. It seems reasonable to specify the date of last crime as the point of termination of offending, recognizing that there are serious measurement problems in ascertaining if in fact a person has stopped committing crimes after a certain point.

Desistance, by contrast, evolves over time in a process. According to Vaughan (1986), "uncoupling" is the process of divorce and separation. The process of uncoupling occurs prior to, during, and after divorce. Like desistance, uncoupling is not abrupt, but a gradual transition out of an intimate relationship. We would similarly argue that desistance, similar to uncoupling or quitting smoking, is best viewed as a process rather than a discrete event (Vaughan 1986; Fisher et al. 1993; see also Bushway et al. 2001). The process is a social transition that entails transformation, for example from a smoker to a non-smoker, or from a married/coupled person to a divorced/uncoupled person, or from an offender to a nonoffender. In addition, like quitting smoking or uncoupling, desistance is not an irreversible transition.

Because low-rate offending is so common, especially during adolescence, we further argue that criminologists will not learn much more than is already known about the near ubiquity of delinquency during the teen years. This logic suggests that it is not fruitful for criminologists to spend much time studying termination or desistance for low-rate offenders (defined as involvement in a single event or a series of relatively isolated events in the teenage years). Furthermore, it follows that termination and desistance should be studied among those who reach some reasonable threshold of frequent and serious criminal offending. The precise details of measurement depend upon the data set and the research question under investigation. For example, we have argued for a focus on desistance from persistent and serious delinquency, operationalized in our own research using the Gluecks' delinquent group of 500 formerly incarcerated juveniles with lengthy and serious criminal records (Sampson and Laub 1993).

Our position, then, is that whether or not one embraces the criminal career paradigm (Blumstein et al. 1986), good theories of crime ought to account for the onset, continuation, and desistance from criminal behavior across the life span. At the heart of this focus on persistence and desistance is a conceptualization of stability and change over the life course. Consider that desistance can occur when there is a change in criminal propensity or a change in opportunities to commit crime. Is desistance related to one or both of these domains? Defining criminality as the stable propensity to offend, Gottfredson and Hirschi (1990) argue that desistance occurs when there is a change in the opportunity to offend. In their view, because criminality is stable over the life course, it cannot account for desistance from crime. We of course agree that observed acts of crime change over time (Sampson and Laub 1993), but we have also contended that criminal opportunities are either ubiquitous (Sampson and Laub 1995) or not sufficiently variable to account for the sharp declines in crime by age. We have thus been silent as to whether an individual's propensity to crime changes or remains stable over time, although we have implied that traits like self-control can change over time as a consequence of changes in the quality or strength of social ties (Sampson and Laub 1995).

Here we wish to make our position on propensity more explicit, especially in relation to Gottfredson and Hirschi's (1990) position. We believe that an individual's propensity to crime can change over time because of a variety of factors (for example, aging, changes in informal social control, the increasing deterrent effect of sanctions). In Chapters 5 and 9, we use statistical approaches (for example, Poisson modeling of event rates) that treat the underlying rate of criminal offending as a latent construct that generates a probabilistic distribution. The problem with such methods arises when the idea of propensity to crime is assumed to mean stable individual differences, and when theories focus more on alleged unobserved causes than on demonstrated variability in the commission of criminal acts. In other words, there is an implicit theory underlying the concept of propensity in most criminological circles—the positing of fixed individual attributes that are related to crime yet never observed. It should be clear that propensity is in the end a "black box," and that propensity is the result of a variety of individual, situational, and community factors.

As we have implied thus far and will investigate more thoroughly in the next chapter, we see persistent offending and desistance from crime as two sides of the same coin. There are three broad and distinct processes that can be used to understand these intertwined phenomena. To illustrate the differences in these processes, we return to the two individuals whose life histories were introduced in Chapter 1, Arthur and Michael. One process stems from what has been labeled *population heterogeneity* but which might be better described as a "kinds of people" argument. This perspective argues that behavior over the life course is a reflection of differences that vary between persons (usually, but not necessarily, individual differences or traits) and that are established early in life with consequent stability over time. Hence this can be referred to as a theory about differences in persons and the consequences of those differences for persisting in or desisting from crime. For example, Nagin and Paternoster argue that "there may be differences between individuals in socialization, personality, or biological/constitutional attributes which makes crime more likely over time" (2000, 119). Once identified, time-stable traits like self-control, temperament, and intelligence are thought to account for continuity in antisocial behavior—indeed, all behavior—over time. Applying this notion to the lives of Arthur and Michael means that the different life-course outcomes we observe are due to some trait like self-control, temperament, or intelligence.

A second process has been labeled *state dependence* but which might be better thought of as a "kinds of contexts" argument. According to the notion of state dependence, past behavior constrains or influences future events (contexts), and these in turn can causally affect current and future behavior. For example, getting arrested may weaken one's future employment prospects, which in turn leads to an increased risk for later crime. This can thus be referred to as a theory about differences in situations or contexts and their consequences for persisting in and desisting from crime. As Nagin and Paternoster point out, "committing crimes has the two-pronged effect of both weakening restraints/inhibitions and strengthening incentives for additional criminal behavior" (2000, 118). For example, Arthur's life-course outcomes might be partly explained by the influence of incarceration on weakened social ties that in turn work to keep him on a trajectory of antisocial behavior. Once identified, such time-varying characteristics and social contexts (for example, unemployment status, marital disruptions) can explain continuity in offending behavior over time.

A third process is one that combines the ideas of population heterogeneity (differences in people) and state dependence (differences in contexts) into one explanation. In this "mixed model," both differences in persons and contexts matter. For example, it may be that population heterogeneity constrains state dependence. If we follow a mixed model, differences in life-course outcomes for Arthur and Michael are due not only to their individual traits but also to the effects of later life events. This compromise perspective recognizes both time-stable traits and time-varying characteristics as important in explaining continuity and change in offending over time.

What is still lacking in all three of these models, however, is a concerted focus on and a theoretical explanation of change in behavior, especially from criminal behavior to conventional behavior. For instance, if Arthur and Michael share the same individual traits that increase their propensity to crime and these traits are stable over time, how can one explain Michael's desistance from criminal behavior? If the idea of state dependence is that "criminal behavior has a genuine causal effect on subsequent criminality by eroding constraints and strengthening incentives to crime" (Nagin and Paternoster 2000, 117), it is not readily apparent how "state dependence can also explain why there is change or cessation in offending over time" (2000, 127).[2] Although state dependence models are theoretically able to account for desistance from crime (see Nagin and Paternoster 2000, 118–119, 124–125), the fact of the matter is that most criminologists use state dependence to explain the positive correlation between past and future criminal offending (for a recent example, see Piquero, Farrington, and Blumstein 2003, 38–39).

The result is that population heterogeneity and state dependence models tend to emphasize one side of the coin—continuity in offending—and do not provide insight into the processes of change. Combining the processes of population heterogeneity and state dependence is a step in the right direction, but still begs the theoretical issue of change. In our view, ultimately the only way for population heterogeneity and state dependence models to provide an adequate explanation of continuity and change in criminal behavior is to adopt a typological approach, which argues that different offenders have different causal pathways to crime and, as a result, different prospects for persistence versus desistance. As our data will indicate, this is not a satisfactory solution.

## Theoretical Frameworks of the Desistance Process

To explain change in offending over time we turn to conceptual accounts that focus primarily on desistance from crime. Implicit in each of these theoretical accounts, however, is an explanation or image of the offender that helps explain persistence in crime as well. Although there is overlap across these frameworks, we highlight what we see as the differing elements of emphasis within each framework. We then make the case that the life-course perspective is the most promising approach for advancing the state of knowledge regarding continuity (persistence) *and* change (desistance) in crime and other problem behaviors.

### Maturation and Aging

The Gluecks developed the idea of maturation as the key factor in explaining desistance from crime. Their theory was that "the physical and mental changes which enter into the natural process of maturation offer a chief explanation of improvement of conduct with the passing of years" (Glueck and Glueck 1974, 149). Desistance occurred with the passage of time; specifically, there was a "decline in recidivism during the late twenties and early thirties" (1974, 175). Thus for the Gluecks desistance was normative and expected unless an offender had serious biological or environmental deficits. At the same time, the Gluecks argued that persistent recidivism could be explained by a lack of maturity; offenders who eventually desisted experienced delayed or belated maturation. Although their argument was perhaps tautological in nature, the Gluecks stressed that the men under study "finally achieved enough integration and stability to make their intelligence and emotional-volitional equipment effective in convincing them that crime does not lead to satisfaction and in enhancing their capacity for self-control" (1974, 170).

The Gluecks believed that maturation was a complex concept and process. They wrote that maturation "embraces the development of a stage of physical, intellectual, and affective capacity and stability, and a sufficient degree of integration of all major constituents of temperament, personality and intelligence to be adequate to the demands and restrictions of life in organized society" (1974, 170). The Gluecks were quite clear that desistance "cannot be attributed to external en-

vironmental transformations" (1974, 173). They called for more research into the "striking maturation" phenomenon from biological,
psychological, and sociological perspectives, with the goal to "dissect
maturation into its components" (Glueck and Glueck 1940, 270). Interestingly, for the Gluecks age and maturation were not one and the
same. It was the case that as age increased, recidivism declined. But
age alone was not enough to explain maturation. "It was not the
achievement of any particular age, but rather the achievement of adequate maturation regardless of the chronological age at which it occurred that was the significant influence in the behavior change of our
criminals" (Glueck and Glueck 1945, 81). Nonetheless, the basic idea
of this approach is that desistance results when offenders grow out of
crime and settle down.

A variation of the Gluecks' approach is found in Gottfredson and
Hirschi's *General Theory of Crime* (1990). Like the Gluecks, Gottfredson and Hirschi argue that crime declines with age for all offenders (see also Hirschi and Gottfredson 1983). Gottfredson and Hirschi
contend that the age distribution of crime—including onset, frequency, and desistance—is, for all intents and purposes, invariant
across time, space, and historical context and therefore cannot be explained by variables currently proposed in mainstream criminology
(for example, poverty, subculture, delinquent peers). Gottfredson and
Hirschi state, "This explanation suggests that maturational reform is
just that, change in behavior that comes with maturation; it suggests
that spontaneous desistance is just that, change in behavior that cannot be explained and change that occurs regardless of what else happens" (1990, 136).

A fundamental aspect of the Gottfredson and Hirschi account
(1990) of desistance is the distinction between crime and criminality.
According to Gottfredson and Hirschi, crimes are short-term, circumscribed events that presuppose a set of conditions. In contrast, criminality refers to relatively stable differences across individuals in the
propensity to commit crime. Gottfredson and Hirschi go on to argue
that while crime everywhere declines with age, criminality—differences in propensities, like self-control—remains relatively stable over
the life course. They write, "Desistance theory asserts that crime declines with age because of factors associated with age that reduce or
change the criminality of the actor. The age theory asserts that crime,

independent of criminality, declines with age" (1990, 137). For Gottfredson and Hirschi, criminality is impervious to institutional involvement and impact.

Unlike the Gluecks, Gottfredson and Hirschi do not invoke the process of maturation, but rather see a direct effect of age on crime. Decreases in offending over time are "due to the inexorable aging of the organism" (1990, 141). From this theoretical perspective it follows that criminal behavior is largely unaffected by life-course events—marriage, employment, education—or any situational or institutional influences. The problem with maturational or "ontogenetic" accounts, well noted by Dannefer (1984), is that they do not really offer an explanation—things are thought to just naturally happen. The basic idea is that desistance "just happens" and that the age effect cannot be explained with the available terms and concepts.

## Developmental Accounts

A similar problem is seen in developmental accounts that are rooted in ontogenetic reasoning (Dannefer 1984). One explanation is that changes in identity account for reductions or cessation in crime (see Maruna 2001; Giordano, Cernkovich, and Rudolph 2002; Gartner and Piliavin 1988; and Shover 1996). Mulvey and LaRosa (1986) focus on the period from age 17 to 20, the period they call the time of natural recovery. They argue that desistance is the result of shifts in behavioral patterns that characterize adolescence, especially late adolescence (see Mulvey and Aber 1988 for details on this developmental perspective). This developmental process is similar to the one advanced by Shover in his study of behavioral shifts among aging men involved in crime (see Shover 1985, 1996). Shover contends that changes in offending are linked to age and aging, especially the changing calculus of decision making. This process is similar to age-related changes in the lives of nonoffenders. Aging influences subjective contingencies or what Shover calls "orientational, resolve-enhancing contingencies" (1996, 130). Men turn away from crime because they take fewer risks and become more rational; gain a new perspective on self; have a growing awareness of time as a diminishing resource; and experience a change in their aspirations and goals (1996, 131). Such accounts of desistance suggest two themes. First, desistance is normative (ontogenetic) and expected across the life span. Some rough and tumble toddlers will desist from antisocial behavior as they enter school, some adolescent delinquents will desist while in high school, and some older delinquents will desist as they make the transition to young adulthood, and so on. Second, cognitive change is a precursor to behavioral change. What Maruna (2001) calls "identity deconstruction" is necessary to begin the long-term process of desistance.[3]

A second developmental account of desistance is offered by Gove (1985). He argues that explanations of the cessation of various forms of crime and deviance must incorporate biological, psychological, and sociological variables. Like Hirschi and Gottfredson (1983), Gove maintains that sociological theories of crime are unable to explain patterns of desistance revealed in the data. Gove reviews six sociological theories of deviance, including labeling, conflict, differential association, control, anomie, and functional theory, and concludes that "all of these theoretical perspectives either explicitly or implicitly suggest that deviant behavior is an amplifying process leading to further and more serious deviance" (1985, 118). By contrast, changes in socially structured roles, psychological well-being, psychological maturation, and biological factors such as physical strength, physical energy, psychological drive, and the need for stimulation provide reasonable accounts of desistance from crime with age. Gove concludes that "biological and psychological factors appear to play a critical role in the termination of deviant behavior" (1985, 136). The peak and decline in physical strength, energy, psychological drive, and the need for stimulation maps fairly well with the peak and decline in deviant behavior.

A third developmental account of persistence in and desistance from crime and perhaps the most influential to date is found in Moffitt's writings (1993, 1994). Moffitt spells out two distinct categories of individuals, each possessing a unique natural history of antisocial behavior over the life course. From a desistance standpoint, what is important is that these two antisocial trajectories have unique etiologies that in part account for the differences in desistance. Life-course-persistent offenders start early in childhood and persist in offending well into adulthood. For this small group of offenders, neuropsychological deficits in conjunction with disrupted attachment relationships and academic failure drive long-term antisocial behaviors. Simply put, life-course-persistent offenders do not desist from crime. As Moffitt states, it is not the traits or the environment per se that account for continuity. Rather her theory of continuous antisocial behavior (and by definition, no desistance) "emphasizes the constant *process* of reciprocal interaction between personal traits and environmental reactions to them" (Moffitt 1994, 28). Antisocial dispositions infiltrate into all domains of adolescence and adulthood and this "diminishes the likelihood of change" (1994, 28).

The adolescence-limited offenders are involved in antisocial behavior only during adolescence. This large group of offenders has no history of antisocial behavior in childhood. The delinquency of the adolescence-limited group is situational and, as a result, virtually all of these offenders desist from criminal behavior over time. Adolescence-limited offenders seek to enjoy the spoils of adulthood (what Moffitt calls the maturity gap) and mimic the antisocial styles of life-course persisters, and, in turn, they are socially reinforced by the negative consequences of delinquent behavior (Moffitt 1994, 30–33). Adolescence-limited offenders desist from crime in response to changing contingencies and reinforcements. For this group desistance, like delinquency, is normative. Because adolescence-limiteds have no history of childhood antisocial behavior resulting from neuropsychological deficits, the forces of cumulative continuity are much weaker. Simultaneously, adolescence-limited offenders have more prosocial skills, more academic achievement, and stronger attachments than their life-course-persistent counterparts, characteristics that facilitate desistance from crime.

In sum, Moffitt argues that "the age of desistance from criminal offending will be a function of age of onset of antisocial behavior, mastery of conventional prosocial skills, and the number and severity of 'snares' encountered during the foray into delinquency. Snares are consequences of crime, such as incarceration or injury, that constrain conventional behavior" (1994, 45). Moreover, "Adolescence-Limited delinquents can profit from opportunities for desistance, because they retain the option of successfully resuming a conventional lifestyle. Life-Course-Persistent delinquents may make transitions into marriage or work, but their injurious childhoods make it less likely that they can leave their past selves behind" (1994, 45).

## Rational Choice Accounts

The main idea of the rational choice framework is that the decision to continue or give up crime is based on a conscious reappraisal of the costs and benefits of crime (Clarke and Cornish 1985; Cornish and

Clarke 1986; and Gartner and Piliavin 1988). In this perspective, persisters and desisters are seen as "reasoning decisionmakers" (Cornish and Clarke 1986, 13). One important component of this decision is the increasing fear of punishment with aging as found in Shover's (1996) qualitative study (see also Cromwell, Olson, and Avary 1991, but compare Shover and Thompson 1992). However, as we have seen, aging is not necessarily tied to the decision to give up crime.

Some researchers have tried to understand the context of rational decisions to stop offending. Cusson and Pinsonneault (1986) contend that the decision to give up crime is triggered by a shock of some sort (for example, a shoot-out during a crime) or "delayed deterrence" (for example, increased fear of doing more time) or both. Cusson and Pinsonneault found the decision to give up crime was "voluntary and autonomous" (1986, 78). These findings are highly speculative, as conceded by the authors, since the study was based primarily on interviews with 17 ex-robbers in Canada. In a similar vein, Leibrich (1996) studied 37 men and women in New Zealand who were on probation and in the process of going straight. She found that shame, as the most commonly identified cost of offending, was the primary factor in the desistance process. Three kinds of shame were reported: public humiliation, personal disgrace, and private remorse. As Leibrich stated, "shame was the thing which most often dissuaded people from offending and the growth of self-respect was the thing which most often persuaded them to go straight" (1996, 297). In another interesting study, Paternoster (1989) integrated deterrence and rational choice perspectives in an attempt to understand decisions to participate in and desist from delinquency (that is, marijuana use, drinking liquor, petty theft, and vandalism). Drawing on data from 1,250 high school students surveyed at three points in time, Paternoster found that the decision to desist was not related to formal sanction threats (for example, the perceived severity and certainty of punishment). Such decisions were, however, related to changes in moral tolerance of the delinquent act. Those offenders who made a decision to stop offending began to have stronger moral reservations about the illegal acts in question. This finding held for all four delinquent offenses. It is noteworthy that changes in moral beliefs were associated with changes in peer delinquency and degree of peer support for delinquency. Whether changes in beliefs and tolerance can be properly understood to support rational choice theory is questionable. What seems important to know is *why* individuals underwent changes in moral reasoning.

## Social Learning

Social learning has been offered as an integrative framework to provide explanations of desistance from crime and other forms of problem behavior. In fact, Akers (1990) has forcefully argued that social learning incorporates all of the major elements of rational choice and deterrence frameworks, including moral reasoning. One of the strengths of the social learning approach is its application to all crime types as well as to illicit drug use, alcohol abuse, and other problem behaviors (see Akers 1998 for an extensive review of the research literature).

In the social learning framework, the basic variables that explain initiation into crime are the same variables that account for cessation from crime. That is, for the most part, the account of desistance is the account of initiation in reverse. For example, differential association with noncriminal friends and significant others, less exposure to or opportunities to model or imitate criminal behavior, developing definitions and attitudes favorable to conformity and abiding by the law, and differential reinforcement (social and nonsocial) discouraging continued involvement in crime are all part of the desistance story. Imitation appears less important after onset; social and nonsocial reinforcements become more important (see Akers 1998). As for onset and continuation, the most important factor in desistance is peer associations.

In perhaps the most important application of social learning theory to desistance, Warr (1993) argued that differential association accounts for the decline in crime with age. Using data from the first five waves of the National Youth Survey for respondents aged 11–21, he found that peer associations (exposure to delinquent peers, time spent with peers, and loyalty to peers) changed dramatically with age. With respect to desistance, declines in crime were linked with declines in peer associations. When peer variables were controlled for, "the association between age and crime is substantially weakened and, for some offenses, disappears entirely" (Warr 1993, 35). Along similar lines, Warr (1998) has argued that changing peer relations account for the association between marital status and desistance from crime. Using longitudinal data, again from the National Youth Survey, he finds that the transition to marriage is followed by "a dramatic decline in time spent with friends" and "reduced exposure to delinquent peers" (1998, 183). Warr concludes that marriage is important because it reduces peer influences, a finding consistent with social learning theory but also with other perspectives. For example, marriage may lead to the greater social control of men (Sampson and Laub 1993) and thus explain their desistance. A theory of desistance needs to better account for such mediating social processes.[4]

## A Life-Course View

We believe the life-course framework offers a number of advantages, developed further in the next chapter, over the traditional accounts of persistence and desistance from crime, even developmental perspectives.[5] According to Elder (1998), the life-course perspective is based on several principles: (1) a focus on the historical time and place that recognizes that lives are embedded and shaped by context; (2) the recognition that the developmental impact of life events is contingent on when they occur in a person's life—that is, timing matters; (3) the acknowledgment of intergenerational transmission of social patterns—the notion of linked lives and interdependency; and (4) the view that human agency plays a key role in making choices and constructing one's life course. The major objective of the life-course perspective is to link social history and social structure to the unfolding of human lives. A life-course perspective thus looks to within-individual variations over time, regardless of whether one is interested in understanding persistence or desistance in crime. Applying the life-course framework leads to a focus on continuity and change in criminal behavior over time, especially its embeddedness in historical and other contextual features of social life.

Developmental accounts, especially from developmental psychology, focus on regular or lawlike individual development over the life span. Implicit in developmental approaches are the notions of stages, progressions, growth, and evolution (Dannefer 1984; Lewontin 2000). The resulting emphasis is on systematic pathways of development (change) over time, with the imagery being one of the execution of a program written at an earlier point in time. Although there are aspects of developmental approaches that rely on pure population heterogeneity models, some developmental theorists, like Moffitt, explicitly recognize the possibility of change. Still, change is usually explained by childhood characteristics and experiences—some people are simply more programmed early on for change than others. In other words, desistance is possible only for those with the "right" characteristics, which have been previously determined. Developmental models are thus ultimately forced to assume that there are "groups" or "types" of offenders (for example, life-course persisters) that display distinct and different causal pathways and probabilities of continuity and change, even if the manifestations of these pathways vary by age.

In contrast, life-course approaches, while incorporating individual differences and notions of lawlike development such as aging, emphasize variability and exogenous influences on the course of development over time that cannot be predicted by focusing solely on enduring individual traits (population heterogeneity) or even past experiences (state dependence). Flowing mainly from sociology and history, life-course accounts embrace the notion that lives are often unpredictable and dynamic and that exogenously induced changes are ever present. Some changes in the life course result from chance or random events; other changes stem from macro-level shocks largely beyond the pale of individual choice (for example, war, depression, natural disasters, revolutions, plant closings, industrial restructuring). Another important aspect of life-course criminology is a focus on situations and time-varying social contexts that impede or facilitate criminal events.

At the end of the day, however, our fundamental disagreement with developmental (especially psychological) accounts concerns a theoretical commitment to the idea of social malleability across the life course and a focus on the constancy of change, including the dynamic processes that serve to socially reproduce stability (Dannefer 1984). A life-course focus recognizes emergent properties and rejects the metaphor of "unfolding" that is inextricably part of the developmental paradigm. To be more specific, like Lewontin (2000), we reject the idea of determinism and lawful predictability from childhood factors. It follows that we must reject the pure version of the so-called population heterogeneity models. We argue that the traits that are at the heart of this perspective, whether derived from genetics or childhood experiences, do not sufficiently predict behavior over the long haul. In our view, the full life course matters, especially post-childhood, adolescence, and adult experiences.[6] We are also compelled to reject the pure version of state dependence. Although state dependence models improve upon population heterogeneity models, they too do not sufficiently account for change—there are simply too many outcomes that cannot be explained by focusing on the past.

Although the life-course perspective is compatible with several criminological theories (for example, social control, social learning, and rational choice), for both theoretical and empirical reasons elaborated in the next chapter, we favor a modified version of social control theory. Because of the life-course perspective's explicit focus on lives in social context, we link it with a revised and expanded age-graded theory of informal social control as a means of understanding onset, continuation, and desistance from criminal behavior (see Sampson and Laub 1993 for background). We thus focus on the structural sources of both continuity and change and their role in the processes of persistent offending and desistance from crime. The idea of "turning points" plays a central role in our theory, especially when linked to the interaction of human agency, life-course events, situations, and historical context. Highlighting emergent experiences that result from person-environment interactions, our framework thus builds in contingencies and returns us to an appreciation of the role of chance, or what Short and Strodtbeck (1965) once called "aleatory elements."

# CHAPTER THREE

# Explaining the
# Life Course of Crime

We need to take seriously the remarkable heterogeneity in criminal offending over the life span. Some offenders have short careers in violence, theft, and public order crimes; other offenders have very long careers. From a theoretical perspective, rather than thinking in simplistic, rigid offender/nonoffender categories, Matza (1964) offered the image of "drift" to capture the instability of offending over time. Along similar lines, Glaser (1969) suggests that it is more appropriate to view criminality as a "zig-zag path" consisting of a crime and noncrime cycle. In his research on ex-offenders, Glaser showed that men typically do not commit crime for long periods of time. Instead, they "follow a zig-zag path . . . going from noncrime to crime and to noncrime again. Sometimes this sequence is repeated many times, but sometimes they clearly go to crime only once; sometimes these shifts are for long duration or even permanent, and sometimes they are short lived" (1969, 58).

This view of criminal careers is a poor fit with the static person-based conceptualizations reviewed in Chapter 2. At the same time, the zigzag image of offending is consistent with more relational studies of personality (see Emirbayer 1997, 302–303). This line of research examines what a person does in particular situations rather than what broad traits a person possesses. By contrast, traditional criminology measures delinquency in an invariant manner in constant settings, inducing more stability than is likely to be found in the everyday lives of its subjects. The point we wish to stress is that criminality is a dynamic concept, especially when viewed over long periods of time. From this starting point, persistent offending and desistance from crime are inextricably tied together—theoretically, methodologically, and analytically.

Although at first it may seem counterintuitive, our fundamental beginning argument is that persistence and desistance can be meaningfully understood within the same theoretical framework. In its strong form, our argument is that persistence in crime is explained by a lack of social controls, few structured routine activities, and purposeful human agency. Simultaneously, desistance from crime is explained by a confluence of social controls, structured routine activities, and purposeful human agency. In this version of our argument the fundamental causes of offending are thus the same for all persons, although for some there may be a single pathway to crime or desistance, whereas for others there are multiple pathways. Regardless of the number of pathways, then, it is possible that the same causal mechanisms account for trajectories (pathways) of criminal behavior over the life course. This framework is similar to the stance we have taken in our prior work regarding crime-specific analyses (see Sampson and Laub 1993). In the current argument, the specific manifestations of violence may be different than the specific manifestations of property crime, but both are explained by the same general processes, namely, informal social control, routine activities, and human agency. The dynamics of persistence in crime may be different from the dynamics of desistance from crime, but the same general processes of social control, routine activities, and human agency explain both. We approached the follow-up study for this book with these general premises in mind, while allowing for a revision of our thinking along the way in light of discoveries in the data.

## A Theory of Persistent Offending and Desistance from Crime

We seek a theory of social control that will identify sources of persistence in and desistance from crime. What sustains persistent offending? What keeps some offenders from moving to more conventional pathways? In a similar vein, how do offenders go straight? How do offenders shift from crime and deviance to more conventional pathways? How do ex-offenders maintain conformity to the law? The central question we seek to answer is: what are the mechanisms underlying the processes of persistent offending and desistance from crime?

One of our theoretical goals is to expand the understanding of informal and formal social control across the life course. In the follow-up, we focused our attention on work, family, the military, community organizations, and neighborhood hangouts (for example, taverns) as well as on formal social control institutions like the police, prison, and parole. Thus we propose to examine a wide array of institutions that we believe influence both formal and informal social control. At the same time, we explicitly recognize that these institutions are embedded in a specific local culture (place) as well as a specific historical context (time).

Consider next the topic of delinquent peer influences (see Warr 2002). Our life-history data suggest that delinquent peers are important not only in the development of antisocial behavior in adolescence but in sustaining offending over the life course. Perhaps people who persist in offending over the life course are in a state of "arrested development" as they age. Consistent with that notion, Glaser (1969, 325–326) notes that association with deviant peers is especially appealing to people who are unsuccessful in securing satisfying and meaningful relationships in other domains such as family and work. This does not mean that social learning explanations are necessarily correct; rather, peer relations are important in structuring routine activities and opportunities for crime over the life course.

We also believe that human agency (or personal choice) and situational context, especially routine activities, are vitally important for understanding patterns of stability and change in criminal behavior over the life course. Individuals make choices and are active participants in the construction of their lives. For example, as revealed in more detail in Chapter 7, calculated and articulated resistance to authority is a recurrent theme in the lives of persistent offenders. At times crime is attractive because it is exciting and seductive (see Katz 1988). In crucial ways, then, crime is more than a weakening of social bonds—human agency must be recognized as an important element of understanding crime and deviance over the life course.

Situational contingencies and routine activities may also lure individuals toward or away from crime, and these contingencies and activities need to be systematically incorporated into our understanding of criminal trajectories over the life course. For example, we found persistent offenders to have rather chaotic and unstructured lives across multiple dimensions (such as living arrangements, work, and family). Routine activities for these men were loaded with opportunities for crime and extensive associations with like-minded offenders. Thus situational variation, especially in lifestyle activities, needs to be taken into account when explaining continuity and change in criminal behavior over the life course.

Aging is another significant feature in understanding the life course of crime. There are "natural sanctions" associated with criminal offending—early mortality, for example. Moreover, there are health costs associated with crime and deviance. It is also apparent that both formal and informal social controls become more salient with age. That is, the influence of social bonds interacts with age and life experiences. As seen in work by Shover (1996) and by Graham and Bowling (1995) in Great Britain, we find in our life-history narratives that, for some offenders, there has to be an "accumulation of losses" before one becomes sensitive to the inhibiting power of informal social controls. Likewise, it seems to be the case in our life-history data that fear of doing more time in prison becomes more acute with age (see also Shover 1996).

Our conception of crime builds on our previous work (Sampson and Laub 1993), wherein we posited an age-graded theory of informal social control. In *Crime in the Making*, we concluded that marriage, work, and military service represent "turning points" in the life course and are crucial for understanding the processes of change in criminal activity. Abbott contends that "turning points are narrative concepts, referring to two points in time at once" (1997, 85). He notes that "what makes a turning point a turning point rather than a minor ripple is the passage of sufficient time 'on a new course' such that it becomes clear that direction has indeed been changed" (1997, 89). Turning points are often retrospective constructions, but Abbott claims they do not have to be. Abbott identifies several types of turning points—focal, randomizing, and contingent (1997, 94)—but all turning points are "consequential shifts that redirect a process" (1997, 101). In a similar vein, Denzin emphasizes "epiphanies," defined as a "moment of problematic experience that illuminates personal character, and often signifies a turning point in a person's life" (1989, 141). Like Abbott, Denzin identifies several types of epiphanies—major, cumulative, illuminative, and relived (see Denzin 1989,

129–131). Turning points and epiphanies are more likely to be implicated in the desistance process than in the persistence process.

Although a wide range of experiences have been associated with the notion of a turning point (for example, residential moves, marriage, and military experience), Rutter (1996) warns that turning points should not be equated with major life experiences or expectable transitions (see also Maughan and Rutter 1998; Clausen 1998). First, some transitions lead to no change in a life trajectory. Second, some transitions merely accentuate preexisting characteristics rather than promoting change. Despite these difficulties, Rutter concludes that "there is convincing evidence" of turning-point effects, defined as change involving "a lasting shift in direction of life trajectory" (1996, 621). Thus in our view, the turning-point idea reveals the interactive nature of human agency and life events such as marriage, work, and serving in the military. Nevertheless, more needs to be learned about the mechanisms underlying turning points in the life course.

It is noteworthy that Maruna argues that the value of the turning-point idea to understanding desistance has "probably been overstated" because "nothing inherent in a situation makes it [an event] a turning point" (2001, 42–43). For Maruna, a more promising strategy is to focus on individuals as agents of their own change. This view underscores desistance as a process, not an event (Laub and Sampson 2001), but our theory focuses on the potential of structural turning points and the subsequent within-individual change in behavior that results. From this perspective, desistance from crime can be initiated by a "disorienting episode" (Lofland 1969) or a "triggering event" (Laub, Nagin, and Sampson 1998) seemingly independent of an individual's cognitive restructuring.[1]

To be sure, turning points take place in a larger structural and cultural context. Group processes and structural determinants (for example, race and ethnicity, social class, and neighborhood) need to be considered in the process of continuity and change in criminal behavior (see also Sullivan 1989). In other words, concepts such as crime, agency, choice, and informal social control need to be contextualized, because their meaning and significance varies by context.

In this chapter we therefore revisit the areas of marriage, employment, and military service, examined in our previous study (1993), as well as uncover some previously unexplored sources of turning points. Our goal is to further unpack the processes of persistence and desistance, or why some offenders stop offending and why other offenders continue offending throughout large portions of their life. Our approach illuminates why marriage, employment, the military, and other institutions have the potency to reshape life-course trajectories for those previously involved in crime. As will be developed in detail below, a major part of the answer is that involvement in these institutions reorders short-term situational inducements to crime and, over time, redirects long-term commitments to conformity (Briar and Piliavin 1965). We then examine the criminal justice system, especially prison, and ask whether this institution facilitates persistence or desistance in offending. After examining the institutional sources of informal and formal social control, we move to a discussion of human agency, situational influences, and local culture and historical contexts. These elements play a key role in our modified version of informal social control theory. We conclude the chapter by arguing that person-based life-history narratives are required to fully capture the processes of persistence in and desistance from crime.

### Marriage and Family

Marriage, especially strong marital attachment, has been implicated as a predictor of desistance from crime among men (for a detailed review, see Laub and Sampson 2001).[2] This idea was illustrated most directly by a former delinquent who had been married for forty-nine years when we interviewed him at age 70: "If I hadn't met my wife at the time I did, I'd probably be dead. It just changed my whole life . . . that's my turning point right there." These kinds of declarations raise fundamental questions. What is it about marriage that fosters desistance from crime? And must changes be recognized by the men? There are several possibilities.

First, a change in criminal behavior may not necessarily result from marriage alone. Rather, change may occur in response to an enduring attachment that emerges from entering into a marriage. From this perspective, the growth of social bonds is like an investment process (Laub and Sampson 1993, 310–311; Nagin and Paternoster 1994, 586–588). As the investment in social bonds grows, the incentive for avoiding crime increases, because more is at stake. Our past position has been that social ties in marriage are important insofar as they create interdependent systems of obligation and restraint that impose significant costs for translating criminal propensities into action. In this scheme, adults will be inhibited from committing crime to the extent that they accumulate social capital in their marital relationships.

Empirical support for the idea of marriage as an investment process comes from Laub, Nagin, and Sampson (1998), who showed that early marriages characterized by social cohesiveness led to a growing preventive effect. Consistent with the informal social control theory of Sampson and Laub (1993) and Nagin and Paternoster (1994), the data support the investment-quality character of good marriages. The effect of a good marriage takes time to appear, and it grows slowly, gradually inhibiting crime. These findings accord well with studies using contemporary data. For example, Horney, Osgood, and Marshall (1995) showed that large within-individual variations in criminal offending for a sample of high-rate convicted felons were systematically associated with local life circumstances (for example, employment and marriage). As the authors noted, some of the time, some high-rate offenders enter into circumstances, like marriage, that provide the potential for informal social control (see also Farrington and West 1995).

Marriage also influences desistance because it frequently leads to significant changes in everyday routines. It is well known that lifestyles and routine activities are a major source of variation in exposure to crime and victimization (Hindelang, Gottfredson, and Garofalo 1978; Cohen and Felson 1979). Osgood and colleagues (1996) have shown that participation in unstructured socializing activities with peers increased the frequency of deviant behaviors among those aged 18 to 26. Marriage, however, has the potential to radically change routine activities, especially with regard to one's peer group. As Osgood and Lee (1993) have argued, marriage entails obligations that tend to reduce leisure activities outside of the family. It is reasonable to assume that married people will spend more time together than with their same-sex peers. We already noted that there is supporting empirical evidence that the transition to marriage is followed by a decline in time spent with friends and exposure to delinquent peers (Warr 1998, 183). Marriage, therefore, has the potential to cut off an ex-offender from his delinquent peer group (see also Graham and Bowling 1995). Shover (1996, 126) notes that "successful establishment of bonds with conventional others and participation in conventional activities are major contingencies on the path that leads to termination of a criminal career."

Marriage often means the introduction of new friends and family (in-laws), who can affect routine activities as well. These changes hold the promise of new opportunities for socialization and changed routines. Marriage can also lead to a residential change—moving from the old neighborhood to the suburbs or to a different state altogether—and this physical relocation changes one's routine. In addition, parenting responsibilities lead to changes in routine activities as more and more time is spent in family-centered activities rather than in unstructured time with peers.

Further, marriage may lead to desistance because of the direct social control exerted by spouses. This may be particularly true of marriages in the 1950s and 1960s, which we partially examined in our previous work (Sampson and Laub 1993). Along with providing a base of social support, wives in this era took primary control of the planning and management of the household and often acted as informal guardians of their husbands' activities. Implicit was an obligation to family by the male partner, especially concerning economic support. Married men thus felt responsible for more than just themselves. Spouses provided additional support by exercising direct supervision. Supporting evidence for this idea can be found in Umberson (1992). Umberson hypothesizes that marriage is beneficial to health because spouses monitor and attempt to control their spouse's behavior. She finds that women "nag" about health more than men and that men engage in more risky behaviors compared with women. Thus marriage has the capacity to generate both informal social control and emotionally sustaining features.

Finally, marriage can change one's sense of self. For some, getting married connotes getting "serious"; in other words, becoming an adult. Although it now may seem retrograde, the men we are studying came of age when getting married meant becoming a man and taking responsibility. Marriage also meant having someone to care for and having someone to take care of you. This view became even more evident once children entered the family.

A key unanswered question is whether there is something unique about marriage from the standpoint of desistance from crime. Or can the apparent crime suppression benefits of marriage extend to those that are involved in cohabitation or other arrangements as well? This question is important for criminology in light of recent work by Waite (1995), who makes a strong case that marriage is indeed different and better for participants across several domains (see also Waite and Gallagher 2000).[3] Horney and her colleagues have shown that marriage is different than cohabitation with respect to crime suppression effects (Horney, Osgood, and Marshall 1995; Horney, Roberts, and Hassell 2000). That is, marriage reduces crime; cohabitation appears to increase criminal behavior.

Overall, we would agree with Waite and Gallagher, who have argued that "marriage actually changes people's goals and behavior in ways that are profoundly and powerfully life enhancing" (2000, 17). This is especially true with respect to those with damaged backgrounds and who have offended in the past. Waite and Gallagher add, "Marriage makes people better off in part because it constrains them from certain kinds of behavior, which, while perhaps immediately attractive (i.e., staying up all night drinking beer, or cheating on your partner) do not pay off in the long run" (2000, 24). Thus marriage, and the subsequent marital attachment, is an important source of desistance from crime. If marriage is absent, or characterized by weak or nonexistent attachment, continued offending will occur. From our perspective, the influence of marriage is nonetheless complex, operating through multiple mechanisms, not all of which necessitate cognitive transformation.

### Is Marriage a Selection Effect?

Of course, some researchers have argued that marital bonds do not just happen but are created by individual choice, therefore rendering the marriage-crime relationship spurious (for example, Gottfredson and Hirschi, 1990; Hirschi and Gottfredson, 1995). For theoretical and empirical reasons, we reject selection as a simple explanation of the marriage effect (see Sampson and Laub 1995 for details). For one thing, Laub, Nagin, and Sampson (1998) demonstrated that childhood and juvenile characteristics were insufficient for predicting patterns of future offending in a high-rate group of juvenile offenders. Individual differences presumed to influence the marriage process (for example, temperament, intelligence, aggressive behavior) were explicitly controlled. These findings imply that many of the classic predictors of the onset and frequency of delinquency do not explain desistance, much less explain away the marriage effect.

More generally, in an intriguing study, Johnson and Booth (1998) examine the question of whether stability in marital quality is due to the dyadic properties of the relationship or to personality or to social factors that individuals bring into the marriage. Using data from a national probability sample of persons married in 1980, these authors analyzed marital quality for those with two successive unions compared with data on marital quality over time for those with the same partner. The data suggest that stability in marital quality is due largely to the dyadic relationship environment. This finding suggests that while individuals bring personality and interactional styles to any relationship, these characteristics are malleable and can be altered by emergent qualities of the marriage itself. In other words, although one cannot deny selection effects, the resulting marital relationships can be quite powerful.

Selection into marriage also appears to be less systematic than many think. As we shall demonstrate, many men cannot even articulate why they got married or how they began relationships, which often just seemed to happen by chance. There is a long history of research on marriage that reveals strong effects for prosaic factors such as residential propinquity (Blau 1977). Selection is surely operating at some level, but most marriages originate in fortuitous contacts rooted in everyday routine activities. Frank Cullen has also pointed out that such fortuitous contacts almost always result in deviant men ending up with less deviant women. According to Cullen: (1) men are more criminal and deviant than women; (2) there are many more men than women with low self-control (in the parlance of Gottfredson and Hirschi); (3) therefore the composition of the marriage pool for women results in a short supply of high self-control men as marital partners, so a certain proportion of women must marry or otherwise associate with men who have less self-control than they do; (4) thus, from an ecological or routine activities perspective, women come into contact with men who have less self-control (Cullen, pers. comm., May 25, 1996).

We could perhaps put it more bluntly—given the crime differences between men and women, it is almost invariably the case that men marry "up" and women "down" when it comes to exposure to violence and crime. For this reason alone it is little wonder that marriage, to virtually any woman, could benefit men. We admit this position is crude and pessimistic regarding the character of men, but would defend it as empirically correct. Indeed feminists are justified, by this logic, in recoiling at arguments about "good marriage" effects. Good for whom, we must ask. Yet given the gendered nature of the Glueck sample along with the historical context, we cannot help but focus here on male outcomes. We look to other scholars to uncover the role of marriage, if any, in the offending careers of women (for example, Giordano, Cernkovich, and Rudolph 2002).

## Work

Like marital bonds, strong ties to work can lead to desistance from crime. In our previous analyses (Sampson and Laub 1993), we found that job stability was strongly related to desistance. In a similar vein, using qualitative data, Shover (1996) determined that acquiring a satisfying job was an important contingency in the lives of men who desisted from crime. It is therefore important to examine the mechanisms underlying the desistance process for work. We contend that the processes for work are similar to those for marriage.

First, in *Crime in the Making*, we argued that job stability, commitment to work, and mutual ties binding workers and employers increase informal social control and, all else equal, lead to a cessation in criminal behavior. As with spouses, here we emphasize the reciprocal nature of social capital invested by employers. For example, employers often take chances in hiring workers, hoping that their investment will pay off. This investment by the employer may trigger a return investment in social capital by the employee. The theoretical point is that interdependency is reciprocal and embedded in the social ties between individuals and social institutions. This conception may help explain how change in delinquent behavior is initiated, as when an employer takes a chance on a former delinquent, fostering a return investment in the job, which in turn inhibits the deviant behavior of the employee. This was the experience of one former delinquent, who said to the Gluecks' interviewer at his age 25 interview, "My employer . . . was good to me. He trusted me with the money, put his confidence in me, and I learned to respect such confidence and was loyal to him." Work provided the Glueck men clear benefits as well as responsibilities and obligations.

Second, even more than marriage, work, especially full-time work, leads to a meaningful change in routine activities. Work restricts many criminal opportunities and thus reduces the probability that criminal propensities will be translated into action. For example, men in stable employment situations are typically subject to more structured activities and have less free time than those not employed or employed intermittently. As William Julius Wilson argues, work is important as a "central experience of adult life" and is a "regulating" force in life (1996, 52). Like marriage, full-time legal employment gives structure to one's time and provides fewer opportunities for offending and other forms of deviance. Work is central to structured routines. The simple fact is that people who work are kept busy and are less likely to get into trouble.

Third, depending upon the nature of the work, employers, like wives, can provide direct social control. In other words, employers can keep their employees in line. For example, one former delinquent told us that his employer was "like a strict father. He went after me a few times. He also took me under his wing. We would have a few drinks together." This man was such a valued and dedicated employee that the company bought him the house he now lives in and provides him with a luxury car every two or three years for his good work.

Finally, work can give a man a sense of identity and meaning to his life. Paul Goodman (1956), for example, wrote about "man's work" as work that allows one to keep "one's honor and dignity." For Goodman, having a good job is one of the principal mechanisms enabling young men to be taken seriously, to be seen as useful, and, indeed, to grow up. Young men who fail to work may get stuck in a state of arrested development (see also Graham and Bowling 1995, 97). This was especially true during the 1950s and 1960s, when men were viewed as the sole household breadwinner and women's work outside of the home was perceived as "extra." Writing from a different disciplinary vantage point, Vaillant and Vaillant (1981, 1434) have argued that work can "reflect competence, social utility, and self-esteem" and is central to mental health.

As for marriage, a selection argument can be made on the spurious nature of the work-crime connection. It is likely that selection contamination is even greater for employment, if for no other reason than that there are sorting mechanisms (for example, applications, interviews) for work that are not found in informal marriage markets. Perhaps the most convincing attempt to counteract selection bias comes from a recent analysis of data from a national work experiment that drew participants from poor ghetto areas in nine U.S. cities. Uggen (2000) found that overall, those given jobs showed no reduction in crime relative to those in a control group. Age, however, significantly interacted with employment to affect the timing of illegal earnings and arrest. Those aged 27 or older were more likely to desist when provided marginal employment. Among those younger, the experimental job treatment had no effect on desistance. This is an important finding, because the experimental nature of the data addresses the selectivity that has plagued much research in this area. By specifying event history models accounting for assignment to, eligibility for, and participation in the National Supported Work Demonstration Project, Uggen provides more refined estimates of the effects of work as a turning point in the lives of criminal offenders. Furthermore, we would maintain that although individual factors most certainly matter, employment relationships, like marriage, generate emergent properties that take on a life of their own and are not easily reducible to the character of the person. The whole idea of "vacancy chains" (White 1970) in the employment literature was to show that getting a job is an interdependent system not reducible to individual decisions. In any case, we treat selection and work as an empirical question to be resolved in analysis.

### Military Service

In our previous work (Sampson and Laub 1996), we have argued that military service is a turning point in the transition to young adulthood (see also Elder 1986). Using quantitative data from the Gluecks' study, we found strong evidence that military service in the World War II era fostered long-term socioeconomic achievement among men raised in poverty areas of Boston during the Great Depression. Military service during World War II stands out as the defining moment for an entire generation, touching the lives of three in four American men and yielding one of the largest social interventions in U.S. history—the G.I. Bill of Rights. Our results revealed that overseas duty, in-service schooling, and G.I. Bill training at ages 17 to 25 generally enhanced subsequent occupational status, job stability, and economic well-being, independent of childhood differences and socioeconomic background. The benefits of the G.I. Bill were also larger for veterans stigmatized with an officially delinquent past, especially those who served in the military earlier rather than later in life (see Sampson and Laub 1996 for more details).

Some evidence, though limited, suggests that the military presents a unique setting for men with a disadvantaged past in yet another arena—the stigma of prior criminal conviction. Mattick (1960) compared the recidivism rates of men paroled to the army with those of a group of civil parolees, and found that the rates among army parolees were much lower. An eight-year follow-up revealed lasting positive effects of the army experience: the recidivism rate for the army parolees was 10.5 percent, compared with the national average of 66.6 percent. Mattick, however, could not identify the aspects of the army experience that may have accounted for this difference.

Our age-graded conceptualization of the life course suggests that military service sets in motion a chain of events (or experiences) in individuals' lives that progressively shape future outcomes. What is it about the military that facilitated change in behavior, especially for those who were involved in crime prior to entering?

First, military service exemplifies change by removing disadvantaged youths from prior adverse influences (for example, bad neighborhoods, delinquent peers) and social stigma (for example, criminal record). As Elder (1986, 244) argued, war and serving in the military can profoundly affect a person's development by introducing a major source of discontinuity in the life course. Caspi and Moffitt (1993, 247) also point out that the military is a strong situational transition because it includes institutional discouragement of previous responses and provides clear direction and novel opportunities for behavioral adaptation. Beginning with basic training, the military provides a basic education and socialization designed to reorient newcomers to a world with different rules and structures. Past accomplishments and past deficits alike have diminished influence. Thus a prominent feature of serving in the military is the "knifing off" of past experience and its potential for reorganizing social roles and life opportunities (see Brotz and Wilson 1946; Janowitz 1972). One former delinquent told us, "The military cured me. It took a young hoodlum off the street. My neighborhood in East Boston was a jumping-off place for jail."

Second, the military provided opportunities such as in-service training and subsequent training or education under the G.I. Bill. In this way military service may offer additional structural benefits that in turn enhance later attachment to work and marriage, which may in turn encourage desistance. As evident in the life-history narratives described in Chapter 6, the military provided a bridging environment for disadvantaged men, especially those with a delinquent past (Browning, Lopreato, and Poston 1973; Cutright 1974, 318).

In short, similar to marriage and work, but more by conscious design, the military changes routine activities, provides direct supervision and social support, and allows for the possibility of identity change. In addition, the military setting provides qualities often missing from the homes of disadvantaged men, such as firm discipline, cooperative relations or teamwork, strong leadership, social responsibility, and competent male models for emulation (Elder 1986, 236–238). The military also entails new options and experiences, especially travel to diverse places and corresponding exposure to all sorts of people and situations—varied backgrounds, talents, interests, goals, and even new conceptions of meaning (Elder 1986, 238–240; see also Elder and Hareven 1993, 53).[4] For some, the military even provided basic necessities—food, shelter, and clothes, for example. One man we talked to said, "I liked the uniform. It seems like it's [the military] altogether different from my childhood. From what I went through." For some, the attraction of the military was so great that they went to great lengths to enter. One former delinquent wanted to join the Marines to get away from his father, and he was so desperate to do so that he signed up under another name.

Of course, serving in the military has its downside as well. Some men were seriously injured in the military, affecting their lives dramatically. According to Elder (1986), veterans least likely to benefit from the military experience were those who served in combat, who were wounded or taken captive, or who observed killing by others. War-induced trauma can undermine the stability of marriage or can result in avoiding marriage altogether. Using data from the Terman study, Pavalko and Elder (1990) examined the effects of mass mobilization in World War II and found that veterans were more likely to divorce than nonveterans. Similarly, Laufer and Gallops (1985) suggest that trauma resulting from combat heightens the risk of marital instability. The tragic consequences of military service cannot be ignored, nor can the wider historical context of war be neglected. The Vietnam War unleashed a dimension of military service and strife unknown to our men. Consistent with the life-course perspective, we are thus careful to situate claims about the military in their historical context.

## Justice System Involvement

Do criminal justice sanctions, especially incarceration, foster recidivism or help lead to the termination of offending? This question has had a long and protracted history in criminal justice research, but is becoming ever more relevant given the recent incarceration increases in the United States. Central to life-course research is how early events like juvenile incarceration influence later outcomes. Conventional wisdom suggests that involvement in the juvenile justice system, especially incarceration, can have consequences that reverberate over the life course.

In our research program analyzing the Gluecks' data, we examined the role of both criminal behavior and reactions to it by the criminal justice system, finding that delinquent behavior has a systematic attenuating effect on the social and institutional bonds linking adults to society (for example, labor force attachment, marital cohesion). More specifically, we found that social bonds to employment were directly influenced by criminal sanctions—incarceration as a juvenile and as a young adult had a negative effect on later job stability, which in turn was negatively related to continued involvement in crime over the life course (Sampson and Laub 1993; Laub and Sampson 1995).[5] From this finding as well as other suggestive evidence (see Freeman 1991; Nagin and Waldfogel 1995), we explored the idea of "cumulative continuity," which posits that delinquency incrementally mortgages the future by generating negative consequences for the life chances of stigmatized and institutionalized youth (see Sampson and Laub 1997). For example, arrest and incarceration may spark failure in school, unemployment, and weak community bonds, in turn increasing adult crime. Western and Beckett's recent study (1999, 1048) shows that the negative effects of youth incarceration on adult employment time exceed the large negative effects for dropping out of high school and living in an area with high unemployment. Serious

delinquency can thus cut off future opportunities such that participants have fewer options for a conventional life.

By design, all of the delinquent subjects in the Gluecks' *Unraveling*
study were incarcerated in either the Lyman School for Boys in Westboro or the Industrial School for Boys at Shirley. The Lyman School
was the first state reform school in the United States. George Briggs,
the governor of Massachusetts, stated in 1846 at the opening:

> Of the many and valuable institutions sustained in whole, or in part,
> from the public treasury, we may safely say, that none is of more impor-
> tance, or holds a more intimate connection with the future prosperity
> and moral integrity of the community, than one which promises to take
> neglected, wayward, wandering, idle and vicious boys, with perverse
> minds and corrupted hearts, and cleanse and purify and reform them,
> and thus send them forth in the erectness of manhood and in beauty of
> virtue, educated and prepared to be industrious, useful and virtuous citi-
> zens. (quoted in Miller 1991, 69)

Work by Miller (1991), McCord and McCord (1953), Ohlin, Coates,
and Miller (1974) and an autobiography by a former Lyman inmate,
Devlin (1985), however, make clear that the reality of the Lyman
School was quite different from the lofty hopes expressed by Governor Briggs.

During the 1940s and 1950s (the time period of the Gluecks'
study), the Lyman School was a large custodial institution containing
250 to 350 boys, primarily 13- to 15-year-olds. The institution was
organized as a cottage system that was age-segregated with house parents. The institutional structure was extremely regimented. For instance, inmates marched from their rooms to meals, and each day activities were segmented and marked by a series of bells and whistles.
Credits were earned for privileges like cigarettes and ultimately parole. If an inmate misbehaved, a master could subtract any amount of
credit from the boy's total. Physical punishment and verbal humilia-
tions were common. For instance, boys were kicked for minor infrac-
tions like talking. Other physical punishments included hitting inmates with wooden paddles or straps on the soles of their bare feet.
Cold showers were also used as a form of punishment and intimida-
tion by the masters (see Miller 1991, 96).

Most distressing were the unusual and cruel punishments imposed
by the staff. For example, boys were forced to sit at their lockers for
hours. Haircuts were also used as a form of punishment and punitive

discipline. Jerome Miller, the former director of the Massachusetts Department of Youth Services, writes of staff reporting the need to "hit the little bastards for distance" (Miller 1991, 94). Miller goes on to describe "programs" that included "kneeling in a line in silence, scrubbing the floors with toothbrushes, or being made to stand or sit in odd, peculiarly painful positions" (1991, 94). Along with these demeaning rituals, there were examples of sadistic discipline (such as having to drink from toilets or kneel for hours on the stone floor with a pencil under one's knees) (Miller 1991, 95).

Our analyses in Chapters 6, 7, and 8 aim to uncover the connection between such incarceration experiences and later life. In addition to transmitting information on punishment and length of incarceration, our narrative data provide a unique window from which we can also view subjective understandings of the criminal justice system. One theme that emerged from our interviews is that the criminal justice system is corrupt and a "game." The men we spoke with talked about police planting evidence, cons selling each other down the river, and arbitrary decision making by judges, district attorneys, and probation and parole officers. In the eyes of the men we interviewed, no one was concerned about justice, truth, helping offenders, or even exacting punishment for crimes committed. Everybody was out to get "the best deal," and the deal you got had little to do with what you did. There is a growing body of research on the perceived legitimacy of law and institutions of social control (see, for example, LaFree 1998; Tyler 1990; Sampson and Bartusch 1998) that we draw upon to better understand how attitudes about criminal justice bear on the adult lives of convicted men.

We also hope to understand the consequences of incarceration, especially early on in the adolescent period, across a variety of adult domains, including family, work, and the military. We ask a simple but provocative question: to what extent is incarceration a turning point (positive or negative) in the experience of human lives? It may be the case that the effects of incarceration are variable, especially when viewed from the perspective of the men themselves.

## Expanding Informal Social Control Theory

Reflecting upon developments in life-course criminology over the decade since the publication of *Crime in the Making,* we have concluded that our age-graded theory of informal social control needs to be modified in some significant ways. Perhaps even the language of social control is in need of revision, although we set that question aside for the moment. In this section we identify several components—human agency, situational influences and contexts, and historical context—that should be incorporated into social control theory in order to provide a richer and more complete explanation of criminal behavior over the life course, especially patterns of persistence in offending and desistance from crime.

### Human Agency

Drawing on ethnographic studies and first-person accounts, Katz (1988) argues that crime is purposeful, systematic, and meaningful. Crime is therefore action—"something to do"—which for Matza (1964) evokes the notion of will and desperation.[6] In this regard, crime is a vehicle for demonstrating freedom and agency. Other themes that are evident in the life histories of offenders include the attraction and excitement of crime (the seduction of crime; see Katz 1988) and crime as calculated and articulated resistance to authority (crime as defiance; see Sherman 1993).

Our view is that these agential processes are reciprocally linked to situations and larger structures (cultural, social, and psychological), past, present, and future. Agency is thus best viewed as an emergent process, both spatially and temporally. Kohli makes a similar argument: "The individual life course has to be conceptualized not as a behavioral outcome of macrosocial organizations (or of its interaction with psychological properties of the individual) but as the result of the subject's constructive activity in dealing with the available life course programs" (1986, 272). What is important is the interplay between agency, action, and structure through time, such that "agency is path dependent as well as situationally embedded" (Emirbayer 1997, 294). Emirbayer goes on to argue that "social actors are always embedded in space and time; they respond to specific *situations* (opportunities as well as constraints) rather than pursuing lines of conduct in purely solipsistic fashion" (1997, 307).

The questions asked in the course of collecting our life-history narratives were designed to reveal human agency and the contexts within which criminal and deviant actions occur. Yet as in Katz (1988), narratives have been used in criminology primarily to study persistence in crime, or what keeps offenders going. Less understood are the actions and mechanisms by which offenders stop or withdraw from a life in crime. If crime is so seductive, how does one exit the temptation? This question points to an important gap in the criminological literature on desistance—the actions that active criminals take in order to improve their chances in life need to be recognized (see also Giordano, Cernkovich, and Rudolph 2002). Fortunately, as developed in more detail below, what is most striking in the narratives we collected is the role of human agency in processes of desistance from crime and deviance. The Glueck men are seen to be active players in their destiny, especially when their actions project a new sense of a redeemed self. One man told us how he felt when he left prison: "The heck with you [guards and others in authority]. I made a conscious effort—do my time and get the hell out. And don't come back." There are numerous examples of similar actions in our narrative interviews, with "redemption" emerging as a key process in desistance. We therefore exploit our life-history narratives to better understand the agential processes involved in the lives of former delinquents, especially mechanisms that differentiate the life paths of persistent offenders from desisters.

## The Situational Context of Crime and Violence

It is important to ground crime and social control in their situational context. As Birkbeck and LaFree (1993, 129) point out, "situations vary in the extent to which they constrain behavioral choices." Informal social controls may be contingent on social context. From our life-history narratives, it is apparent that crime and violence are normative in certain settings and in certain situations. This fact has implications for understanding persistence in and desistance from crime over the life course.[7] The men we interviewed made fine shadings in their characterization of violence. In fact, in certain contexts and situations, strong informal social controls can sometimes promote crime rather than prevent it (Black 1983). Black, for example, argues that one kind of social control is "self-help"—"the expression of a grievance by unilateral aggression such as personal violence or property destruction" (1983, 46). Others have argued that there is a great deal of overlap among offenders and victims (Lauritsen, Sampson, and Laub 1991). Thus it is wise to consider crime, especially violent episodes, as situated transactions (Luckenbill 1977).

Routine activities are, of course, linked to situational variations.

We saw that for persistent offenders, the percentage of time spent married, in the military, or in the labor force is very low, especially in contrast to those that desisted. In contrast, the percentage of time spent institutionalized is quite large. Two patterns emerged with respect to persistent offenders: (1) little or no work, relatively speaking—a low percentage of time is spent working or in a marriage situation; and (2) a lot of short-term work—some seasonal—but nothing long term. There is lots of hustling, but few stable, structured work routines are evident. There are also multiple marriages (between two and five) that do not last very long (for example, two to four years). One persistent offender told us that "a change of pasture makes the cow fat." The men also appeared to go back and forth between their wives and their ex-wives fairly frequently. These patterns show a considerable lack of stability in routine activities.

It is also apparent that alcohol sustains crime in part because it makes work and marriage more difficult. One persistent offender told us, "As soon as I started on a drunk, I'd wind up walking off the job." Moreover, if consuming alcohol is a major part of your life— "tonight, I am going drinking"—then your lifestyle activities involve bars, clubs, and parties with others similarly situated, men and women. One man told us that he never met a woman that was not "a drunk." It is no surprise then that heavy drinking was a dominant feature in the group of persistent offenders we interviewed. In contrast, none of the desisters we interviewed were heavy drinkers and those that had been in the past had gotten help to deal with their problem drinking.

Overall our narrative data suggest that criminologists should treat the definition and meaning of crime as problematic. For this generation and in these neighborhoods, some crime is normative. One man said to us, "I don't classify that [fights down at the bar] as crime because it was normal to fight around here anyways." He went on to say that "well, we got black eyes. One guy got a broken jaw and stuff like that. But no serious stuff." In addition, these men are not afraid to take cash for a side job and not report it as income. Fudging on taxes is not viewed as wrong, nor is overcharging on repair jobs. In fact, many of the men seem willing to cut any deal they can.

## Historical Context

Historical context, especially growing up during the Great Depression and World War II era, heavily influenced the objective opportunities and the subjective worldview for the men in our study (see Laub and Sampson 2002). The historical embeddedness of particular turning points (for example, early marriage and children; lack of education and geographic mobility; military service and the G.I. Bill) cannot be overstated. Although not necessarily reflected in the lives of the Glueck men, this period of history was marked by less mass alienation and crime than today, low unemployment, increasing national wealth, expansion of the occupational structure, and, for some, the G.I. Bill with its occupational and educational training.

We believe this time period is a particularly interesting one in which to think about crime and deviance as well as more general developmental patterns over the life course (for example, the adolescence-to-adulthood transition). For example, drugs like crack cocaine were not even known in this period, and the level of criminal violence, especially gun use, was below what we see at present. Pervasive alcohol abuse, coupled with the virtual absence of other drug use, suggests a strong period effect. As already noted, one of the major forces in the lives of some of the men we interviewed was the military. These men were also in a position to take advantage of numerous opportunities offered by the G.I. Bill (see Modell 1989, 204–205). As Modell has argued, "the dominant lasting effect of the war seems to have been the economic forces it unleashed, and the personal optimism and sense of efficacy that it engendered" (1989, 162). This description rings true for the men who desisted from crime in adulthood, as shown in Chapter 6.

In addition to macrolevel historical events, we explore the role of local culture and community context in the lives of the Glueck men. As been said many times, Boston is a city of neighborhoods, and not surprisingly the local context helps us understand the processes of persistent offending and desistance from crime. For too long, individual lives have been examined in isolation, even though it is now clear that historical time and geographic place are crucial for understanding lives in their full complexity (Elder, Modell, and Parke 1993).

### Life Histories

With the exception of single case histories like *The Jack-Roller at Seventy* (Jack-Roller and Snodgrass, 1982), there have been very few long-term qualitative studies of offenders and ex-offenders. Our goal in this book is to explicate and better understand the processes of persistent offending and desistance from crime over the life course. Using a life-history approach has five major advantages.

First, the life-history method uniquely captures the process of both becoming involved in and disengaging from crime and other antisocial behavior. This information is crucial for understanding the relationship between crime and the mechanisms of informal and formal social control. Life histories reveal in the offenders' own words the personal-situational context of their behavior and their views of the larger social and historical circumstances in which their behavior is embedded. For example, life histories can be used to discover how people react to salient life events, the meaning of those events to the persons involved, and most important, how their experience of the events structures later life decisions. In this way, life-history narratives expose human agency and reveal how conceptions of self and others change over time. These personal accounts play a dual role; they represent the past, but they also actively shape future actions (Scott and Lyman 1968).

Second, life histories can uncover complex patterns of continuity and change in individual behavior over time. Life-history narratives focus on the whole life, not just one dimension or one set of variables, and reveal the interconnectedness between life events and situations. Shover has argued that "the notion that most offenders follow a zig-zag path of criminal participation compels us to be sensitive to *turning points* in criminal careers and the reasons for changes in direction at these junctures" (1996, 1–2). Life-history narratives, ordered temporally, can be used to show sequences that are "on-line" and "off-line" over long time spans (Mishler 1996). We are especially interested in detecting systematic patterns in subjective assessments of "turning points," including the nature or type of self-identified turning points, their timing over the life course, and the triggering mechanisms.

A third advantage is that life histories reveal the complexity of criminal behavior. Ernest Burgess pointed out many years ago that "to label behavior does not serve to explain it. In fact, it may act to prevent understanding of the many different kinds of behavior that may be covered under one term" (1931, 235). Multiple pathways to the same outcome may be present, and life histories expose "the heterogeneity of experience that can lead to a given outcome" (Carr et al. 1995, 23; see also Singer et al., 1998). Life-history narratives offer a way of breaking down complex phenomena by providing detailed information about events as they are experienced and the significance of these events for the actors involved.

A fourth advantage is that life histories are grounded in social and historical context. Shover's research on persistent thieves illustrates this notion with respect to choice and social class. Shover asks: what is rational choice for those who are economically marginalized with little hope for the future? He argues that "offenders do calculate in some manner, but the process is constrained severely by their prior choices of identity and lifestyles" (1996, 177). Life chances and views of opportunities for crime depend on historical circumstances and location in the social structure. Moreover, such calculations often change with age. Thus for each offender the rational calculus surrounding the decision to participate in crime becomes quite different over time and place.

A fifth advantage is that the life-history method shows the human side of offenders. Bennett (1981) notes that life histories disclose the "essential humanity of those who offend," and in turn the distance between the offender and nonoffender is reduced. The purpose of life histories is not to romanticize offenders and their lifestyles, but the closer one is to delinquents or adult offenders, the less likely one is to impute pathology (see also Hagan and McCarthy 1997).

In sum, life histories have advantages that cannot be easily obtained using traditional quantitative data on offenders and the patterns of offending. More broadly, life-history research has the potential to change the discipline by "reorienting criminology to the concrete" (Bennett 1981, 157). We concede that the development of quantitative methods has solidified criminology's claim as a scientific enterprise, but what criminology is lacking is a rich, detailed knowledge base about offending from those who commit crime, expressed in their own words. The consequence is that we have little understanding of the circumstances underlying the dynamics of criminal activity and processes of social control. Life histories can provide the human voices to counterbalance the wide range of statistical data in criminology and the social sciences at large (Bennett 1981; Clausen 1993; Hagan and McCarthy 1997).

## Setting the Stage

There is much to learn about persistence in a life of crime versus desistance from crime and other antisocial behavior. We believe that a life-course theory of crime that incorporates a dynamic view of social control, situations, and individual choices that vary within individuals over time provides the best hope for unpacking the processes of persistence and desistance. Furthermore, by drawing on ex-offenders' own words, life-history narratives can more fully illuminate continuity and change in criminal and deviant behaviors as individuals construct their own life course. The data found in our narratives challenge our theory, and we therefore approach the analyses open to subsequent changes in theoretical concepts, the specifics of which unfold in the chapters that follow.

Our approach, then, is to integrate quantitative and qualitative data in both data collection and data analysis. This integration takes two forms. First, we collected, coded, and analyzed criminal record data from criminal histories and death records from vital statistics (see Chapter 5 for results). Second, these quantitative data were combined with an analysis of life-history narratives. In addition, "objective record data" from the Gluecks' earlier studies (1950, 1968) were integrated with the life histories (see Chapters 6, 7, and 8). In Chapter 9, we return to the quantitative data for an analysis of how changes in adult domains—marriage, work, and military—are related to changes in criminal activity within individuals over time. We now turn to the original sources of the data that we collected to resolve these challenging issues in understanding persistent offending and desistance from crime over the life course.

# CHAPTER FOUR

# Finding the Men

Where are they now? How have time and experience changed them? Who has died? Who is still alive? Such questions are the stuff of television specials, high school and college reunions, and gatherings of war veterans. These questions are also important for researchers interested in criminal behavior over time. One objective of life-course research is to examine how events that occur early in life can shape later outcomes. Thus long-term longitudinal studies are needed to understand the pathways of development from childhood, adolescence, and adulthood. It is also true that longitudinal studies allow the uncovering of turning points that may help to explain significant changes in behavioral trajectories over time. One problem in the social sciences generally, and especially in criminology, is the short-term nature of most longitudinal follow-up studies. To rectify this problem, we initiated a comprehensive follow-up study of the original delinquents in Sheldon and Eleanor Glueck's *Unraveling Juvenile Delinquency* study (1950).

As detailed below, the Gluecks' three-wave study of juvenile and adult criminal behavior involved a sample of 500 male delinquents aged 10–17 and 500 male nondelinquents aged 10–17 matched case by case on age, ethnicity, IQ, and low-income residence. Over a twenty-five-year period (1940–1965), the Gluecks' research team collected a wealth of information on these subjects in childhood, adolescence, and adulthood (see Glueck and Glueck 1950, 1968). Subjects were originally interviewed at an average age of 14, at age 25, and again at age 32. The follow-up success was 92 percent when adjusted for mortality—relatively high by current standards in criminological research (for example, Wolfgang, Thornberry, and Figlio 1987). The men were born between 1924 and 1932 and grew up in central Boston; thus when we launched our follow-up study in 1993, the oldest subject was 69 years of age and the youngest was 61 years of age.

We faced enormous obstacles from the outset. First, the Glueck sample of juvenile delinquents was quite large. Moreover, a large and complex amount of data was collected for all three time periods for 438 of the 500 delinquents (88 percent). Second and more important was the significant time gap; the men in the Gluecks' study had last been contacted between 1957 and 1964. The last addresses we had available were thirty-five years old. Few, if any, of the men had telephone numbers recorded in their case files in the Glueck archive. Also, only for roughly one in twenty men was a social security number available, a key identifier for tracking subjects in modern, large-scale databases.

Finally, of course, unlike old college classmates who may want to be found (replete with dedicated websites), we were searching for men who had a criminal past and sometimes a criminal present. Some men continued to lead criminal and deviant lives, and we suspected that they would not necessarily be interested in being located by us. Or in the case of men who had reformed, their current partners, employers, and other significant people in their lives may have been unaware of their delinquent past. Not surprisingly, these concerns were voiced by our human subjects review boards, which were initially less than enthusiastic about our research plans. In short, it was not at all clear we would be able to conduct a follow-up study at all. We were pessimistic about our chances of locating and updating the records for all the men, much less to actually find and re-interview a subsample of them.

Our study nonetheless set out to accomplish three major tasks: (a) the collection of criminal records, at both the state and the national levels; (b) the collection of death records, at both the state and the national levels; and (c) finding a subset of the original delinquent subjects of the Gluecks' study and interviewing them. Below we describe the specific components of the study and then present a summary of the results of our various follow-up strategies. At the end of the chapter, we contextualize the data we collected by describing their origin—the classic *Unraveling Juvenile Delinquency* study.

## Criminal Records Search

We began our follow-up study with a detailed search of the Massachusetts criminal history database. For this record search, we developed "face-sheets" for each delinquent subject in the Gluecks' study. These face-sheets contained the information needed to search the criminal records of the subjects since the date of the last contact by the Gluecks' research team. The requisite information included the subject's name, known aliases (if any), date of birth, social security number (when available), father's name, mother's name, FBI number, MBI (Massachusetts Bureau of Investigation) number, and last known address.

With the aid of these face-sheets, criminal records were manually searched at the Massachusetts Office of the Commissioner of Probation between January and June 1993 for 475 of the original 500 delinquents.[1] Operating since 1926, the Office of the Commissioner of Probation is the central repository of criminal record data for the state of Massachusetts. All criminal offenses presentable to the courts are reported to this central system. These data allowed us to update the official criminal history for the delinquents in the Glueck study after age 31. From these records, we categorized each arrest charge as one of four offense types—violent, property, alcohol/drug, or other.[2] The age of the subject was also coded for each of his arrests.

The Massachusetts data do not provide any information for those subjects who moved out of state or for those men who reside in the state, but may have committed crimes out of state. The extent to which this is a serious concern is not known. It may be that those men who were the most criminally active moved out of state for at least some portion of their career. At the same time, the rates of interstate mobility for this cohort of men are relatively low. Moreover, Widom (1989, 259) found that local police departments accounted for 80 percent of the adult arrests on record in the follow-up to her study. At the very least, it appears that state-level data provide an important foundation for a study of criminal careers over the life span.

Nevertheless, to supplement our state-level data, we obtained criminal histories from the Federal Bureau of Investigation. The process to secure these data took about eighteen months. We ran into many obstacles and went down several blind alleys. However, with the assistance of the National Institute of Justice, we were finally able to gain access to FBI rap sheets for each of the 475 Glueck men.[3] These records were searched during the months of February and March of 1996 and, in effect, cover the period through calendar year 1995. We coded the FBI rap sheets in a similar fashion to the coding of the Massachusetts data—that is, beginning at age 32, age-specific arrests by crime type were coded.[4] Our goal was to use the FBI data to supplement the existing data we had from Massachusetts. Therefore we coded all arrests after age 31 that did not appear in the Massachusetts criminal history data. This consisted of arrests that occurred out of state and arrests that occurred in Massachusetts, but for some reason were not recorded in the state-level data. A much larger proportion of men had a record in Massachusetts but no FBI rap sheet (29 percent) compared with the proportion of men who had an FBI rap sheet but no record in Massachusetts (6 percent). Overall, 55 percent of the men had a record both in Massachusetts and in the FBI data bank. Geerken (1994) has discussed in some detail the various reasons for the lack of consistency between FBI rap sheets and local police records, and it is evident that relying on one source of data for establishing official criminal histories will underestimate the number of arrests. In their study of the criminal careers of white-collar offenders using FBI rap sheets and local agency records, Weisburd and Waring (2001, 29n2) concluded that less serious offenses (for example, traffic violations, passing bad checks, and failure to pay child support) are not likely to be reported to the FBI.

The strategy of collecting information from both state and national criminal history data systems paid off when we consider the distribution of arrests after age 31 in the FBI records, but not in the Massachusetts records. Ninety-eight men were arrested after age 31, but they did not have a record in Massachusetts for those particular arrests. These men were responsible for 414 offenses, with a mean offending rate of 4.22. Thirteen men were responsible for 51 percent of all the offenses recorded on the FBI rap sheets for these 98 men. If we had relied only on records from Massachusetts, we would have missed these offenses and perhaps worse, depending upon crime type, we may have referred to these 98 men as desisters from crime. As expected, the bulk of these offenses were committed outside the state of Massachusetts.

Official criminal records, of course, are limited to offenses committed by the men that came to the attention of the criminal justice system, and hence refer only to official criminal histories. But though limited in scope, official data capture serious offenses (for example, robbery) fairly well (see Gove, Hughes, and Geerken 1985). Moreover, the criminal record data from the Massachusetts Office of the Commissioner of Probation have been successfully used in prior research (see Vaillant 1983; McCord 1979; Sampson and Laub 1993) and data from FBI rap sheets for a long time has been considered the "gold standard" in criminological research on criminal careers (see Blumstein et al. 1986; Belair 1985; and Weisburd and Waring 2001).

## Death Records Search

As we searched the criminal records, we simultaneously began a search of death records as well. We started with the Massachusetts Registry of Vital Records and Statistics during July and August 1993. At that time, the most recent index included Massachusetts deaths through March 1993. In all, 475 subjects were searched from their thirty-second birthday, unless an arrest date showed a later search date was appropriate. We already knew the dates and the cause of death for the 25 subjects who died during the Gluecks' study. Once a record of death was found, we purchased the death certificate from the Registry. From the death certificate itself, information on the date of death, the cause (or causes) of death, the location of death, and marital status at time of death was coded. This information was then integrated into our longitudinal data file of official criminal histories to age 70.

Next we conducted a search for the remaining living men using the National Death Index (NDI) maintained by the National Center for Health Statistics (National Center for Health Statistics 1990).[5] The NDI is a centralized, computerized index of death record information for all fifty states, the District of Columbia, Puerto Rico, and the Virgin Islands. The index begins with deaths in 1979. We searched this index in October and November 1993 and uncovered additional deaths, both in Massachusetts and out of state, through calendar year 1992.

We continued our search of death records periodically throughout the follow-up study. For example, the Massachusetts death records were last searched for all subjects known to be alive in the summer of 1996. The National Death Index was searched again in November of 1996 and those data covered the years 1992 through 1995. Finally, obituaries in the *Boston Globe* were examined on a daily basis throughout the project period (1993–1998).

## Life-History Interviews

The third part of our follow-up study involves collecting detailed life histories for a subset of the delinquent subjects. As argued in the previous chapter, we believe that life-history narratives, more than any other methodology, will allow us to capture the heterogeneity of life-course experiences and uncover the dynamic processes surrounding salient life-course events, turning points, and criminal offending.

Initially our strategy for case selection for interviews was driven by the vagaries of funding. More precisely, selection of the men to be interviewed was influenced by a grant to study violence. With support from the Harry Frank Guggenheim Foundation, we identified eight distinct trajectories of violent criminal behavior across three stages of the life course (juvenile <17, young adult 17–32, and middle/later adulthood 32–70). Our strategy was to capture variation in dynamic trajectories of violence across the life course. To do this we selected eight groups (see Figure 4.1). We sought to interview at least five individuals in each of these eight groupings for a minimum total of forty interviews.

As it turned out, there were not enough men in certain trajectory groups, and in other cases the data on violence were overlapping with predatory offending against property (for example, burglary).[6] We therefore collapsed and revised our classification to be more parsimonious and reflective of offending patterns in the data, regrouping the men we interviewed into five working categories: (1) persistent violent or predatory offenders ($N = 14$); (2) nonviolent juvenile offenders who desisted in adulthood ($N = 15$); (3) juvenile violent offenders who desisted in adulthood ($N = 4$); (4) intermittent (or sporadic) offenders who also had an onset of violence in later adulthood ($N = 5$); and (5) intermittent offenders with an onset of violence in young adulthood and desistance in middle age, or those showing an erratic

offending pattern over their entire life course ($N = 14$). This classification scheme for the narrative interviews is described more fully in
Chapters 6–8.

For the interviews, we developed a modified life-history calendar
(see Freedman et al. 1988) to help subjects place major life events
(for example, marriages, divorces, residential moves, jobs) in time.
See Figure 4.2.[7] The life-history calendar is an important visual aid
that allows the subject and the researcher to contextualize objective
events. From the life-history calendar, one learns the number of events
and their timing, sequence, and duration.

We also used an open-ended interview schedule that covered a variety of life-course domains and brought into focus retrospective views
of the interviewee's life course (Clausen 1993). We asked the Glueck
men to reflect about their educational and work experiences, mili-

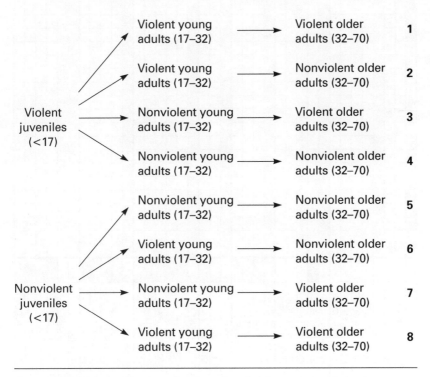

*Figure 4.1* Initial classification of trajectories of violent criminal behavior across
the life course

Subject: _____

| Reference years > | | 30 | 31 | 32 | 33 | 34 | 35 | 36 | 37 | 38 | 39 | 40 | 41 | 42 | 43 | 44 | 45 | 46 | 47 | 48 | 49 | 50 | 51 | 52 | 53 | 54 | 55 | 56 | 57 | 58 | 59 | 60 | 61 | 62 | 63 | 64 | 65 | 66 | 67 | 68 | 69 | 70 |
|---|---|---|---|---|---|---|---|---|---|---|---|---|---|---|---|---|---|---|---|---|---|---|---|---|---|---|---|---|---|---|---|---|---|---|---|---|---|---|---|---|---|---|
| Birthday: | | | | | | | | | | | | | | | | | | | | | | | | | | | | | | | | | | | | | | | | | | |
| MARRIAGES | # | | | | | | | | | | | | | | | | | | | | | | | | | | | | | | | | | | | | | | | | | |
| MARITAL EVENTS | | | | | | | | | | | | | | | | | | | | | | | | | | | | | | | | | | | | | | | | | | |
| LIVING W/ SPOUSE | | | | | | | | | | | | | | | | | | | | | | | | | | | | | | | | | | | | | | | | | | |
| PARTNER EVENTS | | | | | | | | | | | | | | | | | | | | | | | | | | | | | | | | | | | | | | | | | | |
| LIVING W/ PARTNER | | | | | | | | | | | | | | | | | | | | | | | | | | | | | | | | | | | | | | | | | | |
| CHILDREN | # | | | | | | | | | | | | | | | | | | | | | | | | | | | | | | | | | | | | | | | | | |
| BIRTHS/DEATHS | | | | | | | | | | | | | | | | | | | | | | | | | | | | | | | | | | | | | | | | | | |
| HOUSEMATES (if ever lived without spouse/partner) | | | | | | | | | | | | | | | | | | | | | | | | | | | | | | | | | | | | | | | | | | |
| LIVING W/ RELATIVES | | | | | | | | | | | | | | | | | | | | | | | | | | | | | | | | | | | | | | | | | | |
| LIVING W/ FRIENDS | | | | | | | | | | | | | | | | | | | | | | | | | | | | | | | | | | | | | | | | | | |
| FAMILY | | | | | | | | | | | | | | | | | | | | | | | | | | | | | | | | | | | | | | | | | | |
| PARENT DEATH | | | | | | | | | | | | | | | | | | | | | | | | | | | | | | | | | | | | | | | | | | |
| OTHER DEATH | | | | | | | | | | | | | | | | | | | | | | | | | | | | | | | | | | | | | | | | | | |
| OTHER–MISC. | | | | | | | | | | | | | | | | | | | | | | | | | | | | | | | | | | | | | | | | | | |
| EDUCATION | Y/N | | | | | | | | | | | | | | | | | | | | | | | | | | | | | | | | | | | | | | | | | | |
| FULL-TIME | | | | | | | | | | | | | | | | | | | | | | | | | | | | | | | | | | | | | | | | | | | |
| PART-TIME | | | | | | | | | | | | | | | | | | | | | | | | | | | | | | | | | | | | | | | | | | | |
| EMPLOYMENT | # | | | | | | | | | | | | | | | | | | | | | | | | | | | | | | | | | | | | | | | | | | |
| FULL-TIME | | | | | | | | | | | | | | | | | | | | | | | | | | | | | | | | | | | | | | | | | | | |
| PART-TIME | | | | | | | | | | | | | | | | | | | | | | | | | | | | | | | | | | | | | | | | | | | |
| SPOUSE WORK | | | | | | | | | | | | | | | | | | | | | | | | | | | | | | | | | | | | | | | | | | | |
| UNEMPLOYED | | | | | | | | | | | | | | | | | | | | | | | | | | | | | | | | | | | | | | | | | | | |
| DEPENDENT | | | | | | | | | | | | | | | | | | | | | | | | | | | | | | | | | | | | | | | | | | | |
| RESIDENCES | # | | | | | | | | | | | | | | | | | | | | | | | | | | | | | | | | | | | | | | | | | | |
| IN BOSTON | | | | | | | | | | | | | | | | | | | | | | | | | | | | | | | | | | | | | | | | | | | |
| IN MASS. | | | | | | | | | | | | | | | | | | | | | | | | | | | | | | | | | | | | | | | | | | | |
| OUTSIDE MASS. | | | | | | | | | | | | | | | | | | | | | | | | | | | | | | | | | | | | | | | | | | | |
| INSTITUTION | | | | | | | | | | | | | | | | | | | | | | | | | | | | | | | | | | | | | | | | | | | |
| ARRESTS | # | | | | | | | | | | | | | | | | | | | | | | | | | | | | | | | | | | | | | | | | | | |
| CONVICTIONS | # | | | | | | | | | | | | | | | | | | | | | | | | | | | | | | | | | | | | | | | | | | |
| VIOLENT | | | | | | | | | | | | | | | | | | | | | | | | | | | | | | | | | | | | | | | | | | | |
| PROPERTY | | | | | | | | | | | | | | | | | | | | | | | | | | | | | | | | | | | | | | | | | | | |
| DRUG/ALCOHOL | | | | | | | | | | | | | | | | | | | | | | | | | | | | | | | | | | | | | | | | | | | |
| OTHER | | | | | | | | | | | | | | | | | | | | | | | | | | | | | | | | | | | | | | | | | | | |

*Figure* 4.2 Life-history calendar for the follow-up of the Glueck delinquents at age 70

tary service, family relationships, living arrangements, neighborhood characteristics, social activities, and both official and unofficial involvement in crime and violence and alcohol/drug use. Of particular interest are the questions regarding the subject's assessment of his own life, specifically whether he saw it as improving or worsening since childhood, adolescence, or young adulthood, and the subject's self-evaluation of turning points in his life course and their relationship to criminal activity and various life-course transitions, such as marriage, divorce, military service, or residential change.

Although life-history narratives with a long retrospective window should be used with caution (see Janson 1990; Henry et al. 1994), a "catch-up study" such as ours really has no alternative. The key is to ensure that the data collected are valid and reliable, regardless of whether they are collected prospectively or retrospectively, or are quantitative or qualitative (Scott and Alwin 1998). The strength of our approach is that we combined life-history narratives with extensive institutional records, as well as with data in the Glueck archives, to ascertain the validity and reliability of the narratives. We believe that the narrative data are accurate from the actor's point of view, precise in their detail, and full of breadth (see Becker 1996). As we argued earlier, qualitative interviews provide a unique perspective often lacking in criminological research (see also Becker 1966; Katz 1988). We expect that these life-history narratives will provide important clues regarding the course of adult development from the vantage point of the actor, which cannot be obtained from statistical tables. Furthermore, by focusing on several offender subgroups, we will begin to unravel the developmental trajectories of continuity and change in criminal behavior over the life course. These interviews will not provide a full life review, of course, but they provide a rich supplement to the quantitative data we have collected in our follow-ups of official criminal histories and death records and our recoding of information extracted from the original files in the Gluecks' study.

As described in detail below, we conducted life-history interviews with 52 men, well beyond our target of 40.[8] Perhaps the biggest surprise was the fact that the vast majority of the men had little recollection of participating in the Gluecks' study. No one seemed to know, or care, who the Gluecks were. Others seemed shocked to see such a "young" interviewer. Most were expecting someone their age who had been involved in the original study. Interestingly, only one man called the Murray Research Center to verify the authenticity of the study and its investigators. He said, "You can't be too careful today."

Although our preference was to conduct the interview in the subject's home, we made every effort to accommodate the men. Some men wanted to meet at the Murray Research Center in Cambridge or at a locale near Northeastern University in the Fenway area of Boston. Other interviews took place in restaurants such as the 99, Daddy's Donuts, and Burger King. One interview was conducted in the Kennedy Library and another in a subject's car, an old, beat-up brown Ford that reeked of cigarette smoke. Finally, three interviews were conducted in prison with men incarcerated for new offenses committed in their fifties and sixties.

## Tracing and Finding Subjects

Call, Otto, and Spenner (1982) refer to long-term follow-up studies as more craft than science. That sentiment resonates with our experience. We found a small number of men in our study rather easily—for instance, by opening the Boston telephone directory and finding, to our surprise, a valid address and phone number. But most cases were considerably more difficult, taking several months of investigation to track down. Some men were never found even though countless hours were spent searching for them.

Over the course of the project, we employed a variety of means to find the subjects from the original study. Phone books (paper and electronic versions), web-based search engines like *www.switchboard .com*, criminal records, death records, motor vehicle records, and voter lists were used to locate the vast majority of the men. In addition, for targeted subsamples, records from the Massachusetts Department of Corrections and the Massachusetts Parole Board were also used. As a last resort, the Cold Case Squad of the Boston Police Department assisted us.

The most unusual aspect of our follow-up study involved the Cold Case Squad. In September of 1996, a lieutenant detective in the Boston Police Homicide Department's Cold Case Squad and a graduate student at Northeastern University began searching for a subset of subjects interviewed in the original Glueck study. These subjects were classified in two groups: (a) men for whom we had a current address, but had not received a response to their mailings, and therefore we needed a verification of their address, or (b) men whom we could not find. As a first step, the subjects were divided into two categories, those with confirmed social security numbers and those without. It was assumed that the subjects with social security numbers would be easier to find, although this was not always the case. Occasionally the social security numbers were incorrect, probably due to clerical errors somewhere along the line. For instance, we regarded with suspicion any number that did not begin with 01, 02, or 03, which would indicate issuance of the number in Massachusetts, where nearly all of the subjects were born. Once a social security number was confirmed as correct, it was used for a search through the Massachusetts Driver's License Registry (Massachusetts uses a person's social security number as his license number, unless the person requests otherwise.) Once Massachusetts had been exhausted, drivers' license checks and arrest record checks were done in surrounding states (for example, New York, Connecticut, Vermont, New Hampshire) and other states with many non-natives (for example, Florida and California). This process yielded several "hits," especially in the state of California.

Using birth dates and parents' names, the Cold Case Squad was able to obtain social security numbers for some of the subjects whose numbers had previously been unknown.[9] In some instances, we adjusted names to a common Americanization, which permitted us to find more of the subjects. In an ethnically diverse area such as eastern Massachusetts, it is common for people to change their names to Americanize or simplify them, as was evidenced by the discrepancies between the names of fathers and sons in the study. Frequently first names were Americanized (Pasquale becomes Patrick, for example). Another point worth considering when following criminal and deviant subjects is that some names have been changed in order to avoid detection and deceive authorities (Peter Vincent Doyle becomes Vincent Peter Doyle, for example). Similar changes could be made regarding dates of birth, social security numbers, and other forms of identification. Some individuals simply do not want to be found. For the most difficult cases, the Cold Case Squad used several newly developed national on-line systems to track down missing subjects.[10]

### Results of the Multiple Search Strategies

We started our person-based search with 500 delinquent subjects (for an overview see Table 4.1). Unfortunately, the original records for 20

**Table 4.1** Status of the Glueck delinquents follow-up at age 70

| Status | Number | Percentage |
|---|---|---|
| Interviewed[a] | 52 | 11 |
| Refusal | 27 | 6 |
| Refusal–illness | 9 | 2 |
| Unlisted phone number | 53 | 12 |
| Located, but did not contact | 40 | 9 |
| Can't locate | 49 | 11 |
| Dead | 225 | 49 |
| Total number of cases searched | 455 | 100 |
| Not followed by the Gluecks[b] | 25 | |
| Lost cases[c] | 20 | |
| Total number of cases | 500 | |

a. Twelve of those interviewed died after the interview.
b. Three of the 25 died.
c. Seven of the 20 died.

cases were lost in the first transfer of the data from the Gluecks to the Harvard Law School Library.[11] Because we lacked the requisite information needed to find these men (for example, names of parents) and because the original interviews were missing, we decided to eliminate these 20 cases (7 of whom were dead in any case) as potential subjects for our interview follow-up study. In addition, we eliminated 25 cases that were not followed up by the Gluecks (22 alive and 3 dead), leaving a base of 455. Overall, 225 of the 455 delinquents have died (49 percent); this number is conservative, based on confirmed death certificates in hand.

We started our search focusing on the 230 members of the original study that we believed were alive at the time of our follow-up study. Of the 230, we could not locate any reliable information on 49 men; thus our location rate was 79 percent. Of the 49 subjects whom we could not locate, we have good reason to believe that 10 are probably alive and 4 are probably dead, leaving a total of 35 that we are uncertain about. It is quite likely that many of these subjects are dead, and have been for some time. Forty men were found, but were never contacted for the study because we had already reached our desired number of interviews. For the remaining 141 men, the distribution is as follows: 52 interviewed; 27 refusals (including nonresponse to messages left on answering machines); 9 refusals due to illness; and 53 men had an unlisted phone number and never contacted the research team in response to multiple mailings requesting them to do so. Several men with unlisted numbers called us and participated in the study. For those subjects we were able to talk with about the study ($N = 88$), 52 (59 percent) were interviewed and 36 (41 percent) refused or were unable for health reasons to be interviewed. Eliminating the refusals due to illness, our participation rate was 66 percent. This figure is much beyond what we had originally expected given the thirty-five-year gap, and compares favorably with other long-term follow-up studies (for example, McCord and Ensminger 1997).

Some of the men we located had moved out of state. There seemed to be two patterns. First, some men left Massachusetts relatively early in their adult lives, with California being the preferred destination. Second, some men moved to Florida, New Hampshire, or Maine when at or near retirement age. We did not have funds to interview these men face to face, but we did send letters to men living out of state with the hope of doing a phone interview.[12] Of the 52 men we interviewed, 21 percent lived out of state. Table 4.2 presents information on the geographic distribution of those interviewed compared with the geographic distribution of those known to be alive, but not interviewed. While 79 percent of those interviewed resided in Massachusetts, 73 percent of those alive but not interviewed resided there.

Both in- and out-of-state study subjects whom we hoped to interview were sent a letter on Murray Research Center stationary—

Dear

You may remember participating in a study conducted by Sheldon and Eleanor Glueck of the Harvard Law School during the 1940s and 50s. For this study, you were interviewed about your work experiences, family life, and general social activities as a teenager and a young adult. Not only is the Gluecks' study famous, it has been enormously helpful to individuals with backgrounds like yours. I am in the process of re-contacting those who were interviewed for that study, and would appreciate your cooperation again.

Your participation is very important to me because you cannot be replaced. As a social scientist, I am interested in the lives of men who grew up in Boston neighborhoods during the Great Depression and World War II. Similar to the interview you gave when you were in your early 30s, I want to learn about your work experiences or retirement, your family life, and social life, as well as your views of how the Boston area has changed over the last 30 to 40 years.

I hope you will be able to participate again. The interview should take

**Table 4.2** Geographic distribution of the Glueck delinquents at age 70

| State/country | Interviewed | | Alive, no interview | |
|---|---|---|---|---|
| | Number | Percentage | Number | Percentage |
| Massachusetts | 41 | 79 | 94 | 73 |
| New Hampshire | 3 | 6 | 4 | 3 |
| Maine | 2 | 4 | 1 | 1 |
| Florida | 2 | 4 | 10 | 8 |
| California | 2 | 4 | 7 | 5 |
| Georgia | 1 | 2 | 0 | 0 |
| Mexico | 1 | 2 | 0 | 0 |
| Connecticut | 0 | 0 | 3 | 2 |
| Alabama | 0 | 0 | 1 | 1 |
| Arizona | 0 | 0 | 1 | 1 |
| Illinois | 0 | 0 | 1 | 1 |
| Maryland | 0 | 0 | 1 | 1 |
| Michigan | 0 | 0 | 1 | 1 |
| New Jersey | 0 | 0 | 1 | 1 |
| Nevada | 0 | 0 | 1 | 1 |
| Oregon | 0 | 0 | 1 | 1 |
| Pennsylvania | 0 | 0 | 1 | 1 |
| Virginia | 0 | 0 | 1 | 1 |
| | N = 52 | | N = 129[a] | |

a. This number excludes those dead (225), cannot find (49), and interviewed (52).

about one hour, and I will pay you $25.00 for your time. All of the information you share with me will be kept strictly confidential. The information I am collecting will be used only for research purposes. I will do everything I can to make the interview as convenient as possible for you. In other words, I will meet you any time, day, and place you want. In fact, I can interview you over the telephone if that is best for you.

For the men for whom we had a phone number, the letter indicated that we would call within a few days to set up an interview. For subjects with an unlisted phone number, we asked that they call us at our research office at the Murray Research Center. Upon receiving our letter, several of the men (both with and without unlisted phone numbers) called us to set up an interview. The human subjects review board prohibited us from visiting a subject at his home without first sending a letter and receiving permission to make a visit. This affected, but did not critically damage, our ability to locate and interview study subjects. Every subject who did not respond to our first letter was sent a second follow-up letter. For a small subset of subjects, we sent yet another letter about six months later asking them once again to participate in the study. In a handful of cases, this third letter generated a positive response.

For each subject who refused to participate, we wrote a follow-up letter thanking him for his consideration and indicated that this was an ongoing study and that if he changed his mind about participating, he should call us. A word on the nature of refusals to participate. All of the men who refused to participate when we telephoned them were asked why. Our hope was to find out their concerns and try to address them. Most of the men indicated that they simply did not feel like participating. Some men elaborated. One man told us, "I don't remember being in the study and I am not interested in talking with anyone." Another said, "I don't want to be bothered. That was a long time ago. I have been out of jail since 1957. I am a senior citizen in good health and that's all I have to say." Some refusals were more hostile. One man called the Murray Center and left the following message: "I am calling about the letter about the survey from thirty-five years ago. Don't send me any more letters. You never interviewed me and you're not going to. Don't bother me anymore. I got two letters from you, stop sending them." Perhaps it is not a coincidence that this man had alleged ties to organized crime.

In sum, our goal was to capture variation in criminal offending, especially predatory offending, over the life course. We were successful in this endeavor, as the following chapters will show. Before we proceed, however, we step back and connect our long-term follow-up data with the data from the *Unraveling Juvenile Delinquency* study and the subsequent follow-ups conducted by the Gluecks' research team. These data have been described in detail elsewhere both by the Gluecks themselves (for example, Glueck and Glueck 1950, 1968) and by us in *Crime in the Making* (chaps. 2–3). Readers familiar with the context of the data may want to skip to the Coda at the end of this chapter.

## Glueck Data on Criminal Careers

The work for which the Gluecks are known best is *Unraveling Juvenile Delinquency* (UJD; 1950). The Gluecks' classic study of the formation and development of delinquent behavior began in the fall of

1939. The sample of 500 "persistent delinquents" contained white males, aged 10 to 17, recently committed to one of two Massachusetts correctional schools—the Lyman School for Boys in Westboro and the Industrial School for Boys in Shirley. The sample of 500 nondelinquents, also white males aged 10 to 17, were chosen from the Boston public schools. Nondelinquent status was determined on the basis of official record checks and interviews with parents, teachers, local police, social workers, and recreational leaders as well as with the boys themselves. The sampling procedure was designed to maximize differences in delinquency, an objective that by all accounts succeeded (see Glueck and Glueck 1950, 27–29). Although not a random selection, the samples appear to be representative of the populations of persistent official delinquents and generally nondelinquent youth in Boston at the time.

A unique aspect of the *UJD* study was the matching design. The 500 officially defined delinquents and 500 nondelinquents were matched case by case on age, race/ethnicity (birthplace of both parents), neighborhood (for example, "boys who are living in clearly defined delinquent areas"), and measured intelligence (Glueck and Glueck 1950). The matching on neighborhood ensured that both delinquents and nondelinquents grew up in lower-class neighborhoods of central Boston. The neighborhoods included Roxbury, East Boston, Charlestown, South Boston, Dorchester, the West End, and the South End. Using census tract data, property inventory data for the city of Boston, and personal observation of the areas themselves, the Gluecks targeted underprivileged neighborhoods—slums and tenement areas—for selection in the study. These areas were regions of poverty, economic dependency, physical deterioration, and were usually adjacent to areas of industry and commerce—what Shaw and McKay (1942) would have termed socially disorganized neighborhoods (Glueck and Glueck 1950, 29). The homes of the subjects also revealed the underprivileged aspect of the neighborhoods. In general, the homes were crowded, and often lacking in basic necessities like sanitary facilities, tubs/showers, and central heating.

Given the similarity in neighborhood conditions, the areas were in essence matched on delinquency rate along with poverty: 59 percent of the delinquents and 55 percent of the nondelinquents lived in neighborhoods in which the delinquency rate was 10–24.9 per thousand; 20 percent of the former and 23 percent of the latter came from areas with a delinquency rate of 25–49.9 per thousand; and 15 percent of the delinquents and 17 percent of the control group resided in areas of high delinquency (50–100 per thousand; Glueck and Glueck 1950, 36).

In addition to growing up in similar high-risk environments of poverty and exposure to antisocial conduct, the delinquent and nondelinquent control groups were further matched on an individual basis by age, IQ, and ethnicity. The delinquents averaged 14 years, 8 months, and the nondelinquents 14 years, 6 months when the study began. As to ethnicity, 25 percent of both groups were of English background, another fourth Italian, a fifth Irish, less than a tenth American, Slavic, or French, and the remaining were Spanish, Scandinavian, German, or Jewish. And as measured by the Wechsler-Bellevue Intelligence test, the delinquents had an average IQ of 92 and nondelinquents, 94.

Thus the 1,000 male subjects in the *UJD* study were matched on key criminological variables thought to influence both delinquent behavior and official reactions by the police and courts (Sampson 1986). That 500 of the boys were persistent delinquents and 500 avoided delinquency in childhood and early adolescence therefore cannot be attributed to residence in urban slum areas, age differences, ethnicity, or IQ.

### Data Sources and Follow-Up

A wealth of information on social, psychological, and biological characteristics, family life, school performance, work experiences, and other life events was collected on the delinquents and nondelinquent controls in the period 1939–1948. Key items regarding families include parental criminality and alcohol use, economic status, family structure (for example, divorce/separation), family relations, and the patterns of supervision and discipline by parents. Items on grades, school-related behavior, and educational/occupational ambitions are included as well. There are also numerous indicators of recreational and leisure-time activities, peer relationships, church attendance, and complete psychiatric profiles gleaned from psychiatric interviews.

These data were collected through detailed investigations by members of the Gluecks' research team. Their work included interviews with the subjects themselves, with their families, and with employers, school teachers, neighbors, and criminal justice/social welfare officials. These interview data were supplemented by extensive record checks across a variety of social agencies. The Gluecks were especially concerned with independent sources of measurement and hence provide a means to validate many of the key concepts (see Sampson and Laub 1993, chap. 3). For example, most of the social variables (such as family income, parental discipline) were collected from a variety of sources, including home interviews conducted by the Gluecks' research team along with independent visits by social welfare agencies. This level of detail and the range of information sources used in the Glueck study will likely never be repeated given contemporary research standards on the protection of human subjects.

The original sample in the *UJD* study was followed up at two different points in time—at the age of 25 and again at the age of 32. This data collection effort took place during the 1949–1963 period (see Glueck and Glueck 1968 for more details). As a result, extensive data are available for analysis relating to criminal career histories, criminal justice interventions, family life, school and employment history, and recreational activities for the matched subjects in childhood, adolescence, and young adulthood. As already noted, the attrition rate for waves two and three was quite low and this was testimony not only to the Gluecks' rigorous research strategy but also to lower residential mobility and interstate migration rates in the 1940s and 1950s compared with today. It should be noted, though, that the follow-up of criminal histories and official records covered thirty-seven states—most commonly California, New York, New Hampshire, Florida, and Illinois (Glueck and Glueck 1968, xix). Overall, criminal history data from first offense to age 32 were gathered through extensive record checks of police, court, and correctional files.

Additionally, follow-up information from interviews and record checks was collected on key life events over the time. Of particular interest are items such as the nature of and change in living arrangements as an adult—including marriage/divorce, frequency of moves, number of children, and military experiences; employment history and work habits (including number and type of jobs, weekly income, unemployment, public assistance); and schooling history (including age at final academic achievement, reason for stopping schooling, adult education). There are also a host of items on factors such as participation in civic affairs, aspirations, types of companions, and nature of leisure-time activities.

As if anticipating future concerns, the Gluecks were able to gather data on criminal careers that overcame a key problem noted by Blumstein et al. (1986) in modern criminological research. Many studies lack a sufficient number of persistent and serious offenders. By contrast, during the age 17–32 period, approximately 90 of the Gluecks' delinquents were arrested for robbery, 225 for burglary, and over 250 for larceny. As for the frequency of offenses, overall the delinquent group generated well over six thousand arrest charges from birth to age 32. The Glueck delinquent group clearly consisted of persistent and serious offenders. Moreover, the fact that the Gluecks followed these individuals from childhood (retrospectively), adolescence (concurrently), and young adulthood (prospectively) allows one to study patterns of continuity and change in criminal offending over time. (For more details on the Gluecks' study and our efforts to reconstruct, computerize, and validate the data, see Sampson and Laub 1993, chaps. 2 and 3).

## Coda

Tracing, locating, and interviewing the men for this study turned out to be an incredible experience. These men revealed life stories that were often filled with sadness and tragedy. The men we interviewed spoke of loved ones lost, missed opportunities and regrets, and personal tragedies that they had experienced and somehow survived. It was not unusual for tears to accompany their life-history narratives.

Each year since the data collection component of the study ended we have sent each man interviewed a Christmas or Seasons Greetings card. We have been amazed at the response to this gesture. About 20 percent of the men have written back. We have received Christmas cards, letters, photos, and other items (one man sent his family tree). Photos included family members at wedding anniversaries and birthday parties, shots of their house and garden, and even photos of artwork from one of the Glueck men's wife. Others shared news about family members, especially their number of grandchildren and great-grandchildren, as if they were speaking with an old family friend. Some letters contained observations about life in old age. One man told us that he had had several stints in the VA hospital and wrote wryly, "Whoever coined the expression 'The Golden Years' should be shot." Echoing the same theme, a wife of a Glueck man wrote, "I don't know how old you are but I can tell you there's nothing gold about the golden years." Not all complained, however. One man wrote, "Health wise I'm doing great. I lift weights and still ride my motorcycle and do a lot of charity work." Another man told us he was into "tour biking" and his longest trip to date was 3,287 miles solo from New Hampshire to Texas, covering 48 days. Others talked of travels through Europe. Some of the men turned their attention to politics. One man wrote, "Clinton made a stupid mistake but in the long view I think he's the best thing that happened to the people of this country since Franklin Roosevelt." Others were less charitable. Referring to President Clinton, one man wrote, "Don't anyone know what truth is? The 'Great American' is a charter member of the Liars Club." The following year the same man wrote, "You haven't been counting ballots have you? What a laugher! I couldn't take another 8 years of a Clinton type administration. Lying, immoral, deceptive, and deceitful." Another man asked for help getting a copy of a proposed bill by Senators Kennedy and Jeffords focusing on work and the disabled. Most poignant were the letters we received from spouses telling us that their husbands had died in the year since the last Christmas card.

# CHAPTER FIVE

# Long-Term Trajectories
# of Crime

Current portraits of the developmental course of criminal offending are sharply divergent. From proponents of the criminal career approach, the idea has emerged that those who are chronic offenders at an earlier age fail to stop as they grow older (Wolfgang, Figlio, and Sellin 1972; Blumstein and Cohen 1979; Blumstein et al. 1986). A variation of the same theme comes from Moffitt (1993, 1994), who argues that, like chronic offenders, a subset of life-course-persistent offenders continue offending as they age. In direct contrast, Gottfredson and Hirschi (1990) contend that the age effect is invariant—regardless of stable between-individual differences, all people will commit fewer crimes as they age. A middle ground is found in Nagin and Paternoster's (2000, 134) position that there are discrete "clumps" of offenders with varying propensities of criminal offending; that is, there are different age-crime curves for different groups of offenders (Nagin and Land 1993).

Yet as noted in previous chapters, most longitudinal research efforts that purport to resolve the age and crime conundrum suffer from two major limitations: (a) criminal careers are typically studied over circumscribed portions of the life course; and (b) trajectories of offending are usually identified retrospectively, on the basis of the outcome, rather than prospectively, on the basis of the causal factors presumed to differentiate groups of offenders. In this chapter we address these limitations directly by analyzing newly collected data on adult criminal involvement among the group of 500 men in the Gluecks' original delinquent group. One of the major strengths of our study is its ability to examine variability in offending over nearly the entire life course—data on crime from age 7 to 70 for a relatively large group of individuals simply do not exist elsewhere. Moreover, the Gluecks' (1950) original design in *Unraveling Juvenile Delinquency* targeted serious, persistent delinquents in adolescence, providing an important opportunity to assess patterns of continuity and change in offending for a population of high interest and concern.

We begin with a detailed examination of within-individual trajectories of age and crime in the lives of the Glueck men from childhood to old age. After assessing basic facts as they bear on the age-crime debate (for example, patterns of onset, frequency, termination), we then turn to trajectories of crime in connection with prospectively and theoretically defined taxonomies based on early risk factors. We next take the opposite tack by defining offending trajectories retrospectively, or ex-post, on the basis of patterns of observed offending over the full life course, and then assessing their predictability from childhood and adolescent risk factors. This dual analytic approach allows us to shed new light on prevailing theories that rest fundamentally on the idea of distinct and predictable groups of offenders.

## Typological Approaches: The New Controversy?

Before the 1980s criminological research tended to focus on between-individual correlates of crime (for example, what factors distinguish offenders from nonoffenders?) and concerns about measuring these correlates using official versus self-report data. The criminal career debate ushered in a new era, most notably the claim that one must distinguish elements of offending (onset, escalation, persistence, and desistance) within the population of offenders (Blumstein et al. 1986; compare Gottfredson and Hirschi 1986). Although the question of whether the aggregate age-crime relationship is invariant or not has generated most of the controversy, we see the debate as a much larger one—how does the field of criminology conceptualize its dependent variable?

Over the last decade, developmental criminologists have similarly promoted the idea of offender types (for example, Moffitt 1993; Patterson and Yoerger 1993; Loeber and LeBlanc 1990). These researchers extend the criminal career position one step further by arguing for the existence of distinctive groups of offenders as defined by criminal trajectories, with each group possessing a distinctive developmental etiology. As in the earlier debate on criminal career research, in effect this position stakes out a claim for the correct conceptualization of the dependent variable in criminological research.

This kind of typological thinking has a largely unrecognized historical background (see also Laub and Sampson 1991). According to Gibbons (1985, 152), typological approaches assume that a number of distinct types or groups of offenses and/or offenders exist that can be identified and studied. This is an old idea in criminology that goes back to the days of Cesare Lombroso's (1912) notion of an atavistic type. Over the last century, some criminologists have taken a more nuanced approach, most commonly with a focus on types of offenses (Clinard and Quinney 1973). Other criminologists have taken a person-centered or offender-centered approach and focused on types of criminal or delinquent persons (Roebuck 1966). Typological approaches promise a great deal. First, as Gibbons has noted, if distinct groupings of offenders and offending exist, "explanations or causal analysis probably requires that we develop separate etiological accounts for each of the forms of lawbreaking or kinds of lawbreakers" (1985, 153). Second, if different causal processes produce distinct groupings, then we will be better positioned to apply interventions matching the person-type and the crime.

It is hard to overestimate the appeal of typological thinking in criminology, especially on the second point. Consider the concept of the recidivist offender. Over seventy years ago, Sheldon and Eleanor Glueck found that virtually all of the 510 reformatory inmates in their study of criminal careers had backgrounds in serious antisocial conduct. Their data were thought to confirm "the early genesis of antisocial careers" (1930, 143), a finding that has reverberated throughout criminology ever since. Indeed, one of the most consistent findings in criminological research is that those offenders with the highest rate of offending have a tendency to begin their involvement in crime at earlier ages than offenders with shorter careers and fewer offenses.

A related, modern example of considerable import is that a small proportion of chronic offenders account for the majority of crime incidents (Wolfgang, Figlio, and Sellin 1972). In an analysis of the famous Philadelphia Birth Cohort data, Wolfgang and associates reported that 6 percent of the subjects (or 18 percent of the delinquents) accounted for nearly 52 percent of the crimes committed by this cohort. Wolfgang, Figlio, and Sellin (1972) also found that chronic offenders were more likely than nonchronic offenders to be nonwhite; come from a lower socioeconomic background; experience more family moves; have lower IQs; have fewer school grades completed; exhibit more school discipline problems; commit more serious offenses; and begin criminal careers early in the life course as measured by age of first arrest. Similar results were soon reported elsewhere in the United States and abroad. Heavily influenced by the pioneering Philadelphia cohort study, criminological inquiry has turned its attention ever since to the subset of chronic offenders known as serious, violent offenders. The idea that there is a distinct group of such offenders that can be distinguished by early life predictors became one of the hallmarks of the criminal career approach (Blumstein et al. 1986).

As discussed in Chapter 2, one of the most influential typological accounts of crime has been offered by Moffitt (1993, 1994). She posits two distinct categories of individuals, each possessing a unique natural history of antisocial behavior over the life course—life-course persisters and adolescence-limited offenders. Moffitt (1993, 695) explicitly argues that life-course persisters have etiological roots traced to childhood risk factors such as difficult temperament, low verbal IQ, and poor self-control. The specific prediction is of distinct developmental trajectories—in her case, two groups of offenders, one of whose lineage (the persisters) is rooted in preexisting differences in childhood and early adolescence. Life-course persisters, though small in number, do enormous damage since they account for the lion's share of adult misconduct. The fundamental point is that the two groups are qualitatively distinct, with the life-course persisters starting early and, as the name implies, persisting through time.

Considerable research and policy attention has been directed toward subgroups of high-rate offenders over the last two decades, most notably the policy of selective incapacitation (Greenwood 1982) and the arrival of "super-predators" (Bennett, DiIulio, and Walters 1996). These theoretical developments culminated in the publication of a report by the Study Group on Serious and Violent Juvenile Offenders (Loeber and Farrington 1998). Funded by the Office of Juvenile Justice and Delinquency Prevention, this study group integrated the literature on risk and protective factors with information on prevention and intervention strategies. One key finding of the study group is that serious and violent juvenile offenders start displaying behavior problems and delinquency at an early age, which implies, we are told, that it is never too early to intervene with at-risk children and their parents.[1] The "risk factor" and associated typology paradigm is now popular in public policy circles; a recent conference even advertised that attending criminal justice officials would be taught how to make an early identification of the life-course-persistent offender.[2] If such groups are so easily identified, surely we should be able to find them prospectively.

In short, developmental theorists and researchers claim different factors at different points (or ages) in the life course lead to different offending trajectories or, more simply, distinct groups of offenders. Moffitt's (1993) theory of a dual taxonomy focusing on life-course-persistent and adolescence-limited offenders is the leading example of this approach. Some critics of the developmental approach see risk factors as being the same for all offender groups. In other words, though the risk factors may vary by degrees, the same underlying causal factors distinguish offenders from nonoffenders, early starters from late starters, persisters from desisters, and so on. Gottfredson and Hirschi (1990) go one step further and argue that there is a single risk factor (and cause) at work—low self-control—and that this factor can explain crime at all ages.

No matter what the preferred risk factor, however, like the criminal career debate, the question of whether there are distinct and ontologically valid groups of offenders has enormous implications for criminological theory, research, and policy. Our study seeks to investigate one of the basic actors in this controversy: the foretold persistent offender.

## Age and Long-Term Crime Patterns

Following our belief that the facts about crime in long-term perspective are not yet fully known, the first set of questions we address are intentionally descriptive and pertain to core patterns of age, crime, and desistance. Is the age-crime curve invariant across the lives of the same individual offenders? How much crime is there in middle age and later life? What types of crime are most common among older offenders? When does desistance occur?

We began by creating person-period observations in our data, starting with the delinquent group of 500 men. For each of up to 63 observations from ages 7 to 70 we coded the number of recorded arrests by crime type.[3] We begin in Figure 5.1 with the almost 31,500 person-by-age crime counts in which mortality is accounted for; each observation is censored after the time of death for men who died. The y-axis is the mean of total recorded offenses. Note the asymmetric but still tepee-shaped age-crime pattern for the total offense rate, representing more than 9,500 recorded and coded crime events. There is a sharp increase peaking in adolescence followed by a less sharp decline through middle adulthood, with eventual disappearance in the fifties. Hence the first and perhaps unexpected point is that the classic age-crime pattern (Hirschi and Gottfredson 1983) is replicated even within a population that was selected for its serious, persistent delinquent activity. It is not obvious from the criminal career model that this should be so, although of course it may be that there are some

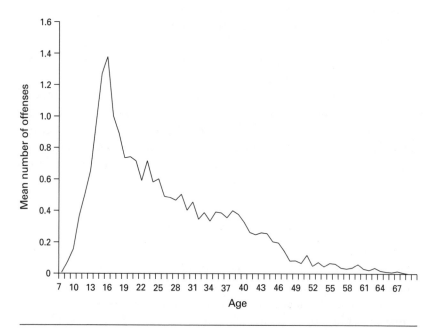

*Figure 5.1* Actual mean number of offenses for total crime (total events = 9,548): Ages 7 to 70

subgroups in the data that do conform to a flatter age-crime pattern. We investigate this possibility below.

Consider next the age-crime curves disaggregated by type of crime displayed in Figure 5.2. The first three graphs display the actual or raw curves for property, violence, and alcohol/drug offenses (Figures 5.2a,b,c, respectively). The total age-crime pattern observed in Figure 5.1 holds up in a rough sense for each type of crime, but the peak age and rate of decline are clearly less sharp for violence and alcohol/drugs. Because a large share of total crime is accounted for by property offenses, virtually the same age-crime pattern is revealed for property crime. For violent crime, however, the peak age of offending is in the twenties and the rate of decline is more erratic over time, with some offenders remaining active well into their forties even though the rate of violent offending is low relative to the other crime types. Perhaps more interestingly, drug and alcohol offending is clustered and remains relatively flat between the ages of 20 and about 47, and then sharply declines. Although this measure contains arrests for alcohol and drug offenses, the vast majority of these arrests are for alcohol crimes. For both violence and alcohol offenses, then, it is apparent that censoring or artificially truncating life-course data on crime in the twenties or even the early thirties, as is typical in criminology and even in Sampson and Laub (1993; see also Laub, Nagin, and Sampson 1998), is problematic at best.

In Figure 5.2d we smooth the age-crime curves for each offense with a simple prediction model consistent with the asymmetric pattern in Figures 5.1 and 5.2a–c. Specifically, we estimated a Poisson regression model of crime-specific counts in each observation period, with the best fit to the data obtained by a cubed polynomial represented by terms for age, age squared, and age cubed (see Osgood and Rowe 1994). The smoothed plots thus reflect the predicted number of offenses by age, $age^2$, and $age^3$. The resulting overlays in Figure 5.2d confirm the distinct differences in peak age and rate of decline for property, violence, and alcohol offenses. The coefficients for age, $age^2$, and $age^3$ were significantly positive, negative, and positive, respectively, reflecting the sharply escalating and then moderating decline in offending. (The small uptick in the predicted property trajectory after age 67 is artifactual, as there are no offenses in that period.) Because of the rarity of some offense counts for each person-year broken out by crime type, we also estimated a logistic regression model predicting

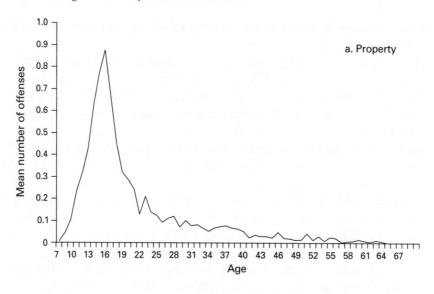

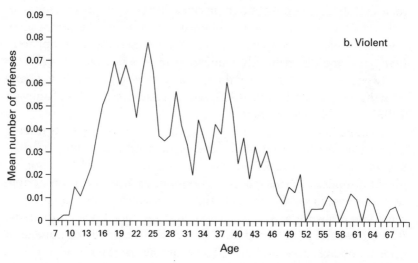

*Figure 5.2a–d* Actual and predicted mean number of offenses by crime type

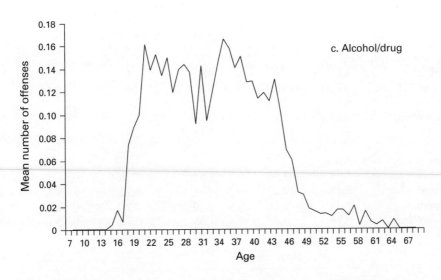

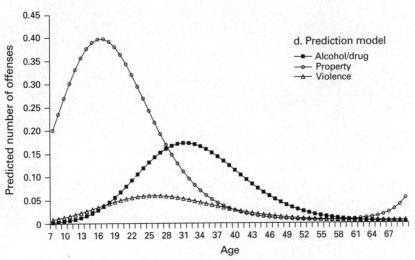

**Table 5.1** Descriptive data on criminal careers in the delinquent group

| | 17–24 | 25–31 | 32–39 | 40–49 | 50–59 | 60–69 |
|---|---|---|---|---|---|---|
| *Percentage arrested by age* | | | | | | |
| Total | 84 | 65 | 60 | 44 | 23 | 12 |
| Violent | 33 | 16 | 18 | 14 | 7 | 3 |
| Property | 61 | 27 | 22 | 14 | 8 | 2 |
| Alcohol/drug | 35 | 29 | 28 | 21 | 9 | 7 |
| Other | 67 | 49 | 44 | 28 | 13 | 5 |
| *Mean number of arrests by age* | | | | | | |
| Total | 5.04 | 2.96 | 2.83 | 1.76 | 0.56 | 0.20 |
| Violent | 0.49 | 0.23 | 0.31 | 0.22 | 0.08 | 0.05 |
| Property | 1.63 | 0.56 | 0.50 | 0.26 | 0.17 | 0.03 |
| Alcohol/drug | 0.96 | 0.87 | 1.05 | 0.72 | 0.13 | 0.07 |
| Other | 1.96 | 1.30 | 0.97 | 0.56 | 0.18 | 0.05 |

| | Mean age of | | Mean career length |
|---|---|---|---|
| | Onset | Desistance | |
| Total | 11.9 | 37.5 | 25.6 |
| Violent | 22.0 | 31.3 | 9.2 |
| Property | 12.6 | 26.2 | 13.6 |
| Alcohol/drug | 25.3 | 36.8 | 11.4 |
| Other | 14.3 | 32.7 | 18.4 |

whether there was a recorded crime (recoded to yes, no) in each period. Violence in particular is very skewed and infrequent in the latter years. The predicted logistic probabilities nonetheless replicated the Poisson models.

Table 5.1 turns to a detailed descriptive analysis of the parameters of the men's criminal careers over the life span. We see that while 84 percent of the Gluecks' delinquents were arrested between ages 17 and 24, the participation rate declines sharply with age. Generally, this declining pattern holds for the crime-specific categories, but note the relatively high participation rates for alcohol/drug offenses that hold rather steadily between early adulthood and age 50. These data suggest that offending in middle adulthood (beyond age 30) is more extensive than commonly believed. Indeed, 44 percent of the men were arrested between the ages of 40 and 49, 23 percent were arrested between the ages of 50 and 59, and 12 percent were arrested between the ages of 60 and 69. Although a relatively small proportion overall, it appears that a nontrivial portion of the Glueck delinquents were arrested in each decade of their life.[4]

Data on incidence, onset, termination, and career length are also shown in Table 5.1. Incidence patterns are similar to those for prevalence. Consistent with Figure 5.2, what is especially noteworthy is that the highest incidence rate of alcohol and drug arrests occurs between the ages of 32 and 39. Incidence rates for violence are also high during this age period. The mean age of onset (defined as first arrest) for total crime is 11.9 and the mean age of desistance (defined as last arrest) for total crime is 37.5. Perhaps foreshadowed by their active juvenile years in crime, the average career length of the delinquent group is a substantial 25.6 years. Consistent with the graphical data, the mean age of onset for violence and alcohol and drug arrests is 22 and 25, respectively. The mean age of desistance for these crimes is 31 and 37, respectively. Violent criminal careers are the shortest (9 years).

Overall, what is most striking is how much variability there is in patterns of offending during adulthood for this sample of serious, persistent delinquents. To illustrate the point a bit differently, we find that for those men who survived to age 50, 24 percent had no arrests for predatory crime (crimes of violence and property) after age 17 (6 percent had no arrests for total crime); 48 percent had no arrests for predatory crime after age 25 (19 percent for total crime); 60 percent had no arrests for predatory crime after age 31 (33 percent for total crime); 79 percent had no arrests for predatory crime after age 40 (57 percent for total crime). Desistance from crime is thus the norm, and most, if not all, serious delinquents desist from crime. Remarkably, the age-crime curve for the general population appears to be replicated, almost in identical (fractal?) fashion, for active, serious delinquents.

### Prospectively Defined Groups

The essential idea of developmental taxonomy approaches is that there are distinct groups of offenders whose etiological significance can be traced to early risk factors. If such typological approaches are valid, then we should be able to see fairly basic and distinctive patterns of adult life-course trajectories that vary by the factors that allegedly produce the groups in the first place. We thus investigate our ability to predict, prospectively, long-term patterns of offending on the basis of childhood and adolescent characteristics. We are posing a simple yet powerful question: does the age-crime trajectory follow a different pattern across the life course of delinquents according to the causal categories specified by typological theories? In a related question, we ask whether those identified as life-course persisters at one point in time remain life-course persisters at a later point in time. We now know there is considerable crime in later adulthood, but are the offenses generated by the same people who committed offenses at a younger age?

To test the ability of typological theories of crime to predict offending trajectories, we present age-crime curves classified according to a variety of prospectively defined risk criteria. To be true to the major extant perspectives, we sought to err on the side of inclusiveness. We selected thirteen measures from multiple sources (parents, teachers, official records, and the boys themselves) that tap either classic individual-difference risk factors or the observed propensity to offend in the early years of the study. Measures of individual differences include some of the most venerable and sturdy predictors of crime, especially cognitive abilities (Moffitt 1994, 16), personality traits (Caspi et al. 1994; Coie et al. 1995; Hawkins et al. 2000), temperament (Moffitt 1993, 695), and childhood behaviors (Caspi 1987; Caspi, Bem, and Elder 1989; Moffitt 1994, 15). In addition, guided by the substantial body of research on criminal careers, we focused on early and frequent involvement in crime and delinquency (Blumstein et al. 1986, 72, 94).

Verbal intelligence (see Moffitt 1993) was assessed using the Wechsler-Bellevue IQ test and coded into eight categories ranging from one (120 and above) to eight (59 and below). The mean verbal IQ for the delinquent sample was 88.6. We also examine the full-scale IQ score that includes both math and verbal skills, unrecoded. From detailed psychiatric assessments of the boy, we use four dichotomous variables of personality traits: extroverted ("uninhibited in regard to motor responses to stimuli"); adventurous ("desirous of change, excitement, or risk"); egocentric ("self-centered"); and aggressive ("inclined to impose one's will on others"). To capture the early onset of childhood behavior we used self-reported age of onset of misbehavior, a dichotomous indicator based on teacher and parent reports of the subject engaging in violent and habitual temper tantrums while growing up, and a report from the mother as to whether the subject was overly restless and irritable growing up (we labeled this "difficult child").

The level of delinquent conduct in adolescence was measured in several ways. We used an indicator of the average annual frequency of arrests in adolescence while not incarcerated and a composite scale (ranging from 1 to 26) based on unofficial self-, parent-, and teacher reports of delinquent behavior (for example, stealing, vandalism) and other misconduct (for example, truancy, running away) not necessarily known to the police. Following the logic of the criminal career approach, we also included measures of the age at first arrest and age at first incarceration for each boy. Overall the delinquency measures capture both the level and the developmental pattern of official and unofficial behavior up to an average of about 14 years of age for each boy.

To assess summary patterns we followed the logic of risk factor theory by giving emphasis to the combination of risks within the same boy. We combined standardized indicators of all thirteen variables in a single childhood risk indicator, with constituent items scored such that a high value indicated either the presence of antisocial behavior or an individual-level risk (for example, low verbal IQ, engaging in tantrums, early age of onset of antisocial behavior, and so on). We then looked at the distribution across all boys and created a group at highest risk for what Moffitt would call life-course-persistent offending—namely, those boys in the upper 20 percent of the distribution. The bottom 80 percent group is defined as low risk. It is important to point out that the groups were defined prospectively, in this case without recourse to information on the boys past their adolescence. Other than delinquency, which we separate out in later analysis, the vast majority of measures refer to individual differences of the boys in childhood. The prospective ability of these measures to predict later involvement in crime was demonstrated in our earlier work (Sampson and Laub 1993, 92). The summary measure that captures boys in the upper quintile of risk is also predictive of levels of offending even up to the late fifties; for example, the child high-risk group accounted for twice as many recorded offenses at ages 50–59 as the nonrisk group ($p < .05$). Thus while retrospective reporting is a concern we fully acknowledge, the multi-method and multi-reporter approach, combined with the diversity of measures and their demonstrated validity in predicting stability of offending, speaks to the utility of considering the link between childhood risk and trajectories of crime throughout life.

The data in Figures 5.3 to 5.5 show long-term trajectories for property crime, violent crime, and alcohol/drug crime, respectively. Separate logistic and Poisson-based regressions of counts were performed for each crime type and childhood risk level with similar results; for simplicity in the subgroup analysis the graphs depict the predicted logistic probabilities for these crime types at each age from 7 to 70 by level of childhood risk. Starting with the predicted probabilities for property (Figure 5.3), which mimics the total crime rate, the data show that the two groups' life-course trajectories share an almost identical path through time, albeit at different levels of offending. That is, there is some stability in offending patterns, but both groups peak and then desist in a process that appears general rather than causally distinct. Although at different peak ages, the same pattern emerges for violence (Figure 5.4) and alcohol/drugs (Figure 5.5). In fact the violent crime patterns yield virtually a textbook example of

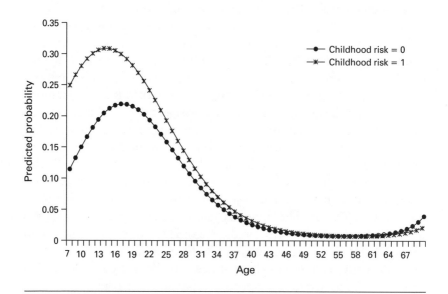

*Figure 5.3* Predicted probability of offending by age for property crime: Comparison between childhood risk = 0 and childhood risk = 1

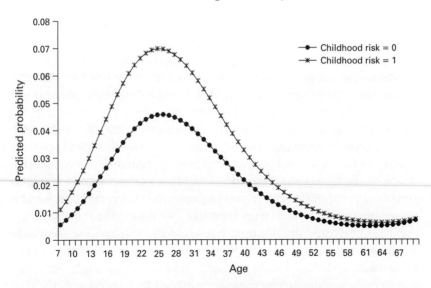

*Figure 5.4* Predicted probability of offending by age for violent crime: Comparison between childhood risk = 0 and childhood risk = 1

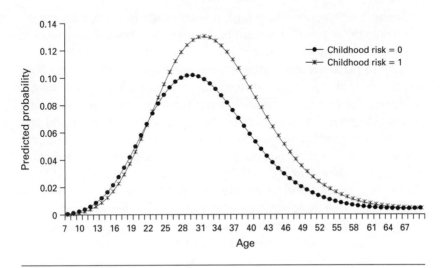

Figure 5.5 Predicted probability of offending by age for alcohol/drug crime: Comparison between childhood risk = 0 and childhood risk = 1

Hirschi and Gottfredson's (1983) argument (allowing for differences in peak ages of offending), even though the two groups were defined according to their risk for divergent developmental patterns.

One might argue that the results so far are confounded by the particular risk factors selected in childhood and adolescence. What if we restricted the comparison to just the individual-difference factors, eliminating the indicators of actual juvenile offending? We performed this analysis, but the patterns were identical—childhood risk factors predict a modest level of stability (between-person differences) but the shape of the trajectories was identical (data not shown). One might further argue that our cutoff points were too lenient, and that we are not capturing the boys at truly high risk. We thus shifted the cutoff to the 10th percentile distribution, but again the results were identical. We also examined the distribution of self-, parent-, and teacher-reported acts up to age 14 (on average) and selected the high-rate juvenile offenders as defined by those boys in the top 10 percent of the distribution. Because we are analyzing data from a sample of delinquent and incarcerated boys to begin with (promising candidates for life-course persisters), by any reasonable definition, the boys in the upper 10 percent of this group should be tapping the small subset (typically thought to represent about 5 percent of males in the general population) that exhibit serious conduct disorder and life-course-persistent offending.

Figure 5.6 compares these high-rate chronic offenders with the offenders in the bottom 90 percent of the juvenile offending distribution for total crime. Again, there is no evidence of differential shape or patterning to the trajectories other than level. Might crime type account for the lack of typological differences, for example by concealing a subset of violent predators? Disaggregation by violence, property, and alcohol/drug trajectories revealed differences in peak ages and frequency, but again the shape was invariant (data not shown). The prospectively identified persisters offend at a higher level but decline markedly in their criminal activity for the last decades of their lives. As an even stricter test we allowed the predictions to be (tautologically?) generated using adult crime data to age 70. We summed the total number of arrests (nearly 10,000 in total) for each man up to age 70. We then selected those men in the upper 10 percent of the distribution, and compared them with the vast majority (9 in 10) of delinquent boys who fell in the bottom of the distribution of lifetime offending frequency (data not shown). Even with this split, the data fail to reveal a distinct pattern of persistent offending over time (again, data not shown). Active adult criminals, it appears, dramatically reduce their activity in criminal offending with advancing age.[5]

Finally, and perhaps most important, we conducted analyses that interacted individual risk factors with key "criminogenic environments" (Moffitt 1993) during the turbulent years of child and adolescent development, especially in the family. A long history of research, including our own, has shown that family structural conditions (for example, poverty, large family size, residential mobility) and family social processes such as poor supervision, erratic/threatening discipline, and weak parental attachment are strong predictors of adolescent delinquency (see Sampson and Laub 1993, chap. 4). Moffitt (1993) argues that when a child's vulnerability is compounded with such negative family conditions, life-course-persistent offending is most likely to occur. Note that the interaction argument undermines the assertion of prospective predictability from early individual differences alone—it can't be "all over" for troubled children at an

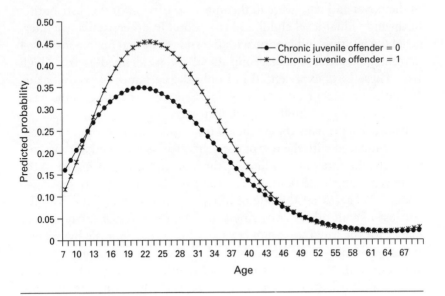

*Figure 5.6* Predicted probability of offending by age for total crime: Comparison between chronic juvenile offending = 0 and chronic juvenile offending = 1

early age if life-course persisters emerge in interaction with later criminogenic environments. In this sense the current widespread promotion of early intervention is not consistent with the logic of Moffitt's (1993) actual argument.

Be that as it may, we can directly examine trajectories of offending for boys who differ according to theoretically defined interactions of child and family risk. Following theory and past research we highlight two major dimensions of criminogenic family environments. Drawing on our past research with the Glueck data, we conducted a principal components analysis that reduced the dimensionality of a set of theoretically selected items. Two key dimensions emerged, the first defined by high residential mobility, parental emotional instability, low maternal supervision, and hostility between father and son. Poverty, large families, and erratic/harsh methods of discipline defined the second dimension. These factors make sense on the basis of prior criminological work, and moreover each "criminogenic family" factor independently predicts the level of adolescent delinquency ($p < .05$) within the delinquent group.

We then selected those boys who were in the upper half of the distribution of each orthogonal factor (hence approximately 25 percent of the boys) and who were in the upper 20 percent of the distribution of the individual-level childhood risk score. In other words, we interacted the multiple indicators, with the end result that approximately 4 percent of the delinquent group members are defined as truly high risk. These boys experienced not only the extremes of criminogenic family environments; they were vulnerable from the start on the basis of the summary of childhood risk factors.

Figure 5.7 presents the predicted trajectories of offending for these boys compared with the rest of the delinquent group. Perhaps not surprisingly, the rate of offending for the high-risk group is higher in the early years up to the point of the traditional peak age of offending—about 15. Thereafter the rate of offending drops off and the boys desist just like all others. Amazingly, in fact, the rates of offending are higher for the low-rate group later in adolescence. But the big picture is clear—the age-crime curves looked the same as in the earlier figures we examined. We see increasing and then declining involvement in crime for all risk groups. Our basic conclusion thus continues to hold, namely that desistance is a general process. Despite the interaction of childhood variables with criminogenic family environments, we see no evidence of a group that, prospectively at least, continues to offend throughout the life course.

For a somewhat different look at the stability and predictive power of the interaction of childhood-family risk, we posed another straightforward question. Are those boys at highest risk for child and adolescent crime the same individuals who account for life-course-persistent offending as adult men? To address this question, we summed the frequency of crime events from ages 25 to 60 (the data confirm that there is little crime past age 60). Then we selected all men with a childhood*family risk score of 1 who survived to 60 (11 of 18) and examined where they stood in the relative rankings of ages 25–60 crime. Of the 11 men with the highest childhood-family risk in the delinquent group, and who accounted for over 200 arrests before age 25, over 50 percent (6 men) were nonetheless in the bottom quartile of adult offending. Only two men were in the upper quartile. To capture persistence of adult offending as opposed to frequency, we also looked at the data from another angle by determining those men who were criminally involved during each decade of adult life. Some 17 percent of boys at high childhood*family risk were persistent adult offenders,

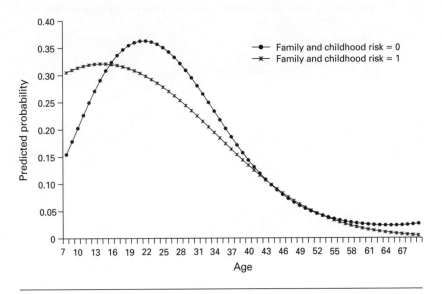

*Figure 5.7* Predicted probability of offending by age for total crime: Comparison between family and childhood risk = 0 and family and childhood risk = 1

compared with 23 percent of boys with no interaction of child and family risk ($p = .40$, ns). Clearly, and yet again, the data are firm in signaling that persistent and frequent offending in the adult years is not easily divined from zeroing in on juvenile offenders at risk.

## Mortality and Incarceration

Largely overlooked in recent thinking about persistent offending and desistance from crime are the issues of mortality and incarceration. Information on deaths is crucial to identify more precisely who has desisted from crime as compared with those who have no criminal records due to death. Some researchers have speculated that in comparison with low-rate offenders, high-rate criminal offenders die earlier and experience more violent deaths; Reiss (1989) refers to this group as "false desisters." Indeed, in the longitudinal follow-up to age 32 for the subjects in the *Unraveling* study, the Gluecks found that the death rate for the delinquents was twice that for the nondelinquent controls (1968, 46), raising the specter of a contaminated age-crime relationship.

For comparison purposes, Figure 5.8 displays the survival curves for the delinquent and the nondelinquent control groups to age 70.

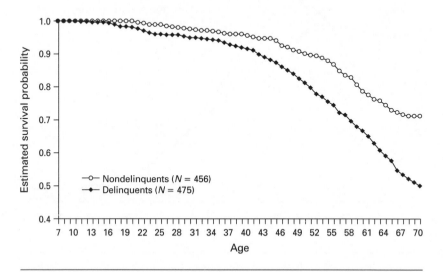

*Figure 5.8* Estimated survival probability among delinquents and nondelinquents: Ages 7 to 70

Note that the death gap maintains and even widens in scope until the end of our observation period. The delinquent group experiences death more quickly, with half of the men dead by age 70 compared with less than 30 percent of the controls. We display this figure to underscore the potential implications for age-crime offending curves. Still, even though half of the delinquent men died, and even though many have argued that involuntary desistance through death accounts for much of the apparent decline in the age-crime relationship, our data instead confirm the persistence of the age effect. Each person-period observation represented in Figures 5.1 to 5.7 censored the observation for death, and hence the mean offense counts were based on the risk pool of men that were alive.[6]

Incapacitation is another concern, given the well-known fact that high-rate, serious offenders are disproportionately more likely to be incarcerated (Blumstein et al. 1986). Neglecting incarceration time in assessing trajectories of offending can have important methodological consequences. For example, Piquero and his colleagues (2001) used data from the California Youth Authority and found that without incarceration time, 92 percent of the sample appeared to be on a desisting trajectory by their late twenties. Once exposure time was added to the model, only 72 percent of the population showed a pattern of desistance (see also Eggleston, Laub, and Sampson 2004). We investigate this issue using data on the number of days incarcerated each year up to the age of 32 in order to provide a more accurate picture of the process of desistance from criminal careers.

Figure 5.9 displays the raw number of days incarcerated. Interestingly, the incarceration careers repeat the classic age-crime pattern that we observe for total and property crime. This is not an obvious outcome, because the common belief is that incarceration is lagged in time from offending, in that it takes some period of offending before one gets to the incapacitation phase. Note also the magnitude of the phenomenon—the average number of days incarcerated per year tops 150 days at age 16. What happens if we take this considerable time off the street into account in assessing criminal offending careers? Using data on the number of days incarcerated each year from childhood to age 32, we estimated a Poisson model of the number of offenses while free by age for our childhood risk groups. As seen in Figure 5.10, the trajectories are again remarkably similar for our main childhood risk indicator, with both groups following a similar path to desistance. This basic result maintains when crime-specific analyses

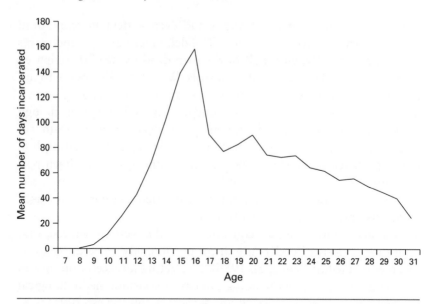

*Figure 5.9* Actual mean number of days incarcerated per year: Ages 7 to 32

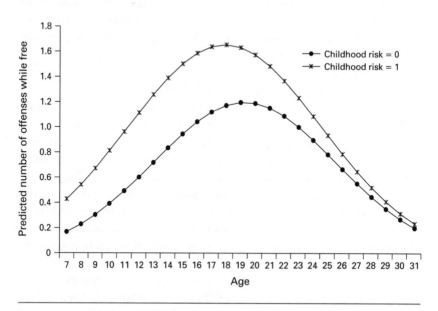

*Figure 5.10* Age-predicted number of offenses while free for total crime, ages 7 to 32: Comparison between childhood risk = 0 and childhood risk = 1

are conducted and Figure 5.7 (childhood*family risk) is replicated (data not shown). Despite the considerable magnitude of death and incarceration associated with criminal offending, the age-crime curve and the similarity of offending trajectories by childhood risk groups is thus remarkably stable.

## Latent Class Models of Desistance

So far we have restricted our analysis to groups of offenders who are prospectively defined on the basis of childhood and adolescent risk factors, as in Figures 5.3 to 5.7. Another, quite different, approach is to take the full life course as a given and ask whether there are distinct and latent offender groups based on ex-post patterns in offending. That is to say, are there latent classes as defined by trajectories of crime over the full life course? And are resulting trajectory groups linked to preexisting or childhood differences? The key difference in this approach is that groups are defined not by early risk factors but rather by the outcome of offending using data to the end of each person's life. In addition, a formal statistical model of desistance is used by estimating individual-level propensity to offend across time and the probability of being in a latent offender group (for further discussion, see Bushway et al. 2001).

Nagin and Land's (1993) semiparametric group-based modeling approach offers an innovative advantage to studying offending trajectories over the life course under the assumption that the population comprises a mixture of several groups with distinct developmental trajectories. Because the specifics of this approach have been discussed in detail elsewhere (for example, Nagin and Land 1993; Nagin 1999; and Jones, Nagin, and Roeder 2001), our description here is restricted to a brief explanation of its key components. In general, the mixed Poisson model assumes that the population comprises discrete Poisson distributions with respect to the rate of offending. Each developmental trajectory assumes a polynomial relationship that links age and offending. On the basis of our earlier analysis we use a cubic function of age for the 7 to 70 models, which allows for more flexibility in the shape of the trajectory over time. We estimated the equation:

$$\log(\lambda_{it}^j) = \beta_0^j + \beta_1^j (\text{AGE})_{it} + \beta_2^j (\text{AGE}^2)_{it} + \beta_3^j (\text{AGE}^3)_{it},$$

where $\lambda_{it}^{j}$ is the predicted rate of offending for person $i$ in group $j$ for time period $t$, $AGE_{it}$ is the age of person $i$ for time period $t$, $AGE_{it}^{2}$ is the squared age of person $i$ for time period $t$, and $AGE_{it}^{3}$ is the cubed age of person $i$ for time period $t$, and the coefficients $\beta_{0}^{j}$, $\beta_{1}^{j}$, $\beta_{2}^{j}$, and $\beta_{3}^{j}$, structure the shape of the trajectory for each group $j$. Although every individual in each group is constrained to the same slope and intercept of that trajectory, these parameters, which determine the level and shape of the trajectory, are free to vary by group.[7] The final result from the semiparametric mixed Poisson method is a number of different groups composed of individuals who demonstrate similar patterns of offending over time.[8]

Using this trajectory method, we are able to address whether the age-crime relationship is invariant over time for all offenders and for all offenses in the Glueck delinquent sample. Figures 5.11 to 5.14 show results using semi-parametric mixed Poisson models for total crime, property crime, violent crime, and alcohol/drug crime, respectively. The ultimate conclusion to be derived from these figures is that the age-crime relationship is *not* invariant for all offenders and offense types. Moreover, the data firmly reject the typology of two offender groups. For example, the analysis reveals that there are six groups of offenders for total crime, each with a distinct shape and time path (Figure 5.11).[9] In particular, there is a small group (3 per-

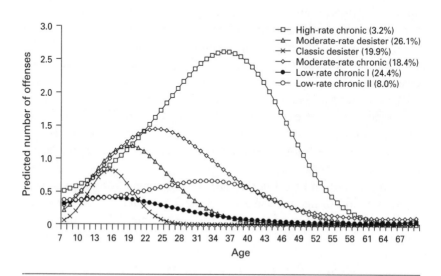

*Figure 5.11* Offending trajectories for total crime: Ages 7 to 70

cent) of high-rate offenders that some would call persistent. But while the peak age of offending for this group is much later compared with the other groups, all groups show declining patterns of offending at some point over the life course. There is no evidence of a flat-trajectory group with age. We believe this is a central finding that has been undetected by most prior research given the middle-adulthood censoring of observations in the major longitudinal studies of crime.

Crime-specific analyses (Figures 5.12, 5.13, 5.14) reveal five groups of offenders for property, violence, and drug and alcohol crime, respectively.[10] Generally, these data show that there are subgroups of offenders who do not display the uniform age-crime relationship alleged by Gottfredson and Hirschi (1990). Once again, though, for each specific type of crime, all offender groups decline in their offending over time.[11] Recall that mortality is accounted for in these models. Moreover, this basic conclusion holds when we account for offending per day free in the community. For example, Figure 5.15 shows the latent class analysis restricted to total offending counts while free during the ages 7–32. There are varying grades of "chronic" and desister groups with distinct peak ages and profiles, but all begin a decline in crime during the twenties. Thus neither mortality nor incarceration serves

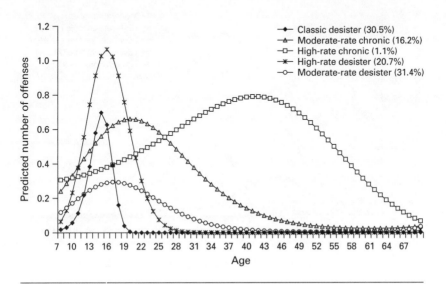

*Figure 5.12* Offending trajectories for property crime: Ages 7 to 70

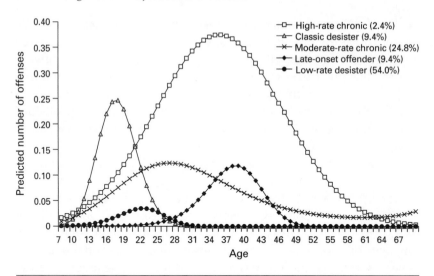

*Figure 5.13* Offending trajectories for violent crime: Ages 7 to 70

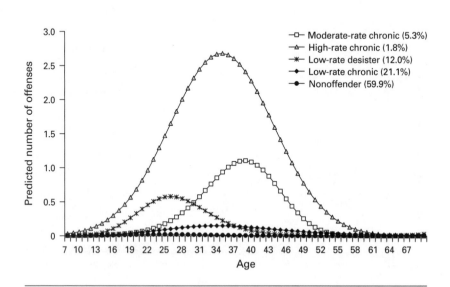

*Figure 5.14* Offending trajectories for alcohol/drug crime: Ages 7 to 70

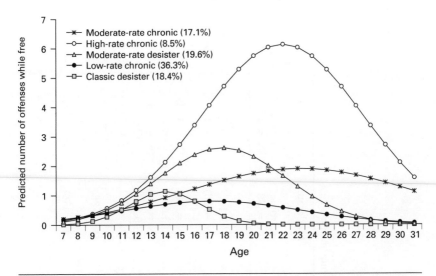

*Figure 5.15* Offending trajectories for total crime: Ages 7 to 32, controlling for incarceration time

to alter our basic conclusion in the latent class analysis, just as was the case for the prospectively defined trajectories.[12]

We are now in a position to (re)turn to a key question: do childhood risk factors distinguish trajectories or, in this case, group membership? Table 5.2 displays the means for key childhood characteristics and individual differences by group membership for total crime. With respect to individual differences and parent/child disposition, there are no statistically significant differences in the means across the six groups of offenders.[13] For example, neither low verbal IQ nor parental crime, two classic risk factors, distinguishes high-rate chronics from classic desisters. Significant differences between groups are noted only for arrest frequency and unofficial delinquency. The main conclusion from these analyses is that once conditioned on delinquency, individual differences and childhood characteristics defined by risk rather than by crime itself do not do a good job of distinguishing different offending trajectories over the long haul.

The basic findings in Table 5.2 were also replicated controlling for incarceration, and in addition, we compared group means for several other risk variables, including low birth weight, poverty, and the "criminogenic family" measures such as parent-child attachment, su-

**Table 5.2** Comparison of selected childhood and adolescent risk factors by group membership

| Characteristic | High-rate chronic N = 15 | Moderate-rate desister N = 126 | Classic desister N = 102 | Moderate-rate chronic N = 88 | Low-rate chronic I N = 113 | Low-rate chronic II N = 36 |
|---|---|---|---|---|---|---|
| *Individual differences* | | | | | | |
| Full-scale IQ | 88.5 | 92.9 | 91.0 | 92.1 | 90.7 | 90.5 |
| | (N = 15) | (N = 126) | (N = 102) | (N = 88) | (N = 113) | (N = 36) |
| Verbal IQ | 2.87 | 3.67 | 3.41 | 3.48 | 3.53 | 3.31 |
| | (N = 15) | (N = 126) | (N = 102) | (N = 88) | (N = 113) | (N = 36) |
| Percentage extroverted | 73.3 | 56.3 | 58.8 | 63.6 | 48.7 | 58.3 |
| | (N = 15) | (N = 126) | (N = 102) | (N = 88) | (N = 113) | (N = 36) |
| Percentage adventurous | 73.3 | 58.7 | 51.0 | 60.2 | 47.8 | 55.6 |
| | (N = 15) | (N = 126) | (N = 102) | (N = 88) | (N = 113) | (N = 36) |
| Percentage egocentric | 6.7 | 11.9 | 15.7 | 11.4 | 14.2 | 13.9 |
| | (N = 15) | (N = 126) | (N = 102) | (N = 88) | (N = 113) | (N = 36) |
| Percentage aggressive | 6.7 | 18.3 | 16.7 | 13.6 | 14.2 | 13.9 |
| | (N = 15) | (N = 126) | (N = 102) | (N = 88) | (N = 113) | (N = 36) |

*Parent/child disposition*

| | | | | | |
|---|---|---|---|---|---|
| Parental crime/alcohol abuse | 2.27 | 2.09 | 1.87 | 2.01 | 1.98 | 1.92 |
| | (N = 15) | (N = 126) | (N = 102) | (N = 88) | (N = 113) | (N = 36) |
| Parental instability | 1.2 | 0.84 | 0.84 | 0.87 | 0.95 | 0.69 |
| | (N = 15) | (N = 120) | (N = 96) | (N = 83) | (N = 111) | (N = 36) |
| Percentage tantrums | 53.3 | 43.7 | 41.2 | 42.0 | 31.9 | 36.1 |
| | (N = 15) | (N = 126) | (N = 102) | (N = 88) | (N = 113) | (N = 36) |
| Percentage difficult child | 57.1 | 54.8 | 57.4 | 63.2 | 60.0 | 62.9 |
| | (N = 14) | (N = 124) | (N = 101) | (N = 87) | (N = 110) | (N = 35) |
| Percentage early onset | 7.1 | 15.6 | 14.8 | 13.0 | 9.3 | 12.5 |
| | (N = 14) | (N = 109) | (N = 88) | (N = 77) | (N = 97) | (N = 32) |

*Adolescent delinquency*

| | | | | | |
|---|---|---|---|---|---|
| Arrest frequency (ages 7–17)[a] | 0.51 | 0.55 | 0.36 | 0.49 | 0.32 | 0.33 |
| | (N = 15) | (N = 124) | (N = 102) | (N = 88) | (N = 113) | (N = 36) |
| Unofficial delinquency[a] | 14.5 | 14.7 | 13.5 | 15.2 | 13.5 | 14.5 |
| | (N = 15) | (N = 126) | (N = 102) | (N = 88) | (N = 113) | (N = 36) |

a. $p < .05$

pervision, and discipline styles examined in Figure 5.7. Overall, we found no statistically significant differences in the means across group membership. These findings, along with the results of the graphical analyses, suggest that life-course-persistent offenders are difficult, if not impossible, to identify prospectively using a wide variety of childhood and adolescent risk factors. The implications for criminological theory and intervention appear considerable.

## Summary

We have attacked the age-crime and "offender group" question from multiple directions, using an unprecedented body of data from childhood to age 70. Although our data certainly have weaknesses, the long-term window allows us to speak to a number of current controversies in the field of theoretical criminology and public policy.

The findings seem quite clear on a number of fronts. First, the criminal career model appears justified if by that we mean the paradigm of studying within-individual trajectories. The aggregate age-crime curve is not the same as individual trajectories, one of the main claims of the criminal career model. On the other hand, crime declines with age even for active offenders,[14] and trajectories of desistance could not be prospectively identified based on typological accounts rooted in childhood and individual differences. While childhood prognoses are moderately accurate in terms of predicting levels of crime, they do not yield distinct groupings that are valid prospectively in a straightforward test. Although peak ages of offending vary by crime type, we found that all offenses decline systematically in the middle adult years for groups identified prospectively according to extant theory and early risk factors. Moreover, when we switched strategies and estimated latent classes of offender groups on an ex-post basis, a similar conclusion was obtained. Namely, although latent classes of offenders appear to yield distinct trajectories of offending, supporting Nagin and Land (1993), group membership is not easily, if at all, predictable from individual, childhood, and adolescent risk factors.

We are hard pressed to attribute these conclusions solely to an artifact based on the data source. It is difficult to imagine why a 45-year-old man, for example, as opposed to the same man at 40, would be any more or less likely to be arrested for the same crime. Recall that these are within-individual trajectories and not the comparison of different groups or cohorts of men with different characteristics (such as race or class) often thought to influence processing. More important, the Glueck men as adults also engaged in all sorts of deviant activities that the Boston police appeared only too happy to record—including drunkenness, domestic violence, receiving stolen goods, failure to pay child support, and so on. To illustrate, there were 1,802 arrests for alcohol and drug use and over 3,000 arrests for other minor offenses. Because of the wide variety of offenses that are captured, the historical nature of the Gluecks' data is analytically strategic. The argument that the men could have been involved in other deviant activities is thus not compelling, in our view, and does not overturn the very strong patterns of desistance in the data.

One might claim that we left out an important childhood or adolescent risk factor, or that some of our measures were retrospectively biased. These are real possibilities, of course, but any such bias would seem to have worked in favor of the typological accounts. If parents reported some of the risk indicators on the basis of the child's actual delinquent behavior rather than the risk indicators themselves, then those children would have increased risk for later life-course-persistent criminal behavior. Moreover, the central argument of Moffitt (1993) and the risk-factor paradigm (for example, Loeber and Farrington 1998; Hawkins et al. 2000) is precisely that risks come in a bundle. What this means is that for our results to be invalid, the critic must point to an isolated risk factor that is uncorrelated with the more than one dozen indicators we summarized. Recall that our strategy was based on the constellation of multiple risk factors within the same boy.

Another possible bias is that high-rate offenders are disproportionately incarcerated, injured, and killed, such that simple trajectories of offending may disguise the existence of persistent offenders who exit involuntarily from the risk pool. When death and incarceration were accounted for, however, the patterns remained remarkably similar even though, as expected, the more the delinquency the greater the likelihood of early death and incarceration.

## Resolution?

That all offenses eventually decline in the middle adult years for all groups of offenders identified according to extant theory and a multitude of childhood and adolescent risk factors suggests that (a) desistance processes are at work even for the highest-risk and predicted life-course-persistent offenders, and (b) while childhood prognoses are modestly accurate in predicting level differences, they do not yield distinct groupings that are valid prospectively for troubled kids. It is precisely for the group of troubled kids, of course, that claims are made about prediction. There is no point intervening in the lives of model children, and we see no policy move to do so. It is only for the sort of boys represented in the Gluecks' delinquent sample do we see clamoring for "early intervention."[15]

What does this mean for developmental theory and the typological question with which we began? Do the data leave us on the side of Gottfredson and Hirschi, the criminal careerists, the developmentalists, or on some middle ground? We think the answer is a "new middle" ground. Paternoster and his colleagues (1997) have pointed out that the life-course perspective of Sampson and Laub (1993) is in important respects more compatible with general theories like that of Gottfredson and Hirschi (1990) than with developmental theories, even though the latter are often viewed as synonymous with life-course perspectives (for a recent example, see Chung et al. 2002, 60).[16] Paternoster and Brame argue, "Gottfredson and Hirschi and Sampson and Laub would predict that the same causal process can be invoked to account for the offending behavior of all individuals" (1997, 57; see also Paternoster et al. 1997). This claim may be true for other theoretical perspectives such as social learning theory (Akers 1998), general strain theory (Agnew 1992), and control balance theory (Tittle 1995) as well, although the authors have not been explicit on the matter. At first reading we were skeptical of Paternoster's assessment, in part because we take issue with key aspects of Gottfredson and Hirschi's theory (see Sampson and Laub 1995 and Hirschi and Gottfredson 1995). On the basis of the data analysis in this chapter, however, we have come to see the wisdom of Paternoster's argument.

We emphasize that our work is not a brief against the latent class method per se. Groups are useful in managing and presenting data because they reduce complexity. And, as we have shown, they capture age heterogeneity in offending trajectories quite well, which was exactly our goal. Groups can also be used as a sampling strategy to maximize variation, which we in fact employed in our follow-up. The problem occurs when empirically derived groups are reified as meaningful entities or analyzed outside a meaningful theoretical concept of the offender. Statistical approaches for data reduction in particular have seduced some criminologists by giving the appearance of distinct groupings in the real world (super-predator, life-course-persistent offender, for example) that are amenable to direct policy intervention. This is not the fault of the method—Nagin and Land (1993) warned as much—but rather the user community.

To be sure, with our data we are not able to definitively assess the validity of the adolescence-limited hypothesis of Moffitt (1993) or many of her specific predictions. Much of the testing of her theory requires a population-based sample. Our data do, however, make it possible to examine long-term trajectories of crime and the existence of life-course-persistent offender groups. Again, it would be hard to write an analytic script that would be more conducive to finding troubled adult men than the one laid out in the behavioral story of the delinquent group in the Gluecks' *Unraveling Juvenile Delinquency* (1950). These 500 men generated some 10,000 criminal and deviant acts to age 70, and yet we have failed to find convincing evidence that a life-course-persistent group can be prospectively or even retrospectively identified on the basis of theoretical risk factors at the individual level in childhood and adolescence. Moreover, even in hindsight (ex post), crime declines with age at the extremes of active offending (compare Blumstein and Cohen 1979; Moffitt 1993, 695). It is difficult to reconcile these findings with the theoretical idea of a life-course-persistent group (Moffitt 1993).

So the fact remains that there are important differences in adult criminal trajectories that cannot be predicted from childhood, contra the "national summits" of the policy world and apparently much yearning among criminologists. The question we are left with is what *does* account for these important (perhaps even group-based) patterns of offending? Many of the original Glueck delinquents did in fact persist, whereas other delinquents desisted soon after adolescence (see Figures 5.11–5.14). To solve this puzzle, we turn to the qualitative data in Chapters 6–8, in the form of life-history narratives. We then return to further analysis of quantitative data on the timing of salient life events in adulthood and variation by crime using dynamic statistical models (Chapter 9).

# CHAPTER SIX

# Why Some Offenders Stop

To better understand the processes of persistent offending and desistance from crime over the life course, in the next three chapters we turn to life-history narratives. We present narratives for men who have desisted from crime (Chapter 6), for men who have persisted (Chapter 7), and for the remaining group of men that reveal the zigzag quality of many criminal careers (Chapter 8). Our rationale for using life-history narratives was explained in Chapter 3 and the strengths and weaknesses of these qualitative data were discussed in Chapter 4.

Our strategy wherever possible is to weave back and forth between quantitative and qualitative data. The life histories that follow are informed not only by the trajectory analyses just completed but by further quantitative data on the criminal histories (for example, number of arrests and time served in prison) and social data (for example, proportion of time married) for the 52 men in the follow-up. Then in Chapter 9 we return to a quantitative analysis of life-course trajectories to explain how changes in adult domains—marriage, military experience, and work—are related to changes in criminal activity within individuals over time. This quantitative analysis is informed, in turn, by the narrative data. In the end, our approach represents a blending of diverse methods of data collection and analysis that could not be achieved by exclusive reliance on a single mode of research.

## Strategy and Background

As discussed in Chapter 2, defining and identifying desistance is problematic. Classification schemes that posit "desisters" as formally distinguishable from "persisters" or other offenders are at some level arbitrary and suspect. At the same time, the concept of desistance has theoretical utility and provides a useful means of organizing our narrative data.

Combining both narrative data and official records, our strategy is to investigate two subgroups of men who desisted from crime. The first group consists of men who were arrested as juveniles (age 7 to 17) for nonviolent crimes only, and were not arrested for any predatory crimes (violence or property) as adults. A few of these men were arrested for speeding or other moving violations as adults as well as for other minor offenses (for example, profanity), but still desisted from interpersonal offending. We interviewed 15 men in this group. The second group consists of 4 men who had at least one arrest for violent crime as a juvenile, but none for predatory crime in adulthood (after the age of 21). Again, we did not consider arrests for minor motor vehicle violations as counting against the men in terms of desistance. Thus we interviewed 19 men we call desisters from serious crime. We compare these two subgroups of desisters to detect any differences in desistance by type of offense.

Criminal history data for the 19 desisters are displayed in Table 6.1, and information regarding other important social characteristics is displayed in Table 6.2. Using available data up to age 70, we find that the "nonviolent desisters" were arrested on average nine times, and by design these men had no arrests for violence at any point in their life. The "violent desisters" were arrested on average twelve times throughout life, and by design all had a violent arrest as a juvenile. Although all of the men were classified as desisters, they did spend time incarcerated in prisons and jails, especially early in their criminal careers. For example, four-fifths, or all but three, of the "nonviolent desisters" stayed out of jail or prison over the adult life course (age 17 to 70), whereas half the "violent desisters" stayed out of jail or prison over their adult life course. Interestingly, both the "nonviolent desisters" and the "violent desisters" were incarcerated as juveniles for 1.4 years on average.

Table 6.1 Desisters: Criminal history data

| Name | Total report | Official offenses <17 | Official offenses 17–32 | Total official offenses[a] | Total official violent offenses[a] | Age first incarcerated | Time served <17 (in years) | Time served 17–32 (in years) | Time served[b] |
|---|---|---|---|---|---|---|---|---|---|
| *Nonviolent offenders* | | | | | | | | | |
| Henry | 13 | 6 | 1 | 7 | 0 | 10 | 2.4 | 0.0 | 0.0 |
| Vinnie | 11 | 8 | 1 | 9 | 0 | 14 | 1.0 | 0.0 | 0.0 |
| Victor | 8 | 4 | 0 | 4 | 0 | 14 | 0.6 | 0.0 | 0.0 |
| John | 10 | 4 | 1 | 6 | 0 | 14 | 1.0 | 0.0 | 0.0 |
| Robert | 17 | 4 | 2 | 10 | 0 | 13 | 1.9 | 0.0 | 0.2 |
| Leon | 19 | 3 | 0 | 4 | 0 | 12 | 1.1 | 0.0 | 0.0 |
| Stanley | 7 | 2 | 0 | 5 | 0 | 15 | 1.0 | 0.0 | 0.0 |
| Norman | 14 | 8 | 2 | 11 | 0 | 14 | 0.7 | 0.0 | 0.0 |
| David | 17 | 4 | 1 | 7 | 0 | 13 | 0.7 | 0.0 | 0.0 |
| Richard | 23 | 7 | 0 | 7 | 0 | 14 | 0.6 | 0.0 | 0.0 |
| William | 17 | 3 | 1 | 4 | 0 | 11 | 2.9 | 0.0 | 0.0 |
| Gilbert | 18 | 9 | 10 | 22 | 0 | 11 | 3.6 | 9.0 | 62.3 |
| Domenic | 15 | 4 | 0 | 4 | 0 | 13 | 1.0 | 0.0 | 0.0 |
| George | 15 | 5 | 1 | 6 | 0 | 14 | 1.1 | 0.0 | 0.0 |
| Edward | 15 | 5 | 18 | 29 | 0 | 15 | 0.9 | 2.6 | 17.9 |
| *Violent juvenile offenders* | | | | | | | | | |
| Leonard | 11 | 15 | 6 | 23 | 1 | 14 | 2.1 | 5.5 | 37.6 |
| Angelo | 6 | 6 | 4 | 10 | 1 | 15 | 0.6 | 0.0 | 0.0 |
| Bruno | 7 | 6 | 3 | 9 | 1 | 15 | 0.5 | 0.0 | 0.0 |
| Michael | 17 | 5 | 0 | 6 | 1 | 10 | 2.3 | 1.0 | 8.0 |
| Mean | 13.7 | 5.7 | 2.7 | 9.6 | 0.21 | 13.2 | 1.4 | 1.0 | 6.6 |

a. Ages 7 to 70.
b. Ages 17 to 70, days incarcerated over lifetime per year.

**Table 6.2** Desisters: Social history data

| Name | Ethnicity | Age at interview | IQ | Adolescent competence | Proportion of time married[a] | Proportion of time divorced/separated[a] | Proportion of time with unstable employment[b] | Proportion of time in military[b] | Military outcome |
|---|---|---|---|---|---|---|---|---|---|
| *Nonviolent offenders* | | | | | | | | | |
| Henry | Swedish | 69 | 93 | 1 | 0.85 | 0.06 | 0.13 | 0.40 | Honorable |
| Vinnie | Italian | 69 | 86 | 3 | 0.96 | 0.00 | 0.40 | 0.20 | Honorable |
| Victor | Lithuanian | 69 | 112 | 3 | 0.89 | 0.00 | 0.20 | 0.20 | Honorable |
| John | Czech. | 70 | 115 | 2 | 0.96 | 0.00 | 0.00 | 0.33 | Honorable |
| Robert | English | 71 | 79 | 0 | 0.87 | 0.00 | 0.13 | 0.33 | Honorable |
| Leon | German | 70 | 103 | 0 | 0.92 | 0.00 | 0.27 | 0.07 | Honorable |
| Stanley | Polish | 69 | 86 | 3 | 0.72 | 0.00 | 0.07 | 0.60 | Honorable |
| Norman | Eng. Can. | 69 | 77 | 0 | 0.62 | 0.11 | 0.13 | 0.00 | N.A. |
| David | American | 67 | 75 | 3 | 0.92 | 0.00 | 0.20 | 0.07 | Honorable |
| Richard | Eng. Can. | 68 | 101 | N.A. | 0.62 | 0.00 | 0.07 | 0.93 | Honorable |
| William | Irish | 64 | 90 | 1 | 0.83 | 0.00 | 0.27 | 0.33 | Dishonorable |
| Gilbert | Eng. Can. | 65 | 104 | 3 | 0.76 | 0.00 | 0.80 | 0.00 | N.A. |
| Domenic | Italian | 67 | 112 | 2 | 0.75 | 0.00 | 0.07 | 0.20 | Honorable |
| George | Eng. Can. | 68 | 80 | 1 | 0.98 | 0.00 | 0.40 | 0.00 | N.A. |
| Edward | English | 67 | 90 | 0 | 0.00 | 0.00 | 0.57 | 0.00 | N.A. |
| *Violent juvenile offenders* | | | | | | | | | |
| Leonard | Fr. Can. | 70 | 90 | 1 | 0.81 | 0.00 | 0.47 | 0.00 | N.A. |
| Angelo | Italian | 70 | 90 | N.A. | 0.92 | 0.00 | 0.27 | 0.13 | Honorable |
| Bruno | Italian | 70 | 92 | 0 | 0.87 | 0.00 | 0.40 | 0.27 | Honorable |
| Michael | Irish | 63 | 89 | 0 | 0.87 | 0.00 | 0.27 | 0.53 | Honorable |
| Mean | | 68.2 | 92.8 | 1.4 | 0.80 | 0.01 | 0.27 | 0.24 | |

*Note:* On adolescent competence, see note 1.
a. Ages 17 to 70.
b. Ages 17 to 32.

Table 6.2 presents social history data for these men. Most revealing is that men who desisted from crime are distinguished by long-term stability in marriage and employment. Most of the desisters also had a successful stint in the military, a pattern of stability that holds for both nonviolent and violent desisters. No discernible pattern emerges with respect to ethnicity, IQ scores, or our measure of adolescent competence.[1]

We begin with a detailed life history of two men in the group of nonviolent desisters. These cases were selected because they highlight different aspects of the desistance process with regard to family life and military service. We then present one life history from the second group of desisters—men who had a record of violence as adolescents, but none as adults. After presenting these life histories, we draw on the remaining interview data to explore in detail several emerging themes regarding the mechanisms involved in the desistance from crime. We believe life-history narratives are especially valuable in uncovering issues overlooked in more traditional quantitative approaches in criminology. In particular, the following narratives provide rich and nuanced information that we use to further develop our theory of why people stop offending.

## Marriage as a Turning Point

If I hadn't met my wife at the time I did, I'd probably be dead.

Consider first the life of Leon. Leon grew up in a large family in a poor neighborhood in Boston. He had nine brothers and sisters, but several of his siblings died young. Leon's father was described as a "heavy drinker." He had been arrested for assault and battery, vandalism, receiving stolen goods, and drunkenness. Leon's mother also had an arrest record for assault and battery and profanity. She too was described in the records as a "heavy drinker." According to the Gluecks' initial investigation in the 1930s, Leon's parents showed little concern for their children, providing lax supervision and erratic discipline. Their home was dirty and the children were neglected. The combination of a large family with inept parenting by two alcoholic parents meant that Leon experienced a rather chaotic family life growing up. As but one example, his family moved more than twenty times while he was a child. In addition, there is some evidence to suggest that Leon's parents condoned his stealing. Despite these unsavory conditions, at his age 14 interview, Leon reported that he was "attached" to both of his parents.

Leon's educational experiences were dismal as well. He went through the seventh grade but quit when he was sent to reform school. Leon's full IQ score was 103, but his verbal IQ score was 83 and his performance IQ was 123—a discrepancy of 40 points. It is well known that verbal deficits are related to delinquency (Moffitt 1993). Because of his poor verbal skills, Leon was placed in a special class, putting him three grades behind other students his age. It comes as no surprise that Leon felt little attachment to school or his teachers, and began skipping school at the age of 7.

Leon was arrested three times as a juvenile for breaking and entering, mainly stores and trucks. He served a little more than one year in reform school. His total self-reported score of "unofficial delinquency" was 19, well above the mean for the delinquent sample (see note 1 for a description of this measure). Like most of the persistent offenders, Leon started his criminal career early—he began playing hooky at the age of 7 and was first arrested at the age of 11. He was also a savvy delinquent. According to notes in his record, Leon became involved in a series of burglaries and lootings of trucks while he was on parole from the Lyman School. The stolen goods included silk stockings that his gang sold around the neighborhood. Leon learned that the police knew who was responsible for the thefts, and he subtly suggested to his parole officer "that he would like to be returned to the Lyman School for having broken his parole by truanting." This strategy enabled Leon to avoid a new set of criminal charges, a potentially longer period of confinement, and a more extensive criminal record.

In contrast to the chaos and disorganization early in his life, Leon's adult life is markedly stable. He lived in only three places in his middle and later years, including a stretch at one address for thirty years. As an adult, he worked as a manager at a donut shop for thirty years and as a laboratory technician at a chemical plant for twelve years. In fact Leon worked more or less continuously from the age of 13. Most of his early employment consisted of low-paying jobs as a movie usher, a furniture mover, a shipper in a bakery, and an attendant in a gasoline station. Despite a seventh-grade education, Leon is now a homeowner who spends his retirement traveling throughout the United States and

Europe with his wife. At the time of our interview, Leon was 70 years old. He looked back on his life with a sense of accomplishment, especially sweetened by the fact that he overcame early hardship and disadvantage. Throughout his adult life, he had been strongly committed to upward mobility and recognized that he could make progress, if only a little bit at a time. What accounts for such change?

Leon served in the U.S. Army between 1946 and 1948. He was drafted at the age of 21, six weeks after he was married. As with many Glueck men, he served a tour of duty in the Far East. After his military service, he used the G.I. Bill to buy a home. Not all is rosy in the military-as-turning point story, however. Leon told us that, like his father, he developed a drinking problem in the service. There is no mention of this fact in his military record (for example, no arrests for drunkenness were recorded), which again underscores the importance of collecting both official and self-report data. As we learn below, Leon still did not become an alcoholic, nor did his early drinking problem hamper his adult development.

At the time of our interview, Leon's major turning point, at least in his own mind, was marriage. He met his wife when he was 17 (she was also 17 years old at the time). Marriage's roles in changing routine activities, as a social investment generating strong social support, and in supplying direct social control all describe Leon's situation. His wife knew he was in trouble as an adolescent, but she decided to take a chance on him anyway. During our interview with Leon, she stated, "I was young and naive." She went on to say,

> It wasn't unusual in those days for kids to be in that kind of trouble and for some reason . . . if my daughter took up with anybody like that, I'd go through the roof! We had so many strikes against us. He had no education, he drank. Not when we were together . . . When you think of it, you know, I can't get over how well we've done with how little we had. He had no occupation. He was a baker. And luckily he learned to bake and then he learned to manage, and he was a go-getter, and actually that's all we had going. And I was a fighter and a go-getter. Even though I had a little bit more education, we got so much in common, that's why we get along so well, we like the same things.

Not only did Leon have a record, his mother, a Catholic, strongly disapproved of his marriage for religious reasons. She did not want one of her sons marrying a Protestant. Leon's wife told us that his mother "put a curse on our marriage" because of her unhappiness with the union.

Despite the long odds and lack of family support, Leon's marriage was a success. As a married man, Leon worked every day, did not go out with the guys, and was home every night. At his age 25 interview, Leon stated that he was "quite content to stay at home." Home life became the center of activity for Leon and most other men who desisted from crime. Leon insisted to us that he would have continued getting into trouble if he had not married. Indeed, some fifty years earlier, when asked for the reasons behind his reformation, Leon stated emphatically, "My wife straightened me out." Even before his actual marriage, Leon's parole officer remarked that he had given up drinking and gambling when he became interested in a 17-year-old woman who would later become his wife.

At Leon's age 25 interview, the Gluecks' interviewer remarked on the beneficial influence of his wife. She was described as "respectable," "decent," and with a "stronger personality" than her husband. During this earlier interview, the interviewer wrote that "the couple seem very much in love and made a display of their attachment in an obvious manner." This was our sense at the age 70 interview as well. During our interview, Leon and his wife completed each other's sentences and displayed a great deal of love and affection.

Along with the social support and love that came from this successful marriage, additional factors help explain why Leon was able to desist from crime. First, perhaps in response to his wife's investment in him and vice versa, Leon took his marital responsibilities very seriously. He often worked overtime to support his family. Moreover, later in his career, he turned down a promotion because it would have taken more time away from his wife and children. Second, as a direct result of his marriage, Leon was cut off from his former peer group. These peers were replaced by his wife's friends. At his age 25 interview, Leon disclosed that one of his delinquent friends "went away" for murder. Leon continued, "On the very night of the murder, I had a date with my wife and we went to a dance. If it weren't for my wife, I'd probably be up for murder." Third, Leon spent more time with his wife's family than he did with his own. In fact, the couple moved to get away from his family. They relocated to another part of Boston and his in-laws moved in on the first floor of their two-family home. This action solidified his new family bonds, both practically and symbolically.

Leon and his wife have a rewarding union and are clearly woven together. One of the more poignant moments in the interview came when they spoke of their son who had died of a heart attack at the age of 45. This heart attack was brought on by drug and alcohol abuse. Rather than dwelling on the loss of their son, the couple focused on the future of their daughter-in-law. Referring to their daughter-in-law, Leon's wife said, "She was an enabler. She did everything for him. All the classic things that you do for alcoholics. She called the boss and told him that he's sick, . . . She learned to be a baker, taking over for [her husband] when he was hung over or drugged over or whatever." The discussion with Leon and his wife continued.

> *Wife:* It was a terrible marriage in that way, because—
> *Leon:* It made it terrible for her, not him.
> *Wife:* It made it terrible for her is right, and it didn't help him at all. I mean, instead of saying, "Look, buddy, you know, get with the program or get out," she didn't. She just kept covering for him and covering for him and covering for him.
> *Leon:* And she's still like a daughter to us today.
> *Wife:* Ruined ten years of her own life.
> *Leon:* An adopted daughter, in fact, . . .
> *Wife:* She remarried a wonderful guy.
> *Leon:* She's doing wonderful, yeah. She's going to school.
> *Wife:* She's a computer expert now. They have these robots that go down to see the fish. She's in charge of that. She does the repair work and everything on those computers, so she's done that all on her own.
> *Leon:* . . . She had ten years of living with a drunken drug addict, and yet she turned her whole life around on her own, once she got away from him.

A second transformative event mentioned in Leon's interview was his institutionalization in the Lyman School. Leon characterized his time at Lyman as a "turning point in his life." He went to Lyman when he was 13 for breaking and entering and skipping school. He described the reform school as offering a "learning environment." Leon recounted:

> I mean it might sound silly—I thought it was great. I mean they taught you a lot of things there. They taught you to respect yourself, and no matter what you did you were dressed up every day, you were clean, you went to school, and they just, I mean even like, I used to set the table,

you learned the proper way to set a table . . . I might have been one out of a thousand that got anything out of it, but still, I go back to that whenever I think of a change in my life . . . And I think it was great, I think they ought to have them today instead of having these places where they stick the kids in the halls [detention centers].

Leon and his wife also became involved with meditation—unusual for our sample of delinquents. They took up the practice when they were in their thirties, and they claim it has given them spiritual peace and an overwhelming sense of well-being. Leon declared, "It made me simmer down." Leon's wife described him as "like a hen on a hot griddle" before he took up meditation.

### Military Service as a Turning Point

I learned a lot of responsibility there [in the military] and . . . how to follow orders.

Here we examine the life history of another desister we call Henry. Like Leon, Henry experienced no arrests for predatory crimes of violence or property as an adult. His narrative brings into play new elements that add further complexity to our understanding of how movement away from criminal behavior is sustained.

Henry, at the age of 69, was interviewed by telephone at his retirement home on the southwest coast of Florida. Although possessing only an eighth-grade education, Henry worked as a machinist nearly all of his adult life. Employed most of his life, he stated emphatically, "I was never without a job." This glimpse of Henry's life as an adult provides a dramatic contrast to his childhood and adolescent experiences.

Henry grew up in slum areas in Boston. At the time of the wave 1 interview, Henry's family lived in a deteriorated wooden tenement district close by the waterfront. Like many delinquents, Henry often changed schools because his family moved excessively (at least once a year). He repeated grades one and four and from age 10 was frequently truant. According to teacher reports, Henry seemed childish and immature. His overall IQ score was 93 (79 verbal and 107 performance).

Henry's home conditions were considered very poor by the Gluecks' research team. At the time of the interview, his mother and father had been separated for four years. Henry and three sisters were living with their mother. She was described as being "careless in her appearance, some of her front teeth missing, and her fingers heavily stained from cigarette smoke." Henry's father was described as a "heavy drinker." In fact, Henry's father was a weekend drinker who went on "benders." When he drank he was verbally abusive to the children and his wife. One illustration from Henry's file described the following: "When the father went to bed, he would stick a knife in the closed bedroom door explaining that if anyone opened the door during the night the knife would fall on them and kill them." Despite this family situation, a psychiatrist noted that Henry "seems very fond of his father" and hoped to be paroled to his father.

Henry's mother had her husband committed to Boston State Hospital for observation. He was "paranoid" and claimed that he could not work because he had to keep an eye on his wife. Furthermore, he questioned the paternity of the children and accused his wife of child neglect. There is a notation in Henry's file that his mother had an affair with his uncle, his maternal aunt's husband. Henry's father had disappeared and was therefore not providing any child support. As a result, the family was living on welfare.

At his wave 1 interview, Henry was described as a stubborn child, a truant, a runaway, and a beggar. He apparently committed thefts to get money for candy and the movies. Henry's first arrest occurred at the age of 10 and the charge was stubbornness. Overall, Henry had six arrests as a juvenile.

One of the most important events in Henry's life was his decision to join the Marine Corps at age 18. He served three years in the Marines (from 1945 to 1948). Henry achieved the rank of corporal, and he received the Good Conduct Medal and the Victory Medal for World War II. Then he joined the Air National Reserves for two years. At the end of the two years, he was called back to the service—"convenience of the government, they called it, COG." He served again from 1950 to 1951. Henry used the G.I. Bill when he left the service to receive on-the-job training as a machinist. Looking back on the military, Henry maintained that it was a very important part of his life. He declared: "I learned a lot. It was just a big part of my life and I liked it." When asked further about the precise change-inducing elements of serving in the military, Henry stated, "It taught me a lot of responsibility and things like that."

The ordeal of reform school was also a transforming experience for Henry, as it was for Leon. When asked whether he experienced any turning points or things that happened that pushed him in a direction other than he might have gone, Henry responded that his turning point was being sent to the Lyman School for Boys. "That was a big turning point in my life . . . I think that helped straighten me out quite a bit that Lyman School." When pressed on what it was about the Lyman School that changed him, Henry said, "Well, I started learning a lot of responsibility. Taking more responsibility—to stay on the good side because I used to do a lot of skipping school and stuff like that. I think that taught me to grow up, I'd just go to school and learn what you can and do what you can." For Henry, going to reform school twice facilitated his desistance from crime. "I didn't want to go back . . . It's not a reform school but like a reform school. It was like a real, private, strict school. They were very strict. If you needed a whack, you'd get a whack . . . I think it helped me a lot."

The parallel experiences between the military and the Lyman School in Henry's life are clear. In both institutions, Henry learned "responsibility" and "how to follow orders." Reflecting back over the long term, Henry considered both experiences as turning points in his life. He described both institutions as "helping him out a lot." Both institutions facilitated and perhaps redirected the natural process of maturation. In large part, Henry was a defiant adolescent who did not like to be told what to do. In his own words, he did not "like to be ordered around." He went on to say, "My main problem I think when I was growing up, not liking school, skipping school, and not taking authority the way I should." This was something that he "grew out of" with the help of the Lyman School and his military experience.

Nevertheless, the story of pure social causation is complicated by Henry's own actions. According to information in his file from his parole officer, Henry was "unable to get along with either his mother or his stepfather," and he "selected the service as his 'out' for his problems." Henry's parole officer further speculated that Henry was "intelligent enough to realize that part of his difficulties existed in his home and that the U.S. Marine Corps might give him a second chance in the service to make good under closer supervision than what the U.S. Maritime Service gave him."

The timing of these institutional engagements and life-course events is also important. After serving a sentence in the Lyman School for

Boys, Henry reported that he joined the Maritime Service at age 16, two years before he joined the Marine Corps. Unfortunately, serving in the Maritime Service did not work out. Henry went AWOL and received a dishonorable discharge. In effect Henry simply continued his antisocial behavior, especially regarding the following of rules and orders. At age 18, however, the Marine Corps was one of his self-described life-course turning points. Although the Maritime Service and the Marine Corps are not strictly comparable, it seems that the timing of these two experiences is crucial. It should be noted that Henry did not reveal to the Marines that he had been dishonorably discharged from the U.S. Maritime Service or that he was on parole from the Lyman School for Boys.

According to Henry, another significant element in his life was a move from the city to what was then a country setting. Henry recalled these residential changes as significant in facilitating desistance: "Well, I think my family—my Mom and Dad—moving out of the Boston area had a lot to do with it also. Originally we had lived in a town about twenty miles north of Boston. And it's a completely different scenario. It's like living out in the country. Getting away from the Boston environment that it had at that time [1930s and 1940s] had a lot to do with it." Given that these moves occurred before his unsuccessful stint in the U.S. Maritime Service, it is not clear what role they played in the desistance process. Nevertheless, Henry described these events as important turning points.

In looking back on his life, Henry saw marked improvement given his childhood and adolescent experiences. He feels "fortunate that things had turned out the way they did," and he has a sense of accomplishment from overcoming disadvantage and hardship early in life. This is true of Leon as well. Displaying a sense of generativity, Henry also believed that things were more promising for his children and that he could help them have a better start in life than he did.

## The Lyman School as a Turning Point

Everybody should do a stretch in Lyman.

The next life history we profile in this chapter comes from a man called Bruno. Bruno grew up in a large Italian family in East Boston. He had seven siblings. Although there is evidence in the Gluecks' interview of strong emotional attachment in the family, Bruno was not well supervised during adolescence. He talked about frequently staying out late at night and returning after his parents went to bed. They never knew what time he came into the house. Bruno also had little interest in school as a kid. He repeated two grades and eventually quit school at age 16. He went up to the ninth grade. Although he had a full-scale IQ score of 92, his teacher thought he reached his "intellectual ceiling" in eighth grade.

As a youth, Bruno was the leader of a small but tough street gang that encouraged his delinquent behavior. He had six arrests as a juvenile, including one for violence (he and two friends were drinking and got involved in a brawl on New Year's Eve). Bruno and his companions were also arrested for "jack rolling," but they were formally charged with larceny, not robbery, for this crime. In total, Bruno spent about six months in the Lyman School for Boys for his crimes.

As an adult, Bruno refrained from any criminal activity. Like Leon, Bruno's adult life displayed remarkable stability across several important life domains. For instance, at the time of our interview, Bruno had been married for forty-six years. He went into business for himself as a plumber when he got married. At age 70 when we spoke to him, he had recently retired from the plumbing business. Bruno spent his entire life in one neighborhood in Boston. At his age 32 interview, he and his wife had lived in his mother's house for about seven years. From there they moved to their current address, where they have lived for the past thirty-eight years. This residence was originally his mother in-law's house.

Bruno maintained close ties to his family by virtue of his living arrangement: "My wife and I live here [the first floor of the three-decker where the interview was conducted]. My son lives upstairs with his wife and their two daughters. My daughter lives up another flight with her husband and baby boy. And then my other guy lives up the street."

As was true for Henry, one of the major self-reported turning points in Bruno's life was serving in the military. He enlisted and served three years in the Marine Corps. Like many of his cohort, he saw action in the war in the Pacific theater. Bruno achieved the rank of corporal, and he received the Good Conduct Medal and the Asiatic-Pacific Campaign Medal with two Bronze Stars. When he returned to Boston, he used the G.I. Bill to become a plumber, a skilled trade. Bruno recounted, "I wouldn't have been able to learn to be a plumber because I didn't have the money for school, but when I went under the G.I. Bill, it cost the government the money to teach me. It was like an apprenticeship."

Like Leon and Henry, and once again surprising to us, Bruno thought one of the other turning points in his life was getting sent to the Lyman School for Boys.

> It was positive, it was good. I'll tell ya', everybody should do a stretch in Lyman, because the people don't hurt you. If you were in a disciplinary cottage, yes. But they deserved to get shellacked. But I never did. While I was up there, I became a painter. We used to paint boats down around the harbor there. Then from that we would . . . you know you pick certain jobs. So, in other words, every chance I had I'd try to do better, because I wanted to get out. I wanted to go home. I missed my mother's cooking.

This account is consistent with what he told the Gluecks' interviewer more than forty years before our interview. In that interview, Bruno admitted that he deserved to be sent to Lyman and that his commitment convinced him to "respect the things that count in life." In addition, Bruno said that Lyman was "the best thing that ever happened" because he was placed under "firm authority and close supervision." There was a definite change in Bruno because of the Lyman experience. Before Lyman, he described himself as a "wise guy—I knew all the answers and no one could tell me anything. My father did the best he could, but I thought I knew more than he did."

In the aftermath of his Lyman experience, Bruno was not allowed to associate with the friends that he got in trouble with earlier in his career. He recalled, "I had two brothers that used to watch me—not watch me—they used to kick the shit out of me in plain English. But never enough to hurt me, but enough for me to think."

For Bruno, then, the crucial factors appeared to be the Lyman School and his military experience. What is significant is that the factors that facilitated Bruno's desistance from crime after adolescence are the same as those that facilitated desistance for Henry and Leon, despite the fact that Bruno was involved in violence as a youth. These narratives, plus those described below, suggest a general process of crime cessation that is not necessarily distinguished by crime type. This perspective on desistance is consistent with the general theory of crime we presented in Chapter 3, which also does not distinguish distinct causal mechanisms for crimes of violence compared with crimes of property. We turn to a deeper exploration of these mechanisms.

## Unpacking the Desistance Process

In examining desistance, several themes emerge in the life histories profiled so far. Despite early instability, rancor, and family chaos, men who desisted from crime exhibited remarkable stability and organization across several adult life domains—work, marriage, and living arrangements. Self-identified turning points included marriage, serving in the military, being sent to the Lyman School for Boys, residential relocation, and becoming involved in meditation. One unexpected finding was the positive aspect of the reform-school experience for these former delinquents. The reform-school experience was especially salient for some men when coupled with serving in the military, a fact that suggests the need to examine further the Lyman School–military connection. A second surprise was that although all three men we profiled displayed remarkable employment stability in light of their childhood and adolescent backgrounds, none of them pointed to work as a major turning point in his life. This suggests that stable work may not trigger a change in an antisocial trajectory in the way that marriage or serving in the military does, even though employment may play an important role in sustaining the process of desistance. In this section, we examine these themes in more detail, drawing on the additional interviews we conducted.

### Lyman School

For some men, the Lyman School provided an important setting in which to acquire the discipline and structure that were absent from their young lives. The Lyman School also was a place where they could perform tasks that they would be rewarded for, in sharp contrast to many of their school and family experiences. For others, the Lyman School represented a purely deterrent force. For example, Angelo did not go back because he "learned that he did not want to do the time." Several others expressed the same feeling. Angelo went on to tell us that he had a "very distinct recollection" of the Lyman School. A guard "gave me a crack on the mouth that I still can remember and feel today. And I have a vengeance for him that you can't believe. But it did teach me to respect society or whoever." He concluded, "If you haven't got the time, you don't do the crime. Lyman was a turning point in the sense that I don't want to do the time." For others, Lyman provided an environment for learning important lessons about life. As Stanley said, "I learned how to be away from home and how to get along with other people."

### The Lyman-Military Nexus

Perhaps even more important, several men alluded to a Lyman-military connection. There are important commonalities in the two experiences for men who later desisted from crime. For instance, Richard identified the parallel themes between the two institutions as "discipline and strictness." In addition, he noted the capacity of both institutions to "give kids something they never had at home." For Richard at both places, "Somebody took me under their wing and that was it. It changed my life." In a similar vein, at his age 25 interview, John said that he believed his correctional school experiences helped him considerably in adjusting to Navy life, as he learned at the Lyman School to accept authority and to live with large groups of other boys harmoniously. In his interview at age 63, Michael also noted the similarities between reform school and the military: "Well a lot of people can't adjust to stuff like that. I was in reform school and all that. Like I told you—You got to get up. Gotta go to bed. You got to eat. It was just like the military. You get up at a certain time. And you eat at a certain time. You do calisthenics at a certain time. You go to bed at a certain time. I'm used to it."

But what is also evident from our interviews is that the Lyman School was not the right experience for all men, nor was it necessarily a turning point, positive or negative. For instance, in his interview at age 67, David told us that staying at Lyman was a horrible experience. He continued:

> It was bad. Real bad. You see these pictures about torturing the kids. Well, they did then, let me tell you. Well, we'd come in from a march out in the cold, and . . . and you were walking beside him [another inmate] and I says "How is everything going today?" and the counselor heard you he'd take you back in the room and take your shoes off and you had to hold your feet up with no shoes on and he had a stick that big [about two feet long] and that thick [about two inches] he'd give you 10 whacks. Now you can't walk. And if you dropped your foot down you'd

get another 10. I mean the pain was right up through your leg. And then they'd take you in the corner and they'd pound the living shit out of you.

When asked how long he had been in reform school, David recalled the exact number of days he was there—"13 months, 2 weeks, and 3 days—made it to Saturday." This was more than fifty years after his Lyman incarceration.

What is harder to untangle is why those who had adverse experiences in Lyman did not react negatively to those experiences by committing crime or displaying other forms of poor adaptation as an adult. For instance, Victor talked about beatings, cold showers, and endless marching at Lyman. His view of the Lyman School experience was prosaic—"I didn't learn anything up there, except not to go back. That's about it." This came from a man who was sent to Lyman because his father was the town drunk and the probation officers had it in for his father. Despite his apparently unjust incarceration, Victor did not go on to commit any more crimes during adolescence or adulthood.

Gilbert, another desister, recalled Lyman:

I was mistreated back then. There was people that ran these cottages and they beat the devil out of you and beat on the bottom of your feet with a stick when you ran away and they'd get you down on the floor and make you scrub the floor with an old bristle brush that was just wood against wood. And demoralize you—make you stand in line with your arms folded and demoralize you as a young person. I was only, cripes, a young kid then. And I remember these points vividly in my mind—how I was treated at Lyman School. I was always running away. Some of the people I couldn't stand—there were sex deviants there too. All kinds of crazy stuff going on.

Remarkably, Gilbert remembered the guard's name who beat him. He exclaimed, "Can you imagine? Here I am talking about how many years ago when I can remember this guy's name . . . It's unbelievable. When I could remember a man's name that used to beat me on the bottom of my feet with a stick, trying to tell me that I won't have any more feet to run away with."

### Military Service

Our quantitative data for the desisters show that several had a successful tour of duty in the military (see Table 6.2). Moreover, several men who desisted from crime described the military as a turning point in their interview (see also Sampson and Laub 1996). The following statement from Victor highlights this point.

> I'd say the turning point was, number one, the Army. You get into an outfit, you had a sense of belonging, you made your friends. I think I became a pretty good judge of character. You met some good ones, you met some foul balls. And things along that line. There was more of a spirit of camaraderie there, togetherness, you know, you come to rely on the friends you make, you know. And even if you didn't like the guy you wouldn't throw him to the dogs. There's no question that the fittest survive and you have to learn to get along with everybody.

The timing of the military experience for this cohort of men, who were raised during the Great Depression, is crucial as well. The military in the 1940s represents something quite different from the military today. Patriotism and pride in the military during the World War II era were abundant. But even more significant, the military offered clothes, shelter, meals, discipline, and structure to men who had little. Several men we talked to about the military mentioned food. John recalled:

> I thought a turning point was joining the Navy. Oh, sure, everybody squawked about the food. And I'm laughing myself, because I had nothing. Where the hell can you have roast beef on a Monday for supper and then have roast pork? If we had roast beef [in Boston], we had it once a month. So I appreciated it. Like I said I only had a couple of bad meals. Like on a Sunday night, that bologna . . . we used to call it. Every other meal, even breakfast, was good. That was my turning point.

For more on what the military offered to disadvantaged youth, we turn again to Victor's interview:

> Well, number one, you had guys that were coming out of the Depression. They got out of school and there were no jobs around, that was number one. And a lot of my friends, they're a little older than I am, a lot of those jumped into the National Guard to pick up a few extra bucks and they got a uniform. A lot of guys went into the service in World War II, a lot of them didn't know what three squares a day was. And I can remember a picture I saw in *Life* magazine pertaining to that. It showed a black from Georgia going back home on leave and everybody's just sitting on the porch and they're feeling his uniform and everything else. They never saw threads like that. He's got shoes on, you

know? But, like I say, put three meals on the table, and then the Army too in those days didn't take any shit. You went and did your thing. If you want to be a wise ass, they had ways of taking care of you. Like I can remember, going out to the obstacle course and dig a 6 × 6. That's 6 feet square, 6 feet deep. He'd throw our newspaper in and then he buried it up, bury it, and say, "What was the headline?" Dig it up, and take a look. Shit details, KP, things like that. They had a way of getting back at you.

Another man we interviewed further added that the military taught him to control his temper, the value of helping others, and the need to follow orders. As William pointed out, "They teach you that you can be your own boss as long as you do what the other people want you to do."

It is also important to note that the military offered something concrete to men when they returned to civilian life—the G.I. Bill. The importance of this voluntary "aftercare" program should not be underestimated (see Sampson and Laub 1996). To illustrate, we examine John's experience in the military. While on parole at the age of 17, John enlisted in the Navy. He received important skill training as an electrician in the Navy, a career he would eventually work in all of his life. When he left the service, he used the G.I. Bill. But even more important for John was the fact that his veteran status overrode his ethnic status in joining the union. He told us,

I worked for [name of company] the last four months of '41. I went to the service from there. Congress passed a law saying that anybody leaving their job voluntarily would come back to the same place—regular seniority. And I went back there [in 1945] and they were non-union. In 1946 they had to go union because they had a bank that they couldn't get on the job unless they were a union shop. And they went, "Hey, sign me up." I happened to be one of the guys there who was working there as non-union and then I got into the union. At the time with my name, which looks real Italian—I'm not Italian—it was an Irish union. "What are you, Ginzo?" But I got in the union. They took 200 veterans. The VA made them do it. I was about the 180th or something like that, that close. That was 1947. I was an apprentice for four years. You had to be an apprentice in the union. So I had my license at the end of three years. I was just hanging for a year—but I was getting the G.I. Bill, which paid up to five cents under an hour. In other words if I was getting $1.80 an hour at the time, I can get up to $1.75 with the G.I. Bill. It was pretty good; it was helpful with four kids. My biggest help was the G.I. Bill of Rights. It raised my pay up to five cents under what a journeyman would make.

As discussed in Chapter 3, military service has the potential to be a transformative experience, especially for those from disadvantaged backgrounds. For some men the military, like the Lyman School, provided the opportunity to learn a new set of skills, both technical and interpersonal, in a new and different environment. Moreover, being in the military meant one could make use of the G.I. Bill, a bridge that allowed disadvantaged men to gain access to jobs, technical training, and even housing to facilitate their efforts to start anew.

### Marriage

Unlike the persistent offenders described in the next chapter, the desisters had stable marriages, with divorce or separation conspicuously absent (see Table 6.2 for details). Indeed, from several narrative accounts, we learned that one of the sources of desistance is a successful marriage. This was illustrated most directly by Leon, who had been married for forty-nine years when he was interviewed at age 70. He said, "If I hadn't met my wife at the time I did, I'd probably be dead. It just changed my whole life . . . that's my turning point right there." Leon is not alone. Several men we interviewed told us that marriage was their turning point and that their criminal and deviant behavior changed as a direct result of getting married. For example, in response to the question "When you look at your life, do you think you've had turning points?" Domenic said, "Oh, sure. My biggest turning point is when I met my wife." Stanley stated proudly, "I gave up drinking after I got married." Similarly, William insisted, "The thing that changed me was marriage. That turned me right straight down the line. She won't put up with any baloney. Well, if you got a job you're supposed to do what the boss wants. I call her the boss. No, we're both the boss, [but] she's got more head than I have. She's got more schooling, she knows more. And I agree with her." For these subjects, marriage was part of "being a man" and that required becoming "serious and responsible."

As discussed in Chapter 3, marriage has the potential to change one's life across several dimensions. We have written extensively about the role of marital attachment and the increased social capital that results from a "good marriage" (see Sampson and Laub 1993; Laub and Sampson 1993; and Laub, Nagin, and Sampson 1998). What has not received enough attention is the role that marriage plays in restructuring routine activities and the direct social control that spouses provide, especially concerning deviant peer group associations.

One wife of a former delinquent, for example, talked about her husband's joining the Elks Club. That club became the place where he spent his leisure time, rather than a bar in Charlestown where his former delinquent friends congregated. She went on to point out that from her perspective, "It is not how many beers you have, it's who you drink with that matters." Graham and Bowling (1995, 71) have shown that continued involvement in offending is closely associated with heavy alcohol use with friends of the same inclination, and wives can provide the triggering influence to extract husbands from this deviant lifestyle (see also Warr 1998; Farrington and West 1995). Marriage can also lead to a residential change. When asked why he left East Boston, Angelo told us, "Because I got married. I got married and I married a girl from Malden and we lived in Malden." As Kenaszchuk (1996) found in his study of good marriages among a subsample of Glueck delinquents up to age 32, a residential change allowed the men to break away from unsatisfactory family and peer relationships that were, or were expected to be, problematic to the husband-wife dyad.

Parenting responsibilities also lead to changes in routine activities, as more time is spent in family-centered activities rather than in unstructured time with peers. Although becoming a parent was not a significant factor in explaining desistance from crime once marital attachment was taken into account (Sampson and Laub 1993), the life-history narratives suggest that parenting was important. For example, shortly after marriage and becoming a father, one former delinquent bought property in New Hampshire and spent each weekend clearing the land and building a summer getaway for his wife and children. Another man told us that he and his wife had one child and they "poured it all out to her." Along with changing routine activities, having children can also influence a person's identity and sense of maturity and responsibility (Graham and Bowling 1995, 72–73).

Perhaps the most unexpected finding emerging from the life histories is that marriage may lead to desistance because of the direct social control effects by spouses. This social control feature may be especially true of marriages in the 1950s and 1960s, which we are examining here. Along with providing a base of social support, wives took primary control of the planning and management of the household and acted as informal "guardians" of their husbands' activities.[2] Some wives "managed" their husband's deviance; others adopted a strict "zero-tolerance" policy. For example, David's wife controlled the pace and timing of his drinking: "Like we had [only] two or three hours [at the bar]. You could drink eight or 10 beers and a couple of shots in that time so that would be enough." His wife also managed to get him to work after a bout with drinking: "What she did is—I went to work every day . . . before I never worked. I'd say, 'The hell with it, why should I go to work?' " David felt an obligation to his family that was reinforced by his wife's presence and constant reminders. "I had to get the money to support the house. If I didn't have that, why would I have to quit drinking and go to work? I think that pushed me to a point anyways."

This view was shared by other men we interviewed. William talked about his sister and later his wife providing supervision and monitoring while he was an adult. Bruno was reluctant to sign the consent form to be interviewed without his wife's permission. He said that he didn't "want to start any trouble with the old lady, you know?" We left the consent form with him and he mailed it back to us after his wife had looked it over.

The experience of a wife taking a direct role in the social control of the man was explicit in the life of one man we interviewed. Before marriage, Leonard's wife told him directly, "Your friends or me." This man was a serious delinquent and had served time as a young adult for burglary, auto theft, and larceny. Upon learning of her impending marriage, friends told her, "Are you out of your mind? He is never going to be anything. He will always be in trouble." Leonard's wife, however, would not tolerate crime or any other misbehavior. At the early stages of their marriage, Leonard wanted to quit his job because he felt he was not making enough money. Like the persistent offenders we describe in Chapter 7, Leonard was not scared of prison and he sought easy money. He told his wife, "I am making peanuts. I can make this money in one day." His wife told him, "You quit, you leave." Leonard took his wife's advice (or followed her orders)—he stayed with his employer for forty-three years and was never involved in crime again. At the time of our interview, furthermore, he had been married for forty-three years and the couple had lived at the same residence for the last thirty-two years. This life story illustrates the reciprocal nature of social support invested by spouses.

For some men, wives were like bosses, but for others, wives played a different role. For some men, a wife was one of the first people to care for them and about them. In this instance, the marriage represented a fusion of interests and shared goals for the future. For instance, George told us that his wife cared for him and that this was the first time in his life that another person had felt this way toward him. Moreover, his in-laws "surrounded" him and adopted him into their family. This acceptance contrasts sharply with his own family, where he had little contact with his siblings and parents. Vaillant has argued that during recovery from alcohol abuse it is valuable for alcoholics to form bonds with people who have not hurt them in the past (1988, 1154; see also Shover 1985, 1996). Satisfying relationships can offer a "new sense of direction and achieve a sense of belonging" (Graham and Bowling 1995, 72).

Additional benefits of marriage deserve mention. Some men married women who were smarter or more talented than they, and the partnership helped them enormously in organizing and managing their affairs as an adult. Many wives finished high school, whereas most of the delinquents did not. Moreover, some delinquents married women from families that were better off economically than they were. "Marrying up" provided many concrete benefits, such as housing, employment, and other material goods.

It should be pointed out that these changes are more gradual than abrupt. Our conceptualization suggests that because investment in social relationships is gradual and cumulative, resulting desistance will be gradual and cumulative (Laub, Nagin, and Sampson 1998). As the wife of a former delinquent said, "The change did not happen overnight." This woman told us that she worried her husband would return to crime. He worked in the neighborhood he grew up in and saw many of his friends who were still involved in criminal activity. For instance, she spoke of worrying each time he was late from work. She went on to say, "It took about five to six years into the marriage before I could relax. Once the company he worked for moved out of Boston, I knew there would be no problem."

## Employment

The men we interviewed who desisted from crime displayed marked stability in employment (see Table 6.2). As we noted in Chapter 3, we believe that the processes for work are similar to those for marriage. In our previous writing, we focused on the role of job stability—length of employment and work habits—in facilitating desistance from crime (Sampson and Laub 1993). Here we broaden our perspective to focus on how work changes routine activities; how employers, like spouses, can provide direct social control; and how work can change one's sense of identity and meaning of life. Following this line of thought, we find that stable work, while not necessarily self-defined as a major turning point, does play an integral role in the process of desistance from crime.

From the life-history narratives, a steady paycheck from work was evidently an indicator of stability and responsibility. As Domenic said, "I had a paycheck coming in every week without fail. I always knew that it was going to be there, or even if I got sick. So that makes you stable and that takes a lot of worry out of your life." This perception rings true particularly for men growing up in the Great Depression.

The men were employed in a wide range of jobs, which included work as a cab driver, fire fighter, boiler maker, construction worker, pipe-covering installer, postal worker, engineer, and stove repairman. Some men clearly enjoyed their work, and for them work was an end in itself. Gilbert claimed that work allowed him to show "what he was best at." He went on to say, "I was best at doing what I enjoy doing and it benefited the world because I got things done. It benefited society because I was able to work at what I felt was good for me because I knew a lot about it. I felt good at doing it." But for most men, work was something that one did as a means to an end. It was simply a way to make money to live as comfortable an existence as possible.[3]

In addition, work served a social control function. Mostly this was an informal by-product of working, but sometimes the social control function was direct. In fact, some employers kept their employees in line. For example, Leonard said that his employer was "like a strict father. He went after me a few times. He also took me under his wing.

We would have a few drinks together." Leonard was such a valued and dedicated employee that the company bought him the house he now lives in and buys him a luxury car every two or three years for his good work. (Recall that Leonard initially wanted to quit this job because he believed he was underpaid.)

Work also provided a structured routine. Perhaps a dramatic example, but John told us that working as an electrician he "averaged 3,400 hours a year." He added, "I didn't work all the time; I was sleeping half the time . . . I did a lot of work. I'd get up at 5:30 in the morning for at least 25 years. I did it for years. You're used to it; it's a trend." Many men who desisted from crime worked extensively. It was also not unusual for men to work nights and/or weekends. If given the opportunity, the men often worked overtime. It was also true that many of the men's wives worked outside the home as well, further structuring routine activities.

Finally, though not common, work gave some men an identity and sense of accomplishment. Gilbert told us, "Being able to work, being able to get a pay check. Being able to spend the money and not have to steal it. Being able to go to the store and buy something and not have to steal it. That's important in life . . . what changed my life is work."

### Other Circumstances

It is possible that desistance can occur "unnaturally"; that is, without any institutional or personal intervention that changes a criminal pathway. As discussed in Chapter 2, desistance by death is possible. Desistance can also result from physical injury. For example, Vinnie was physically disabled because of an injury he received in the military. At the time of the interview (at age 69), he had not worked for the past thirty years or more.

Other circumstances can also lead to desistance from crime. For instance, Norman was a born-again Christian and a strong believer in Alcoholics Anonymous (AA). He is one of the few Glueck men who changed because of either formal religion or AA. According to Norman, he was turned around by his wife's insistence that he leave the household and get help for his drinking. At our interview, he gave the following account:

*Norman:* Well, I had come home drunk and I got into a fight with my wife. I guess I had beaten her and my daughter too—my stepdaughter. They called the cops. That was the only time she ever called the cops on me in her life. That's the best thing she ever done for me. That's when I went out looking for help.

*Q:* So you got arrested then?

*Norman:* Well, I don't know if you call it getting arrested or not. But I was in a cell overnight. They put me in the tank there overnight with the rest of the drunks. And I was ready to face the judge the next morning. And I guess my wife and my daughter came down. They were going to press charges against me. And a clerk of the court called me over out of the group and told me that they were there and that they told me if I would promise to stop drinking and leave the house that they wouldn't press any charges against me. It sounded pretty good so I promised them I would, so I didn't have to face the judge. They let me go. And when I came back home, I went into the house. There was nobody home. I felt pretty lousy, so I dropped into the bed and fell asleep. And when my wife come home she come into the bedroom and she says, "What are you doing here?" I says, "What do you mean what am I doing here? I live here." She says, "Not any more you don't." I says, "Why, what are you talking about?" She said, "You were supposed to leave. You promised me and you told right in front of the cops and everything that you were going to leave and that you were going to get help for yourself. Try to find out what was wrong, why you were drinking so much and all." I got down on my knees and I begged her and stuff, but she stuck to her guns though. As I say it's the best thing she's ever done. Because that's when I went out . . . called my mother and stayed with my mother and father for a while. But they both drank. So they got into arguments and everything and I got into the middle of it and here I am trying to stop drinking. So I moved out and got myself a room over in South Boston, right near the job where I worked. I was working over a boiler over at the [name of company] in South Boston. I could walk to work from where my room was. And then I went and talked to Father [name] with the Gavin House in South Boston.[4]

Norman told us that he had been in all of the correctional institutions in Massachusetts as part of an AA group talking to prisoners.

Some men also benefited from a residential change, independent of marriage. As noted above, Henry moved from a poor Boston neighborhood to a small town twenty miles outside of Boston. Another subject, George, escaped from the Lyman School and went to live with relatives out of state. He told us that he knew he could not go back to his old neighborhood in Boston because he would find himself in jail or dead if he did.

For others, mentors were important in steering them away from crime. Gilbert told us that while he was in federal prison he learned "a lot about life from a guy down there named Jack. He was an amateur radio guy in the service . . . he loved amateur radio. And he got me interested in radio and electrical stuff and things of that nature." Jack was an electrician who worked in the prison. Gilbert went on, "I'm still a young guy. He saw the potentials in me. He saw I enjoyed electricity. I enjoyed radio and stuff like that. He took me under his wing. And I thought an awful lot of this guy in a short ten months I worked with him. He was a prince." Gilbert concluded, "I prepared my whole life in ten months to do something. Think about it. Those ten months I spent in [name of prison] were the most crucial in my life. Because they turned me around. [Name of prison] turned me around. Jack turned me around. Jack was a humanitarian and cared for me as an individual. Let's get down to brass tacks. What if Jack wasn't there? What if I wasn't offered the opportunity? . . . He treated me right. As a matter of fact, after I left [name of prison] year after year on a yearly basis I would take my wife and the kids, we'd drive all the way to [name of prison] to see Jack."

### The Missing Link in Desistance: Human Agency

Not because of my mother and father. Because of me. I'm the one that made it shitty.

We have argued that life histories are especially useful in uncovering ideas that have not been examined in previous research. What is most striking in the narratives we collected is the role of human agency, or choice, in desistance from crime and deviance. The men who desisted are "active" players in the desistance process. Cohler (1982) has noted that a subjective reconstruction of the self is especially likely at times of transition (see also Emirbayer and Mische 1998,

1004). Several examples emerge from the life-history narratives that we collected.

For example, Michael went into the military to avoid trouble. When asked why he entered the service, he answered ironically, "I had no choice. If I'd a gone back out when I left Shirley [a reform school in Massachusetts]—If I'd a gone back out on the corner—I'd get mixed up with the same gang that I got involved with, so I didn't want to do that. So I just went in. And the reason I stayed in was I didn't want to get out, because I would get mixed up with the guys again." This was a conscious decision on Michael's part in light of his perception of the situation. Michael was in the Army for seven years. He told us with a smile that the decision to stay in the military so long "probably saved my bacon." Reflecting back on the importance of the military experience in his life, Michael chuckled and said,

> Well you can say that the army changed me. If I had gotten out the first time, I'd probably [have] gone back with the same crowd that I grew up with. And I probably would have ended in jail, because that's the way I was heading . . . I wouldn't take a million bucks for my experience . . . I loved it. I was brought up in a ghetto. And I struggled my way out. If the military had not been available, I tell you what—I'd hate to say what I would have become.

As we learned above, Norman actively participated in Alcoholics Anonymous to try to get his family back. His wife and daughter left him after tiring of his drinking and violence in the home. Norman told us,

> I used to slap her and [the] kids around and stuff until I was put out. I was out of the house until she ended up in the hospital . . . She had a nervous breakdown and she was under a psychiatrist's care. She had shock treatments and everything. When she got sick and went to the hospital she asked me if I could move home and take care of the children until she got out of the hospital. And I said, "Sure." I've been staying sober all the time. I went to AA and I haven't had a drink since my first meeting.

Norman changed with the help of AA, and what motivated him in large part was the fear of losing his wife and family if he did not straighten out.

Similarly, John worked hard all of his life to provide for his family. He did not want his children to repeat his own experiences growing up. John's parents separated and his father left the family when he was ten years old. His father was arrested for assault and battery and was known as an alcoholic and a wife beater. John was ready and willing to take advantage of opportunities that came his way to avoid repeating what he saw as his father's mistakes. He always worked overtime. John recounted, "If you don't mind working, anybody can do it, really, if you have the opportunity. I really didn't have an opportunity even to get into the union, unless I was a G.I. My main thing at the time, I didn't have an Irish name, although I'm 3/4 Irish. I didn't have the Irish name. That was the union then." John worked as an electrician all of his life up to his retirement in 1990. When we interviewed him at the age of 70, he was living comfortably in retirement in a waterfront condo on the South Shore in metropolitan Boston.

## Accounts in Later Life

The men who desisted from crime accepted responsibility for their actions and freely admitted getting in trouble. Some of the men were "not proud" of what they had done, but they saw that period of their life as long over. They did not, however, offer excuses. Tough times due to the Great Depression, uncaring parents, poor schools, discrimination based on ethnicity and class, and the like were not invoked to explain their criminal pasts. Michael captured this opinion best when he said, "Not because of my mother and father. Because of me. I'm the one that made it shitty." Furthermore, some men claimed that it was merely "luck" that distinguished them from the persistent offenders we present in Chapter 7.

For the men who have desisted from crime, one is struck by the pride they have in their accomplishments and material effects. They are proud of their cars, homes, and possessions such as large-screen TVs and VCRs. Simple, material things are important to them because they did not have material goods in their youth.[5] They were bitten and bitten hard by growing up during the Great Depression in poor, disadvantaged neighborhoods in Boston. They are rightfully proud of what they have now. Michael captured this sense of accomplishment most vividly:

What I done here is a success story. I have no education whatsoever. I have no grammar school. No high school. No nothing . . . In plain English I done all the shit jobs, because I had no education . . . My life now is beautiful. Raised five kids. No education. Worked every day in my life. Whenever I lost one job, I got another. No, I think I done pretty god-damn good.

David echoed this sentiment—"I'd say I had a goddamn good life. Goddamn good. I'm 67 years old now. I'm in pretty good shape. I think I've got a few more years. When I was young I never thought I'd have this age. I think I'm doing pretty good. I've got nice kids, nice wife, can't ask better than that."

Combined with their pride in their possessions and accomplishments, the men who desisted also exhibited generativity (McAdams and St. Aubin 1992). They have worked and are working to make things better for the next generation. The most dramatic evidence is a man and his wife who have taken foster children from state hospitals into their home for many years. Several of the men we talked to have adopted children from teenage mothers. Illustrating the theme of generativity concretely to us, one man we interviewed insisted we send his payment to a local charity in the neighborhood in which he grew up.

The men worry about the apparent lack of generativity in the current generation. For example, Victor deplored young people's failure to take responsibility.

> That's the way I look at it—we've gotten away from everything . . . all these people gave something to the country. . . . You never saw their kids, and it was always working for their kids. And their kids in turn worked so that their kids could be a little better. After that the whole thing started to change. I see like the passing of the box at church Sunday. A bunch of these goons—three of them in the last row. I tell Father [name]: "Why don't you take them and put them down in front?" Comes the time to pass the box under their nose. Out of those three rows, if I get 15 cents, I'm lucky. How the frick is the church going to survive in the future? But, if there is a basketball game, World Series, or baseball game, or rock concert, baby, they can come up with 30 or 45 bucks for a ticket.

In a similar vein, Leon and his wife pointed out the differences between growing up during the Great Depression and today. Leon's wife stated:

> We lived paycheck to paycheck practically until we retired. All our lives, I've always had to worry about money. There's never been enough of it,

but we managed to buy a home, several homes, and buy and sell them, and go up the ladder a little bit more each time. But I think that most parents of our generation were far too generous with their children, and I don't think it gave them the work incentive that our generation had. I think we took that away from them, and I think that's a sad thing. I think things come much too easy to my children's generation. It's much too easy for them to get themselves into debt. We couldn't have got ourselves into debt. They didn't have charge cards that I know of in our day, so if we wanted something, we had to save up for it. Or get it on time and have somebody co-sign for us or something, you know.

Whether these views represent normative generational conflict or a real change is not known.

## What Have We Learned?

Why do some offenders stop offending? It appears that offenders desist as a result of a combination of individual actions (choice) in conjunction with situational contexts and structural influences linked to important institutions that help sustain desistance. This fundamental theme underscores the need to examine both individual motivation and the social context in which individuals are embedded. The processes of desistance operate simultaneously at different levels (individual, situational, and community) and across different contextual environments (family, work, and military). The process of desistance is more than mere aging or "maturational reform" (Matza 1964), and we believe that life-history narratives are useful for unpacking complex person-environment interactions.

Overall it appears that successful cessation from crime occurs when the proximate causes of crime are affected. A central element in the desistance process is the "knifing off" of individual offenders from their immediate environment and offering them a new script for the future (Caspi and Moffitt, 1995). Institutions like the military and reform school have this knifing-off potential, as does marriage, although the knifing-off effect of marriage may not be as dramatic. Another component in the desistance process is the "structured role stability" that emerges across various life domains (for example, marriage, work, residence). The men who desisted from crime shared a daily routine that provided both structure and meaningful activity. The structure was fully embraced by the men, and one result was a disassociation from delinquent peers in adulthood, a major factor in explaining their desistance from crime (see Graham and Bowling 1995; Warr 1998). As discussed in Chapter 3, marriage can change routine activities, especially regarding one's peer group. Wives, for example, may limit the number of nights men can "hang with the guys," so that marriage has the potential to cut off an ex-offender from his delinquent peer group (see Warr 1998, 2002).

This idea is consistent with research on social stratification: successful mobility is a cultural change involving new opportunities and a willingness and ability to accept them. For example, Gans (1962, 254) found that people from the West End of Boston who moved into the middle class had to first break, or have broken for them, their dependence on family and peers. That is, those who strove to get ahead had to shift from peer-group goals to object goals, such as a career, prestige, wealth, or individual development (see Whyte 1993 for a similar discussion of peer groups in Boston's North End).

The routine activities of work and family life and associated informal connections serve two functions. One is to provide social support (Cullen 1994) or emotional "attachment" (Hirschi 1969). The other function is one of monitoring and control through the provision of a set of activities and obligations that are often repeated each day. Many habits are mundane, but they nonetheless give structure to one's time and restrict opportunities for crime. Moreover, these activities result from shifts in role expectations that are not fully explained by age (Osgood and Lee 1993).

What is especially notable in the desistance process is personal agency. A vital feature that emerged from our qualitative data is that personal conceptions about the past and future are apparently transformed as men maneuver through the transition from adolescence to adulthood. The men engage in what can be called "transformative action." Although informed by the past, agency is also oriented toward the future (see Emirbayer and Mische 1998; Cohler 1982; Maruna 2001). Projective actions in the transition from adolescence to adulthood advance a new sense of self and a new identity as a desister from crime or, more aptly, as a family man, hard worker, and good provider. As a result the men we studied were active participants in the decision to give up crime. Thus both objective and subjective contingencies are important in the desistance process (see Giordano, Cernkovich, and Rudolph 2002; Maruna 2001; Shover 1996).

As we observed in our life-history narratives, the men who desisted from crime seem to have acquired a degree of maturity by taking on family and work responsibilities. They forged new commitments, made a fresh start, and found new direction and meaning in life. These commitments were not necessarily made consciously or deliberately, but rather were "by default"—the result of "side bets" (Becker 1960, 38). The men made a commitment to go straight without even realizing it. Before they knew it, they had invested so much in a marriage or a job that they did not want to risk losing their investment (Becker 1960; see also Toby 1957, Hirschi 1969). Involvement in these institutions—work and marriage—reorders short-term situational inducements to crime and, over time, redirects long-term commitments to conformity (Becker 1964; Briar and Piliavin 1965).

It seems that some, but by no means all, men who desisted changed their identity as well, and this in turn affected their outlook and sense of maturity and responsibility (see Maruna 2001). From our life-history narratives, for example, we sense that certain roles and certain behavior are seen as "age inappropriate" (Shover 1996). One former delinquent linked the role of "party boy" to being young and single. In response to the question, "What about your marriage? Has that changed you?" Richard replied with a hearty laugh, "Oh yeah. I mean that's when you really had to settle down." He continued, "Especially when [my oldest son] came." Remaining a delinquent or a party boy or a hell-raiser would signify a state of "arrested development" and be incompatible with adult status (see Gove 1985, 129). This notion is consistent with Hill (1971), who discusses changes in identity over the life cycle as one moves from "a hell-raiser to a family man."

We are by no means claiming an absence of regret in the process of desistance. In his study of the transformation from being a hell-raiser, Hill presented evidence of the ambivalence that men feel regarding their new role and identity as "family men" (1971). This is not surprising because, as Smelser (1998, 8) pointed out, bonded relations are fused with ambivalence—dependence, even when welcomed, "entails a certain entrapment." For example, William told us that if he were not married he would be "wandering" around. He said ruefully, "There's many times I wanted to go back to Alaska to see what it was like now. But we can't do that. We're hoping to go to Disney next March." We heard many such bittersweet remembrances of deviant lives left behind—of exciting moments given up.[6]

The lessons we learned about desistance from our narratives are consistent with the research literature on drug and alcohol relapse. In a study of one hundred hospital-treated heroin addicts and one hundred hospital-treated alcohol-dependent individuals, Vaillant (1988) found that external interventions that restructure a drug addict's or alcoholic's life in the community were often associated with sustained abstinence. The main factors are: (1) compulsory supervision; (2) finding a substitute dependence to compete with drug or alcohol consumption; (3) obtaining new social supports; and (4) membership in an inspirational group and discovery of a sustained source of hope and inspiration (see also Vaillant and Milofsky 1982). Culling the recent literature on treatment, especially from Canada, produces some hopeful signs that offenders can be rehabilitated when proximate causes of crime are targeted. Programs that address dynamic attributes of offenders and their circumstances (for example, antisocial attitudes, involvement with delinquent peers, and employment status) that can change during and after the treatment process appear to be more successful than programs that focus on static factors or background characteristics (Andrews and Bonta 1994; Bonta 1996; Gendreau, Cullen, and Bonta 1994).

What is also striking from our life histories is that there appear to be no major differences in the process of desistance for nonviolent and violent juvenile offenders. Despite contrary expectations put forward by many criminological theories, this finding is consistent with empirical research showing that violent offenders have the same background characteristics as frequent but nonviolent offenders (Farrington 1991; Capaldi and Patterson 1996; Piquero 2000). In fact, Farrington concluded that "the causes of aggression and violence must be essentially the same as the causes of persistent and extreme antisocial, delinquent, and criminal behavior" (1991, 25). Our narratives reveal that the processes of desistance across a wide variety of crime types are very similar.

Overall, then, while there are multiple pathways to desistance, there do appear to be some important general processes or mechanisms of desistance at work. We have found four major self-described turning points implicated in the desistance process: marriage/spouses, the military, reform school, and neighborhood change. Each of these creates new situations that (1) knife off the past from the present; (2) provide not only supervision and monitoring but opportunities for social support and growth; (3) bring change and structure to routine activities; and (4) provide an opportunity for identity transformation. Although some offenders may seek to "make good" (Maruna 2001) or engage in "up-front work" to better their lives (Giordano, Cernkovich, and Rudolph 2002), we believe that most offenders desist in response to structurally induced turning points that serve as the catalyst for sustaining long-term behavioral change. As Becker noted a long time ago,

> A structural explanation of personal change has implications for attempts to deliberately mold human behavior. In particular, it suggests that we need not try to develop deep and lasting interests, be they values or personality traits, in order to produce the behavior we want. It is enough to create situations which will coerce people into behaving as we want them to and then to create the conditions under which other rewards will become linked to continuing this behavior. (1964, 52–53; see also Becker 1960)

# CHAPTER SEVEN

# Why Some Offenders Persist

We now turn to the challenge of understanding the lives of men we call persistent offenders. Approaching the problem from an angle not common in criminal career research, we use narrative data to peer into the lives of men who offend repeatedly throughout their lives, indeed well into middle age. As discussed in Chapter 4, we define persistence in offending as being arrested at multiple phases of the life course. This strategy seems consistent with the idea of persistent offending as enduring, repetitious, and tenacious. As we saw in Chapter 5, however, the rate of offending declines with age even for high-rate and presumably chronic offenders, making the notion of the life-course persister problematic. As with the desister group in the last chapter, we use these labels as a means of organizing our analytic strategy and presenting our narratives, leaving as an empirical question the ultimate validity of such classification schemes.

We set out to examine two types of persistent offenders. The first consisted of men who were arrested as juveniles (aged 7 to 17), young adults (aged 17 to 32), and older adults (aged 32 to 70) for crimes of violence. The second consisted of men who were arrested as juveniles, young adults, and older adults, including arrests for violence in at least two of the three phases of the life course. Altogether, we interviewed 14 men who were not only persistent offenders but serious, violent offenders as well.

Using available criminal history data up to age 70, we find that these men were arrested on average forty times (more than twenty-three times up to age 32). Moreover, they spent an inordinate amount of time in prisons and jails; on average, 1.8 years up to age 17 and 6.4 years from age 17 to 32. Over the full life course, these men were incarcerated on average 75 days each year. Criminal history data for the 14 persistent offenders, along with information on other important social characteristics, are displayed in Tables 7.1 and 7.2. It is notable that whereas these persistent offenders had similar scores for our measure of unofficial delinquency, IQ, and adolescent competence compared with desisters (see Table 6.2), the persisters spent considerably less time married, working, and in the military over the course of their lives.[1]

We begin with a detailed life history of "Boston Billy" from the persistent offender group. We selected this case for intensive analysis because it was one of the most absorbing life histories we collected, and Billy was one of the most interesting and poignant of the men we encountered. Even more important, Boston Billy illustrates many of the emerging themes we develop regarding persistent offending over the full life course. After presenting his life story, we draw on additional narratives from other interviews to explore several themes that emerge from the data. As will be seen below, life-history narratives are especially useful in uncovering issues overlooked in more traditional quantitative approaches in criminology, including our own previous work (see Sampson and Laub 1993).

### The Life of Boston Billy

> My entire record is stealing cars and armed robbery . . . it was so easy and money was so scarce. It was nice to have a couple hundred dollars. To me that was a lot of money. And I had it in my pocket. I couldn't find a good job. And I couldn't find a job where I could learn a trade. And I didn't have no education. So I did the only thing I could.

From early in our follow-up study, Boston Billy stood out as a challenging and intriguing case. Although Billy was worthy of the title "career criminal," he was not a product of a disorganized and chaotic family of immigrants. His parents were native born, and on many counts they would be considered good parents. They provided adequate supervision and "firm, but kindly" discipline. For instance, if

**Table 7.1** Persistent offenders: Criminal history data

| Name | Total report | Official offenses <17 | Official offenses 17–32 | Total official offenses[a] | Total official violent offenses[a] | Age first incarcerated | Time served <17 (in years) | Time served 17–32 (in years) | Time served[b] |
|---|---|---|---|---|---|---|---|---|---|
| Tony | 13 | 8 | 18 | 34 | 6 | 13 | 2.0 | 12.6 | 107.21 |
| Jimmy | 6 | 9 | 20 | 50 | 4 | 13 | 2.8 | 12.6 | 93.66 |
| Harry | 12 | 4 | 5 | 15 | 4 | 12 | 1.8 | 2.0 | 13.74 |
| Buddy | 19 | 4 | 17 | 37 | 5 | 14 | 1.6 | 10.5 | 162.26 |
| Gino | 20 | 5 | 15 | 33 | 2 | 14 | 0.9 | 0.8 | 5.58 |
| Wally | 13 | 4 | 9 | 25 | 3 | 16 | 0.8 | 0.0 | 0.00 |
| Billy | 14 | 10 | 8 | 26 | 7 | 15 | 1.1 | 14.0 | 213.45 |
| Gus | 18 | 7 | 16 | 27 | 4 | 10 | 3.5 | 2.6 | 24.62 |
| Charlie | 17 | 23 | 8 | 37 | 3 | 12 | 3.8 | 11.1 | 129.72 |
| Arthur | 12 | 12 | 20 | 57 | 6 | 12 | 1.8 | 5.2 | 39.24 |
| Frankie | 17 | 5 | 42 | 106 | 4 | 15 | 1.0 | 8.1 | 55.77 |
| Maurice | 23 | 8 | 20 | 54 | 3 | 15 | 1.3 | 9.8 | 106.98 |
| Don | 16 | 5 | 14 | 25 | 3 | 16 | 0.8 | 0.0 | 0.00 |
| Nicky | 13 | 8 | 2 | 27 | 6 | 14 | 1.8 | 0.3 | 100.66 |
| Mean | 15.2 | 8.0 | 15.3 | 39.5 | 4.3 | 13.6 | 1.8 | 6.4 | 75.2 |

a. Ages 7 to 70.
b. Ages 17 to 70, days incarcerated over lifetime per year.

**Table 7.2** Persistent offenders: Social history data

| Name | Ethnicity | Age at interview | IQ | Adolescent competence | Proportion of time married[a] | Proportion of time divorced/ separated[a] | Proportion of time with unstable employment[b] | Proportion of time in military[b] | Military outcome |
|---|---|---|---|---|---|---|---|---|---|
| Tony | Italian | 70 | 102 | 1 | 0.58 | 0.00 | 1.00 | 0.00 | N.A. |
| Jimmy | Irish | 71 | 104 | 2 | 0.66 | 0.00 | 0.93 | 0.00 | N.A. |
| Harry | Jewish | 69 | 69 | 1 | 0.82 | 0.04 | 0.27 | 0.00 | N.A. |
| Buddy | Eng. Can. | 69 | 105 | 1 | 0.00 | 0.00 | 0.80 | 0.27 | Dishonorable |
| Gino | Italian | 70 | 97 | 0 | 0.35 | 0.24 | 0.53 | 0.00 | N.A. |
| Wally | German | 69 | 94 | 1 | 0.82 | 0.08 | 0.27 | 0.47 | Honorable |
| Billy | German | 68 | 87 | N.A. | 0.00 | 0.00 | 1.00 | 0.00 | N.A. |
| Gus | Greek | 63 | 82 | 0 | 0.92 | 0.08 | 0.93 | 0.07 | Dishonorable |
| Charlie | Swedish | 64 | 111 | 2 | 0.69 | 0.25 | 1.00 | 0.00 | Dishonorable |
| Arthur | Italian | 65 | 72 | 1 | 0.12 | 0.82 | 1.00 | 0.00 | N.A. |
| Frankie | Irish | 69 | 84 | 0 | 0.00 | 0.00 | 0.93 | 0.00 | N.A. |
| Maurice | Portuguese | 68 | 105 | 3 | 0.64 | 0.13 | 1.00 | 0.07 | Dishonorable |
| Don | Irish | 68 | 90 | 1 | 0.72 | 0.00 | 0.67 | 0.13 | Honorable |
| Nicky | Italian | 68 | 87 | 1 | 0.87 | 0.11 | 0.53 | 0.20 | Honorable |
| Mean | | 67.9 | 92.1 | 1.1 | 0.51 | 0.13 | 0.78 | 0.09 | |

*Note:* On adolescent competence, see note 1 in chapter 6.
a. Ages 17 to 70.
b. Ages 17 to 32.

Billy returned home past his 9:00 P.M. curfew, his father would keep him in the next night and sometimes the night after.

Billy's father was a plumber and a "good worker." He was employed by the same company for several years. He did not have an arrest record, was not a "drinking man," and was described as "intelligent" and having an "even disposition." Although Billy's mother had been committed twice to the Lancaster School for Girls as a "stubborn child" and for being "idle and disorderly," she had no record of criminal activity or drinking as an adult. Moreover, she was described in one social worker's report as a "mother who has definite interest in her children" and as a mother who keeps a "neat home." Billy's mother worked as a candy dipper three days a week. According to social worker reports, his mother prepared lunch for her children before leaving for work, and one of Billy's sisters gave the children lunch and "kept house" until their mother came home.

Billy's family was also distinguished by its residential stability. Unlike families of the most active delinquents (Sampson and Laub 1993), Billy's family moved only once from the time he was born, and even that move was five and a half blocks down on the same street in Boston to a three-family house that they bought. Billy was the fourth child in a family of six, with two brothers and three sisters. He was the only person in his family to get into serious trouble.

Unlike many of his delinquent counterparts at the time, Billy enjoyed reasonably good living conditions. He had his own bed in his own room and his house also had a bathroom, tub, flush toilet, hot water, central heat, and electricity. The home was "adequately furnished" and well-kept and neat. Perhaps even more important, the family's household routine was depicted as "orderly"—there were regular meal times and sleeping times. Billy's parents encouraged their children to have their friends in the house as a way of avoiding trouble on the streets. They set up a radio and had board games in a "club" in the cellar for Billy's friends. Unlike many families in the neighborhood, the family was also in relatively good shape economically. They owned their home, had a car, and were "careful with their money."

There were early warning signs, however, that the cohesive family life was not sufficient. One of Billy's early obstacles in life was school, in which he had no interest. Billy did not like schoolwork and had to be "prodded" constantly. Despite this lack of interest, his teachers reported that he was not a "behavior problem." He scored 87 on the general Wechsler-Bellevue IQ test (90 verbal and 87 performance). It is perhaps not surprising, given his lack of interest in schoolwork, that Billy repeated first and sixth grade. Yet unlike most persistent offenders, he began skipping school at a relatively late age—12. Billy finished his formal schooling with only an eighth-grade education. His dislike for school was long lasting and consistent. At his age 25 interview with the Gluecks' investigator, Billy stated, "I hated school." Nevertheless, he became an effective jailhouse lawyer during his long career in crime.

As a kid, Billy did not belong to any clubs and expressed a dislike for "supervised recreation." He preferred playing in the streets. He did not belong to a gang, but he did associate with a large number of peers, all boys, some the same age as he and some older. Companions played an important role in Billy's life history.

### Juvenile Delinquency

According to his criminal record, Billy's juvenile delinquency began relatively late for someone who offends persistently over the life course—age 15. As a teenager, Billy stole cars. He was a confirmed "hot boxer" (car thief). Along with other delinquent companions, Billy stole cars for immediate use, not profit. When interviewed at age 15, he estimated that he had stolen about 50 cars.[2] He also reported being drunk on several occasions.

In contrast to his official record regarding the onset of delinquency, Billy's self-report indicated that he began his criminal career at age 6, when he started stealing from the 5 & 10. Sounding like Stanley from *The Jack-Roller* (Shaw 1930), Billy said that older friends took him to Codman Square (a shopping district in Dorchester) on Saturdays and initiated him into the art of snatching items (such as candy, jackknives, toys, and comic books) from the 5 & 10 store counter. This earlier age of onset is consistent with much research on criminal careers and points out the need for multiple sources of data (Farrington, Loeber, et al. 1990; Patterson, Crosby, and Vuchinich 1992). Billy also reported running away, gambling, late hours, drinking, truancy, hopping trucks, and sneaking admission into shows. His total unofficial delinquency score was 14, about average for the delinquent sample from the Gluecks' study.

Billy's delinquent companions also taught him how to "fish" cars (steal items from cars) and steal cars. In his file, the Gluecks' investigator wrote,

> As a little boy, probably not old enough to be held legally responsible for criminal acts, he used to toddle along with older delinquent boys who would let him go with them to "fish" cars. This merged into going to ride with them in "hot boxes" so that he became trained by imitation of experts in all the techniques of fishing and stealing cars, or rather, stealing especially those cars that appeared to contain "good fishing." To follow, look on, help, become expert and finally to be one of the most sought for and most welcome partners in these automotive delinquent projects was and probably still is a great emotional satisfaction to the boy. In this way he found what in reality for him is the joy of life. Long before his commitment to Shirley [Industrial School for Boys], he had arrived at the status of what we may call a consulting engineer in all the knotty problems of getting into, starting, and driving locked cars.

This is suggestive evidence for the significance of peer influences in the onset of crime in Billy's life (see Warr 2002).

With respect to personality, Billy was described in his psychiatric report at age 15 as "stubborn, extraverted in action and feeling, and having poor insight." The psychiatrist also noted that Billy was "suggestible" and that he suffered from "social insecurity." Billy's mother reported in the home investigation that he was "always stubborn and very nervous." His Rorschach assessment revealed "marked hostile and aggressive trends."

Billy and his parents attributed his involvement in delinquency to his association with delinquent companions. In fact, "hot-boxing" (stealing cars) was the preferred type of delinquency in the neighborhood. Several sources reported that Billy insisted in going out with his delinquent friends. Billy's official criminal record consisted of ten arrests as a juvenile (before age 17 in Massachusetts). He was committed to the Industrial School for Boys at Shirley on three different occasions, serving a total of 392 days.

When Billy was sent to the Shirley School for the first time (at age 15), he said, "it was the greatest." From Billy's vantage point, the reform school at Shirley had everything, even a swimming pool. For Billy, it was "exciting . . . like going to a farm." Significantly, he did not see his incarceration as punishment at all—"it was just going away for a while and then you came home." When you returned home, "of course, you made it sound like it was kind of tough but you made it. But it wasn't." Despite all of the fun, Billy did reveal that for the first month he was there he "cried his head off" because he had never been away from home before. He wrote to his parents every week, and they maintained contact by visiting him frequently. Nevertheless, when he was released he met the "old gang again and was back into trouble."

## Crime in Young Adulthood

Billy logged eight arrests between ages 17 and 25. During a two-month crime spree when he was 18, Billy and a co-offender committed at least twenty armed robberies. The pair spent their illegal gains on alcohol, women, and gambling. During this period, Billy also committed auto theft, larceny, and burglary. Between the ages of 17 and 25, Billy spent 7¼ years in prison (first at the Massachusetts Reformatory, then at the state prison at Charlestown).

At his age 25 interview, conducted in prison, Billy said that when he found out he could not get a job, he decided to get "big money" fast by robbing people. At the time of the interview, he was classified as one of the "eight most dangerous inmates" at state prison, although this designation may mean that he was "dangerous to the Department of Corrections" because Billy was outspoken and critical of the correctional system. At his age 25 interview, Billy also related that he feared his life would be "nothing but a continuous prison term." He had lost hope for any kind of "civilian job." Billy experienced no arrests between ages 25 and 32, perhaps only because of his prison confinement throughout virtually the whole period.

When asked for the reasons he was delinquent, at age 25 Billy responded, "I have no one but myself to blame for my troubles. You need help to go straight—I did not get any—hence I went back with my old companions, and drifted into crime." Perhaps surprisingly, Billy initially maintained close family ties during his confinement, and his family frequently visited him in prison. His father was described as "loyal and interested." Billy had planned on working with him as a plumber's helper when he was released from prison. Later, however, during the 1960s, Billy "lost" his family when he was sent to state prison. Although his father still visited him regularly, Billy said later that his father hated him for what he had done. His mother also visited him when she could, but eventually she went into a nursing home. The rest of Billy's family "disowned him." When Billy was released from prison in the 1970s, he lived with his two sisters, but eventually they asked him to find his own place. When he left, he never saw his family again until recently, at the age of 68. Much of Billy's mid-life experiences outside of prison consisted of floating from place to place looking for a spot to stay.

### Crime in Mid-Life and Beyond, Ages 32 to 70

Billy was arrested eight times after age 32 for a variety of crimes, including armed robbery (twelve counts), larceny, possession of a deadly weapon, auto theft, and assault and battery with a deadly weapon. Not surprisingly in light of this record, Billy spent considerable time in prison after age 32—we estimate a total of seventeen years. For instance, at age 32 his parole was revoked when he was implicated in twelve armed robberies. In 1960 he was sentenced to state prison to serve a term of five to eight years for these robberies. Then, about two years after his release on parole in 1965, he was arrested again for armed robbery (seven counts) of several package and convenience stores in the greater Boston area and sentenced again to prison for a term of seven to ten years. He served six years and was released in 1973, as we shall see. Billy was then arrested in 1981 for receiving stolen property (a motor vehicle). He was given a suspended sentence and placed on probation with an order to pay over $5,000 in restitution. At age 58, he was arrested again for receiving stolen goods and resisting arrest. He served one year in the house of correction in New Hampshire for this crime; this was his first arrest and commitment outside of Massachusetts. Still not finished, Billy was arrested at age 59 for armed bank robbery, conspiracy to commit bank robbery, and bank robbery with force and violence. He was sentenced to ten years in the federal correctional system for this offense.

Yet according to prison reports, at the age of 46, Billy was described as "courteous, polite, and cooperative." When he was 58 years old, Billy received his high school equivalency diploma in the house of correction. Earlier in his life, despite an eighth-grade education, Billy became an effective jailhouse lawyer.[3] In fact, he won a case that led to his outright release in the early 1970s. Billy also challenged his convictions on the federal charges of bank robbery, but he was unsuccessful in these legal challenges.[4]

## Pathways to Desistance in Young Adulthood: The Road Not Taken

From our prior research (Sampson and Laub 1993; Laub and Sampson 1993) and the life histories presented in the previous chapter, we identified at least three pathways leading away from crime in the transition from adolescence to young adulthood—strong bonds to work, strong ties to a spouse, and a successful military experience. From our narratives, we also discovered that for some men who desisted from crime, incarceration in the Lyman School was a "turning point" that deflected them away from crime. Here we look at Billy's life experiences in each of these domains.

### Employment

Billy never really worked at an everyday job through most of his adult life. From his age 25 interview, we learned that the longest job he ever had was at age 16, when he worked as a plumber's helper for eight months. This fact was confirmed in our interview at age 68. Billy did, however, hold a variety of other jobs for a brief period of time. For example, he worked as a painter, parking attendant, pipe fitter, laundry attendant, and helper on an ice truck, and he did odd jobs around the house. At age 68, Billy recounted his work experiences: "I was more or less doing odds-and-ends jobs like helping people move and whatever I could find to make a few bucks. I never really had a good job." Billy often did chores in exchange for food and lodging. For instance, he would baby-sit for friends, or he would drive his friends and their children to work and school. Billy was in this kind of work and family situation for most of his adult life when he was not incarcerated.[5]

### Marriage

Billy was married once during the 1950s. He met his wife in a restaurant in Boston. He recalled that she was going out with some "bike-y" and was having a problem with him.

> She wanted to get away from him so she came with me and lived with me. We got married and then the bills started piling up and I just got in trouble again. I couldn't make it. So we started stealing and robbing and I got myself back in prison. And she divorced me. I was only married a very short time, probably about nine months. I tried to straighten out but I couldn't. I was in too deep.

## Military Service

Billy tried to volunteer for the service at the age of 23, but he was rejected because of his record. When we asked him about this incident during his interview, however, Billy said that he tried to enlist, but was not accepted because of his health. "The health I think is the thing that turned me down. I don't know why."

At a second interview, the military came up again. Billy was asked if he thought that the military could have turned him around. He answered,

> I tried to get into the military. Yes, I did. I tried. And the reason they wouldn't let me in was because I was stealing cars. My record really hurt me. Once you get arrested, you're going to pay for it the rest of your life. Even though you did your time. I feel that once you did your time that should be it. But then again, three strikes you're out.

## Reform School

As we have seen, Billy thought the reform school at Shirley was "the greatest." The only thing that Billy did not like was "that you had to go to bed early." Reform school seemed to have little positive or negative effect on his subsequent criminal behavior. What is evident is that for Billy reform school had no deterrent effect, as it did for some men we interviewed (see Chapter 6). Billy told us, "Actually it wasn't punishment at all. It was just going away for a while and then you came home."

## The Lack of Positive Turning Points

Billy seems to have had little opportunity or ability to engage successfully in the traditional pathways away from crime. He did not serve in the military, he did not have a steady job that he was willing to invest in (or an employer to invest in him), and he did not have any strong ties to a spouse. Moreover, the effect of being sent to reform school was apparently innocuous. Of course, a critical issue is whether these are the factors that influenced Billy's continued involvement in crime or whether they are the consequences of his rather obvious propensity for trouble. Without any structural turning points and subsequent social ties to deflect his criminal trajectory toward conformity, his remaining social networks consisted of like-minded delinquent peers.

Even the concept of a life-altering turning point was different for Billy. When asked if he had any turning points in his life, Billy responded,

> Well, the turning point—it may sound silly to you—but I got to learn how to drive when I was real young and I enjoyed it. And I remember going over to Somerville and I bought a car. I put a down payment on it. And at that time I was working with a guy that was doing plumbing work. And he was paying me so much money a week and I was putting it away because I had been living with my mother and father and didn't have to pay no rent. So I saved up a little bit of money and I saw this car that I liked very, very much and I bought it. I put the down payment down and I was paying the rest the following week. And I had thought at that time because I put the down payment that . . . my father would help me to pay for the rest of it, which was probably a lot then for him. But it seemed so little to me [the amount was about $300]. And he refused to help me. And they took the car back and I lost the down payment. That's when I said to myself, "Well, I'll get a car." And I went out and stole it. And I kept stealing them. When they would run out of gas, I would just leave them. I never wrecked one. I never had one longer than like a week. And then I would only drive it in the daytime. Because in the day time, you could see the police car a mile away; in the night time they could be right behind you and you wouldn't know it.

Billy was only 15 years old when this incident took place, and yet his trouble seemed to start well before. Perhaps for Billy this was the turning point that solidified his path to persistent offending. Or perhaps Billy's account merely reveals the potential for distortion inherent in retrospective self-reports of salient life events and their significance for understanding lives. This conundrum presents a major challenge for narrative analysis, one that we shall keep addressing. Our strategy is to probe deeper into the narratives and then reevaluate the emergent framework with further analysis of our quantitative data.

### What Sustains Crime in Adulthood?

What sustains crime in adulthood, and what accounts for persistent offending over the life course? It would be easy to conclude that Billy continued to commit crime as an adult because he lacked the human and social capital necessary to desist. Indeed, Billy lacked social bonds, and informal social control was not a factor in his adult life. Formal sanctions had little influence as well. But we are not willing to accept this explanation for Billy's persistent offending as the whole story.

There are many puzzles in Billy's life history. Probably most significant is that little in his early life record portended a life of adult crime and violence and more than thirty years in prison. Many of the delinquents in the Gluecks' study had more extensive and more violent juvenile records. To dig deeper into Billy's life, we draw on detailed information culled from our interviews. We first interviewed Billy for this study when he was 68 years old and on parole from federal prison. The interview took place in his home in a working-class neighborhood in Boston. Subsequently we interviewed Billy again at his home and on occasion met over lunch at a local restaurant.

Here we explore the role of personal agency, the immediate situation (or what Katz (1988) calls the foreground), and the changing social controls in the course of Billy's criminal career. More precisely, life-history narratives let us examine the motivations underlying crime, the planning of crime, the meaning of crime, and the sense of self that emerges—all from the perspective of offenders in their own words. Several important domains that emerged from Billy's narrative shed additional light on the natural history of persistent offending. We describe these domains below and conclude that a theoretical focus on informal social control needs to be augmented as well as more nuanced.

### Personal Agency and Persistent Offending

From Billy's perspective, "everybody" was stealing cars in his neighborhood when he was a youth. Everybody was breaking into houses too, which Billy claimed he did not want to do. Although Billy certainly exaggerated, the kind of criminal cultural milieu in disadvantaged neighborhoods in 1940s Boston seemed to lead to even bigger things for Billy. He recalled hearing about the money one could make robbing people and he tried it and it worked. Billy asserted, "It was so easy, it was pathetic. I just kept saying to myself, 'I'm going to get caught.' But I never did [sic]. It was easy."

When Billy robbed liquor stores and other commercial establishments, he typically worked with a partner. One or both of them would carry a gun. Most of the robberies occurred during the evenings, around dinner or closing time. Billy and his partner didn't put much thought into what store they would rob. Billy recalled,

I was desperate. I would steal a car. And I would drive around until I thought it was safe for me to go in, and rob the store. And hope that a person wouldn't put up a fight, which they never did. And I'm glad. Because I don't know what I would have done. I'm glad it never turned out that way. But when I went in—and I was desperate—it was possible I could have done anything. Because when I was desperate—I don't know if you know what it's like to be without—it's not easy. I got to the point where I had to have money and it was the only way I could get it. I couldn't get a job because I couldn't do any kind of work.

Yet Billy does not see himself as a violent person. When asked if he had any kind of violence in his history, Billy said, "None whatsoever. I've been shot by the police, but I never hurt anyone. I have never shot anybody. I have never struck anybody . . . in my life actually."[6] For Billy, it is as if violence is distinct from crime. He remarked, "If I hurt a person, I'm not just hurting that person, but I'm hurting his family . . . But I could never do that. I'm probably capable of doing it, but I just don't want to do it."

Billy used a gun to commit robberies just to make the theft of cash easier. He said that using the gun was just a "phony front" to get money. When asked if he was prepared to use his gun, Billy replied, "I don't know what I would have did. I can't say because it never happened. But when I would go in there I would go in there because I needed that money. And that's what I would go in there to get—that money."

Billy went on to say that he selected liquor stores because they were easy to rob and "I figured they had more money than a delicatessen or whatever or any of them places." Billy avoided other kinds of more lucrative robbery (for example, banks, armored cars) and dealing drugs.[7] "I just didn't want to go into banks then. I didn't run with the drugs. I was offered a billion times to go into drugs and I said, 'No. I don't like drugs.' " Billy also shunned burglary. He explained, "Well, I just didn't want to go in anyone's house. Because I look back watching my mother and my father—what little they had. If somebody came in and took it, it probably would have killed them. And when I rob a liquor store, I figure, 'Well, they're insured.' " Billy also observed, "I knew that if I took $500 from the liquor store, those people in the liquor store would say I took $2000 and their insurance company would pay them back $2000. They would say I took $900 when I took $100. Because I would see it in the paper. And at the trial sometimes they would say, 'Well, he took $5000 out of my store.' And I only took probably $100 or $150. And there's nothing I could say to prove different."

Billy's rationalizations are familiar. Sykes and Matza (1957) some time ago discussed techniques of neutralization that facilitate the commission of crime. Billy seems to be evoking the idea of "denial of injury"—for example, no one was really hurt here. Or that the money was insured. Equally important is the allusion to a cynical worldview that implies everyone is corrupt. For Billy, even so-called straights commit crime in their own way. Ultimately, however, Billy openly admitted his crimes and claimed that he "alone was responsible—I knew it was wrong."

### The Initial Attraction and Excitement of Crime

Billy was attracted to crime early in life, despite relatively strong informal social control by his family. Of course, his predilection may have been due in part to the influence of delinquent peers. There is evidence that delinquent peers play a major role in the onset of delinquency (see, for example, Warr 2002). Moreover, Billy lacked strong ties to school, an important indicator of delinquency (see Sampson and Laub 1993). Billy did feel rejected as a kid, and he believed that he was treated unfairly (see, for example, Patterson 1982; Coie and Dodge 1998). Whatever the underlying reason, however, Billy was clearly drawn to crime at a young age, and he persisted in criminal activity until he was in his late fifties. As a kid he stole cars and as an adult he was an armed robber. Billy told us proudly, "My entire record is stealing cars and armed robbery."[8] He was attracted to this kind of crime because it was "easy" and, as indicated above, his values steered him away from other forms of criminal activity.

We asked Billy what motivated these crime sprees. He stated emphatically that his main motive was to get money. He went on, "I just ran amuck. Why I did it—like I said, I needed money. But I got in so deep I couldn't get out, so I kept going. I flipped right out. I didn't care what happened to me. I just did everything." Billy would spend the money he obtained in the robberies on rent, food, cigarettes, booze, gambling, and women.

In addition, Billy believed that he would never get caught, and that if he did get caught once, he would learn from that mistake to avoid being caught in the future. The idea of deterrence as a means to prevent crime did not seem to affect Billy's decision making (see also Shover 1996; Wright and Decker 1994, 1997). What is clear from Billy's narrative is that crime was an attractive alternative to conformity. It was exciting.

At age 68, Billy was asked what he remembered the most from his adolescence. Being shot at by the police and getting away, he responded. He was 16 years old at the time and had run away from the reform school at Shirley. He and another inmate had stolen a car and were heading to New York City. Although the police had set up a roadblock to capture them, Billy and his co-offender managed to escape, albeit not without a gunshot wound. Billy also recalled the excitement of participating in a prison riot at the state prison at Charlestown. More than forty years later, he told both stories with great animation. As we discuss below, Billy's narrative suggests that social scientists should pay more attention to the attractive elements of crime (Katz 1988). Bordua (1961a) argued long ago that crime can be, and often is, fun.

### A Long-Standing Resentment of Authority

Willis (1977) points out that a central element of working-class male culture is opposition to authority and rejection of the conformist. Willis argues that "this opposition involves an apparent inversion of the usual values [for example, diligence, deference, respect] held up by authority." (1977, 12; see also Cohen 1955). Resisting authority is thus part of the attraction of crime (Katz 1988). In Fox Butterfield's *All God's Children* (1995), Butch and Willie, who as children would not obey their parents, bullied their neighbors, and defied their teachers at school, are illustrative examples of this defiance toward authority. Sherman (1993) extends the idea of defiance to explain the conditions under which criminal sanctions backfire and increase crime.

Consistent with these works, another theme that emerges in Billy's narrative is defiance and resentment of authority. Billy did not want to do anything that was "forced" on him. From early on, he resented having to go to school. Billy was also not swayed by his parents' attempts to control him. Once when he was upset with his parents, he stole his father's car, left it on the steps of the courthouse, and told his father he did it. Billy said, "I knew it was wrong. At the time I just didn't care about nothing."

Even the Gluecks' investigator noted that Billy was not respectful of authority, especially the police, because he thought they were "dumb." Following on this point, Billy's parole officer in 1945 found him "thoroughly uncooperative, antisocial, and a vicious criminal who has absolutely no respect whatever for any kind of decency or law enforcing agency."

### Alcohol Abuse and Losing Control

When Billy described his crime sprees in more detail, his life seemed out of control.

> What got me off track was when I came out I stayed with my sisters for a while and it was hard. Then I just took off. I never came back. I quit my job and I went from one friend to another friend. I didn't want to impose on anyone. "Damn it," I said to myself, "I got to get another job." So I got another job and I was painting and I was getting sick from the paint. So I quit that. I tried again. In the meantime I had no meals and every time I went on the train it was costing me money. It wasn't much but I didn't have much. So from there I said, "Well, I don't know what to do?"—so I'd go out and steal a car, sell the car. Doing things like that. Buy food here from the money I got for the car. Actually that's all I really was into was cars at that time. And even when I came out, it was my way of moving around. I didn't like trains. I didn't like buses. And I couldn't afford a car, so I stole them. I think if I had a good car and a halfway decent job like I got now I could have made it. But things got tighter and tighter and then I got arrested in New Hampshire.

Billy served one year in New Hampshire on a charge of receiving stolen goods, in this case, a car. Incidentally, Billy's reputation from Massachusetts affected his stay in the New Hampshire jail. He reported, "I was a trustee and I got a job—they created it for me—just to keep me happy." This was because, they said, "you was in a riot at Charlestown. We don't want no riots here. And we're going to try to make you happy while you're here." Billy was serving a one-year sentence, and one week before his release, the FBI arrested him for a bank robbery in Maine.

When he was not in jail during this period, Billy was drinking quite heavily. He told us,

> I was drinking everything. I couldn't sit here without drinking and talking to you. I'd have to drink. I was drinking vodka, Southern Comfort, and Jack Daniels. Drinking all them three, yeah, heavy. I passed out drinking them. Pretty close to every day. Now I don't drink because of

my heart. And it was one of two evils I got rid of: cigarettes or the booze. I got rid of the booze, and I continued with the cigarettes. And I'm trying to stop that but it's not that easy. I've been smoking all my life, and I had been drinking very heavily. And the reason I'm able to stay off that is you can't buy beer or liquor in prison. But you can buy cigarettes.

Like many persistent offenders, Billy had a serious problem with alcohol that contributed to his sense of losing control over his life (Katz 1988; Shover 1996). In Shover's research on criminal careers, there is evidence that alcohol abuse promotes a mood of desperation. Vaillant (1983) notes that over time progressive alcoholism involves a loss of control.

### The Prison Experience

One of the most striking aspects of Billy's life history is the amount of time he spent in prisons and jails. By our estimate, Billy had spent about half his life in these institutions (roughly thirty-two years), experiencing what Sykes (1958) called the "pains of imprisonment." Most recently, Billy did a stint in a federal prison for bank robbery. During the 1980s, he spent time in the house of correction in New Hampshire. During the 1960s and 1970s, he spent time in state prison in Massachusetts. In the 1950s, Billy was in state prison and served time in forestry camps. At age 68, Billy stated that prisons were "terrible." He went on to say, "I've seen everything in prison. Everything!"

One salient event in Billy's time in prison was a riot at the Charlestown State Prison in the early 1950s. The riot was precipitated by concerns about food. Billy explained,

I don't know if you've heard anything or know anything about Charlestown [the state prison at the time], but they never had a kitchen where you could eat, a dining room where you could eat. What they did was open the door in the morning and you came down and you went to the window and you had guys with hash barrels there. And they had stew in this barrel, potatoes in this barrel. And they gave you one scoop each. You could see bugs and everything else in it. The place was infested with cockroaches. There was no way you could look you'd see nothing but cockroaches. Thousands of them. And you took your food back to your cell. You sat down and you ate. You had no toilet in your room and no sink. Every morning on the way to work you had to take your bucket, carry it down and empty it, rinse it and put some white stuff in there to take the smell away. And water was brought to you like maybe twice a night. An inmate that was trusted was out and he'd walk around with a pitcher and you'd put your little tin cup out and he'd fill it up. That was your water. And if you wanted to shave, you had a little metal dish and in the morning they'd bring warm water and let you shave. Now you've got to time yourself. You had to eat and shave and get out the door on time or you're in trouble. When you came out, you stepped out your door, put your hand on the shoulder of the guy in front of you and carried your bucket in this hand. And you couldn't take your hand off that guy's shoulder until you reached the bucket; that's where you emptied it, rinsed it and put stuff in it. Then they have a crew of guys that brought them back. Because the number of your cell was on the bucket. They used to bring the buckets back—like the west wing, south wing, north wing, east wing. And it was tough. It was tough.

Regarding the riot, Billy provided the following account: "There was 52 of us; I was one of them. I destroyed the dentist's room. We took over the whole prison." Billy was especially angry with the dentist from a previous encounter.

I went into the dentist one time and I asked him to pull a tooth; it hurt. And he says, "I'll pull it for you." And he got me in the chair and stuck the needle in. And he started pulling and I said, "It's hurting." I was trying to tell him it's hurting. I was trying to push his hand away but he forced his hand back in and he yanked it out. I mean he did an awful job when he pulled it. I was mad at him. Then when the riot come off, I got into it. And the first thing I did was go up there and destroy the whole dentist's office—destroyed the whole thing. And I told him afterwards, "That's why I did it."

Like many criminal acts, this one had a context and a history. Billy's punishment for participating in the riot was confinement in "the hole" on bread and water for 10 days. In addition, he lost all of his good time.

The question remains: why wasn't prison a turning point for Billy? When asked that question, he admitted that it was hard to say: "Like I said, prisons are horrible places. I have seen more people get killed in prison than on the street. I think prisons toughen you up to a point that you don't care. Just like today, the average kid will shoot another kid in the head and don't care about the consequences." Billy has strong feelings on the inability of prison to reduce crime. He explained,

I went in for stealing cars. I wouldn't dream of robbing anybody or breaking into a house. When I was in there I used to see these guys there with money and they could go to the commissary and whatever. And they were all in for armed robberies and things like that. And they used to brag about it. And I used to listen. They were telling me how easy it was. And it was that easy. And it still is that easy. But the consequences, I never thought of them. I never gave it a thought. And then when I did it was too late, you know.

Billy continued, "A prison will either break ya or make ya. And if it breaks ya, you don't want to do time. And if it makes ya, you don't care about nobody but yourself. And if someone nabs you with a knife, you're going to go back at them. But if they break ya, you ain't going back."

Billy's long experiences of confinement suggest a pattern of "institutional dependency" (Straus 1974). Straus describes this as a characteristic of people who have lived long periods of time in institutions where their basic needs are provided, their expression of initiative is prohibited, and they are cut off from normal socializing experiences of family and work so that they are unable to cope satisfactorily with independent living in the larger society (1974, 334). Along similar lines, Glaser (1969, 325) pointed out that "a lack of long-range focus on either criminal or conventional life after prison seems to distinguish the most highly institutionalized individuals who may prove relatively inept at both criminal and noncriminal pursuits after release."

## The Long-Term Consequences of Crime

Billy currently rents a one-bedroom apartment in a working-class neighborhood in Boston for $450 a month. When we first met him, he told us that this was the first time in his life he had a place of his own. "It's the first apartment I've ever had!" he gushed with the excitement of a 18-year-old moving out on his own for the first time. Previously, Billy had lived in rooming houses, with friends, or in prisons.

Billy works as a bus driver and has held his job for more than three years. He was able to get his driver's license with the help of his parole officer. Billy had no work skills, but he could drive. All he needed was a license. Despite a steady job, there is still uncertainty and an edge to Billy's future. He explained:

I still feel kind of uncomfortable, even though I've been out like three years now. It's actually the first time I ever held a job this long. I haven't been in trouble. No police officers have ever came over and asked me anything or anything like that. And it makes me feel good because I know I'm in here and they can't say I'm doing something out there. I work every day, except Saturdays and Sundays now. I stopped working on Saturdays and Sundays because I don't want these people [Social Security] to think I'm trying to buy a Cadillac or a home.

Although working and trying to avoid trouble that would lead to a return to prison, Billy still hopes to get a big score from the lottery. His lucky number is 8104, which was his mother's phone number before she died. When asked why he plays the lottery with his small discretionary income, he reasoned,

I keep thinking it's going to keep coming up. And it has. That's how I am. I get desperate and I'm trying to say, "I don't want to go out and do nothing wrong. So I'm going to put in this number." I put in 5 Quick Picks and I always have my 8104 there. When I get a little extra money I'll pour it all into a couple of those.

Perhaps most striking is the routine in Billy's life now, especially in contrast to the carefree days of his youth and nearly all of his adulthood when he was involved in crime. Billy works all week long driving a bus, two shifts a day. He leaves his house at 5 o'clock in the morning and gets home about 10 or 10:30 A.M. He leaves again for work at 1:30 and gets home about 7:30 P.M. Saturday mornings he usually stays in and cleans his house. Then he does his food shopping. On Sundays, he goes over to his sisters' or his brother's house and helps them out with chores.

There is still a precariousness to Billy's everyday life that we believe is tied to the consequences of a life of crime. We assess some of these consequences below.

### Family

During the interview, Billy talked about the importance of reconnecting with his family. "I just wanted to be—you know, back with the family. I had never seen my family for all them years. Never. Never got a visit all the time I was in the federal prison. Never. I never got letters, never got Christmas cards, never got nothing."

Billy's mother died while he was in prison in Massachusetts. He recalled being taken to the funeral parlor in handcuffs while he paid his last respects. His father died shortly after Billy was released from prison in the early 1970s, and he had had little relationship with him during his long incarceration.

Now Billy's family situation is very different. Billy summarized:

> But now I see the difference. They wanted to help me but I just didn't give them a chance. And since then, since I've been out, I've been going every week over to my sister's. I did her back stairs for her, because she is older than I am. And I did her front steps. I painted everything for her. I cut down trees for her. And once in a while I go up to my sister's in New Hampshire. Plus I can only stop at her place when I'm working because I can't leave the state without permission.

According to information from Billy's age 25 interview, these two sisters were described as loyal to their brother.

## Health

Billy had two heart attacks while in federal prison. "I thought it worked out fine until six months later I almost dropped dead. I was working . . . The next thing I knew I was on a plane, being shipped to Missouri. They did four bypasses. And they opened my leg up, took the vein out of the leg. The scar goes all the way up. And my leg hasn't been right since then." Billy developed diabetes in prison too. We asked him if he worried about his health and he said, "No, because sometimes I don't care." He smokes a pack of cigarettes a day, but he is trying to quit. "I know I shouldn't [smoke] but I do. I'm very nervous and it's the only thing—it may not help me but I feel it helps me." Billy has tried to stop smoking. In fact, he says his doctors have told him a hundred times to quit, but he can't.

Billy still drinks alcohol, but "just a little bit." In a week, he probably drinks four small cans of beer. When Billy does drink, he drinks at home. The serious problem he had with alcohol when he was younger has abated. "That was one of my big problems. I drank too much." Billy experienced blackouts and tried to cut down, but he was not successful in reducing his alcohol intake until he was sent to prison. "Then I had no choice." After Billy was released from prison, he got sick when he drank. "I was away from the liquor for so long I tried it when I come out and I got so sick. I just couldn't take it."

## A Last Chance at Redemption?

Looking back on his life, Billy viewed it as "a waste, a real waste." He admits that when he was younger he didn't care about anything and he didn't think about the consequences of his actions. He continued, "I'm just going along thinking back all the years that I've wasted. I think if I had what I had now I don't believe I would have had to do what I did as I was coming up, you know. There's no reason for me to do anything wrong (now). But before I had no choice." As Billy told us of his regret, he wept considerably.

Although it may be too late, Billy said, "Today I have a lot of good friends again. Hopefully, I just hope that I can make it." About a year later, Billy said that he was the "happiest he had ever been." He went on to declare, "I licked it, I really have. It feels good." He joked, "I don't think I will need to get the old pistole again," making the shape of a gun with his fingers.

## Unpacking the Process of Persistent Offending

Data from additional persistent offenders' narratives will allow us to develop in more detail some of the themes that emerged in Boston Billy's life history. One intriguing idea concerns the lack of positive turning points in Billy's life. It was as if Billy was never structurally positioned to experience any concerted effort moving him toward desistance. Several other themes also appeared important in sustaining Billy's criminal activity over the long haul. The most striking of these included actions taken by Billy himself (human agency), serious alcohol abuse, and long-term institutional confinement in prison. These emergent themes fit within our expanded version of informal social control theory, aiding our effort to explain both continuity and discontinuity in offending over the life course.

### The Lifestyles of Persistent Offenders

The life-course persistent offenders we interviewed exhibited chaotic lives in multiple dimensions (residences, work, family). When asked about residential arrangements, Buddy told us, "Oh, my God, I bounced all around. Well, I've been in and out of jail all my life." He guessed that he had lived in about twenty places in the last thirty-five years (when he was not in jail or prison). By his own account, he worked about five years of his life, "except when I was in the can." Buddy never married, although he "lived with broads." Like Boston Billy, Buddy displayed remarkable continuity in antisocial behavior in several domains. He engaged in illegal and deviant activities in the community, the military, and prison. He was arrested thirty-seven times. He guesses that for every robbery for which he got caught, he probably committed two.

Nor were other persistent offenders we interviewed well positioned to take advantage of available opportunities to desist from crime. This situation was exacerbated by long periods of confinement in prison or several short-term incarcerations. It was not unusual for this group of offenders to have spent most of their young adulthood (ages 17 to 32) in prison or jail (see Table 7.1 for more details). Many of these men had unstable living arrangements. Several moved frequently, including being in and out of jail. Others were in "off-time" family situations for their cohort. For example, one man we interviewed was a new father at age 53 and another at age 57.

As for work, virtually none of the persistent offenders held a steady job or had a trade. Table 7.2 displays a measure of job instability for each of the 14 men. The average for the group is .78 (with 1.00 equaling unstable). Among those who did work, many worked seasonal jobs in construction, in roofing, or as a longshoreman. Others worked on and off as painters, day laborers, or bartenders.

The persistent offenders also had difficulty in the military. Most saw their participation (or attempts to participate) in the military as, upon reflection, a big mistake. Some of the men tried to enter the military through fraudulent means (most commonly using an assumed name or reporting their age to be older than it was).[9] Others who entered legally went AWOL or generally disregarded orders. One man was in the military for a little more than six months and spent most of this time in the guardhouse. Ultimately the vast majority of persistent offenders either could not enter the military because of their record or received a dishonorable (undesirable or bad conduct) discharge once they did serve (see Table 7.2).

Finally, most of the persistent offenders were divorced or had never married at the time we interviewed them. Some had a history of marital instability, marrying several times (see Table 7.2). For example, Gino was married five times. He is the persistent offender whom we quoted in Chapter 3 as saying "a change of pasture makes the cow fat." A few of the men were married for lengthy periods, yet they continued their pattern of persistent offending. Although marriage was not a turning point for these men, the idea of marriage to the right woman appealed to most of them.

### Turning Points in the Lives of Persistent Offenders

Unlike the desisters, who pointed to turning points in their lives such as marriage, work, the military, and reform school that helped move them away from crime, in general turning points are absent or of a different kind in the lives of persistent offenders. For some persistent offenders, typical turning points—marriage or serving in the military—are even seen as "backfiring" and making offenders worse off than when they started.

Some of the persistent offenders we interviewed claimed that they had no turning points. When Nicky was asked if he had any turning points in his life, he responded, "No, not really. I've had wasted years, you know." Others were more direct and emphatic. Harry said in response to the same question, "I don't think so, sir. I can't recall of any." He continued, "Well, whatever I did with my life, I can blame myself for it. Because I had nobody to influence me or steer me in a certain direction. Whatever I did was pretty much on my own."

Some of the men described turning points that accounted for their persistence in criminal offending. Looking back on his life, Buddy thought he kept getting in trouble because of his Lyman School experience, which made him "so mad" that he "just hated society for the rest of his life." At age 69, he told the following story:

> I was threw in with guys your size [6 feet, 2 inches, 200 lbs.] and I'm only a kid twelve years old. They'd punch you right in the face, you know. Beat the hell out of you; like if you pissed in bed, which I used to do when I was a kid. I was very nervous or something. They'd scrub you with scrubbing brushes and stuff like that. They'd scrub you until you was raw; your skin was all raw. So I got so aggravated because of this experience that I hated any kind of rules or regulations, you know, when I got out. And I'd do things just because I wanted to aggravate people. You know what I'm saying? I wasn't mean. I wouldn't try to hurt people. But I'd take their money away from them. Like walk into a store and stick them up or something like that. But the only reason I did that—I don't think it was because I was so greedy. Because I didn't look for a whole bunch of money. It was just that I wanted something and that was where I was going to get it.

We asked Buddy if he still felt a sense of injustice about the system and what it did to him. He replied, "I probably do because I look for it in everything." Buddy expounded this theme of perceived victimization as a turning point in his life as he described an earlier incident.

> I'd say I was only 9 or 10 years old when I started my running away. I wound up in Vermont for a while. The Children's Aid Society took me in and put me in a foster home in Vermont. But anyway I come home one day and all the little things that I had done—you know, I'd break a dish or something or I'd put a little duckling in a thing of water. I'm only a kid and I figured ducks know how to swim when they're small. And this thing just sunk and before I got him out he was drowned. But anyway all this stuff was listed. Mr. [name]—he was my social worker at the time—he used to come up and see me every once in a while. So he made an agreement with me. He says, "Listen, it's a long way to school. You'd like to have a bike, wouldn't you?" I'd say, "Oh, yeah." So he says, "If you save half, I'll put the other half with it and buy you a bike." So I had the jar in the chest, in the bureau—so I used to put all my nickels and dimes and pennies. So anyway we were out picking blueberries one day and I come home and I went to my jar. So I looked in the thing—so I was going to count how much money I had saved and there was a note in there that everything that I had done wrong—like any dish that I had broke, and she was going to take all of the money that I saved. [Buddy became very upset and teary at this point in retelling this story.] Anyway I took all of my money, you know, out of the jar and put it in my pocket, put on my Sunday shoes, and went through the woods, got on a highway and tried to hitchhike back to Boston.

Although this touching story may be true, there is no record of the incident as Buddy described it in the Gluecks' records. We did find a statement from a social worker indicating that Buddy left his foster home in Vermont because he "missed the excitement and the activity of the city" and the country was "too quiet for him." Nevertheless, Buddy recalled the episode as one of disappointment and unfairness.

One can speculate that Buddy's disappointments began with the unexpected death of his father. He had no record of persistent delinquency before his father's death when he was 10 years old. Buddy's life began to unravel from that point on and his cascade of trouble began. His mother remarried a man who was a drunk, and Buddy was left without any adequate supervision.

Although turning points can be either positive or negative, not all turning points are necessarily discrete events. Some are reactions to objective experiences and part of an ongoing process of change. Buddy related that "most of the turning points in my life were disappointments in people that I figured were friends, like Jimmy. He grew up with me and he wound up ratting on me. That's been the story of my life." Buddy went on to say, "See, I have a strict sense of loyalty and I never hurt a friend, you know what I'm saying. So, those things like that happened to me are . . . you could define them as crises because they're so disturbing. Like I hate this Jimmy. Those things—hell, they're really a disturbing thing to my life, you know."

Other persistent offenders referred to turning points as missed opportunities. Gus recounted the following:

> I don't know, I feel that I could have made something out of myself real big, if I got the education. I know that, I always said that. If I ever had a chance to finish schooling, maybe get to college, I could have made something of myself. Because I was always inquisitive about things. I was always reading something on the attorney's side, or doctor's side, I always got involved in reading things that I didn't even understand. I was interested in it, but I didn't understand. So I know it was the education part. And then I kind of realized, I says, well you ain't got the education, you are what you are. Don't look for nothing in life, just be satisfied with what you got.

Gus later returned to this theme: "Like with me, education. That was my turning point. If I didn't get married at a young age, finished my high school. Who knows if I would have got a scholarship to college. See? This is it."

For other men timing of the potential turning point seemed to have made a difference in retrospect. For example, Maurice said, "As for a change, I think what happened when I was 17 in that army made things worse for me. That was down. That was really the downer, what happened there. Because I think if I had been able to go into the service after the war had ended and I would have been serving as the peace thing instead of actually being in the war. I might have liked it. I might have learned to accept discipline, which was hard for me to accept. I might have been able to continue my education while I was in the service."

### Desisting Persisters?

We do not wish to imply that none of the persistent offenders ever desisted from crime. In fact, as we showed in Chapter 5, all offenders eventually desist. It is just that some do so later or at different rates than predicted by the conventional wisdom in criminology. Boston

Billy, for example, took until his sixties to finally give up on a life in crime. But another persister stopped committing crime at age 43. Without any solicitation or discussion of the turning point idea, this persistent offender said that his sister's death was his positive turning point. Charlie was in prison at the time and he was brought to the hospital to see his sister, who was dying. According to Charlie, his sister said, "I want you to promise me something." I said, "What?" She said, "You won't get in trouble again. And watch out for the kids [she had 8 children]." I said, "You've got my word." Charlie continued his account of this event: "And that was it, I haven't been in any trouble since . . . I think that was a turning point in my life; my sister dying." He returned to this incident later in his interview. "It was just, you know, what my sister asked me to do. And it was hard, believe me, because I had many opportunities to make a fast buck. I just didn't want to get in trouble again and I didn't want to break my word to her. And ever since then I've been working, made good money, good hourly wage. For the last twenty years I've made some big money working. Up until I got sick I was working fourteen, sixteen hours a day, seven days a week. It didn't bother me at all." Charlie said that his wife helped him keep out of trouble, as well. When Charlie would get nervous and anxious about bills, she encouraged him to hang in there and not revert to his old ways.

One might scoff at this description as a doubtful turning point and wonder if the interviewee is merely spinning a good tale, but a longitudinal record can shed important light on the life history. At his age 25 interview, there was considerable mention in the Gluecks' file regarding Charlie's attachment to his sister. For instance, it was noted that he and his sister corresponded weekly while he was in prison. In addition, at his age 32 interview, one of the Gluecks' investigators again remarked on Charlie's loyalty to his sister. Thus some objective data in the record confirm Charlie's strong regard for this older sibling.

Other men eventually changed because of processes similar to those that desisters experienced earlier in their lives. One wife of a persistent offender stated, "The marriage, he did a complete turnaround, you know. I wouldn't put up with that. He was a changed man." Similarly, Don described his "wife" (he was not officially married) as a "good woman." He elaborated, "I used to go out a lot—I like women myself. So I went out quite a bit, just girlfriends I had. They liked to have a few drinks. But as soon as I got around with her, she never drank much . . . So, then I wasn't consuming what I would have normally done if I was out with the guys or the other women. So after I said, 'Hey, this thing is pretty good.' She did very good to me." Another man pointed to the military as his turning point. He stated, "Oh, the military helped me a lot. Gave me an education. Helped me know right from wrong, discipline. Be neat and clean. Yeah. In other words, the Marine Corps was like a mother and father to me . . . Like a closely knit family."

The issues surrounding turning points and change are thus complex. In discussing why some kids may have changed for the better as a result of serving a sentence in the Lyman School, Buddy remarked,

> Well, I think the difference is kids that get out [of Lyman] and straighten out have weak natures—some of them—I don't mean all of them. I'm talking about some of them. The majority of them have weak natures. They conform because that's the thing to do. Because that's the easiest way. Others figure it out. Like I finally figured it out that this is a losing game. I've wasted my goddamn life by just hating; by hating the system, you know. So, I finally figured it out. Some of the kids have got that ability to get that understanding early. Maybe they've had in their early life they've had some experience with being . . . of good and bad, you know. Where my experience for me has been mostly bad. So I responded in that way, by not wanting to take part in any goddamn thing.

There are also contingencies even in the lives of hardened offenders. It seems as though all persistent offenders had chances to go straight, but things did not work out. For Buddy, his perceived window of opportunity for change came when he was nearly forty years old. By then he was ready for change even if it ultimately did not materialize. Looking back, he said,

> Well, I figured I done enough time; I learned a trade and I was working and I was making good money. Things were going reasonably well. Except this broad would get me upset every once in a while by not showing up . . . I guess I was in love with her. Like I say, she was worse than I was. She was an alcoholic. She'd go out and be gone for a week and be back—that's why I finally got rid of her. I eventually moved over to Southie [South Boston] and went back to my old ways.

Buddy claimed that if he had met somebody "decent" (his word) he could have changed at that point. In other words, Buddy thinks that the right marriage could be a turning point for some offenders. He explained, "Positively—stability, having somebody else to take care of and give to, you know. It didn't matter too much on the take; it was to give that's important. To have somebody to help become something." Buddy mourned that he had never met a woman who wasn't a drunk.

### Personal Agency and the Motivation for Persistent Offending

The motivation for those persistent offenders who were involved in robbery, burglary, and other forms of theft was clear and straightforward—"fast money." For example, when asked why he committed burglaries, Arthur responded, "Why does anybody do anything? Either because it's money, or fast money." Although some offenders preferred robbery to burglary or vice versa, there is little evidence of offender specialization.

For some men, however, the motivation for crime is more complicated. In response to the question "Why did you do it?" Jimmy replied, "Self-punishment—that is the only thing I can think of now. I didn't do it for the money. I don't care about money now or then. It was stupid. I did not steal for the money. To a certain extent, it was something to do. Once when I was drunk, I broke a window and got charged with B&E. It was stupid." Jimmy's account of his crime evokes Matza's idea of crime as infraction. "An infraction is among the few acts that immediately and demonstrably make things happen. Infraction properly and predictably invokes the criminal process. Thus, it may serve well as a symbol of restored potency" (Matza 1964, 190).

Of course, not all of the persistent offenders that we interviewed were armed robbers or burglars. Some were also involved in assaultive violence. (See Table 7.1 for the number of violent arrests for each of the 14 persistent offenders.) For example, Gus was described by the Gluecks' investigator as "evasive," "deceptive," and "vicious" at age 14. In his first arrest, Gus was accused of stealing from a blind woman at the age of 10. He was so determined to go out each night against his mother's wishes that when she resorted to hiding all of his clothes, he got around this problem by hiding an extra set of clothes himself to wear on his nightly excursions. Gus was arrested for assault and battery as a juvenile, as a young adult, and in mid-life. For offenders like Gus, individual choice (or to use Matza's term, "will") seems to be important in understanding patterns of offending (Matza 1964). From our narratives it is clear that "will"—the mental faculty by which one deliberately chooses or decides upon a course of action—is necessary to activate crime, whether crimes of violence or crimes of theft.

We found three types of violent offenders in our persistent offender group. First, there is the Boston Billy type—men who are committed to armed robbery involving guns, but for the most part engage in little physical violence toward others. The second category of violence is a variation of what Chaiken and Chaiken (1982) call "violent predators." These men are involved in domestic violence (especially on wives), assaults on nonfamily members, larcenies, burglaries, drug dealing, and all other forms of criminal behavior. Unlike the Chaikens' violent predators, none of these men committed robbery as well. The third category comprises offenders who are continually involved in drinking and assaultive behavior. In this instance, local neighborhood values, barroom culture, and assaultive behavior are joined.

Among the persistent offenders, some calculus went into the selection of targets. For example, Charlie said that he tried to take money from the people who had it and couldn't say anything about the theft to the police. So he robbed bookies. Other robbers, such as Buddy, told us that they avoided potential targets like cabbies because they were "out struggling" to make a living. Buddy made it clear to us that he would do anything, but that he "preferred the robbery, because the money was right there." He especially liked robbing commercial establishments, because they represented those with "more power" in society. Thus Buddy used crime as a means of transcending his circumstances and triumphing over people with more power (Katz 1988).

The robbers we interviewed carried guns or knives or both. They were fully prepared to use them, if the situation demanded it. Charlie quipped, "I carried a gun. And I knew in my own mind that if somebody tried to stop me I would shoot them, I knew that." Fortunately, most of the offenders we interviewed did not have to use their weapons except for display. Importantly, and apparently unlike present-day offenders, these men chose not to carry their weapons unless they were going to commit a robbery. Charlie stated emphatically, "I never carried a gun unless I was going out to commit a crime [a robbery]. I never carried it just to be carrying one." The ramifications of this secular change in gun carrying are enormous. The persistent offenders we interviewed did not carry a gun to a bar when they went out drinking or in other social settings. The weapon had a solely instrumental purpose and was carried only on those occasions.[10] Nicky elaborated on this point:

> No, in them days you never did [carry a gun to a bar]. Yeah. When I was in trouble, . . . I don't know if you heard of Winter Hill gang [a well-known gang connected to organized crime during the 1960s]. Well, I knew every one of them. They were the only ones that carried guns at them times. But the only people they used to shoot were their enemies. It was taboo to shoot—"suckers," they'd call ordinary people. You'd be a sucker—a clean, ordinary guy. It's different today though. I think it is the dope.

Nicky seems to imply that abuse of drugs other than alcohol and changes regarding norms of gun carrying led to a change in the incidence of violence.

Finally, like Boston Billy, the men who were persistently involved in crime never thought about getting caught. That is not to say that they liked doing time—they did not. The point is that fear of punishment by the criminal justice system did not seem to influence their decision making about crime. Ironically, not being caught the first time seemed to incite further criminal activity. One persistent offender offers this insight.

> *Nicky:* The worst thing that can happen to a kid, I think, or a guy—is to go out and do something and be successful the first time out. Boy, I'll tell you, money comes easy. Then you figure. Yeah, I was driving trucks . . . I was making big money then at that time. In the '60s I was making $700 or $800 a week. Of course, I was working 100 hours a week. I got a proposition to drive a car in a bank job, so I went. Everything went off good. . . . I got a good offer, you know. Like I say, I got an offer to drive a car in a job. I was making good money. I was offered like $30,000—you know that was in the '60s. That was big money.
>
> *Q:* So was it simply then the attraction of it? Or was it also the excitement?
>
> *Nicky:* No. I was just going to drive a car once; I'd give it a try. And it worked out good, so, like I say, if you're a success, it feels

> good. So we kept going . . . it wasn't excitement. It was the money, let's face it.

Recall that Boston Billy reported that crime was so easy it was "pathetic." It would be a mistake, however, to conclude that sanctions make no difference whatsoever, especially as the men aged. Gino, for example, knew about sanctions for nonpayment of child support. He told us that if you skip paying support for two weeks you are all right, but if you skip three weeks the court will hold you in contempt. As a result, he routinely paid his child support two weeks late.

### The Attraction and Excitement of Crime

According to his record in the Gluecks' file, Charlie "enjoyed delinquency" at the age of 12. Many of the persistent offenders described themselves as "hell-raisers." They seemed to possess a strong desire for action and adventure. Frankie, a confirmed "hot boxer" like Boston Billy, described himself as a "seeker" who would often hop freight trains as a kid. This group of persistent offenders was also fearless. As noted by the Gluecks' interviewer, for these boys the "Lyman School holds no terror."

Perhaps most troubling is the fact that in their adulthood as well as in their youth, these men didn't seem to care about anything or anybody. This lack of caring can be viewed as a form of alienation and seems quite different from a bumbling impulsivity or lack of self-control. The men had an "edge" about them that seemed to indicate that because they had nothing, they had nothing to lose. Thus the consequences of their actions were ignored rather than unforeseen.

Supporting the idea of the sensuality of crime, Maurice discussed the "sneaky thrill" he received from breaking and entering (see Katz 1988, 52–79). He recounted:

> The thing at that time was breaking and entering because doing that, you did it under the guise of nobody could see you. You had less chances of getting caught if you did it at the right time and there was, to me—I used to get a charge. I used to get a feeling. You know, you get euphoria, you know you're getting away with something. It's like a high, you know. And I just kept doing it, you know. And I kept getting caught.

### Calculated and Articulated Resistance to Authority

Persistent offenders have a difficult time with all types of authority, rules, and structure. One of the investigators on the Gluecks' research project described Buddy at age 14 as having an "ingrown resentment for any authority." This subject was also described as having a negative and hostile attitude and a "quiet resentfulness." At age 69, Buddy told us, "I never made it on parole. I just couldn't stand any supervision." Buddy could not make it in the military either. He was in the Navy and the Army, but he got kicked out of both branches of the service. "I just couldn't conform. You know, my previous experience was in the Lyman School and being told what to do—I couldn't handle any kind of regulation. When somebody told me to do something, if I didn't think it was right I'd tell them to go and fuck themselves."

This defiant outlook was captured succinctly by Jimmy, who noted, "Ask me and I will do it. Demand it, forget it." Jimmy went on to describe crime as "a struggle for power. The more you say don't, the more I will." Similarly, Frankie was depicted as "deeply suspicious of, and hostile against, authoritative adults," according to his Rorschach assessment taken at age 14. The report went on, "He would like to get rid of them, of their rules, standards, commands, and prohibitions." Another subject, Don, was described in the Gluecks' record as "unmanageable and defiant" at age 14. As an adult, he was a drinker and a brawler. In his age 32 interview, the Gluecks' investigator said that Don was defiant toward any symbol of authority. When we spoke with him at the age of 68, he stated that as a young adult, "I was a son of a gun. I didn't care." Maurice too had problems in the military. When told that he did not have enough time in to get a furlough to see his family, Maurice remembered that he responded, "Is that right? You should have never told me that. My hackles backed right up. I said, screw him, you know. So I went AWOL."

The Gluecks' investigators were not spared from the defiance of authority by the persistent offenders. When interviewed at Deer Island House of Correction for his age 25 interview, Jimmy came into the room with a "hostile attitude." He stated, "I don't mean any disrespect to you and I have no hard feelings but we might as well get it straight right now that if you're after personal information I have nothing to say." Jimmy also expressed resentment at the Gluecks' investigators' continued interference in his "personal affairs."

For some, defiance does not diminish with age. In his interview at age 69, Harry told us, "I like to tell people off when they don't do me right." Likewise, when asked if he was still defiant at age 69, Buddy responded, "No . . . I have changed. [But] there's still a lot of that in me. Like if I get mad at somebody, I'll tell them to go and fuck themselves. You know, just stay away from them and avoid them. If I find out they're the kind of people that I can't handle, that have nothing to offer or that I have nothing to offer them."

The men's defiance may have been fueled by a perceived sense of injustice resulting from contact with officials of the criminal justice system. Many persistent offenders see the system as unfair and corrupt. Moreover, many of the men talked about "setups" by the police (for example, planting evidence and then arresting them), being "shaken down" by the police (for example, having their money and property taken illegally in a routine traffic stop), and general harassment (for example, showing up at the place of employment of the ex-offender to question him about alleged crimes). Similar evidence was found by Glaser (1969, 258), who reveals that a recurrent theme in the stories of prison inmates is alleged police harassment. Furthermore, some of the men we interviewed were charged with assault and battery on a police officer. Arthur told us that he did not assault any cop. They try to "break your ass, that's all. Like I said, if they don't find you guilty of something, they know you didn't do anything, they'll come up with something else."

Frankie told us he had a run-in with a police captain who afterward targeted him. The captain's officers were told to bring Frankie in any time they saw him—"these are guys [the police officers] that never even knew me, never seen me before." Frankie claimed that the captain said, "If you ever see him, bring him in. I don't give a shit if he's doing nothing. Bring him in." According to Frankie, most of his early crime consisted of automobile theft because "this bum [the police captain] up here wouldn't give me my license." According to Frankie's account, the dispute stemmed from the fact that Frankie witnessed the captain engaged in police brutality. "I got him killing a guy in the cell one time. He beat the shit out of him. Oh yeah. He would OK it. He was the captain. I told him—I got him fucking a guy in a cell next to me. The guy was screaming. The guy was drunk." Frankie also asserted that this police captain was on "the take." "He'd walk around all these bar rooms, walk in . . . I want $100. I want $100 or you're going to get locked, closed up. He went to every bar in the neighborhood . . . , [he] wanted to get $100 off of each bartender." Frankie lamented, "He never forgot me, in forty years he never forgot me. The rotten bastard." The extent to which these accounts are exaggerated is not known.[11] It is possible that the men are employing the technique of "condemnation of the condemners" as a way of justifying their own criminality (Sykes and Matza 1957; Matza 1964).

For Frankie and others, the justice system is viewed as a game (see Blumberg 1967). Plea bargains, corrupt cops, deals for testimony, false charges, and a courtroom workgroup wherein prosecutors, defense attorneys, and judges act in concert to achieve their mutual interests are the images our men see when they view the system. Frankie complained,

> The same shit. They always hit me with something. I'd walk in drunk or something—they'd always hit you with two or three other charges. This is what I'm trying to tell you. Everything was . . . when they walked in, they looked at this piece of paper. Now they say, "for the month of January, there's 35 breaks, there was six cars stolen in the area. There was a couple of houses broken into, a couple of stores. All right put him down for three breaks. We've got to clear this. We've got to clear the books up." . . . Instead of being smart enough, which you ain't because you ain't got no money for a lawyer or anything else—your lawyer [a public defender] will say, "Here, plead guilty. The judge is not going to send you away." That's good for the cops because that clears the record. And the judge lets you go on a two months' probation. That's why you read the paper today and you say to the guy, "Jesus Christ, if that judge let that guy off, he just knifed a guy and almost killed him." The poor bastard might have admitted that the other charges he wasn't even around to do. But this is what society *is*.

A large portion of the defiant stance is class based. Recall that these men were raised in poor, working-class neighborhoods in Boston. The notion that forms of deviance and the probability of state sanctions vary across social class and the dominant hierarchy was uncovered in our narratives. Jimmy, who grew up in Charlestown, said, "If you've got the money, you're going out the door. If you haven't got the money, you're going to stay right there [meaning prison]. You don't have to be 19, 20 years old to understand that." Jimmy went on to point out that no kids from Needham or Newton [middle-class suburbs of Boston] were sent to Lyman or Shirley. Instead reform schools were for kids from Charlestown, East Boston, and Roxbury. Jimmy concluded, "It is all social class." Extending this view, Frankie claimed that all of the prison guards at Concord were "sadistic, Protestant bastards . . . And where do you think they all came from? Nine-tenths of them? Concord, Lexington, Belmont [middle-class suburbs of Boston]—where all the high Republican— . . . high-class money people [live]." The defiant stance of Jimmy and Frankie (men of Irish descent) was influenced by class, ethnic, and religious prejudices.

This outlook has wider ramifications for the men's view of society. Most persistent offenders (as well as ex-offenders) see society as a whole as corrupt. Buddy provided the following account:

> From my experiences with . . . well, my main experience has been with convicts so I figured that most people are generally the same way. Well, business people, they cut their friend's throat just to get ahead in business. They'll beat their friends for money. So I think the nature of man is evil. They're just polluted. If you're offered more money to do something that will hurt your partner you will go ahead and do it. It's the nature of man, I think. There's good and there's evil and I think the evil outweighs the good in human nature.

The view of the world as corrupt and no one in it as trustworthy enhanced the importance of being a "stand-up guy" at the local level—a person with values in a world without values, so to speak (MacDonald 1999, chap. 8). One of the important values on the street was loyalty. Buddy described his friend as being loyal in the following way: "If you got pinched on a job, he'd stand there and shoot somebody to protect you, you know." For Buddy, this was the honorable action for a stand-up guy.

### Alcohol Abuse and Persistent Offending

A major problem for these persistent offenders was alcohol abuse. It is apparent that during the decades these offenders were active, the drug of choice was alcohol. These men were part of a culture that encouraged drinking, where going out drinking was an evening's activity. Moreover, there are indications that their crime sprees were linked to binge drinking. Fighting in bars was part of the drinking culture as well. Buddy told us that he drank at home all the time because he knew he would wind up in trouble at the bars, especially in "strange areas where nobody knows [you] . . . you're a target."

Many of the persistent offenders suffered from chronic alcoholism and called themselves alcoholics. Most started excessive drinking in late adolescence and early adulthood. For instance, Buddy described himself as a "drunk." Although he reported that he had been sober for eight years at the time of the interview, alcohol was a major catalyst and sustainer of his criminal career. He committed robberies and other thefts to get money for booze. His problems with alcohol also hampered his acquisition of stable employment and a steady mate. Buddy related that as soon as he started on a drunk, he would walk off his job. "I really enjoyed the work [printing], but I couldn't stay off the booze." For a time, he was able to manage work and drinking. "See, what I'd do is all week I wouldn't drink, especially when I was with somebody [a woman]. And over the weekend, I'd drink Friday night and Saturday and then sober up Sunday and be ready to get back to work." All of the women he met were drinkers, so relationships did not provide a passage away from crime and deviance. Buddy told us, "The places I hung around—I'd run into nobody but drinkers. That's probably why I drank so much."

Alcohol was also a major factor in Charlie's offending. He reported to us that he committed robberies only when he was drunk, none when he was sober. He said, "I drank like a fish. And half the time I didn't even know where I was."

Don's drinking problem was worsened by his job—he was a bartender. He said that his girlfriend tried to monitor his drinking without success. He recounted to us, "See, this bartending—one week I'd work nights. The next week I'd work days. Well, I worked from 8 to 4:30. [At] 4:30 I'd stop, sit in with all the guys—'come on, have a drink.' My wife would call me—not my wife, but I call her my wife— 'When the hell you coming home?' I'll be home. I'll be home." Later in the interview, Don did confess that he did not consume as much alcohol when he went out with his steady girlfriend as he did with the guys, indicating the potential of marital (or quasi-marital) attachments to modify deviance such as excessive drinking.

The long-term effects of alcohol abuse are painfully evident. At his age 69 interview, Buddy stated that he is a "confirmed alcoholic." He continued, "Every time I'd drink I'd go into a blackout. I'd wake up on the floor. Hopefully there would be another drink in the bottle and I'd drink that and pass out again. I was just a stoned alcoholic. I just drank. Probably I was trying to kill myself. I don't know." Buddy is currently sober. Like many Glueck men, he disdains Alcoholics Anonymous and prefers to stay away from booze on his own.[12]

As a matter of fact, when I first came here [to his present residence] they caught me on the floor one day—I was stoned. They took me to a detox. Well, I checked out of the detox the next day and the lady that runs the place told me she's going to kick me out. She just threatened. I told her "I'll just go down to Pine Street [a shelter in Boston]." She said, "Well, listen, let's talk about it." She tried to get me to go to AA and I convinced her that I couldn't stand the AA because the time I went to an AA meeting I stay a drunk, you know. I can't stand people telling their sad stories . . . it just makes me angry. Because these people are fools. They come to one meeting and they'll tell one story and you go to another meeting and they're there telling another story or they lied. That's another thing about me, I can't stand people who lie. I just don't like lying. But anyway, I convinced her that I wouldn't go to AA meetings. So she made me promise to get meals every day and come down and see her every day twice. So I did that for about a year and finally I talked her out of making me go to meals.

The threat of being evicted clearly facilitated Buddy's attempt to stop drinking. As he recounted,

I would have got kicked out if I didn't quit. When I thought about it, I said, "Where am I going from here? What the hell is the matter with me? I've got a nice place here. I'm content. I'm out of the city. I'm out"—and I finally decided—all them years that I was drinking I was a goddamn fool because there was nothing to drink for anymore, you know. I used to drink this to escape from the goddamn world, you know. But I didn't need any escape anymore because I was content.

### Prison Experiences of Persistent Offenders

What distinguishes persistent offenders from all other offenders we interviewed is the exorbitant amount of time they served in jails and prisons (see Table 7.1 for details). It is especially important to learn how these men viewed the prison experience and what effect they believed it had on their lives.

Uniformly, the persistent offenders we interviewed did not regard adult prison as a positive turning point. "Bullshit" is what Frankie called prison. Charlie told us, "All they did in state prison was teach you how to be a better thief. All you did was make number plates. There was nothing there, no incentive to do better, to be better. If you didn't do it on your own, you were dead." Others confirmed that they didn't learn any useful skills in prison and hence they returned to their communities, often in the same place they were before they were incarcerated, though now with the burden of a longer record.

There is also evidence of violence in prison—by staff and by other inmates. For example, Jimmy was one of the youngest inmates in the Concord Reformatory during the 1940s. He said it was a "strange" experience: "The guards at Concord were pricks. They used leaded canes to beat you." Later in the interview, Jimmy told us, "I said put me in the goddamn hole. Up yours. I refused to do whatever they said. I did not care." Because of this attitude, Jimmy spent a fair share of his time in prison in solitary confinement. In the words of Sykes's classic study *The Society of Captives,* Jimmy was a "ball buster." "Blatant disobedience, physical and verbal assaults on the officials, the constant creation of disturbances—these are the patterns of behavior of the typical ball buster" (Sykes 1958, 99).

Frankie said that Concord was a "terrible place." In fact, the word he used the most was "sadistic." Frankie continued,

> They had a saying, "the Protestant bastard." That's what they used to call [the guards] . . . They were very, very, very, very sadistic. There was no reasoning whatsoever. They were very, very sadistic. They would take you or me through the mess hall, shut the lights out and bang you with the leaden cane—the cane loaded with lead—whacking you in the head, the back, your spine.

An example of inmate-on-inmate violence comes from Tony, a well-known offender in the Boston area. Tony participated in a home invasion during the 1950s that involved terrorizing a family in the process of committing a $4,300 robbery. Tony received a long prison term (a 48- to 55-year sentence) for various charges stemming from the incident, including assault to murder, kidnapping, and armed robbery. No stranger to violence, Tony had a long criminal record dating from his juvenile years, including a charge of manslaughter when he was 20 years old. According to information provided by Tony's wife and newspaper accounts, Tony was in his cell one night when he was attacked by three inmates. In the attack, Tony was stabbed in the stomach, hit on the head with a pipe, and blinded from acid thrown in his face by his attackers. A Boston newspaper reported that Tony was stabbed in a "typical gangland attempt at revenge."

Our group of persistent offenders saw their juvenile incarceration experiences as especially deleterious. Don remembered "cold showers" in the wintertime. He went on, "These guys that run this place were no good. I mean, I wasn't up there for being a good boy; I stole a couple of cars. But, Jesus Christ, we didn't deserve this kind of shit."

When asked about his recollections of the Lyman School, Jimmy remarked that Lyman had the "dregs of humanity" and "sadistic bastards." He commented on the humiliating showers and beatings (for example, being handcuffed to a pipe with his pants down and beaten with a strap on his bare buttocks). He expressed extreme bitterness toward Lyman.[13]

Finally, there is some support for the idea of institutional dependency, especially among long-term prisoners. Jimmy said that prison was easier than being on the street. "When I came out of Concord I had nothing. I was completely lost. I lasted three days." Overall, Jimmy was incarcerated 15.3 years before age 32. Similarly, Buddy, who was incarcerated for almost half his life (about 35 years), maintained, "The fact that I've been in jail most of my life . . . I'm sort of like a half cripple."

### Accounts in Later Life

Many of the persistent offenders we interviewed fully accepted responsibility for their misdeeds—there was little or no denial of criminal events. It is possible that there is less need to invoke "techniques of neutralization" in later life. Jimmy maintained that his involvement in crime was "stupid." He went on to say that "I can't blame it on my friends—other guys turned out O.K. I wasn't abused or anything like that."

Although not widely appreciated, there is considerable ambivalence toward crime among persistent offenders. Competing with the attraction and seduction of crime is the simultaneous recognition of the downside of crime (for example, injury, anxiety, prison). The latter seems to increase with age (see, for example, Shover 1985, 1996). As Smelser (1998, 5) points out, ambivalence implies instability, contradiction, and uncertainty in individual behavior and the relationship between individuals and social institutions, especially with those in positions of authority.

Most striking is the sobering recognition by the persistent offenders of their lives as "damaged" and "wasted." For example, when we asked Buddy what he saw when he looked back on his life, he replied, "A big loss." Undoubtedly aging plays a role in this. Again, Buddy told us, "Twelve years ago, the last time I got out of the can, I said, 'To hell with it. I'm sick of this life. I'm going to try to correct'—by then it was pretty late." Buddy noted that it is harder to fight the things that disturb you when you get older.

Revealing the vacillation between the seduction of crime and the reality of punishment and its costs as one ages, Gino pointed out, "There is money to be had without committing crime. You have to work for it. You can't be lazy. Also, I do not want to go to jail at my age." Arthur noted, "Yeah, the last time I did time it changed me because I said what am I wasting my life in the can for? Why don't I waste it on the street, forget about it. And that's what I'm doing. I'm 65 years old, how much can I push? How much time I'm going to do before I drop dead. So, either I live the right life or I don't. Like I said, when you're growing up you think you're a wise guy, you think you can do anything and get away with it until you get caught two or three times, and then you say hey, I'm wasting my life." When we asked Arthur at the age of 65 whether he would get involved in crime again, he replied, "Oh forget it. I am too old. I can't run no more."

Although the persistent offenders we interviewed are still alive, a life of crime has taken its toll. Most are heavy smokers with more than their fair share of health problems. Some have lingering injuries due to their criminal and deviant escapades that resulted in accidents or direct injuries from crimes. For instance, at the age of 40, Buddy described being chased by the police after robbing a store. While driving drunk, he hit the back of a truck and broke his neck. He also had a piece of his lung taken out and was in a cast from head to toe. Whether his account is somewhat exaggerated or not, Buddy still suffers serious health problems stemming from this incident.

Another compelling example is Frankie, who was struck by a train at age 30 and had his right arm severed in the accident. Up to that time, Frankie was one of the more active delinquents in the Glueck study. He had been arrested 47 times before age 32, including arrests for robbery, drunkenness, loitering, breaking and entering, auto theft, larceny, receiving stolen goods, and violation of probation. After the accident he could not work, but he was still arrested a number of times. He also never married. Frankie spent his life living with his sister in the house in which he grew up.

Ironically, many of the men we interviewed expressed a fear of crime, especially by young "hoodlums." These aging offenders described life as different today, largely because of guns, drugs, and a perception that communities and neighborhoods no longer exist. For example, Charlie noted,

> I think, you know, when we were growing up we were into sports and things. That's all we had were sports. We didn't have TV or nothing. In the wintertime we used to go out and shovel off the field and play football and all we'd do is put on a bunch of sweaters. And after the game we'd . . . play the kids in South Boston. After the game we automatically had a fight, a fistfight. But a fistfight, we did it with our hands. If you argue with a kid today you're going to pull a gun on them, because they don't care. Nothing can be done to them and they know it.

When asked about crime today, Nicky responded,

> Crime? Crime is terrible. I'll tell you, the kids today are dangerous. Let me tell you. I'll tell you, if someone said to us, "Halt," you know, that was it. Today if they're robbing you, you give them your money and they shoot you anyways. Kids today are crazy. Yeah, really. I think it's the dope. Eight and nine years old—they're killing kids. That's bad.

For most of the men we interviewed we detected a last attempt at "redemption." These activities are often tied to seemingly mundane things, but, especially for men with chaotic backgrounds, they represent stable and reassuring routines. Buddy has a series of chores he does in his building. "I go down every noontime—that lady I told you about that runs the place—I get lunch for her. And I deliver the mail to a couple of the older women in here that can't get up to the mailboxes." For others, redemption is expressed through generativity. Jimmy coaches a baseball team in the Babe Ruth League and helps kids with soccer. Recently, with his son-in-law, he raised money to develop three soccer fields, three baseball diamonds, and a clubhouse in his town. Along somewhat different lines, Charlie told us that his life was full of "twists and turns," but that despite his troubles the "last twenty-five years have been the happiest." He continued,

> I've had good success working; I've raised four kids. I see them and the grandkids; I look back and say, "Gee, I did that." I still have a problem with one of them [a son who is involved with drugs], but I've got him, he's straightening his act out . . . He was into it heavy but I got him off it. I got him a good job, and I just got him his license back. And he's getting his car this week so he can get back and forth to work because I've

been driving him for the last six months every morning. I think he's all set now.

## What Have We Learned?

What draws persistent offenders to crime and keeps them there? Is it an inability or unwillingness to conform? Is it the result of long-term cumulative disadvantage brought about by a difficult childhood temperament? Is persistence due to a lack of structural turning points and a reduced exposure to situations and commitments that facilitate change? Or does abuse of alcohol or other drugs sustain persistent offending? This chapter begins to grapple with these questions by drawing on life-history narratives from a group of men who have persisted in offending over much of their life course.

From a methodological standpoint, the persistent offender represents challenges with respect to the validity of the narrative data acquired. Perhaps surprisingly, there appeared to be a substantial amount of cover-up by only a small subset of the offenders we interviewed. As the Gluecks' investigator remarked more than fifty years ago after an interview—"What he did say was the truth, but what he left unsaid is probably more important than the admissions he made." A few of the men even denied being in reform school, which was the basis for being selected for the Gluecks' study. As with all criminological data, one must be cautious, and to the extent possible, use supplemental sources of information as we have done throughout this study, moving from interview data to records gathered from multiple sources. This issue is compounded, of course, by the interpretation of life-course events under investigation, especially in light of our long retrospective window.

Given the long-term nature of our data, the men we interviewed for this chapter sounded a lot like what are commonly called "life-course persisters" (Moffitt 1993). Moffitt uses this term to describe a relatively small group of offenders who offend during each developmental stage of their life course. For Moffitt, the life-course persister has distinct traits such as personality disorder and cognitive deficits. These offenders have inadequate social skills, do poorly in school, have fragile mental health, lack the capacity to forge close attachment, have inadequate self-control, and have low intelligence. These characteristics emerge early in life, typically between ages 7 and 12.

As the career of the life-course persister unfolds, salient life events in adolescence and adulthood become problematic. Life-course persisters often leave school early, become fathers as teenagers, experience unemployment, divorce, and separation, abuse alcohol and drugs, and continue criminal activity that often leads to incarceration.

At first glance, looking back over the course of lives, support for Moffitt's portrait of persistent offending can be found in our narratives. Much of the support, however, is illusory. What is most striking about the persistent offenders we interviewed is that their childhood traits are the same as those who desisted from crime (see Chapters 5 and 6 for more details). What is particularly striking is that men who exhibited childhood and adolescent risk factors for "life-course-persistent" offending according to Moffitt's theory just as often desisted from crime in adulthood. Consistent with Chapter 5, in our narrative data we find no evidence that a group of "life-course-persistent" offenders can be identified prospectively. As the case of Boston Billy aptly demonstrates, there is something at each stage of the life course—childhood, adolescence, young adulthood, and mid-life—that sustains involvement in crime.

These narratives also convey the richness and complexity of examining lives over time. Even the most hardened offender is not a persistent offender in the true sense of the term, and all offenders eventually desist albeit at different rates and ages (Chapter 5). The question becomes, What is it about frequent and persistent, but eventually desisting, offenders that distinguishes them from low-rate offenders and those who desist earlier? In our view, rather than being identified by a single trait like poor intelligence or even a series of static traits, the persistent offender seems devoid of connective structures at each phase of his life course, especially involving relationships that can provide informal social control and social support (Sampson and Laub 1993; Cullen 1994). Generally, the persistent offenders we interviewed experienced residential, marital, and job instability, failure in the school and the military, and relatively long periods of incarceration. Men who desisted from crime led rather orderly lives, whereas the life of the persistent offender was marked by frequent churning, almost as in adolescence. Surely part of this chaos reflects an inability to forge close attachments or make any connection to anybody or anything. One can view the men as possessing a distorted sense of autonomy without any commitment or concern for others.

In turn, the lack of structure these men experienced offered more situations conducive to crime and encouraged a downward spiral. Routine activities are different for those without jobs, permanent addresses, spouses, children, or other stable forms of life (Osgood et al. 1996). As a consequence, one has increased contact with those individuals who are similarly situated—in this case, similarly unattached and free from informal social control. Thus the influence of deviant peers, criminal networks, and prison is especially strong in the lives of persistent offenders,[14] although their criminal activity does not necessarily depend on learning crime from a supportive peer group, as Sutherland (1947) claimed. Rather, as Matsueda and Heimer argue, the lack of role structure affects behavior by "delimiting opportunities, and affecting the generalized other and identities by affecting communication networks, peer associations, and subcultural affiliation" (1997, 175).

Like men who desist from crime, persistent offenders also articulate personal agency and imbue meaning to their actions. This group of persistent offenders did not apologize for their behavior, nor, for the most part, did they make excuses. Generally they saw themselves as responsible agents, though not in a moral sense. Moreover, the men appeared to be painfully aware of the choices they had made and, as they looked back, they saw a life filled with misery and missed opportunities. The sense of loss is profound, and they will carry their broken dreams with them forever.

# CHAPTER EIGHT

# Zigzag Criminal Careers

So far we have concentrated on two groups of offenders: persisters and desisters. As we have seen, however, the rather neat typologies offered by criminological theory often conflict with the messy and complicated nature of the actual lives of the Glueck men. This chapter investigates the relatively large number of criminal offenders who fall into a residual category. Some of the men we will meet committed disturbing acts of violence late in life, others desisted at very late ages, and a quirky group seem to be "intermittent" offenders who follow a zigzag pattern of crime (Blumstein et al. 1986; Nagin and Land, 1993).

When we began writing this book we envisioned an entire chapter on what appeared to be an intriguing phenomenon—the onset of violence in later adulthood (see also Figure 4.1). In reading the narratives, however, we soon realized that using official records to determine the late onset of violent events induces too much error. One of the reasons to collect qualitative data is to "make room for the unanticipated" (Becker 1996, 61), which is exactly what happened. Our detailed life-history narratives reveal that while some men in our group of "late desisters" followed the pathway of classic desistance with respect to turning points like marriage, other men stopped committing crime but did not cease, for example, excessive drinking. Still other men maintained a lively defiance of authority and engaged in problematic behavior in the domains of family and work. These narratives thus raise the question—what exactly do we mean by desistance? By late onset? Moreover, the lives of the remaining group of intermittent offenders are so varied that little systematic patterning is revealed.[1] When we investigate more thoroughly the vast middle ground of offending between the end points of persistent offending and desistance, the validity of distinguishable "groups" becomes even more tenuous.

Although the lives described in this chapter are messy and difficult, the payoff from our narrative strategy extends beyond a critique of groups to a more nuanced understanding of the nature of crime across the life course. New topics such as homelessness due to alcoholism, the aftermath of combat experiences and wartime injuries, racism, organized crime, class and ethnic conflict, and physical and sexual assault emerge as salient themes. We were also surprised to discover that the narratives of these men were filled with noticeably more pathos, pain, and personal destruction than the narratives presented in Chapters 6 and 7. Why this is so presents a challenge not only for interpretation but also for the confident nature of prediction and trait-based models in criminology.

## Strategy and Background

To shed light on these and other dilemmas, we examine life-history narratives for a group of men who displayed trajectories in officially recognized offending that do not fit neatly in either our persister or our desister categories. For this group of men ($N = 19$), there appear to be at least three subtypes of offending patterns. The first consists of offenders who experienced their first arrest for violence in later adulthood, after age 35. We interviewed 5 offenders who display this trajectory and whom we initially call "the late onset of violence" group. The men in this group were arrested in later adulthood for violent acts ranging from spouse assault to homicide to sexual assault on children. The late onset of violence distinguished these men from the persistent offenders who displayed violence early and often as they aged.

The second group consists of offenders who had at least one arrest at each segment of their life course (juvenile, young adult, and older adult) but experienced their first arrest for violence in young adulthood, between the ages of 17 to 32, rather than in adolescence. We interviewed 14 offenders who fit this pattern of offending. Although some of the men could be called persistent offenders on the basis of their overall arrest histories, as a group they spent considerably less time incarcerated (on average, 3.5 years of their life up to age 32) compared with the persistent offenders we discussed in Chapter 7. Interestingly, most of these men desisted from crime as they aged. We designate the men who desisted in their late twenties to their thirties as "late desisters" ($N = 7$). The remaining 7 men are a hybrid group displaying more intermittent patterns of offending over their life course. We label them "intermittent" or "hybrid" offenders. What distinguished the "late desisters" was that all of the men had four consecutive time periods (ages 25–31, 32–39, 40–49, and 50–59) in which they did not get arrested for violence.

Data for all three categories of offending are summarized in Tables 8.1, 8.2, and 8.3. With regard to their unofficial and official delinquency, the three groups do not look much different. Not surprisingly, on average the intermittent group and the late onset group were arrested more often than the late desisters (mean = 33.3, 32.4, and 19.0, respectively). Although the late desister group on average spent more days incarcerated before age 32 than the intermittent and late onset group, over the full life course, the late onset group was incarcerated 28.2 days per year, followed by the intermittent group (21.1 days per year), and the late desisters (16.5 days per year).

Data relating to other aspects of the life course are also provided in Tables 8.1–8.3. Two items stand out. First, the average IQ for the late onset group was 102, about 10 points above the mean for the full sample of delinquents and the mean for the late desister group. Second, the late onset group spent less time married and more time divorced/separated compared with the late desisters and the intermittent offender groups.

Following the analytic logic of Chapters 6 and 7, our strategy is to present narrative life histories capturing broad topics related to the onset of violence in later adulthood, desistance in later adulthood, and intermittent offending. Because so little is known about the onset of violence in adulthood, especially after age 35 (see Eggleston and Laub 2002), we spend a considerable amount of time presenting life-history narratives from the five men in this category. In our presentation, we pay particular attention to the men's descriptions of violent incidents and the meaning they attribute to them. We then turn to the late desisters and hybrid offenders that exhibit zigzag patterns of

**Table 8.1** Late onset of violence offenders

Criminal history data

| Name | Total report | Official offenses <17 | Official offenses 17–32 | Total official offenses[a] | Total official violent offenses[a] | Age first incarcerated | Time served <17 (in years) | Time served 17–32 (in years) | Time served[b] |
|---|---|---|---|---|---|---|---|---|---|
| Alberto | 15 | 5 | 14 | 32 | 1 | 11 | 1.99 | 0.82 | 5.70 |
| Rocco | 20 | 6 | 10 | 32 | 1 | 16 | 0.47 | 3.36 | 23.34 |
| Giuseppe | 15 | 13 | 25 | 48 | 2 | 14 | 0.74 | 1.68 | 54.58 |
| Roger | 17 | 5 | 8 | 26 | 4 | 11 | 1.91 | 0.00 | 0.00 |
| Paul | 16 | 6 | 6 | 24 | 2 | 14 | 0.92 | 6.44 | 57.30 |
| Mean | 16.6 | 7.0 | 12.6 | 32.4 | 2 | 13.2 | 1.21 | 2.46 | 28.18 |

Social history data

| Name | Ethnicity | Age at interview | IQ | Adolescent competence | Proportion of time married[c] | Proportion of time divorced/separated[c] | Proportion of time with unstable employment[d] | Proportion of time in military[d] | Military outcome |
|---|---|---|---|---|---|---|---|---|---|
| Alberto | Italian | 69 | 93 | 1 | 0.00 | 0.00 | 0.53 | 0.00 | N.A. |
| Rocco | Italian | 70 | 102 | 1 | 0.28 | 0.62 | 0.33 | 0.00 | N.A. |
| Giuseppe | Italian | 67 | 98 | 0 | 0.68 | 0.25 | 0.53 | 0.13 | Dishonorable |
| Roger | French | 68 | 105 | 0 | 0.79 | 0.02 | 0.20 | 0.27 | Honorable |
| Paul | Belgian | 68 | 111 | 1 | 0.43 | 0.41 | 0.93 | 0.07 | N.A. |
| Mean | | 68.4 | 101.8 | 0.6 | 0.44 | 0.26 | 0.50 | 0.09 | |

*Note:* On adolescent competence, see note 1 in chapter 6.

a. Ages 7 to 70.
b. Ages 17 to 70, days incarcerated over lifetime per year.
c. Ages 17 to 70.
d. Ages 17 to 32.

Table 8.2 Late desisters

| Name | Total report | Official offenses <17 | Official offenses 17–32 | Total official offenses[a] | Total official violent offenses[a] | Age first incarcerated | Time served <17 (in years) | Time served 17–32 (in years) | Time served[b] |
|---|---|---|---|---|---|---|---|---|---|
| Art | 12 | 5 | 8 | 18 | 3 | 12 | 3.10 | 9.96 | 68.6 |
| Donald | 16 | 8 | 12 | 20 | 2 | 12 | 2.69 | 1.17 | 8.1 |
| Edmund | 13 | 3 | 9 | 20 | 3 | 15 | 1.25 | 0.00 | 0.0 |
| Ralph | 16 | 6 | 9 | 17 | 1 | 13 | 2.44 | 2.02 | 14.0 |
| Carlo | 13 | 4 | 4 | 8 | 1 | 16 | 0.77 | 0.00 | 0.0 |
| Allen | 14 | 7 | 7 | 16 | 1 | 14 | 0.98 | 2.13 | 15.3 |
| Mark | 7 | 6 | 28 | 38 | 2 | 15 | 0.89 | 1.39 | 9.6 |
| Mean | 13.0 | 5.6 | 10.4 | 19.0 | 1.6 | 13.9 | 1.73 | 2.38 | 16.5 |

Criminal history data

Social history data

| | Ethnicity | Age at interview | IQ | Adolescent competence | Proportion of time married[c] | Proportion of time divorced/separated[c] | Proportion of time with unstable employment[d] | Proportion of time in military[d] | Military outcome |
|---|---|---|---|---|---|---|---|---|---|
| Art | American | 71 | 110 | 2 | 0.58 | 0.00 | 0.93 | 0.20 | Dishonorable |
| Donald | Syrian | 68 | 78 | 2 | 0.75 | 0.15 | 0.67 | 0.13 | Dishonorable |
| Edmund | Irish | 70 | 79 | 0 | 0.81 | 0.00 | 0.13 | 0.53 | Honorable |
| Ralph | Eng. Can. | 68 | 88 | 3 | 0.92 | 0.00 | 0.60 | 0.00 | N.A. |
| Carlo | Italian | 70 | 87 | 0 | 0.89 | 0.04 | 0.53 | 0.20 | Honorable |
| Allen | Eng. Can. | 67 | 106 | 1 | 0.82 | 0.00 | 0.67 | 0.27 | Honorable |
| Mark | Italian | 67 | 95 | 0 | 0.27 | 0.20 | 0.67 | 0.07 | Dishonorable |
| Mean | | 68.7 | 91.9 | 1.1 | 0.66 | 0.09 | 0.60 | 0.10 | |

*Note*: On adolescent competence, see note 1 in chapter 6.
a. Ages 7 to 70.
b. Ages 17 to 70, days incarcerated over lifetime per year.
c. Ages 17 to 70.
d. Ages 17 to 32.

Table 8.3 Intermittent offenders

| | | | | | | Criminal history data | | | |
|---|---|---|---|---|---|---|---|---|---|
| Name | Total report | Official offenses <17 | Official offenses 17–32 | Total official offenses[a] | Total official violent offenses[a] | Age first incarcerated | Time served <17 (in years) | Time served 17–32 (in years) | Time served[b] |
| Sal | 10 | 9 | 22 | 44 | 2 | 13 | 2.55 | 3.64 | 25.19 |
| Patrick | 17 | 7 | 20 | 30 | 6 | 12 | 1.08 | 0.00 | 0.00 |
| Mickey | 17 | 8 | 15 | 24 | 1 | 15 | 1.10 | 0.03 | 0.23 |
| Pasquale | 11 | 2 | 7 | 11 | 1 | 15 | 0.95 | 0.69 | 4.77 |
| Sean | 13 | 14 | 32 | 82 | 2 | 13 | 1.70 | 3.78 | 46.87 |
| Ron | 20 | 9 | 3 | 14 | 2 | 13 | 1.02 | 1.25 | 8.66 |
| Bernard | 11 | 11 | 12 | 28 | 2 | 13 | 1.88 | 0.96 | 61.72 |
| Mean | 14.1 | 8.6 | 15.9 | 33.3 | 2.3 | 13.4 | 1.47 | 1.48 | 21.06 |

Social history data

| | Ethnicity | Age at interview | IQ | Adolescent competence | Proportion of time married[c] | Proportion of time divorced/separated[c] | Proportion of time with unstable employment[d] | Proportion of time in military[d] | Military outcome |
|---|---|---|---|---|---|---|---|---|---|
| Sal | Italian | 67 | 73 | 0 | 0.58 | 0.02 | 1.00 | 0.00 | N.A. |
| Patrick | Irish | 66 | 96 | N.A. | 0.70 | 0.00 | 0.73 | 0.20 | Honorable |
| Mickey | Irish | 69 | 109 | N.A. | 0.94 | 0.00 | 0.53 | 0.20 | Honorable |
| Pasquale | Italian | 69 | 102 | N.A. | 0.68 | 0.00 | 0.27 | 0.07 | Honorable |
| Sean | Irish | 66 | 92 | 1 | 0.26 | 0.62 | 0.87 | 0.00 | N.A. |
| Ron | Fr. Can. | 67 | 111 | 2 | 0.58 | 0.17 | 0.13 | 0.93 | Honorable |
| Bernard | Italian | 65 | 89 | 0 | 0.51 | 0.00 | 0.87 | 0.00 | N.A. |
| Mean | | 67.0 | 96.0 | 0.8 | 0.61 | 0.12 | 0.63 | 0.20 | |

Note: On adolescent competence, see note 1 in chapter 6.
a. Ages 7 to 70.
b. Ages 17 to 70, days incarcerated over lifetime per year.
c. Ages 17 to 70.
d. Ages 17 to 32.

offending over the life course. The analytical strategy we adopt here, as in the previous narrative chapters, is to constantly question the idea of distinct offending groups and official histories of crime through the narratives from the men themselves, supplemented with data from the Glueck archive.

### The Onset of Violence in Later Adulthood: The Life History of Giuseppe

So I grabbed the knife, grabbed the end of the bedpost, and I got up. That's the last thing I remember. Then I opened my eyes and I was propped up against the wall between the kitchen sink and the doorway. [My roommate] was on the floor, a little round hole in the middle.

Giuseppe experienced his first arrest for violence after age 32. However, from an examination of information from other records in the Glueck archive, including his own self-report, it appears that Giuseppe was no stranger to either crime or violence much earlier in his life. In fact he was a persistent offender who committed crimes in childhood, adolescence, and adulthood. On the basis of his arrest history, one could make a case that Giuseppe was one of the "baddest" men in our study. For example, he had thirty-eight arrests before age 32 and forty-eight overall (from age 7 to 70). Surprisingly, before age 32, he had spent only 2.4 years of his life incarcerated. He later spent significant time in prison, because at the age of 55 Giuseppe was arrested for murder. He was accused of killing his roommate and was eventually convicted of manslaughter.

Giuseppe's criminal career started early. In his first interview for the Gluecks' study at the age of 14, he reported that his involvement in crime had begun at the age of 5. He was arrested thirteen times as a juvenile, primarily for burglary and larceny. His involvement in crime did not diminish in adulthood. He was arrested twenty-five times in young adulthood (17 to 32), and his record included arrests for burglary, larceny, receiving stolen goods, forgery, nonsupport, and drunkenness.

Giuseppe never completed grammar school, along the way repeating grades 1, 2, 4, and 5. His Wechsler-Bellevue IQ scores were as follows: full scale 98, verbal 93, and performance 104. As a juvenile, he spent only nine months in reform school despite his rather lengthy juvenile arrest record. Giuseppe joined the Merchant Marines at the age of 16. He needed his mother's consent to get into the merchant service because of his young age. He told us that there were two notary publics in the neighborhood he grew up in. One was Irish and one was Italian. He took his mother to the Irish notary because she did not understand English, only Italian. The Irish notary asked his mother if she realized her son was going to maritime school. His mother heard the word school and signed the papers.

Giuseppe's adult life consisted of considerable job instability, multiple marriages, nonsupport, adultery, gambling, and extended periods of drunkenness (see Table 8.1 for quantitative details). He was described in the Gluecks' files as a "chronic loafer," because he worked about two months a year over an eight-year period. There is evidence that Giuseppe purposely loafed to avoid support payments for his former wives. At age 31, his probation officer stated that Giuseppe was "nothing but a bum with big ideas." Giuseppe did not fare well in the military either. After seven months he received an undesirable discharge from the Army because he was persistently AWOL. He maintained that he hated Fort Dix because it was "too big."

At his age 25 interview, when asked for the reasons he was delinquent, Giuseppe stated, "I never had a decent home or even the ordinary things most children should expect from their parents. I was always adventurous and would never be tied down—loved to go to different places and see different things. I still believe that money can buy anything and most of my stealing has been motivated by this belief. I was out to get what I could, no matter how."

In his thirties, Giuseppe was caught in a pattern of heavy drinking and crime. He and a partner were in the junking business, but as Giuseppe pointed out, "[we were] stealing more of the junk than we were finding." Giuseppe then clarified, "It wasn't really stealing . . . it was taking it without consent." Giuseppe and his friend would start drinking at 10:00 A.M. in a bar and stay there until 3:00 the following morning. "At 5:00 in the morning we'd go out and get some more junk, get a couple hours' sleep, and go back. So that kept on, kept on."

It was during this period that Giuseppe married and had his first experience with violence, an incident that did not appear in his official criminal record. As Giuseppe recounted,

Heavy arguments started. She was a beautiful son-of-a-bitch and I can't take that away from her. So one night I come home, and I've been drinking, but I was never violent or loud or anything like that. And she started on me. She started scratching up my face. I tried to hold her back and she was scratching up my face. I mean, real scratches. I didn't hit her that night, but she says, "Get out." And I said, "What? You shitting me? Get out? It's my house." So she called the police. Meanwhile, I was washing my face, and the police came as I was washing my face. The combination of the blood and the water without drying it, I looked horrible. The cops wanted me to get out. I said, "You can't throw me out of here!" He said, "I'm going to take you down to the station house." I said, "Who looks bad? Me or her?" I said, "Do you see a bruise on her? Look at me!" So he says, "You're rowdy and noisy." I says, "Do I sound like I'm rowdy and noisy? I came home, yeah I had a few drinks, what's the big deal?"

Giuseppe eventually divorced this woman and went to live in a small town in rural Massachusetts. At the time, he was doing carpentry work. A friend of his who was recently divorced had no place to live, so he was staying with Giuseppe. Both were heavy drinkers. Giuseppe was also taking medication (Valium) because of an earlier injury to his back. Giuseppe claimed that he was unaware of the danger of combining Valium and whiskey.

Giuseppe tells the story of his drinking that culminated with Giuseppe killing his roommate.

I started out buying a pint of whiskey. So I'd sit down in the house, the television, and have a whiskey and a beer, and next thing you know it went to a quart. I was drinking that. Meanwhile I'm doing all this sitting, sitting, sitting, no exercise and I'm taking the Valium. By this time I'm taking the Valium with the whiskey. So then I thought, there's no sense buying two quarts, I'll buy a half gallon. So strange as it may sound to you, I was drinking a whole half gallon a night. I was rushed to the hospital twice. My blood count was 375. Four hundred [and] you're dead. My brother-in-law found me in a field, my mouth was split open, and all my teeth out. My nose was broken. Oh then, somebody found me in the snow bank. Anyway, I went through several, several cases of detox. The last one I was determined I was going to stay and make it work. At this particular place, [name of hospital], I had walked out on them once before. This time they took all my clothes away and gave me a bathrobe and slippers . . . I told the doctor, I want a pair of pants. He wouldn't give them to me, so I swore, I'll walk out of here like this. The next thing you know they actually struck me down on the bed. Struck me down on the bed. I was angry. Furious. So finally they had me committed to a mental hospital. Anyways, I was there for about three months. And by this time my legs had gone, and I still walk with a cane. So my legs had gone. So finally I talked my sisters into getting me out of there. So they got me out of there and took me back to my home.

Giuseppe continued his account, leading up to the violent incident.

By this time I got my license back and I started working again at [name of company]. And the next thing you know I started drinking again. And it didn't take long to build up to half a gallon again. I can remember nights, in order to get to bed—Marty was staying with me again in the front room—in order for me to get to bed I had to crawl across the floor, and I remember one time grabbing onto the bedpost to put myself in bed. Meanwhile, Marty came home one day and he won a ham down at the market. I get real sad when it comes to this. So, he come home with the ham, and he opened it up and put it on a plate, took a couple slices, put it in the refrigerator. Then, Marty was friendly with this nutcake called J.D. A nutcake. He tried to kill Marty with a big long monkey knife one time when Marty was sleeping. So I knew he was a fruitcake. And he comes in the house, with Marty, they were both drunk. What you got to eat, Marty? He says, oh, there's ham in the refrigerator. So he takes out the ham. Instead of cutting it like a human being, J.D. starts to rip it apart with his fingers. I says, "What the fuck, you an animal? Use a knife." He says, "Who the hell you calling an animal?" The next thing you know he's taking a knife out of his pocket. Marty comes running in and grabs a hold of him. So I had a spatula and I hit J.D. in the face with the spatula and I cut him over here (points to his right eye). So finally we got him out of the house. I knew he was a nutcake. And I knew Marty never locked the front door. So I put a knife alongside the bed. Well, later that night, I was laying down. First I was drinking, drinking real heavy, and taking the Valium. I heard the door slam and I woke up. Marty comes in the room and he grabs me—get up, yeah, he's grabbing me, he's pulling me like this. I said, "What the fuck's wrong with you?" He said, "I'm getting rid of those two guys next door, the two I rented the house to. I'm going over and I'm going to get rid of them right now." I knew Marty was afraid of knives. I had put the knife on the end table in case J.D. came in. I had to stop him from bothering my tenants. So I grabbed the knife, grabbed the end of the bedpost, and I got up. That's the last thing I remember. Then I opened my eyes and I was propped up against the wall between the kitchen sink and the doorway. Marty was on the floor, a little round hole in the middle. I had lost my phone . . . I didn't have the money to pay for it, so I went next door and I banged on the window for help. I was bouncing off the walls. I did make my mistake. He didn't hear me or the District Attorney told him not to say it. I said to him and I remember saying it, "I think I stabbed Marty." So he comes over. If I had tried the case knowing what I know today I would have won. He comes over, Marty is on the floor, he puts his hand on his neck and says, "There's a very weak pulse." I says, "Well, call an ambulance." Now he didn't move from that floor, 'cause I sat at the kitchen table still drinking. And I was looking at him. He didn't move. So in comes the other tenant. They were both named B. One was B.D. and the other had a real French name . . . it will come to me. He comes in. The next thing you know the sirens are going and the paramedics come in. Marty had not moved an inch. So they fooled around with him for about 10 minutes. They too lied when they got to court. They were there 10 minutes before they took him to the hospital. So meanwhile the cop finds the knife under Marty and he says, "Giuseppe, is this the knife you used?" I says, "I think so." I didn't say I did, I said I think so. So they took him out and they took me down to the station. Put me in the cell with a cop right outside. Suicide watch they call it . . . At three o'clock in the morning I heard the desk sergeant say, "Marty is dead. Book him, murder one." So they booked me murder one.

At his trial, Giuseppe was found guilty of manslaughter and was sentenced to nine to twelve years in prison. He was paroled after serving nearly six years. When we met Giuseppe, he was living in senior citizen housing in Boston. He was still drinking, despite the fact that his fourth wife had just left him for that reason. When drinking, Giuseppe tried to avoid detection both by the police and by his wife. He told us about his rather amazing strategy.

This is how I do it. When I'm facing my car toward the hotel, right, I have two shots and a beer. When the car is facing the auto shop, I have one shot and a beer. 'Cause the state police patrol that area like a son-of-a-bitch. And if I'm facing the other way, I take the very first right, which is only about 200 feet, and I take another right, a left, the second right, and I'm in the parking lot. I have the number one spot for handicapped. [Discussion shifts to his wife] . . . she was so afraid of what happened last time. You know, I said, "O.K., I won't do it any more." A couple of times she'd come up the stairs in the bar, she'd look in, she'd see me having one. So . . . Saturday night she was supposed to have been gone up to see the baby up in [name of town], but she didn't go because her girlfriend changed her mind, they didn't want to go up that far. Meanwhile I had bought half a pint and I had it here and I was sitting here drinking it. And that did it. She said, "O.K., that's it."

Such motivated behavior seems almost immune to common strategies of deterrence and rehabilitation. Indeed, Giuseppe went to say,

I'm not going to stop my ways. I mean, it's not that I'm drinking heavy like I used to before. And I didn't buy any booze last night, and I didn't buy any booze the night before, and I just had my two and had my beer. And that's where I'm stopping now. 'Cause I try to remember how it started before, how I got started. So I says to myself, don't let it get started. I could lose my license because right away the Hackney Bureau takes your license forever. So I only have what I know I can handle, and I come home and drink my beer. And that's it.

We interviewed Giuseppe two times, and during each interview he had a beer by his side.

Giuseppe led a chaotic life, comparable to the lives led by many persistent offenders described in Chapter 7. For example, Giuseppe lived many places, he was married and divorced or separated at least four times, he had an erratic employment history with long periods of loafing, and he received a dishonorable discharge from the Army. Giuseppe also had an extensive criminal record and on average he spent 55 days incarcerated per year over his adult life (see Table 8.1). At age 14, an analysis of Giuseppe's Rorschach read, "So completely irresponsible, flighty, unreliable, he lacks so completely any sense of self-discipline, control, persistence . . . He would like to have everything, get everything. He has strong wishes and impulses, but is unable to control them for any great length of time." Perhaps foreshadowing his adult life, his prognosis derived from this Rorschach analysis read, "It is difficult to see how he could be appealed to or educated, and it is likely that the psychopathic trends will remain dominating or even become more pronounced."

Toward the end of our interview, we asked Giuseppe to reflect on his life. Like the persisters we examined in Chapter 7, Giuseppe saw his life as "wasted." He went on,

Totally wasted. I didn't know I had the intelligence I have. The man in the GED school said to me, "Did your mother and father speak English?" I said, "No." He says, "It's the biggest shame that ever happened to [you]. Who used to look at your report cards?" I said, "Nobody. I used to sign them and bring them back." He said, "You had great potential . . . you could have gone to college with no problem at all." I didn't know I had a lot of intelligence. I passed with no sweat. I could have gone to college. I could have been somebody. Hey, I'm not blaming my mother and father, they just didn't speak English. And my brothers and sisters were not that much older than I was so nobody cared to help me with my report card. If my father or mother spoke English, or a little

English, and knew what the hell was going on, they would have kicked the shit out of me and I would have got better grades. And wouldn't have just gone up to school and sign a paper myself and quit at 16. I already was in the eighth grade . . . I quit school and joined the Merchant Marines and that was it.

Like some of the persistent offenders, Giuseppe characterizes his lack of education as a missed turning point. Except for the rather dramatic act of violence in late adulthood, Giuseppe's life history is much like the lives of persistent offenders we investigated in Chapter 7.

### Additional Narrative Accounts of Adult Violence

We examined four additional life-history narratives from men who in later adulthood were involved in violence that came to the attention of the authorities. The types of crimes involved varied markedly and added to the complexity of understanding the "late onset" of violence. For example, Roger's most serious incident of violence involved a dispute with a neighbor. Unlike Giuseppe's narrative, this particular incident of violence was not tied to drinking, although other incidents of violence in Roger's life were alcohol related. He recounted the following:

> *Roger:* I had one. I just remembered. '65 or '66—a neighbor, a guy
>   that lived on the same street I lived on, his dog was out—a
>   German shepherd. He was attacking small dogs on the street
>   and he grabbed one one day and literally tore it apart practically.
> *Q:* This was a dog who attacked other dogs?
> *Roger:* Yeah. And I had grabbed a broken shovel handle and went
>   after the dog. The guy was up the street and I went up and I
>   turned around and told him, "Do something to the goddamn
>   dog or I would." He made a comment about being pretty brave
>   with a club in my hands, and I turned around and handed the
>   club back to my wife, saying, "Here, get rid of this goddamn
>   thing. I don't need it with this asshole." And when I did, he went
>   to the back of his car and come back with a bumper jack and
>   started swinging. He hit my wife on the side of the head,
>   fractured her skull. And he swung at me like he was chopping a
>   tree. I put my arm up. Got this part of my arm all smashed up

[points to his forearm]. I had a double compound fracture with a reverse dislocation. And I got away from him, went into my house, and come out with a 30–30 rifle that didn't have stock on it. And fortunately he had three kids standing in front of him. Otherwise he would have been dead today. So he went in assault and battery with a dangerous weapon. And they got a cause complaint on me—assault with a dangerous weapon. They sentenced me to five years in state's prison and suspended the sentence. But that was it. I haven't had any more trouble with the law or anything else. What pisses me off is when I went to court on it, the D.A. turned around and said there was nothing he could do, but if I had shot and killed him it could have been justifiable homicide.

Q: So you received a suspended sentence, did you get put on probation or anything?

Roger: Actually yes, but the probation officer was the kind of a guy that let it slide.

Q: Do you think you could have killed him?

Roger: Oh, absolutely. That's one of the things the judge asked me. He said, "Would you have killed him?" And my exact words, and I can never forget them, was "In order to protect my wife, yes." That's exactly what I told him, and I would have. If those three young kids weren't in front of that guy, he'd be dead. That's the only thing that saved his life was them three young kids. I didn't want to hurt them.

Q: Now did you have any trouble with him afterward?

Roger: No, he was sentenced to five years, and he went away.

Roger had three arrests for assault and battery along with the arrest for assault and battery with a dangerous weapon just described. More precisely, he was arrested for assault and battery at ages 35, 36, and 37 and in two of these cases he was convicted, but did not receive any jail time. In fact, all of Roger's time in confinement occurred during his juvenile years (see Table 8.1). The last time he was arrested for violence was at age 42. All three of the earlier arrests for assault were part of a larger set of domestic problems coupled with alcohol abuse. Roger was classified by the Gluecks' research team as an excessive drinker; he had five arrests for drunkenness on his record, the first occurring at age 19. In our interview, Roger claimed that his first wife was "running around all the time. I just didn't go for it and I ended up getting grabbed for abuse." Roger and his wife divorced shortly after his arrests for domestic violence.

In another narrative, Rocco described an incident of domestic violence when asked if he had any trouble with the law. Tellingly, Rocco appeared to distinguish crime from involvement in violence between nonstrangers. In response to our question, Rocco exclaimed, "What do you mean, like a criminal thing?" He then provided the following account:

> *Rocco:* Oh, oh they even got me involved with one of my sister-in-laws. They tried to pull my hack license. I forgot about that, see just pulled that one out. So, we went out dancing, to have a couple of drinks [me, my wife, and my sister-in-law]. We got back to my place, the sister, [name]. And I mentioned to her, I says [name], you know you got a couple of children at home. And she had mentioned that she you know fell for another guy. And this guy was no bargain, either. I knew her husband, too. He was a boozer, but he was a hard worker. And I'm trying to explain to her, I says you know you're making a big mistake, you're going from the frying pan into the fire. And in the course of back and forth, you know, I'm reasoning with her, and remember the background she has, and she was half in the bag, so her smarts are completely gone. She came after me with a bottle. This is at my house now.
>
> *Q:* Now how old were you? Do you remember?
>
> *Rocco:* Yeah, about 34. She was about, probably, late twenties. So, I picked up a chair, to defend myself against the bottle and she coming rushing at me—it was like a chrome legging chair. And she injured something in her neck or something, you know the doctor. And Jesus within a week she had a collar, a Dormers[?] collar. Is that what you call them? And they swear out a warrant on me for assault and battery. I never hit her. She ran into the chair, I was ducking that bottle, O.K.? So, with the help, of course, of the mother in-law. She hated my guts. She called me a guinea, you eff-ing guinea, see the resentment was there, you know? So, they swore the warrant.
>
> *Q:* Well, what happened?

*Rocco:* Oh, I was found guilty, fined $50. He [his lawyer] told me, don't put your wife on the stand. I should've listened to him. 'Cause she got all confused. She sunk me, ok.

The following exchange with Rocco reveals the varying perceptions of violence and crime held by the Glueck men.

*Q:* So was that the last time in your life that you had any kind of violence?
*Rocco:* Oh I didn't instigate no violence.
*Q:* No, I know.
*Rocco:* What do you mean by that? Did I instigate it?
*Q:* No, I didn't say you . . .
*Rocco:* Of course I had minor altercations over my life.
*Q:* Just arguments or . . .
*Rocco:* Oh, no, I got, in fact I could've got this guy fired. Years later, I was in a club. I knew everybody in the place, you know the neighborhood area and being in the cab industry. Half the people around there were taxi drivers. And I sat at the bar, cold sober. Now, I don't bother any women who are with their guys, unless I know them. You know, have a conversation with them. And I guess this guy was bottled. He was an Irish guy, too. He goes to the john, she instigates a conversation with me, starts a conversation. I was happy, cheerful. I had no desire for her, I know she was with this bloke, ok? And he come back and tapped me on the shoulder and I turn around and he sucker punched me.

We now turn to Paul's account of the violence in his criminal career. We interviewed Paul in prison where he was serving a term of five to seven years for sexual assault on a child. After he served this term, he was to serve an additional term of five to twelve years for the same crime in another state. As it turns out, Paul had a history of involvement with teenaged girls as an adult, although this was the first time he was ever arrested for sexual assault and it was the first time that he had been involved with children. For example, Paul told us that at the age of 29 he "took off" with a 16-year-old girl. Paul left New England for a southern state because the girl's father was after them. This was the second of at least four 16 year-old girls Paul was involved with as an adult. He said, "Sixteen wasn't, I don't know, an unlucky number for me as far as ages were concerned." Some of these young women Paul married, some he did not. In total, Paul was married three times and had seven children with these three women. In addition to the sexual assault in his history, Paul was also arrested for one other incident of violence—violating a restraining order—as well as a series of nonviolent incidents as a juvenile and as an adult (for example, burglary, larceny, and drunk driving). Overall, he was arrested twenty-four times.

The detailed narratives from our interview with Paul regarding the incidents of sexual assault are revealing and disturbing at the same time.

*Q:* They were both sexual abuse charges?

*Paul:* Yeah. One of them, I don't understand what happened. I just don't understand why it happened, the one up in [name of state]. The one in [name of town in Massachusetts] that I'm here for, it was five to seven years, I mean, and I just turned around, you know. I loved this kid, known her since she was like six years old. Nothing ever happened at all until she started screwing around and doing things out on the street. And then I got a stupid idea in my head that if she can give it away to everybody out on the damn street then she can she ought to be able to do a little bit to me. But we didn't. We got involved sexually, but not . . . I don't care if anybody knows about this because I mean it's already on the court records and the police records anyway. We got involved sexually but it was nothing to do . . . there was no penetration or anything else like that. It was sexually fooling around with her and oral sex, as far as I was concerned, with her. Nothing else on her part. She told the police department the same thing and that was it. There was another girl that was involved—so that she claims she was involved but she never was—and I proved that she was a damn liar in court.

*Q:* And in the case in [name of other state] was the one that . . . ?

*Paul:* That was something that should never have happened, but it happened. I was drinking, but I don't blame it on the booze. I should have had brains enough to know better and everything else. I was taking care of two girls—V. was almost seven years old at the time and C. was going on nine. They used to fool around. I used to take them to school, bring them back home, take them to school, bring them back home, take them to stores, take them to shows, everything else. It started earlier. V. would jump up on my lap and she would start fooling around with me and everything else. I'd say, "Hey, cool it. Don't be doing that." She'd say, "Why?" And put her hands down inside my pants and everything else like that. I'd just, I should have cut it. I should have just said, "Look, either cut it out or I'm giving you back to your grandmother and let your grandmother take care of you." I didn't. I got to the point where I was enjoying it. I let it happen. One night we were fooling around and I was going to bed and they wouldn't get out of the damn bed. They wanted to stay in the bed. Their grandmother lived right next to us. Their mother was living in goddamn New Mexico someplace. She was gone . . .

*Q:* She had left the kids?

*Paul:* But their grandmother took care of them. They were staying in the bed and I'd say, "Why don't you go home? Go home and let me get some sleep, would ya?" And I was half drunk anyway. No, we want to stay over here. I said, "All right, stay over here but shut up and leave me alone." I crawled into bed and then they crawled into bed with me and then I'm fooling around and this and that and that. The grandmother . . . I told V. to get the hell out of there. V. used to be my favorite because she was young but she was a nut. But she used to be my favorite. And then she'd turn around and I would sit there with C. And C. and I would watch the television. And I would squeeze C.'s ass and everything else like that. And V. turned around and said, I don't know, something about, "I want to stay with you, I want to stay with you." I said, "No, why don't you get the hell out? Why don't you go home?" And I guess she got mad. She went home and she told her grandmother what we did to her. So her grandmother came home and she came over and took C. out of there and then she didn't know what she was going to do and she had undecided. And I said, "Yeah, O.K." So after she did that I got up and got dressed and went over to my friend's house over across the street and told him. He said, "They're going to nail your ass, you know that?" I said, "Yeah I know." So I turn around and I give him the keys to my house and I said, "Take the stuff out for me, will you, and put it away and do what you want with it." He said, "All right, where are you going?" I said, "I don't know. I think I'll go to [name of town]. See what's going on down there. I'll let you know. I'll get in touch with you." He said, "All right." So I just hitchhiked and went down to [name of town]. The next day they had a goddamn warrant out for me and I knew they would.

The following passage from Paul's interview further reveals the difficulty of treating sex offenders because of their differing perceptions of what is or is not a crime of violence.

I don't really know what to say about that. All I know is I was told by the judge in New Hampshire that if I finish up the sex offender program down here and showed them that I have finished it, that they will suspend the five and put me on parole for the other seven. So I am doing the sex offender program down here but it is hard because I didn't have any schooling and there is a lot of this damn program I can't understand. And parts of it I can understand I keep getting an attitude. It keeps coming back and saying, what the hell does this got to do with me? You know, I was in love with this girl. And this is two kids, and they're talking about male and they're talking about females that are being raped! I wouldn't rape a girl, for Christ sake. I mean, if she was laying in front of me with her clothes off, I wouldn't waste my time, you know. That's just the way I am. I'm just hoping for the best, you know. Because I'm going to go from here, I have to go to [name of institution] and do eighteen months of extensive, intensive sexual therapy down there too. That's part of the program.

The final narrative about violence comes from a man who was a bookie for a good share of his adult life. Alberto's first arrest for violence was a charge of assault and battery on a police officer. He was convicted for this offense and was fined. A few years later, he was arrested for illegally carrying a firearm. He was convicted and given a one-year term in prison, which was suspended. However, in our interview he revealed other acts of violence, information that again underscores the limitations of using official records to describe the onset and desistance of violence in a criminal career. To illustrate, when asked if he was in the military, Alberto told us that he tried to get in, but was rejected. When we asked why, he responded, "Well, because one time I hung a guy. I didn't kill him, but I hung him, so they had that on my record. I never went to jail or anything, no." This was in retaliation for an earlier incident. Alberto told us, "One time he [the boy he hung] hit me across the hand and cut my hand with a knife. So we were playing one time and I threw a rope around this pipe and I put it on his neck. And he was on a ladder and I kicked the ladder and I hung him." Alberto said that he was about 10 or 11 years old when this incident occurred. It does not, however, appear on the criminal record we have. The arrests in Alberto's early career are for burglary and larceny. At the same time, it is noted in his file in the Glueck archive that he was rejected for military service because of his criminal record and "psychopathic personality."

In response to a question about growing up in the West End of Boston, Alberto disclosed his cultural stance on race relations—indeed on racially motivated violence. Such admissions of hatred are rare, even if the sentiments may not be uncommon for this cohort of men.

> *Alberto:* It's changing now. People are going crazy down there.
> You see, when you have a section, when you grow up in that
> section, everybody in it keeps going that same way. It's beautiful.
> Because you have no prejudices because everybody's the same
> there. When you have people coming in, these colored people
> come in, they want to own the place. You know, I'm prejudiced.
> I don't care. I had an argument in there. See that place over
> there? [This interview took place in a McDonald's in a shopping
> mall outside of Boston.] I was standing in line, just like we were,
> and this little girl, I don't know, she came here, her mother said,
> "See how many lines there is." This little girl, I guess she went
> back and told her mother this guy went in front of me. You
> know, I would never go in front of a little kid. The mother stood
> right aside of me and said, "You dirty white trash bastards." I
> said, "You fucking nigger." She was slapping me and I hit her a
> fucking punch. She picked up that thing, one of those, that the
> napkins are in and tried to hit me on the head. She hit me a
> little bit.
>
> *Q:* In this place?
>
> *Alberto:* In this place. Oh, about, almost a year ago. I hit her a
> fucking punch. I went walking in. But there was a girl there, I
> still got her name, a couple of girls, they heard her calling me a
> white motherfucker, a white trash motherfucker. They were
> prejudiced. They teach it in their churches and everything. And

they say not to be prejudiced. But you watch television. Did you ever see that woman? "And we rise . . . and we rise . . ." That's prejudiced. They have it on television. What do you see stand up? All niggers. I am prejudiced, but I'm telling you right.

*Q:* So what happened? Did the security come in?

*Alberto:* Yeah. Well, they grabbed her. There was some white guys, they jumped in. There was a colored guy. He didn't even make a move. The white guys jumped in.

*Q:* Did the police ever come?

*Alberto:* Yeah, the police came, but nothing ever happened. While they were there, the police and everything, I said "You bunch of fucking niggers." I was so fucking mad.

### Emerging Themes Regarding Late Onset

One of the more remarkable aspects of these narratives was the powerful effect that being sent to reform school had on these men. Paul told us that he was quite concerned about the interview and his ability to recall past events. Yet despite years of alcohol abuse, in response to the question, "Do you remember how old you were when you got sent to Lyman?" he answered, "To Lyman? 1942. I think it was in May." He was committed to the Lyman School May 17, 1942. Speaking about the masters at the Shirley Industrial School, Rocco stated that they were "mean" and "if you looked at one of them cross-eyed, he'd give you a backhander. I mean there was a lot of physical abuse." Rocco told us about one stark incident.

I remember one bad experience when I was in there. We were packing ice in an icehouse. It was about 20 below and I slipped and fell into the pool, into the water. The guard, when I got out of the pool, punched me in the nose, broke my nose and put me in the corner, had me sitting in the corner at 20 below temperature, soaking wet, for two hours. You know I had that thermal problem, whatever. I mean that son of a bitch, cocksucker. When I get that memory it bothers me. That was one of my saddest experiences. He was a drunkard, his name was [recalls the guard's name]. He's long dead and I hope he's rotting in hell, because it's not only me he abused, but he abused everybody else.

Some of the men saw their commitment in and of itself as unjust. Alberto told us that he was sent to reform school for breaking windows and being a "pain" in school. He lamented, "You know, today you shoot someone, you can't go to the can, but in my time . . ." In fact, Alberto revealed that he had three commitments. In total, he served 725 days in reform school, more than any of the other men in the late onset of violence group. "In those times, if you do anything, that's all they'd send you to those places and you go out and you go back." When asked if the experiences at Lyman changed him in any way, Alberto replied,

Well, in this respect . . . they took my ranks [privileges] away. In other words, it wasn't called for. It wasn't called for. Today, murder, they don't go to the can today. Oh, he's only a minor. You see it every day. There's a lot of nutcrackers in the world. You know something, I can remember when I was shining shoes. I didn't have a twenty-five-cent license and the cop pinched me and took my shine box away. To make a living. How's that? I remember that distinctively. Ain't that something? I had to go get a license. He was hanging on twenty-five cents. I almost got pinched for selling papers. There was nothing else in them times. They had to find something to pinch you for. You can make a record, that's what I'm talking about, it was so bad, the kid, trying to make an honest living . . . The only thing that was bad was that in my time we took advantage of kids. Of the poor kids, like the West End and North End, they took advantage. Like, you go to court, you were guilty. Because our parents had no schooling, you know. Like my father had no schooling at all. My father spoke broken English. My mother was a village woman. Like, she didn't know laws or anything like that. They have laws, they have lawyers, they have this, and they have that. At that time, if you had nothing, you were a victim. I'm telling you, you could sell papers and go to court.

It was clear that Alberto felt singled out because of his social class and ethnic status. Such feelings lead to cynicism about the world, especially the criminal justice system (see, for example, Sampson and Bartusch 1998). Like other men we interviewed, Alberto discussed the corruption of the criminal justice system. "Who do you think are the biggest crooks? Cops. If I ever wrote a book about how they get paid, and the things I have seen and done. I'm talking about the cops! Christ, they're going to have to put them all in jail. Every one of them! You know, one time when I got pinched for numbers, the guy was like, hey . . . I said, 'I put plenty of bread on your table.' He shut his mouth. He knew what I was talking about." He concluded, "Tell me who ain't a thief today?" referring to politicians, judges, lawyers, and police officers.[2]

On the whole, this group of men did not report many turning

points. In fact, what stood out was a lack of turning points. The typical response to the question—Do you think you have had any turning points in your life?—was "Nah" or "I don't think so." In this regard, as well as others, these men resemble persistent offenders. Alberto, for example, never served in the military, had no long-term employment that had any intrinsic or extrinsic meaning, was a street urchin as a kid, ran "numbers" as an adult, and developed no genuine relationships and remained single throughout his whole life (see Table 8.1 for quantitative details). Similarly, Rocco did not serve in the military, although he "really wanted to serve." A psychiatrist said he could not stand the discipline or authority of the Army, and he was rejected as unfit for military service. He was employed as a cab driver for forty-five years—a job that implies transience and impermanence. Rocco was married and divorced twice plus he lived with several women. He spoke fondly of a woman he had been with who was a good deal older than he was—"we got along really good, almost like a second mother for me." Roger indicated that he did not think he had any turning points, because "I've done basically the same as I've always done. I don't think I've changed anything. I know there's been no radical changes." Paul talked about missed opportunities as his turning point, as we shall see. Ironically, the one man who had a turning point was Giuseppe. He stated that "moving to [name of town outside of Boston] was the turning point. That was a turning point. It was a happy thirteen years, Jesus Christ. I had beautiful land, a garden. I had a sixty-five-foot deck and a three-hundred-foot frontage lawn, the same amount in the back, plus all the land. And the pond. It was great. It was great. And I used to have a garden, by about 60 by 43. And I used to plant tomatoes, and peppers and cucumbers. It was great." This was also the place where Giuseppe stabbed and killed his roommate.

In addition, these narratives show the prominent role that alcohol abuse plays in violence and crime in general. These men drank large amounts of alcohol. When asked how much he drank, Paul told us, "Oh God, you don't want to know that. I drank until I couldn't drink no more. That's all I can tell you." He continued, "It would start off with beer and then it would go from beer to Jack Daniels. And then from Jack Daniels it would change over to vodka. And then it would be beer and vodka. And then it would be anything I could get my hands on. When I ran out of money, then I went down into Wild Irish

Rose and Thunderbird and all the good stuff on the wine list, you know? Wild Irish Rose, Thunderbird, Mad Dog." Recognizing the connection between drinking in bars and violence (see, for example, Cook, Moore, and Braga 2002), Paul told us that he drank at home most of the time, because "bars are too easy to have fights in. Everybody wants to fight. I stay away from them. I'm not a fighter."

The costs of alcohol abuse did not seem to deter future drinking, as we saw in Giuseppe's narrative. Roger too was labeled an "excessive drinker" by the Gluecks' research team, and the bulk of his violence was alcohol related. Along the same lines, Paul stated that he "constantly" experienced blackouts from drinking. He went on, "The last few years it's been worse and worse. I'd wake up and not even know where I am, what my name was sometimes or anything. And I couldn't understand why. You know, Jesus, it seemed like it was getting worse and worse all the time, you know. And I'd keep saying, stop, this is crazy. But I wouldn't do it [stop drinking]. I'd just keep on doing it." Paul started drinking at age 15. "My old man was an alcoholic. My old man got up in the morning and the first thing he would do is go in the closet and take a drink of goddamn port wine and wash it down with a little bit of stock ale or beer. I knew all his favorite ones because, I mean, after he used to go to work, or after he used to go down to the bar, I should say, then I would go into the closet and I would take a little bit of it. Where he had it marked I'd fill it up with water." Paul was thrown out of the Army for drinking. In fact, he claimed that every crime he was involved in was related to drinking. For example, he described a burglary on his record—"The one in Maine was for breaking and entering into the store, but we broke into the store to steal some beer. And we stole the beer and sat there and drank it until the cops came. So that was that."[3]

Our narratives also reveal the role that human agency plays in life-course outcomes. Rocco claimed with respect to Lyman, "I could have gone out of there with anger and become a crook, but that wasn't my desire." This is from a man who has no concerns about using violence as a problem-solving tool. Like the persistent offenders in Chapter 7, these men did not make excuses for their crimes. For example, Paul said, "I blamed all my troubles on the fact that I was there in South Boston, that I lived in South Boston and I had a reputation to uphold and everything else. So everything else was their fault. But it wasn't. It's my fault. It wasn't South Boston's fault." Although Paul had a "pretty lousy" life, he recognized that he "had an opportunity to do something," but he didn't take advantage of the opportunity.

### Desistance in Later Adulthood: The Life History of Art

> I'm an impulse guy as far as violence. I mean I can't consciously plan a violent thing, but if somebody come along and hit me the wrong way, I'd just turn around and let him have it. He who hits first hits last, that was the way I was brought up. [But not now?] . . . Oh, I could do it, but I'd put a brake on it. Well, when my physical condition more or less prevented me from really following through on something.

Art had a record of violence as a juvenile and a young adult, but he desisted later in life (after age 32). His case illustrates the complex nature of both continuity and change present within the same life. Moreover, this particular case demonstrates why long-term data on crime are needed and the importance of questioning official criminal histories on the basis of data from narratives. Looking at Art's life, especially the first thirty years, one sees plenty of evidence for continuity in antisocial behavior across a variety of life domains. For example, Art was involved in criminal activity during childhood, adolescence, and young adulthood. In addition, he received a bad conduct discharge from the Navy, violated his parole and was sent back to prison, had problems with his boss, and once hit his wife during an argument.

This continuity in antisocial behavior is not surprising when observed in the context of Art's upbringing. His life record reveals a wide array of risk factors for serious trouble. Art was an "illegitimate" child; during childhood he engaged in various forms of conduct disorder (for example, running away, truancy, and smoking); he was placed in several foster homes as a child; his family moved excessively (nineteen moves and ten schools before age 14); he was poorly supervised by his parents; he had a criminal and alcoholic father; he was exposed to domestic violence in his home; he suffered child abuse and neglect as well as erratic discipline; he had a weak emotional attachment to his parents; he repeated grades one and five; and he engaged in serious delinquency leading to multiple incarcerations in reform school. When asked at age 71 if he had had any troubles as a kid, Art responded that he had some "minor problems." He talked about stealing and an incident of arson. What he did not reveal was the extent of his early criminal behavior, including two unofficial reports of violence. In one incident, Art attacked another child in foster care with a tree limb, and in another incident he pulled a knife on an acquaintance. His official record included five arrests as a juvenile and eight arrests as a young adult (from age 17 to age 32). Perhaps the only thing that Art had going for him was an IQ score of 110, about 18 points above the average for the delinquents in the Gluecks' study.

At his age 32 interview Art was in prison, where he had spent a considerable amount of time during his adult life: fifty-eight months between the ages of 17 and 25 and sixty-five months between the ages of 25 and 32. Including his juvenile career, Art spent a total of thirteen years incarcerated in reform school, prison, or jail. As evidence of the difficulties he had with authority, Art had trouble getting along with his parole officer. His parole was subsequently revoked and he served another eighteen months in prison. Art "maxed out" his sentence and subsequently did not return to parole status. He proudly stated, "I didn't owe them anything. I just thumbed my nose at them and I walked out."

Despite this bad start in life and substantial continuity in antisocial behavior across key developmental stages, Art's later life—after age 32—reveals equally stunning change. One of the most significant changes in Art's later life was his marriage at the age of 39. Another major event was finding permanent employment through his father-in-law. Art was not afraid of hard work. Unlike many of the Glueck men, Art took educational and vocational courses during adulthood. For example, he went to radio and electronics school full time in hopes of becoming a radio operator for the Merchant Marines, in which he served after his unsuccessful stint in the Navy. While he was going to radio school, he was working nights, part time, at a local university as a maintenance man. When he ran out of money, he took a full-time job doing radio and TV repair at age 38.

Unlike some of the Glueck men who desisted from crime, Art did not have a successful career in the military. In fact, the opposite is true; he received a bad conduct discharge from the Navy. This is surprising because Art went into the service early (at age 17) and was assigned to overseas duty. According to previous analyses these are two of the key elements of a successful transition from the military to adulthood (Sampson and Laub 1996). Clearly Art's is not a simple story regarding the military and desistance from crime.

Art also had opportunities for skill development, although he admits that he did not take advantage of those prospects. Of course, his bad conduct discharge prohibited him from using the G.I. Bill. Nevertheless, Art regarded the military experience as an important event in his life and he recognized it as a missed opportunity. At age 71, he said, "It was an important role. But I mean . . . I wasn't smart enough to take advantage of it, because I rebelled against the discipline. And as far as I can tell, the B.C.D. was a bad decision. All I got it for was for mouthing off. I had a summary court martial, not a general, and I swear the reason I got it was because I gave the planning officer a smart answer." Again Art's inability to function in situations demanding conformity and rule-abiding behavior is evident. But at his age 71 interview, Art understood this aspect of his life. Reflecting on his regrets, he said, "Well, in the first place, I wouldn't have got in trouble with the law, okay, for one thing. I wouldn't have been so smart when I was in the service. And I wouldn't have gone over—when I was a kid I wanted to go over—they say, 'No liberty.' I says, 'See you later.' Boom, I go, you know what I mean? I think my attitude would have changed. But in retrospect, hindsight is better than foresight."

Art's marriage was the chief turning point that helped steer his criminal trajectory toward one of conformity with the law. Like many of the Glueck men, Art is not sure what he would have done without his wife. "If I didn't meet her, I don't know what I would have been doing. That's my honest opinion. When I met her, my life changed. My ideas of responsibility changed. Up to the time I met her, I didn't have a care in the world." Art went on to say that his marriage "more or less tamed" him, because it gave him a "responsibility" that he never had. We pressed him about how and why marriage changed him. We present his detailed response because it helps reveal our emerging understanding of the nature of turning points for many of the Glueck men.

*Q:* How did that happen? How did you get from that point?
*Art:* Transitional period, I don't know. It just happened.
*Q:* It just happened?
*Art:* It just happened. I mean I sat there, and now I was sitting there [pointing toward two different places]. It wasn't conscious. It was unconscious.
*Q:* Were you looking to get married?

*Art:* Not really, not really. I guess I was in the right mood, the right time, and the right girl.

*Q:* All right, I'm trying to figure this out, since this is important. Because we're hearing a lot from guys that marriage changed them. And I'm trying to figure out why.

*Art:* Responsibility.

*Q:* Responsibility, is that it?

*Art:* Right. It's a gradual process.

*Q:* You just try to think about things a little differently.

*Art:* I mean, it wasn't a conscious, say, "Hey, I've got to do this. Hey, I got married here. Now I've got to do this." It was just a gradual thing. It just more or less fell into a niche.

*Q:* But it's a niche that felt comfortable?

*Art:* Right. Oh, yeah. I feel fine, entirely comfortable.

*Q:* And do you think it's a timing thing? Do you think if you met, could you have met somebody at twenty and turned your life around?

*Art:* I don't think so. I was too young and stupid.

*Q:* Do you think that there are turning points in people's lives?

*Art:* Yes, but see, it's conditional on happenstance. It's conditional on your feeling, the event, the time the event occurs, or who you were with. It's something that's, I'd say, strictly emotional. I mean there's nothing you can put down on a piece of paper, after X amount of years, you gotta do this. You can't, because I know people, for crying out loud.

In addition to changing his perceptions of responsibility, Art's wife was also instrumental in helping him find work. His father-in-law's connections were "very important" in helping him to get his chance working for the city. He went in as a temporary employee and then worked his way up from there. As Art told us, "He got me the job. The rest I had to do myself. He got me in, but then I had to perform myself." Despite an unstable work career and more than ten years of prison time as an adult, Art worked twenty-seven straight years for one employer.

For Art, desistance was linked to key turning points, especially marriage and work, human agency, and age. Art talked in particular about the impulsive nature of violence and the "braking effect" of aging. He told us, "I mean I can't consciously plan a violent thing, but if somebody come along and hit me the wrong way, I'd just turn around and let him have it." When asked whether this behavior had changed over time, Art said that he could engage in violence even now at age 71, but he tries to "put a brake on it." He went on to discuss the "brake" idea.

> *Q:* When did you feel you started to put a brake on it in your life?
> *Art:* Well, when my physical condition more or less prevented me from really following through on something. I mean I had it happen a couple of times around the city, some guy was sitting in the car, he come over and give me a lot of hard time, you know. I wasn't right, but he reached in for me, so as he reached in I just popped him. I mean, I didn't know if he was going to try to hit me or what. But I got in first, I wasn't taking no chances. He who hits first hits last, that was the way I was brought up.
> *Q:* And how old were you when this guy did this?
> *Art:* Oh God, this was about—let me see, . . . I was in my sixties. So I mean I couldn't—at that time I wasn't going to get out there—this kid was about 30 years old. I mean he could have wiped me up probably, you know what I mean? Because I didn't have the physical stamina. In fact I had my back, that's when I had my back injury.

An interesting question is whether situations can be manipulated to allow the "braking effect" to take place earlier in the life course of individuals.

On many accounts, Art is one of the success stories among the delinquents we interviewed, especially in light of his earlier adversity. First off, he was alive at age 71; almost half of the delinquents had died by age 70. Second, he worked for twenty-seven years at one job and rose through the ranks to become a supervisor. Third, he had loved the same woman for thirty-two years of marriage. As Vaillant (1977) points out, living, working, and loving are the principal elements of successful adaptation to life, and Art had them all.

### Emerging Themes Regarding Late Desistance

For late desisters, similar to desisters in Chapter 6, key institutions involved in the desistance process were marriage, employment, reform school, and the military. Our other interviews support this view. As was true for Art, Donald's wife played a key role in the process of desistance. The following exchange with Donald and his wife provides the details.

Q: What happened though? I'm curious about this—you were in Lyman [reform school], then you went to Concord [an adult prison in Massachusetts], and then suddenly you stopped your involvement in crime. Did something happen to you?

*Donald:* No, I met her and she stopped it.

Q: How did you guys meet?

*Wife:* In a bar room.

Q: In a bar room.

*Donald:* Through a friend of hers.

*Wife:* Yeah.

Q: And what year was that, that you met?

*Donald:* '55. [Donald was 27 years old.]

*Wife:* Yeah.

*Donald:* '55. And I was married before I met her.

*Wife:* He was married before me.

*Donald:* But it didn't last.

*Wife:* So that's probably one reason he stopped too, you know.

Q: And did you know about his past when you met him?

*Wife:* Not when I first met him. But he started telling me, you know.

Q: It didn't scare you?

*Wife:* I liked him, oh yeah.

Q: It didn't worry you?

*Wife:* No.

Q: Did you ever have to worry about keeping him in line?

*Wife:* No. He never, you know, did anything after that. I mean robbing people and anything like that or breaking into a store.

In our discussion, the timing of his marriage came up relative to Donald's desistance from crime. Donald noted that he was out of trouble before he met his second and current wife. But she clearly helped him stay out of trouble, reflecting the dual interplay of choice and constraint. "I met her in '55 and like I say I got out [of prison] in 1950 so there's a five-year difference that I wasn't in trouble." Donald married his first wife about seven or eight months after he got out, and stayed married for about five years. His first wife was an "everyday drinker."

Donald pointed out, "And I wasn't going nowhere with that. Because I was making the money and she'd be drinking it and where was I going? I wasn't going nowhere." Donald thought he was influenced by his family—"like all my relations—all up in Canada—they're all well off. They earned it. They all worked. And what they got, they got plenty. They had nothing and they weren't nothing. They were just poor farmers. They all turned out good. I went 'geez, if they can do it, I can do something.' At least they had their own homes and everything like that. I wasn't getting nothing. So I said this is a turning point somewhere."

Thus, while marriage was clearly important in Donald's life, his own actions played a significant role in making the transition from a criminal to a conventional trajectory. "Well, I think I could do better outside than I could do inside. I wasn't making nothing on this side here. Right? I wasn't make nothing this side. I was doing time for nothing. At least outside you could get—you're free and you're making money." Donald continued, "Yeah, I'm 68. I've been out of trouble [not in prison] since 1949. That will be forty-seven years . . . Like I say, well, I met her and got married. But what you gaining when you're inside? You ain't gaining nothing. Right? You're not going nowhere. You don't own nothing. I didn't have a car, for Christ's sake. I bought a Cadillac, my first car."

For Ralph, as one grows older, the investment in family outweighs the apparent benefits of crime, which suggests an interaction between age and perceptions of informal social controls (Shover 1996). He told us, "I guess you get older—your family—you start to think a little bit more of what would happen if you got in any serious trouble. You're always . . . I used to think about making a score. That's about as far as you'd go . . . Like I say, I don't have a clean mind. Like I say, I always fantasize about scores and so on so forth." Ralph elaborated his thoughts on this point:

> By having more money, I mean not my personal gain now because what I would have liked to done—I always feel bad about was not being able to put my kids through college, you know. But now, like I say, the only reason I would need money now is buying houses for the kids, pay off their mortgage and stuff like that. So in this sense, you say Jesus, I've got to make a score. But it's out of the question. It ain't something I'd want to try now. I'm 68.

The bottom line for Ralph was a fear of what doing more time would mean, not for him, but for his family. Like other men who desisted from crime, Ralph's turning point was getting married.

As will be seen below, Carlo had an especially difficult time in reform school and adjusting to civilian life after serving in the military. Carlo told us, "My wife and children keep me living on. They gave me a goal." He continued, "My wife stuck by me. She gave me incentive to live . . . to put behind the hatred." With the support of his wife, Carlo worked hard to give his kids what he never had. Perhaps remembering his difficult start in life, Carlo stated, "I am glad I gave them a start. Now I am ready to die." Carlo's wife was an important influence. "We love each other like a blanket that you lose like when you are a little kid."

For Allen, the military was a transformative experience. "I think it was kind of important. It taught you basically how to get along with different types of people, you know, like blacks and whites, . . . there were a lot of Filipinos in my outfit. Just getting along with different cultures. I found it good."

For Edmund, his reported turning point was a specific incident in the service—getting wounded. Edmund served in the Navy during World War II and in the Army during the Korean War. He said that "after I was wounded I was changed." We pressed him on this point:

Q: How so?
Edmund: I don't know, I settled down more after I got wounded. I guess I got the hell scared out of me so many times. I guess, I wasn't as wild, I used to be a wild kid.
Q: So the wounding—
Edmund: I think that was it.
Q: That was during the Korean War?
A: Yeah.

Edmund also told us that reform school changed him as well. "After the Shirley incident I [swore] I'd never go through anything like that again and I never did. That was a pretty tough place. I think, that's probably one of the best things that happened . . . getting sent there. Otherwise I probably would have gotten into serious crime. Now that I look back on it, it was the best thing for me." This from a man who displayed long-term residential stability, a continuous marriage, and a successful work history throughout his adult life.

In a similar vein, Allen's turning point was a sentence served at Concord for an unarmed robbery. When asked if he kept in line after his stint in prison, he responded, "Oh, yeah. Very much in line. If anybody mentioned going out in a hot car, pulled somebody up or even arguing with somebody, I said no way! I even walked away from a fight. I had to get out of there." Allen continued, "You'd think one dose of prison, like Concord Reformatory, should have been enough for anybody, really . . . I don't know, some guys probably figure they're getting easy money if they stick somebody up or something like that, but you know, it's maybe get a hundred bucks and when that runs out they stick somebody else up. I mean, I can admire a guy who goes out and robs a bank and comes off with twenty-five or thirty thousand dollars. That's compared to the guy that sticks up somebody for a hundred bucks, you know. But to make it for a living, I don't know, I can't see it. You're always running, you know."

Some of the men recalled more vividly their early experiences in reform school or adult prison. For instance, Donald told us that the Lyman School was "rough." He continued, "That was bad. They used to say, "You want to feed the goldfish?" If you did something wrong, you fed the goldfish. You put your feet up on the table and they hit you on the bottom of your feet with a radiator brush. Feeding the goldfish."

Ralph was also embittered by his experience at the Lyman School. He recounted his stay there in detail:

> *Ralph:* I think that I may be more bitter than anything. I've seen things that you wouldn't believe. And I would never, never tell my mother they hit me there. A lot of kids probably did, you know, cry on their mother's shoulder when they come up there. But I would never say a word. I would never let my mother think that I was being harmed or hurt. I got there one time—in fact, I screwed [ran away] a couple of days later. This one guy he hit me—he hit me—I always remembered his name, Mr. [recalls name], and he had a hand like a frigging ham. And he'd give me a . . . cut. He caught me nice.
>
> *Q:* What were you doing?
>
> *Ralph:* He was in his room and it was noisy. He come running up

to me. He never liked me anyway. I had an argument with him before he even became a guard there. He was a student; they were breaking him in. I guess he must have pegged me for a wise guy. He said, "I told you to keep quiet." I says, "Hey, I'm not making any noise." He went whack. I don't know, I said something. And he come at me. I bent down like this. He caught me beautiful. My goddamn face swelled up. You wouldn't recognize me. I was like that for a couple of days. A day or two later, I screwed. I got out of there. I got a key. I come all the way home. My mother used to make me go back all the time. Some of the guys up there, I'll tell you, bad.

Echoing a similar theme, Edmund recounted that the guards at Shirley were "mean as hell. They'd smack you in the face as hard as they could, grown men." Edmund was sent to Shirley for armed robbery. He was with another kid who hit a guy in the head with a two by four and robbed him. He claimed that he did not do anything, but he was there.

Of all the men we spoke with in the late desister group, Carlo seemed to be the most negatively affected by reform school. He was "beaten up, scarred, and torn up" by his experiences in the Shirley School. For instance, he said his teeth were broken when the guards punched him in the face. He also told us that he was handcuffed to a tree naked for eight to nine hours at a time. Furthermore, he reported that he saw boys with sacks over their heads being "screwed in the ass" by guards. He was told, "What are you looking at, asshole? You're next." He recounted a trip to the dentist where the dentist said, "open your fucking mouth you bastard," and he pulled three teeth without any novocaine. He concluded, "I hate fucking people like that. I can't forget things." These experiences became aggravated in the military during World War II. At the age of 18, Carlo entered the Army with enormous hostility and aggression. In his words, he "started to kill human beings." He further stated that "killing allowed me to get my anger and frustration out." The negative effects of the war experience continued when he returned to the States. In his record, the Gluecks' researcher reported that after he came out of the service Carlo claimed that "he started to push people around just like we did over in Germany, but he . . . found out he could not get away with it over here." In adulthood, Carlo was arrested for domestic violence with his first wife, was identified as an "excessive drinker" in his Glueck file, and it was reported that he had difficulties on the job. Apparently he did not get along with his bosses, and he deliberately "loafed" to avoid paying child support. In our interview at age 70, Carlo stated that he carried his bad memories for a long time, although he tried to forget them. He talked repeatedly of his hatred of the state—"the bastards"—for what it did to him and for its failure to respond to his cries for help.

Institutional experiences and labels can have effects that extend into the community in other ways. Ralph reported that when he came out of the Lyman School and was at high school the principal had targeted him—

> anything that was stolen in the school, he'd have me up in that office and he threatened me, you know. I felt like chopping that son-of-a-bitch's head off. He even went so far one time to calling my parole officer, Mr. [name]—I always remembered his name. He actually had him come up to school and that son-of-a-bitch, he threatened me too. And they were blaming me for something I didn't do . . . I don't know why, you know. They always threatened to send me back, and this and that. I wouldn't mind but I minded my own business up there. I see what the situation was. I said, "Shit, these guys—they just don't like the idea of me being there, I guess."

Ralph eventually left school, in part because of this perceived harassment. "I figure, 'Hey, I'm headed for trouble here,' you know."

Despite negative experiences in reform school and prison, the men were still drawn to the seductions of crime and attracted to illicit activity. The importance of local culture and the situational contexts underlying crime and deviance were revealed in Donald's narrative—"I think that's what it is. Every time I drank I got in trouble. If I didn't drink I would never have gotten in trouble I think. [The] South End was loaded with bars years ago—next to each other—everywhere. Everywhere. Everywhere you looked there was bars. And they were all busy. Yeah, day and night." This situational context was conducive to violence. Donald elaborated, ". . . get to drinking, starting fighting. Yeah, that's what it was . . . People—they drank, and then got into fights." Donald was also attracted to a "deviant" lifestyle. He told us that he liked "seasonal" jobs. His wife concurred, with laughter in her voice. Donald explained, "Well, it was better because you worked seven months and you collected [unemployment] for five months."

Ralph's narrative on violence involved armed robbery and assault with attempt to murder. When offering his account, he confided,

*Ralph:* Between you and I, I could remember how many fist fights I've had in my life. I'm not a violent person. When we held up this guy—well, that's a crime of violence, I mean. I never went in with any intentions of shooting anybody or even hitting them or anything. But this kid I was with—he's the one who done the whacking. He hit this guy over the head, you know. I wasn't even at the spot at the time. I had gone out to the front of the store to see if anybody was—

*Q:* This was a store robbery?

*A:* Yeah. He was a Jewish fellow. Jesus, when I got out to the front to look around—it was at night—he had stayed in the shop ironing—he used to have rental tuxedos and stuff. And Jesus all of a sudden I heard this screaming. I turned around, I ran back in. The store was in darkness except for the back, you know. And this kid was—he just whacked him over the goddamn head. I grabbed his hand. I yelled at him, "What the hell are you doing?" Well, anyway, that charge was assault with intent to murder. You get tagged with these titles.

This account highlights the salience of situational and cultural inducements—peers, drinking, guns, and a perceived attractive target to obtain "easy cash."

*Q:* This was a situation where this guy had a lot of money and you knew about that?

*Ralph:* We were going over to Chelsea to drink. He wanted to see this gun—we had been talking about guns. And I stopped off and got the gun. The gun was empty anyway, by the way. It wasn't loaded. It was an old Japanese gun. In fact, the kid that I was with—I hardly knew him—he was a friend of my friends . . . And on the way over he was talking about—we're drinking— we're talking about holding up guys. And then finally we went into this goddamn tailor shop. And the kid who was driving the car, by the way, he got away. Because we had rented a car. He stayed out in the car. But he was a block from the place.

*Q:* Did you get a lot of money?

*Ralph:* We got shit—nothing.

*Q:* What set off this guy that he started hitting—did the guy try to resist?

*Ralph:* Well, when we first come in he [the tailor] got a little hysterical there, you know. We were looking for the money. We were looking around in the back room there. He just started yelling, "Keep quiet, keep quiet." He was making so much noise that I says to this [name of co-offender] I says, "I'm going to take a look up front." So I walked the length of the store, from here probably to the sidewalk. And the store was dark. And there was a restaurant next door. I just looked out—about this time I heard them . . . he let out a yell, I turn around, in the light I could see him holding his head, goddamn blood running down. I ran back and says, "What the hell are you doing?" I grabbed the gun out of his hand. So I says, "Let's get the hell out of here." We bolted out the door and at the same time they come out of this restaurant next door—they heard the yelling and everything. They just stayed with us close enough that we couldn't make it to the car, you know.

*Q:* Now you said that was the only time that you were involved in violence. Right?

*Ralph:* Yeah.

*Q:* Do you have any idea why?

*Ralph:* Well, it's just the way things developed. You went in there—not with the intention to kill anybody or shoot—like I say, the gun was unloaded. But you don't go in there with the intentions of hurting anybody, you know.

*Q:* Had you committed any burglaries before?

*Ralph:* Oh, yes, yes. But I never robbed anybody before. In fact, I always thought of the consequences. Because I always knew that when you start messing with a gun you're going to increase your time in jail. I was always kind of conscious of that, you know, even though I was a little on the wild side. I like guns. I used to like shooting them, not to the extent that I wanted a gun to protect myself or commit any kind of violence with them.

He went on to offer another description of a violent incident.

*Ralph:* The other one was . . . in fact that's not even on my record. Because I sent for my records . . . they are written out in little photocopies. You can hardly see it. I shot a guy in 1949. [Ralph was 21 years old.] I got six months. I had a state lawyer and he told me to appeal. I says, "Appeal? What the hell, are you crazy?" So he says, "Appeal." So, geez, I appealed it. I went back over to Charles Street [the site of the local jail in Boston at the time]. There was a guy over there who I used to go to school with. He says, "What did you get?" I says, "Six months." He says, "Six months? You lucky son-of-a-bitch." So I says, "I appealed." He says "You dumb son-of-a-bitch." He's cursing me out, you know. So I says, "Look, I just done what the lawyer told me."

But anyway the shooting basically—it was an accident. We were drinking there around New Year's, you know. And fooling around with the goddamn gun. And this kid, he told me, "Go ahead, shoot me." So I went across the room. I wrapped the goddamn gun in a blanket. So I figure I am going to hit the goddamn wall. I didn't. I got him under the goddamn armpit. They told me I shot him twice, which was a crock of shit anyway when they grabbed us. Anyway, I'm still friendly with this guy. There was no hard feelings, you know. I walked him down to the police station there. . . .

Q: So what did you get on your appeal? What happened?

A: So I went back to court and I got ten days (laughter). I was lucky on that one.

For at least one man with a long record of crime and violence that included arrests for assault, armed robbery, firearm violations, as well as drugs, gambling, and pimping, the main theme that emerges from his narrative was defiance against authority. In the Glueck files, Mark was described as a "chronic liar," "a-moral," and a "rat—who would for a dime cut his grandmother's throat." His Rorschach assessment taken at age 14 read: "He views relations between people as basically not friendly, but rather as a battle in which one either catches or is caught." In his interview at age 67, it was clear to us that Mark did not like authority. He described himself as "dead set against authority"—and he appeared to have maintained this stance throughout his adult life. For instance, he told us that he was in the Navy, but he did not like to be told what to do. So he "took a walk and overstayed his leave." He received a bad conduct discharge for his behavior. He had five marriages and several jobs as well as periods of unemployment throughout his life. He was a bitter man, who stated emphatically that he "did not care" if he woke up. When asked to assess his life, he concluded, "A waste of time—my whole life has been a waste." Although classified as a late desister because of his official criminal record, Mark's attitudes and behavior in other adult domains besides crime appear akin to those of a persistent offender.

On many dimensions, then, the group of late desisters (with the exception of Mark) look like the desisters we discussed in Chapter 6. Many of these men eventually achieved stability in at least two of the three domains of interest here—marriage, work, and residential location. Also, more explicit in these narratives are the effects of aging on criminal behavior. At the same time, there was and is an edge to the men's lives. There is more crime, more violence, especially domestic violence, and more drinking problems compared with classic desisters. Reading the narratives is an emotionally draining experience, for the accounts underscore the hopelessness, pain, anger, and racism in many of the men's lives.

### Intermittent Offending: The Life History of Patrick

> Roofers and painters are hard drinkers . . . On rainy days you'd always have the excuse, "Well, there's nothing else to do. No place else to go." You'd go to the bar. And then go home and fight with the wife.

We met Patrick, a stereotypical ruddy, round-faced Irishman, about 5 foot, 3 inches, weighing 165 pounds, at the John F. Kennedy Library in Dorchester. With a flair for the dramatic, he insisted that we interview him at this location on Dorchester Bay. Looking out the large-pane glass windows, he said, "The reason I picked this place to meet you is because there's so much history here. I learned to swim over there. My father used to take me out to L Street. We swam out through here. This is where my life began." Like many of the men we spoke with about their upbringing, Patrick observed, "We were not disadvantaged. We were poor, but happy."

Patrick was 66 years old at the time of our interview. In his criminal career, he had six arrests for violent crimes (all assault and battery offenses) during adulthood (after age 17). The first arrest occurred when he was 17½, the second at age 18, the third at age 20, the fourth at age 26, the fifth at age 29, and the sixth at age 30. The last three arrests were accompanied by additional charges for drunkenness. Two arrests were for assaults on his wife and one was for an assault on a police officer. Patrick's life-history narrative reveals the links between ethnicity, work, local culture and social organization, drinking, and assaultive violence.

Growing up, Patrick was part of a gang—the Dripping Daggers. Patrick said that they were not as violent and vicious as today's gangs, because there are more guns available today and they are more widely used. "I always frowned on anybody using a knife or their shoes or anything like that. No, I never . . . it was always a fair fight. Of course there were gang fights and stuff."

When asked about the Lyman School for Boys, Patrick stated that he learned that he never wanted to be incarcerated again. "It taught me one thing—for our era anyhow—the hardest thing you can do in life is stay out of jail." When pressed more on this point, Patrick elaborated:

> In the culture that we grew up in, yeah. My mother told me and I didn't realize what she was talking about until I got older . . . she knew that we'd be doing these things. She never ostracized us. She'd grab us by the ear and give us castor oil and stuff like that, whatever it took when we were little kids. She used to say, "You cannot get caught. If you get caught, you pay the consequences." She never said, "You're forbidden to do this." You see? "You better not get caught." Because she knew that we were going to get in trouble and they were willing to accept it. She just hoped that it wouldn't be too much. "Don't get yourself killed." Yet she was the most law-abiding, church-going, Irish Catholic woman that you could meet. And I didn't realize what she meant when she said, "You better not"—until I got older. She knew we were going to do these things. So all she could do was pray that we would be all right.

Patrick remarked that this situation was a matter of "survival." He referred to himself as a "throwaway kid" from society's vantage point. Kids stole goods to obtain things they did not have or to acquire money. Some of this money was shared with their parents. Organized crime was also present in the local neighborhoods of Boston.

> Everybody knew what everybody was doing. I don't know where Whitey is today, but I wish him luck. [Whitey Bulger, an alleged organized crime figure from South Boston, is currently a fugitive from justice and something of a local hero.] I hope they never get him . . . They accuse him of everything. All I can say as far as he's concerned when I

needed somebody to put some pressure on, to straighten out something, not to hurt anybody, he was always there for me.

As we have heard throughout our interviews, in certain neighborhoods the law-abiding world and the criminal underworld exist side by side and, at times, overlap. In other words, two cultures coexist—one conventional and one criminal, but there is also the recognition of where one belongs. This is a theme developed by Pattillo-McCoy (1999) in her study of a contemporary African-American community striving to negotiate middle-class culture while also struggling with the internal presence of gangs.

Patrick talked about the effects of his involvement in crime on his family. For example, when his father came to see him in Lyman, he had tears in his eyes. Yet Patrick was not aware of the depth of his father's pain until he was older and became a father himself. Yet his mother assured him that everything was all right. Part of the development process is realizing some loss before one can heal. It was not possible for Patrick at age 15 to be moved by his father. Alternatively, this may be an example of not realizing something is important until it is gone. Patrick told us that during his wife's sickness and subsequent death, he realized that he hadn't really appreciated her until she became ill. Interestingly, Patrick revealed that his wife never knew that he had been in reform school. "It was something she didn't have to know. Some things you're not supposed to know," he declared.

The cultural milieu that Patrick grew up in tolerated extensive drinking of alcohol, sometimes leading to alcohol abuse. Patrick reported, "My father drank, yeah. The same as any Irish worker—you know, Irish people—that was a God-given right to them, to be able to take a cold glass of beer. It wasn't a compulsion the way an alcoholic drinks nowadays. It was a way of life. Because they didn't know anything and they didn't—they used to make their own [out] of potato peel and stuff like that." Patrick went into detail regarding his father's production of alcohol during Prohibition.

> My parents . . . came here as kids during the '20s—Prohibition was in. My father couldn't get a regular job. He used to make bathtub gin. And he made good stuff so that people from Galway said, "You knew [name]" . . . The cops had come up the front door—my mother used to have to take the gallon of alcohol on the clothes line which ran from our

street to the next and shoot it over there. But on Saturday nights there would be no booze making in my house because Saturday night . . . my mother and father, everybody went to confession and we had to receive the next day. Saturday night he used to make tonic for everybody in the neighborhood. Now Prohibition was repealed—my father was out of a job. That's like selling pot now. That was an extra way of making a few bucks at that time, making vats of gin. You see. This was before I was born. But remember even during the '30s they used to make—the booze that he made—pachine they used to call it, Irish whiskey. And the neighbors liked it—they wouldn't buy it out of the liquor store. They liked my father's Irish whiskey. He had a little—what I can draw a parallel with is pot—the way pot is now. It's a way of making a quick buck. It's not their livelihood, but it's a way.

As an adult, Patrick worked as roofer. He was also heavily involved in the union, both locally and nationally. From our quantitative data from age 17 to 32, Patrick had a fairly unstable employment history (see Table 8.3). He stated, "Roofers and painters are hard drinkers and hard workers." He told us that he went out after work for drinks. Weekends he spent mostly at home. He recalled, "If I wasn't home, I was in the doghouse. I didn't drink at home. Only with friends and associates. On rainy days you'd always have the excuse, 'Well, there's nothing else to do. No place else to go.' You'd go to the bar. And then go home and fight with the wife."

Patrick stopped drinking in 1968. "I hit my bottom. I knew I was capable of better things. I mean I was going 100 miles an hour and getting nowhere." Patrick was drinking with friends in bars for entertainment after work. He said, "You might go in for one or two after work and get out of the joint at one or two in the morning. Things like that make you start to see. And then go home. Like I said I had enough. I went to AA in 1968 and I haven't had a drink since. I think a turning point in my life was AA." For Patrick, hitting bottom meant experiencing blackouts, having a car accident, and getting in fights—"bar fights, that's all. Drunken brawls." He stated as a matter of fact that "when you drink, you're out of control. When you're drinking you can't do wrong right. If you got to rob a bank you'll probably screw it up." We asked Patrick what he thought would have happened to him if he hadn't stopped drinking. His response revealed his sense of humor, "Who knows? I probably wouldn't be here. Woodstock was the following year. So, who knows? (laughter)." On a more serious note, Patrick said that change has to come from within. "My mother and my wife and my friends had enough of my drinking when I was 18 years old. I didn't have enough of my drinking until I was really . . . The only one that can stop is yourself." Patrick's brother died in a car accident in which alcohol played a role. "He was coming home from the Cape. The driver was drunk and he was hit in the passenger seat. They hit a tree doing 90 miles an hour and he was killed. My other brother was in the back seat and he was injured severely but he came out of it all right. There was four in the car and my brother got killed." Patrick also confided to us that he worried about his own son's drinking. Patrick concluded, "The last thing in the world I wanted to do when I stopped drinking was stop drinking . . . But I knew that something had to be done. There had to be a change in my life and the only thing that I could change is myself. And I was fortunate enough to be steered in the right direction by a friend of mine. And I quit. I met some great people. I met some great people in the program."

Throughout Patrick's interview, the pervasive influence of local culture on crime and alcohol use was striking. This was coupled with a strong defiance and distrust of authority. For example, in a discussion about the service, Patrick said, "Once I got in the service I didn't like authority. I never really appreciated authority. I had rebel blood in me." Patrick told us that he went from being a candidate for officers training school to being discharged as a private. "I got busted when I got back from Korea because I blew my leave and I stayed home for the weekend and—call it article 15—it wasn't a court martial. It was article 15. They took my one stripe that I had. AWOL. Just for the weekend. They wanted me to do KP and I chose not to. I was up in [name of the base] at the time waiting to be discharged and I got busted. No big problem." Patrick received an honorable discharge from the Army.

### Emergent Themes Regarding Erratic Offending

At times the intermittent offenders look like desisters, and at other times they resemble persistent offenders. Such complexity emerges because of the long-term longitudinal data derived from multiple sources that we have at our disposal; the longer the time frame, the more uncertain the simple taxonomy becomes. Nevertheless, a common pattern that emerges in these life-history narratives is that inter-mittent, erratic offenders have a serious problem with alcohol. In ret-rospect it is perhaps not surprising that alcoholic men exhibit such inconsistent offending (Vaillant 1983), with crime sprees often associated with binges or episodes of extreme intoxication.

Mickey, for example, had remarkable marital stability (forty-nine years), residential stability (eighteen years) and home ownership, and long-term job stability (more than twenty years with one company) yet he developed a drinking problem as a way of medicating the pain from a war-related disability. During World War II, Mickey was hit in the head with shrapnel from an exploding hand grenade. He lost an eye, among other serious head injuries. He told us, "The pain would just rip the hell out of me. I was loaded with shrapnel in the skull, on the nerve systems . . . I'd take the medication and drink. Anything to get rid of the pain." Mickey was arrested at least eight times for drunkenness, and he was arrested once for assault and battery at the age of 31. Eventually Mickey did give up drinking and smoking—about fifteen years before we met him at the age of 69.[4]

Sean was an alcoholic who lived several years on the streets of Boston "in and out of detox" and jail.[5] "I lived in the alleys. I bummed money. I wasn't very good at it, wasn't very good at bumming. For some reasons, my legs used to go. But I didn't want to approach people; I was always afraid somebody was going to hit me, which they did. I had a big beard and dirty face—it depends on where you slept. If you slept on a place that had oil then you'd come out the next day and you had oil stuff all over you. I didn't care. Some drunks gave a shit about their appearance. I never did. I just wanted the next drink. I didn't care what I looked like or anything."

When we met Sean at age 66, he told us that "I was drinking even when you people were interviewing me as a teenager." Not surprisingly, his recall of earlier life events was poor; large chunks of his life were blank. In fact, he asked us if he was married at a certain age. Sean's involvement in delinquency started early. He reported, "Well, I was always stealing, always running away, it's 8 or 9." He also said, "I remember being drunk when I was about 9 and loving it." Sean was sent to the Lyman School at the age of 13 for receiving stolen goods. He experienced his first arrest for burglary at the age of 10. For Sean, Lyman was a "farce"—the challenge was "how to beat the system." Sean went on to say that as a kid he "always had moxie. Never had any fear of being hurt, dying, you know." Sean's arrests for violence were alcohol related—an assault and battery on a police officer when he was 24 and an assault on his wife at age 27. He had numerous arrests for drinking and nonsupport as an adult, and he served several terms in local jails (see Table 8.3 for quantitative details).

Regarding his drinking, Sean recounted his early days.

> It was getting rough. I drank wine. The reason people drink wine, it's the easiest thing to get. It was the cheapest drink you could buy. And when you don't live like normal people, you are not a normal person. You have no control of the time. The most horrible feeling in the world is when you look at the clock every morning, you see it's fifteen minutes to eight, you can't get to that package store. The big decision is, hey, man, do I go up and try to hit the bootlegger, spend that extra money on that, or wait fifteen minutes? That fifteen minutes is an eternity. Those things are scary.

Sean's father was a drinker as well. Sean recalled an incident concerning his father.

> I remember him drinking. I'm saying, I don't remember him ever being drunk in the house, I only remember one incident. Him standing down the street, defying the police, defying anybody to stop him, coming up the street, in them days the cops would beat you up. You know, if you were big. My father was a giant . . . But my mother was a midget, more or less, she was only about five feet. But she was the control of my father. She is things you might hear about the Irish women with the frying pan . . . Hit him over the head, and then they'd put him to bed. He'd sleep and go to work the next day.

Finally, in reflecting on his life, Sean referred to it as a "nightmare." He continued, "Things happen, continuously happen, to me. They never seem to end. I never seem to find that time when everything's peaceful. The only joy I ever felt was that short time in AA, when everything was great." Sean told us that he has "no trust."

Sean is one of the few men we interviewed who used AA to help him stop drinking. Although Sean has not been to an AA meeting in over twenty years, he offered this view of AA:

> When I hit AA it was a different world. Sobriety had a form of life that was unbelievable to me. If you could put your trust in that program. For a guy like me who was brought up in reform school and that stuff, we trusted nobody. You just don't. You figure there was a gimmick to every-

thing . . . I believed in it, I preached it, of course, the AA, . . . it was beautiful.

Although Sean has quit drinking, he still smokes three or four packs of cigarettes a day and, in his words, carries "a lot of anger."

Another pattern for the intermittent offenders, as was also true for the other men we interviewed, concerns their perspective on crime. Crime, especially violence in specific situations (for example, domestic disputes), is regarded as normative and "not real crime." This was true for many of the men we call intermittent offenders as well as for those who desisted or persisted in offending over the life course. For instance, Sal provided the following account of an incident of domestic violence. "I hit my sister for having sailors in the house, you know, not realizing that the government said have a sailor in for supper, you know, on the holidays and all that weekends. But I just hit her and they shipped me back to Concord Reformatory. Then I got out. But I never did nothing serious. I was never arrested for nothing serious. That was it." Sal was also arrested and convicted twice for assault and battery on his wife; he did not reveal these arrests in our interview. These incidents occurred when Sal was 26 and 27. His criminal record did not show any arrests for violence after age 32, but he was arrested thirteen times for other offenses. Along similar lines, the men's views of what constituted serious crime were interesting and provocative. In discussing his commitment for auto theft, Mickey stated, "No big deal. It wasn't armed robbery or killing."

Other offenders denied or rationalized entire criminal lifestyles. Consider Bernard, who had ties to organized crime. When we interviewed him at the age of 65 he was doing time in prison for trafficking cocaine and conspiracy to violate state narcotics law. Bernard and a co-offender were arrested after the police found four kilograms of cocaine inside their rental car. Bernard told us that he did not commit this crime and that he was "set up" by organized crime or the police. Bernard had a fairly extensive criminal record, including arrests for rape and assault at age 21 and assault at age 26. Like some of the other intermittent offenders we interviewed, Bernard denied being involved in crime, not only for his current offense but for his initial commitment to the Lyman School as well. Bernard recounted,

See, when I was young and went to the Lyman School, I was not guilty of the crime I committed. What happened, somebody did something and gave me the tool. And the cop said, "Well, you've got the tool." And they charged me for it. And I had nothing to do with it at all. Just somebody gave me an axe. And they sent me to Lyman School for it. Well, I was ignorant. My family didn't come out. My mother doesn't know, my father went to work. You know, these people, they're from the old country. I never told my mother because I didn't want my mother to come to the court and embarrass me. I remember one time I got caught shining shoes. The cops insulted her. I hate the Irish for that. I want to kill the cop. I was only a kid. For what, shining shoes? Made her cry, insulted her? Called her all names? Get your idiot son out of this. I'll never forget it. You wop. Bunch of wops. He's an Irish cop, they're supposed to be intelligent men, they're an officer of the law. From that day on I hated him with a passion.

But that was the beginning. Then I went back for something else. I had nothing to do with it. Oh, my brother. That's when I went to prison, to Concord. They railroaded me again. My brother stole something. I won't squeal on my brother and I took the blame. My brother didn't come up and say he was guilty. Nobody showed up. The prosecutor—he says to me, "Plead guilty and go home." I was turned, I admitted this. I couldn't understand life because I was ignorant. And then I had different values too as a kid. I looked up to kids on the corner. I call them today pimps. They'd just brag about somebody else and they'd make them feel they had to look up to them, I want to be part of it, you know, stuff. So I had that mentality.

Bernard contended that his lack of education, fueled by class and ethnic conflict, accounted for his criminal behavior. "So whenever I went through life, and I broke laws . . . believe me, I had to, because I had no education. So I ended up on the streets. Streetwise." Bernard pointed out the effects of his minimal education. "You know, at that time you could hit me, it's like you could whack at me right in the nose with your word, so how could I defend myself? I don't know the English language to come back. So I'd have to give a whack with my hand. That's the only thing to get the frustration out, you know. Well, you hurt me, so I'm going to hurt you back my own way. I mean, that's what I've been doing all my life. Even in prison here."

Despite this outlook, Bernard claimed that he had "principles." He continued,

I would not hurt somebody. I would not rob a man who had to work all week and went into a bar, got drunk, and take his money. I can't do that. I go into a business or store and clean them out because he's got enough money there. What, could I take a few bucks off him? He's got insurance and can collect it. Do you understand what I mean? He has the brains to make more money. So he'll never be hurt. Do you understand what I mean? But if I take a guy who's a poor working slob who has got to feed his family or pay his bills, I can't do it. I can't do that. I can't cheat at cards. So what kind of crook am I really? You know, I've always thought of that. But if I'm broke and got to survive, so if I see something, a refrigerator the guy didn't bring it in fast enough, that fridge is going to be disappeared. That box, whatever, left out there when he was lugging out from the truck, that box is going to disappear. You understand what I mean? What are they going to say? Well, it disappeared . . . So I had my different values. I was still breaking the law, don't get me wrong. But I wasn't a traditional thief. I'm not that proud of it. Because I'm ashamed. I'm a man, a person, you know, I exist. I could never steal from friends. My mother and father told me you can't do things like that.

The juxtaposition of a cultural framing of certain kinds of crime as normal with bitter memories of incarceration in reform school was also salient. Despite the fact that these incidents occurred more than fifty years ago, many of the men we interviewed remembered precise dates of incarceration, names of the guards who hit them, and their commitment number in reform school. Sal even remembered that when they "shipped me to Concord Reformatory, my number was 22123." Tellingly, Mickey distinguished reform school from the military even though both are total institutions with hierarchical structures. He had run away from Lyman School:

> *Mickey:* I just couldn't stay there any longer. Very pissed off at confinement like that. It wasn't the regimentation; it was the confinement. You went to work for this particular job and you heard the bells and whistles. Yeah. When I went to military, it was the same thing—regimentation. But it wasn't as enforced. It wasn't lax, but it wasn't enforced. And you weren't put away. You were in the military because you wanted to. There [at Lyman] you were sent. So there was a domination there you didn't particularly care for.
>
> *Q:* When you say the military—do you think that was an important factor in keeping you out of crime as an adult?
>
> *Mickey:* Oh yes. Very much so.

Mickey concluded by saying that the military gave him a "line to follow," similar to the support line of his marriage. He claimed that if he hadn't gotten married, he "would have lost it all. So marriage was the biggest thing." Mickey went on to declare emphatically, "If it wasn't for her [his wife], I wouldn't be here talking to you." Mickey's wife stood by him while he had a serious drinking problem related to the war-related injury described above. Mickey said, "But meanwhile my wife stayed with me—solid. She backed me all the way. She took care of me." He still maintains a close relationship with his ex-wife, though now from a distance.

The cynicism about crime and incarceration that we uncovered in many of the narratives extended to other domains as well, religion in particular. We asked Mickey, an Irish Catholic, about religion and whether he thought that religion could play an important role in turning lives around. His reply in many ways typified the views of the Glueck men on religion.

> No, it's a crock of shit. All my mother's people, all Irish, all Catholic school. My father's people, all Irish, Scotch, Catholic, parochial school. My sisters and brothers, parochial school. My children, parochial school. But not me. I had nothing to do with the church. Right in the beginning, early reading, 10, 11, 12, 13 years old, the church was a crock of shit. Not the belief; belief is everybody's right. I'm talking about the structure. I would never go for it. They threw me out of Sunday school and they wouldn't let me make my confirmation and communion. They call[ed] my father . . . and they said they'd enroll me in school, but they didn't want anything to do with me.

He continued,

> But yet, when it came to religion, catechism, Bible, I had all the advice. My sisters and brothers and my children would all come to me, even my sister, Hail Mary and holy water, she'd say, "Mickey, what's this, what's that." They don't—see, they only know what they're told. They never go beyond. The church says that's what it says, and that's what they believe. I want to know where the priest got his information. I wonder how he came to this conclusion, and I read and I read and I read and I read. So I could argue about anything, and I would, and I did, and I will now. That is as far as I went with religion. I never went to church. I never made any application to try to learn from them, because they were only going to tell me what they wanted me to hear, not to know, but to hear. So I just left it.

Still, in keeping with many of the surprises we have uncovered, Mickey reflected on his life rather contentedly.

Well, for what I've gone through and what's happened to me and the fact that I'm here, I'm pretty goddamned lucky. I had a pretty good life. I've [been] loaded with pain, problems, but I've been able to overcome them. I've got a house, a car, and the kids are doing fine. The jobs have always been good. I've always been able to take care of myself. And I think I have done pretty good. I can't point fingers at anybody and say I could have done better. I can't look back and say if someone had helped me. There's nothing out there that I couldn't have done. And there's nothing I didn't do to help myself. That's it. I think I've done pretty well. The gang that I grew up with—thirty to thirty-five kids—there's only about half a dozen of us left. There's been jail, there's been suicides, there's been cancer, there's been heart attacks . . . I can't complain about anything.

## What Have We Learned?

A major concern in criminology is whether one can use arrest histories to classify individuals as offenders or not. Examining specific types of offenses such as violence in some ways clouds this concern even more. Put simply, attempts to subdivide the offender population into meaningful explanatory categories is fraught with difficulty. Examining official arrest histories in conjunction with life-history narratives and data drawn from the Glueck archives, we uncovered some anomalies suggesting that arrest records are crude instruments for classification purposes. Alberto was arrested for assault and battery on a police officer, for example, which we learned may be a phony charge that says more about police perceptions and decision making than the actual behavior of the suspect. Another man was arrested for making threats of violence, a charge that largely depends upon the context in which the threats are made and the discretion of the police officer to carry out an arrest. Another example concerned an incident in which one of our men beat up his wife and daughter while he was drunk. He was subsequently arrested and charged with drunkenness, not domestic violence.

The limitations of official records have serious implications for longitudinal studies of crime generally and studies of the timing or onset of specific forms of crime like violence. In this chapter, we were interested in cases involving what we called "late" onset of violence (defined as being arrested for a violent crime after age 35). An enduring question in the criminal career literature concerns the onset of crime and violence, with researchers searching for instances of "early" offending, "normative" or "on-time" offending, as well as "late onset" offending. Yet these terms, like persistence and desistance, contain ambiguity, and their ultimate utility for criminology is not evident. Critics such as Hirschi and Gottfredson (1983) have long argued that the timing of onset merely reflects differences in rates or propensity and does not add anything meaningful to the study of crime. Moreover, onset and desistance are influenced by random opportunities, and the timing of events varies with the source of data on criminal activity. For example, age of onset of crime is usually reported by mothers as relatively "early" while age of onset of arrest or conviction is relatively "late."

In short, we are compelled by the data to conclude that terms like "early" and "late" have questionable intrinsic meaning. Because arrest records do not always accurately reflect the exact nature and timing of criminal behavior, our approach has been to explore multiple sources of data (especially narratives and life records) and look for basic patterns over a long period of time within each man's life. Within this framework, discrete incidents and the timing of events become only one piece in fitting together the larger puzzle.

Even more unsettling than the ambiguities and gaps in official records is the overall utility of the offender classification schemes that have proliferated recently in criminology. What does it mean to call someone a persistent offender? An intermittent offender? A desister? We will revisit this issue in Chapter 10, but for now we suggest that these terms are at best a loose reflection of reality and, as revealed in our interviews, do not capture the patterning or complexity of criminal offending over the full life course. We do not believe that this issue can be solved by better statistical tools to identify groups of offenders. Nor do we believe that simply expanding the apparently simple classificatory schemes will advance the field either, and we further acknowledge that our previous work is not immune to this criticism (for example, see Laub, Nagin, and Sampson 1998).

The biggest surprise in this chapter, but consistent with a critique of group-based typologies, was learning that men who commit violence in later adulthood do so for reasons similar to those who commit violence earlier in the life course; for example, to obtain money or goods using a weapon, as a means to solve problems with family members and neighbors, or a means of gaining sexual power over females. (For more details, see Chapter 7 for a discussion of persistent offending.) Moreover, in this chapter we learned that intermittent offenders at times look like desisters and, at other times, resemble persistent offenders. Such complexity emerges because of the long-term longitudinal data we are using—again, the longer the time frame and the more data sources one combines, the more uncertain the simple taxonomy becomes other than that all offenders desist.

Another important issue that emerged in these data concerns the perception of crime and violence. As discussed above, several of the men we interviewed viewed certain kinds of crime and violence as "not really crime," but rather as normative behavior in certain situations or contexts. In addition, as noted by some men, crime and violence are sometimes used as a form of social control (Black 1983). For others, "real" criminal acts were considered to be things like "going out holding up people, breaking and entering, stealing automobiles."[6]

In the end, however, there is a similarity in the self-reported turning points that did matter. Men who desist from crime do so when they, on the one hand, experience structural turning points (for example, marriage, the military) that lead to a strengthening of their social support systems and, on the other hand, make an inner resolve to change their lives. They are thus better positioned situationally to respond to the monitoring and control and the love and social support around them—turning points are not deterministic. In other words, the men who changed had identifiable turning points that they noted changed their life-course trajectories. Men who did not change referred to their lack of turning points and/or their own inability (often due to immaturity) to take advantage of turning points when they presented themselves. Turning points are thus simultaneously structural and subjectivist. Finally, in a painful and tragic way, these narratives point to the destructive power of alcohol, brutal institutional confinement, anger, racial and ethnic division, domestic conflict, and horrific war experiences in shaping an individual's life course and in reciprocally inducing further negative turning points.

# CHAPTER NINE

# Modeling Change in Crime

Our qualitative analysis of the Glueck men's narratives has made a compelling case for the importance of turning points in explaining changes in criminal activity over the adult life course of troubled boys. The in-depth examination in Chapters 6–8 is fundamentally linked to the discovery in Chapter 5, using quantitative analysis of trajectory patterns, of considerable heterogeneity in criminal offending through time and of widely disparate ages of desistance. We thus asked the men themselves, and probed as well as we could with in-depth interviews, for possible explanations of the many changes in crime we observed, such as deflections of criminal trajectories to desistance, acceleration of offending, and intermittent patterns of offending. What is intriguing here, once again, is the marked variability even within a highly disadvantaged group of men.

As we detailed throughout Chapters 6–8, changes in criminal behavior were associated in the narratives with a number of themes, including aging, employment, marriage, military service, excessive drinking, and personal choice. Of all the themes we have investigated, marriage comes up again and again in the narratives as a turning point. Recall Leon's narrative wherein he attributed his life-course change to his marriage and his wife's influence, like many of the men we interviewed who desisted from crime. Contrast that with the narrative from Buddy, a man who never married and spent half of his life incarcerated, who told us that he longed for a chance to meet a "decent woman," a chance that never materialized. Does this apparent salience of marriage (or its absence) as a turning point hold up under a different kind of rigorous analysis?

This chapter answers that question with a targeted move back to quantitative analysis, this time through a systematic analysis of variations in crime linked to time-varying (within-individual) and between-individual explanatory factors. Although the methods are quite different, perhaps jarringly so at first, we believe they are in service of the same theoretical goals that animate our investigation throughout the book. In the case of the present chapter, the strength of our analysis is the ability to model quantitative variations in crime both between and within persons up to age 70, along with time-varying covariates at each age. Data limitations preclude our ability to empirically examine factors such as time-varying personal choice. We can and do, however, focus squarely on the themes that emerged most clearly from the narrative analysis and that can be objectively measured in our sample of 52 men—especially marriage. Because we administered a life-history calendar during the personal interviews, we were able to code yearly changes in incarceration and marital status over the full life course, enabling a long-term dynamic look at marriage's influence on crime while the men were free in the community. In addition, by recoding a set of yearly data from our work in *Crime in the Making* on all 500 of the Glueck men up to age 32, a secondary goal is to examine an even wider set of life events (for example, military service, employment) from late adolescence to the early thirties for both the long-term follow-up group and the full delinquent group sample of 500 men.

## Research Strategy

Our analytic strategy was constructed to serve the theoretical goal of simultaneously modeling within-individual change and between-person "propensity" differences in crime. Because of our focus on the life course, we chose age-years as the unit of within-individual change. Moreover, we aim to assess changes in adult crime, especially desistance, using both adult turning points and childhood risk factors measured well before the point of adulthood. To meet these goals we coded person-year observations for each of the 52 men we interviewed starting from age 17, which marks the transition to young adulthood and the peak of overall offending, up to age 70. During the course of our interviews, we asked each man to fill out a life-history calendar of major life events (see Chapter 4). In general it was relatively easy for the men to do this for events such as marriage, divorce, having children, stays in prison, and retirement. Considering the period of recall, which could be almost forty years, we were not surprised to encounter considerable difficulty collecting employment data by year. For example, it was common to get very general answers, and for the men to forget sequences of employment during the volatile young-adult years (for example, one man reported dozens of jobs in one year). After preliminary analysis and confronting considerable missing data, we dropped the hope of examining employment over the full life course and turned to a primary focus on time-varying states of marriage from ages 17 to 70.[1]

The outcome of interest is the criminal activity of each man during these years. On the basis of a combination of Massachusetts's criminal histories, a national FBI search, and death records as described in Chapter 4, we coded the number of criminal events, by crime type, for each year ages 17 up to 70, adjusting for mortality. The outcome of crime is thereby generated from a source independent of the life-history calendar. As argued earlier, our main focus is on within-individual change, where stable characteristics of the person often associated with police bias (race, class, IQ) are not confounded. We did ask about self-reported crime during the interviews, but the retrospective placing of events within specific years going back so far in time proved too difficult for the men. Wherever possible, however, we compared life-history narratives with official records in an effort to discover anomalies. For both major crime episodes and prison stays, the interviews with the men yielded a generally consistent picture.

At the between-individual level, we considered in Chapter 5 a wide-ranging number of stable and early risk factors. Combined with our analyses in *Crime in the Making,* there is a long set to choose from. We experimented with a number of specifications, but the results were surprisingly robust. For simplicity we present here a small number of specifications that best represent the overall pattern. In terms of factors that are exogenous to adulthood and measured before the start of the desistance process, we focus on intelligence (full-score Wechsler-Bellevue test), total number of juvenile delinquencies as reported by self, parents, and teachers, and the validated childhood risk measure introduced in Chapter 5. To match the within-individual analysis, we also examine stable person-level differences in marriage, and in a subanalysis, we use available data in early adulthood to examine unemployment and military service.

### Hierarchical Statistical Models of Change

Our goal is to simultaneously estimate variations in crime within individuals over time and between-individual differences in the latent propensity to offend. As already demonstrated, the Glueck men generated thousands of crimes in total, a repeated outcome not well suited to event-history analysis of single events. We therefore use generalized hierarchical models for nested or repeated measures data (Mason, Wong, and Entwisle 1983; Raudenbush and Bryk 2002). In our case, time periods are nested within individuals, so that level 1 of the hierarchical model becomes the change analysis and level 2 the between-individual analysis. The interdependence of observations within individuals is thus explicitly modeled.

The hierarchical statistical model we estimate was modified to incorporate three important features of our data. The first is a conception of crime as a rare event in any one year, especially in older age. The second is the likely unexplained variation between individuals in the underlying propensity to offend (heterogeneity). The third is that there is variation across time and individuals in incarceration, yielding a varying "street time" during which one has the opportunity to commit crime (see also Blumstein et al. 1986). To accommodate these three important features, our model views the count of crime $Y_{it}$ for a given person $i$ at time $t$ as sampled from an overdispersed Poisson distribution with mean $n_{it}\lambda_{it}$, where $n_{it}$ is the number of days free on the street for person $i$ at time $t$ and $\lambda_{it}$ is the latent or "true" offending rate for person $i$ per days free in year $t$. Recall that we collected data on the number of days incarcerated for each year. We view the resulting log-event rates of crime as normally distributed across persons. Specifically, using a hierarchical generalized linear model (Raudenbush et al. 2000; Raudenbush and Bryk 2002), we set the natural log link $\eta_{it} = \log(\lambda_{it})$ equal to a mixed linear model that includes relevant covariates, and a random effect for each person to account for heterogeneity.[2]

This model serves well our theoretical goals. The individual offending rate conforms to an overdispersed Poisson distribution, incorporating the skewed nature of crime with its many values of zero in any given year, while at the same time creating a metric that defines meaningful effect sizes. For example, exponentiating the regression coefficient in our model allows us to estimate percentage changes in the rate of individual offending associated with a change in marital status and other predictors. Our approach also incorporates unique unobserved differences between persons via random effects (see also Horney, Osgood, and Marshall 1995, 661). To the extent that individuals have unique stable features that affect crime, these random effects are important in accounting for variation not explainable by the structural model.

Let's consider a simple manifestation of this model, which we later generalize with more predictors. Conceptualizing a criminal trajectory, we begin by modeling the log of a person's crime rate per days free as a linear function of age and marriage. On the basis of preliminary analyses of best-fitting models, prior research, and the fact that the age window for the transition to young adulthood (and hence marriage) begins at or near the average peak age of total offending (17) and our follow-up extends up to age 70, we specify a linear and quadratic function of age. Using the above notation the basic elements of this within-person model become:

$$E(\text{CRIME}_{it} \mid \beta_i) = n_{it} * \lambda_{it}$$

$$\log(\lambda_{it}) = \beta_{0,i} + \beta_{1,i}\,(\text{AGE})_{it} + \beta_{2,i}\,(\text{AGE}^2)_{it} + \beta_{3,i}\,(\text{MARRIAGE})_{it} + r_{it},$$

where $i$ is the index for individuals, $t$ is for longitudinal observations, and $n_{it}$ is the number of days free on the street for person $i$ at time $t$. MARRIAGE is a time-varying covariate that can take on values of 0 (unmarried) or 1 (married) during each year from 17 to 70. The intercept, $\beta_{0,i}$, is the estimated log event-rate of crime while free when the predictors are set to zero.

To increase meaningful interpretation of the age effect, we center AGE at the mean of the observed age-person distribution, which for our data is age 43. As Raudenbush and Bryk (2002, 182) note, such centering "in the middle" has two desirable results. First, our centering scheme means that the change parameter, $\beta_{1,i}$, is defined not only as the average rate of change in crime at 43, but as the average rate of change (or, in effect, desistance) over the observation period. Second, by centering at the mean, the age and age-squared terms are orthogonal and thus allow more stable estimation procedures. Quadratic models of age effects are typically plagued by high correlation among the age terms.[3] Overall, then, our centering scheme yields an interpretation of the intercept in the above equation as the log event rate of crime for 43-year-old unmarried men in our follow-up. The $\beta_{1,i}$ and $\beta_{2,i}$ parameters estimate the average rate of change and curvature (rate of acceleration or deceleration), and $\beta_{3,i}$ estimates the time-varying marriage effect.

The between-person model takes the following general form, again using AGE and MARRIAGE:

$$\beta_{0,i} = \gamma_{0,0} + \gamma_{0,1}\,(\text{MARRIAGE})_i + u_{0,i}$$

$$\beta_{1,i} = \gamma_{1,0} + u_{1,i}$$

$$\beta_{2,i} = \gamma_{2,0}$$

$$\beta_{3,i} = \gamma_{3,0}$$

According to this model, the latent rate of offending and the main desistance parameter for age are allowed to vary across persons, as indicated by the presence of an error term. Put differently, the model allows for persistent heterogeneity across individuals (compare Nagin and Land 1993), not just in levels of offending, but in the rate of change. If the age effect is as invariant as Gottfredson and Hirschi (1990) hypothesize, there should be minimal, if any, variation across individuals in $u_{1,i}$; our theoretical perspective suggests otherwise. On the other hand, we assume fixed effects for the error terms for marriage and the age-squared term. There is no theoretical reason to expect randomly varying marriage effects, and the error term for the age-squared term was not estimable in models where age itself was allowed to randomly vary.

We modify the above equations and then generalize in the analysis below to take into account additional predictors at the within-individual and between-individual levels. As noted, we examine stable person traits like measured intelligence, childhood risk, and prior delinquency. Recoding archival material from the Gluecks' follow-up to age 32, we also examine states of unemployment, military service, and marriage for each year during ages 17–32. This strategy allows us to replicate the marriage analysis and then add in employment and military service for both the 52 men in the long-term follow-up and the full delinquent sample. In these analyses unemployment takes on the value 1 if the person was unemployed for at least four months during the year and 0 otherwise; similarly, military service is coded as 1 if the person was in the military for any portion of the yearly period, 0 otherwise.

One important feature of our model, similar to Horney, Osgood, and Marshall (1995), concerns the centering of the time-varying covariates. We center all such covariates, with the exception of the age specification already described, around each person's life-time mean (that is, person-mean centered). Importantly, this centering scheme allows us to account for the possibility that some men are in a state of marriage because they have a higher personal propensity to marry (a selection argument). To examine change within individuals we thus examine deviations in any given year from each person's overall mean level of marriage, which we then link to the latent probability of offending in that year. At level 2, or between persons, we estimate the simultaneous association of the mean time spent in marriage on crime, allowing us to decompose the relationship of marriage (and later, unemployment and military service) to crime into its average within-individual or time-varying component and the stable propensity of men to be married.[4]

### Age, Crime, and Variability

One of the simplest and yet most informative results concerns the level of variability in both crime and key covariates over time. After all, if there is not much change in men's lives, then the validity of our conceptual scheme and the explanatory power of our change models will be inherently limited (see also Horney, Osgood, and Marshall 1995, 662). As it turns out, the percentage of men that produced at least one change in status over time was large: 90 percent for marriage, 87 percent for unemployment, and 64 percent for military service. As previewed in Chapter 5, crime also changes significantly within persons over time, such that all 52 men in the interview follow-up contribute at least one change in criminal status over the yearly observations. More revealing, the total variation in the estimated event rate of criminal offending while free that lies within individuals (over

time) is a substantial 64 percent for total crimes. Corresponding figures for violent, property, and alcohol/drug offenses are 62, 60, and
16 percent, respectively.

It is also the case that our sampling scheme in selecting the 52 men
for follow-up produced an age-crime distribution that is reflective of
aggregate patterns in the criminological literature and Chapter 5. For
example, Figure 9.1 displays the raw mean number of offenses and
the Poisson-predicted number of total crimes while free from ages 7 to
70. Similar to the patterns for the full delinquent group in Chapter 5,
we see the rapidly rising rate of observed crime counts until the late
teens, and then a gradual and erratic decline throughout adulthood.
Because of this asymmetric nature of the decline by age, the predicted
peak age of offending is pulled slightly to the right. Still, for both observed and predicted counts while free, Figure 9.1 demonstrates
the general aggregate pattern of increasing and then decreasing crime
by age.

On the other hand, we know from our sampling design for the follow-up, coupled with the analysis from Chapter 5, that there should
be significant heterogeneity around the aggregate pattern, with some

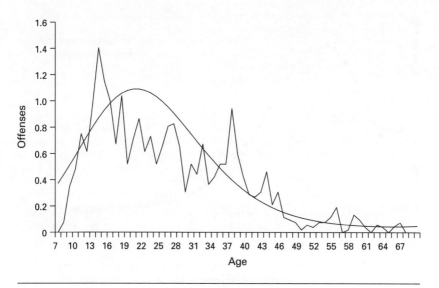

*Figure 9.1* Actual mean number of offenses and age-predicted number of
offenses while free for total crime: 52 interviewed men, ages 7 to 70

men desisting from crime earlier than others. We also know that there are differences by crime type, with violent crimes peaking in the twenties and alcohol/drug offenses at around age 30. In the interest of parsimony, and because violence is extremely rare in any given person-year, we combined violence with property crime on the argument that both are predatory in nature, at least in comparison with offenses related to substance abuse. Figure 9.2 presents predicted age-crime curves for predatory and alcohol/drug offenses generated from a Poisson count model adjusting for days free in each person-year. Once again we see the decline by age for both offense types, but at a significantly later age for alcohol/drug offenses.

### Explanatory Models of Change in Crime

The major goal of this chapter is to account for the variability in crime in relation to stable personal attributes, age, and time-varying life events. Because our analysis is focused on the transition to young adulthood (age 17) up to age 70, Figures 9.1 and 9.2 tell us that the age effects will be mainly a story of differential desistance (decline)

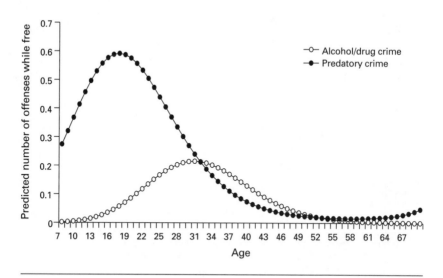

*Figure* 9.2 Age-predicted number of offenses while free by crime type: 52 interviewed men, ages 7 to 70

over the adult life course. In addition to the direct effects of age, we seek to examine social transitions related to marriage, employment, and military service. We begin in Table 9.1 by estimating variability in the log event rate of total crime.

As described in the methods section, this is an overdispersed Poisson model that accounts for exposure time on the street and persistent heterogeneity in unobserved causes of offending. We estimate a series of models that begin with age and then sequentially introduce time-varying and stable person-level predictors. Model 1 enters just the age terms, which basically amounts to an analysis of the average rate of change and its curvature. Exponentiation of the intercept informs us that the average annualized rate of offending at the average age of 43 is about .29 crimes while free on the streets ($e^{-7.149}$ * 365). Both age and age squared are significantly negative, but the coefficient for age (−.0933) is much larger. Exponentiating this coefficient tells us that the average rate of change is fairly steep (about a 9 percent decline in crimes while free at age 43), with a downward curvature as indicated by the negative quadratic coefficient. The main age slope variance is highly significant as well, indicating that there is substantial individual variation around the estimated desistance slope. This latter finding is consistent with our overall theoretical expectations regarding variability in desistance, as opposed to an invariant age distribution imposed on all offenders.[5]

Model 2 enters the time-varying covariate of marriage, and Table 9.1 presents the average within-individual estimate of its effect. The coefficient is −.44, yielding an estimate of a 36 percent reduction in overall crime associated with being in the state of marriage. In other words, the same delinquent man, when married, is considerably less likely to offend given the opportunity than when he is not married. But what about individual differences in the propensity to be married a long time and hence in any given year? To address this question, in Model 3 we estimate the effect of mean years married, effectively decomposing the marriage association into its within-individual and between-level components. Note that the between-individual estimate is highly significant as well—married men, as opposed to unmarried men, are less likely to commit crime ($t$-ratio = −10.06). However, the more interesting result is that the coefficient for within-individual change in marriage barely budges. Controlling for marriage propen-

**Table 9.1** Hierarchical overdispersed Poisson models of total crime counts: 52 follow-up men and change from ages 17 to 70 ($N = 2{,}433$ complete observations)

| | Model 1 | | Model 2 | | Model 3 | | Model 4 | | Model 5 | |
|---|---|---|---|---|---|---|---|---|---|---|
| | Coeff. (se) | t-ratio | Coeff. (se) | t-ratio | Coeff. (se) | t-ratio | Coeff. (se) | t-ratio | Coeff. (se) | t-ratio |
| Intercept | -7.149 (.1525) | -46.866** | -7.095 (.1551) | -45.749** | -5.605 (.1784) | -31.426** | -6.928 (.9907) | -6.993** | -8.745 (.8324) | -10.506** |
| Within-individual | | | | | | | | | | |
| Age | -.0933 (.0067) | -13.906** | -.0948 (.0071) | -13.389** | -.0939 (.0084) | -11.191** | -.0920 (.0080) | -11.439** | -.0808 (.0065) | -12.396** |
| Age$^2$ | -.0010 (.0003) | -2.943** | -.0014 (.0004) | -3.757** | -.0014 (.0004) | -3.889** | -.0014 (.0003) | -4.088** | -.0013 (.0003) | -3.945** |
| Marriage | | | -.4434 (.0893) | -4.964** | -.4072 (.1093) | -3.726** | -.4135 (.0988) | -4.185** | -.3889 (.0917) | -4.243** |
| Between-individual | | | | | | | | | | |
| Marriage | | | | | -2.723 (.2707) | -10.059** | -2.895 (.3120) | -9.278** | -1.327 (.2843) | -4.667** |
| Unofficial delinquency | | | | | | | -.0094 (.0577) | -.163 | -.0141 (.0251) | -.561 |
| IQ | | | | | | | .0150 (.0113) | 1.331 | .0101 (.0090) | 1.119 |
| Childhood risk | | | | | | | .5333 (.2049) | 2.603* | .4363 (.2182) | 1.999* |

|  | | | | | |
|---|---|---|---|---|---|
| Unemployment |  |  |  |  | 2.752 (.4029) | 6.832** |
| Military |  |  |  |  | −.0576 (.6919) | −.083 |
| Variance components |  |  |  |  |  |  |
| Between-individual | 1.492** | 1.453** | .8040** | .8764** | .9290** |  |
| Within-individual | 1.531 | 1.551 | 1.550 | 1.577 | 1.818 |  |
| Age slope | .0013** | .0012** | .0013** | .0012** | .0010** |  |

$*p < .05.$  $**p < .01.$

sity and age effects, Model 3 tells us that the percentage change in crime associated with a change in marriage is approximately 33 percent, compared with 36 percent in the unconditional marriage model.

Model 4 continues the logic of controlling for between-individual differences, this time measured in childhood and adolescence. Surprisingly, neither of the traditional predictors of crime—frequency of unofficial juvenile delinquency and measured intelligence—are significantly related to the average level of adult offending across men. In contrast, the childhood risk indicator created in Chapter 5 is positively associated with later average levels of offending. Those entering adulthood with a history of early trouble and vulnerability exhibit a 70 percent higher rate of later offending than low-risk adolescents. These analyses once again demonstrate the ability of early risk factors to predict levels of later offending, even though trajectory patterns are another story (see also Chapter 5).

Model 5 adds two more between-person predictors measured during the early adulthood years. Specifically, controlling for average time spent unemployed and in the military in the period 17–32, the coefficient for the effect of changes in marriage (from 17 to 70) on total crime is barely changed. The magnitude of the between-person marriage coefficient is cut by about half, on the other hand, suggesting that some of the observed "propensity" association of marriage with desistance is due to the negative association of marriage with unemployment. Nevertheless, the basic pattern holds for our key within-individual factors of age and marriage.

### Crime-Type Patterns

It may well be that there are important crime-type patterns in the data. To explore this possibility, in Table 9.2 we present models for alcohol/drug offenses and predatory crimes, respectively.[6] Although the linear age effect is negative across the two crime types ($-.136$ and $-.050$), the quadratic age term shows a positive curvature for predatory crime and a negative curvature for alcohol/drugs (Models 1 and 2). This pattern reflects an attenuation of the age effect for predatory crimes at older ages (see also Figure 9.2). Further analysis suggests that the positive curvature for predatory crime is somewhat sensitive, however, for it does not hold up when the variance of the desistance parameter is fixed. Apparently heterogeneity in the desistance rate by age, perhaps induced by our sampling scheme that captured late-onset violent offenders, leads to a somewhat unexpected tailing off of the desistance effect at higher ages.

By contrast, the marriage change analysis is remarkably similar in pattern across crime types. The event rate of offending while free is significantly and negatively associated with marriage transitions within persons for both alcohol/drugs and predatory offenses. The estimated percentage decline is greater for alcohol-related offenses than predatory crimes (40 percent versus 21 percent). At the between-individual level we also control for marriage propensity, which is significantly negative for both crime types, and three child-related factors. Childhood risk predicts overall levels of later offending, whereas the IQ estimate is unexpectedly positive for predatory crimes (Model 2). We are reluctant to put much stock in this latter isolated result.

On theoretical grounds and as a further empirical test we investigate the relationship between excessive drinking and predatory crime. Previous research by Horney and her colleagues (1995) suggests that during periods of heavy drinking or substance abuse, men may be more likely to be in situations (for example, bars, drug transactions) where the risks of violence and theft are enhanced. Our narratives in Chapters 6–8 also uncovered evidence that drinking lifestyles and criminal offending were tightly linked. Although alcohol/drug offenses and predatory crimes are both measured with official records, creating a potential artifactual correlation because of the same measurement source, the two types of crime are nonetheless distinct on conceptual grounds. Therefore, by controlling for within-individual and between-individual propensity differences in substance abuse as measured by alcohol- and drug-related arrests, we provide another way to counteract potential selection bias associated with marriage.

In Model 3 of Table 9.2 we re-estimate variations in predatory crime by entering the frequency of alcohol/drug offenses in both the within- and the between-individual equations. The results are intriguing in that changes in drinking are *not* significantly related to the rate of predatory crime. The marriage coefficients, however, remained virtually unchanged—the within-individual marriage coefficient, controlling for within-individual changes in drinking/drug offenses, is −.2386 compared with −.2389 in Model 2. Being in a state of marriage, then, is still associated with a 21 percent reduction in predatory crime controlling for not just marriage propensity, but also changes in drinking and the overall propensity to excessive alcohol/drug use. To

**Table 9.2** Hierarchical overdispersed Poisson models of alcohol/drug crime and predatory crime (violent/property): 52 follow-up men and change from ages 17 to 70 ($N = 2{,}433$ complete observations)

| | Alcohol/drug crime | | Predatory crime | | | |
| | Model 1 | | Model 2 | | Model 3 | |
| | Coeff. (se) | $t$-ratio | Coeff. (se) | $t$-ratio | Coeff. (se) | $t$-ratio |
|---|---|---|---|---|---|---|
| Intercept | -8.383 (1.390) | -6.030** | -10.00 (1.173) | -8.528** | -9.870 (1.102) | -8.956** |
| Within-individual | | | | | | |
| Age | -.1365 (.0095) | -14.342** | -.0502 (.0057) | -8.759** | -.0506 (.0056) | -9.013** |
| Age$^2$ | -.0014 (.0003) | -4.432** | .0011 (.0002) | 5.061** | .0012 (.0002) | 4.965** |
| Marriage | -.5107 (.0449) | -11.371** | -.2389 (.0846) | -2.824** | -.2386 (.0858) | -2.781** |
| Alcohol/drugs | | | | | .0352 (.0597) | .590 |

| | | | | | | |
|---|---|---|---|---|---|---|
| Between-individual | | | | | | |
| Marriage | -4.231 | -8.065** | -3.294 | -9.425** | -3.421 | -10.231** |
| | (.5246) | | (.3495) | | (.3344) | |
| Unofficial delinquency | -.0611 | -.916 | -.0132 | -.220 | -.0141 | -.245 |
| | (.0667) | | (.0601) | | (.0578) | |
| IQ | .0281 | 1.503 | .0400 | 3.370** | .0401 | 3.435** |
| | (.0187) | | (.0119) | | (.0117) | |
| Childhood risk | .8212 | 2.273* | .6830 | 2.781** | .7634 | 3.349** |
| | (.3613) | | (.2456) | | (.2280) | |
| Alcohol/drugs | | | | | -.6880 | -2.530* |
| | | | | | (.2719) | |
| Variance components | | | | | | |
| Between-individual | 2.716** | | 2.834** | | 2.786** | |
| Within-individual | .3620 | | .8816 | | .8807 | |
| Age slope | .0103** | | .0046** | | .0046** | |

* $p < .05$.  ** $p < .01$.

the extent that drinking/drug arrests are an indicator of criminal propensity (for example, Gottfredson and Hirschi 1990), Model 3 is a strict test of the time-varying marriage effect. In other words, the possible simultaneous influence of criminality on marriage within any observation period is addressed in the models where drinking/drugs are controlled. The results in Model 3 thus add further evidence to the marriage-as-turning-point hypothesis.[7]

### Competing Adult Life Events

A limitation of the analysis so far is that it has not permitted the simultaneous estimation of change in life transitions related to employment and military service. That is because we do not have accurate yearly measures of employment for men in their middle and older adult years. On the other hand, military service is essentially a constant (zero) once the men reached their thirties and beyond. We therefore replicate the core analysis in young adulthood (ages 17–32) by relying on raw data we collected for *Crime in the Making* from the Glueck archives. We specifically recoded evidence of unemployment spells and military service for each yearly segment. Because of the short age window and considerable loss of degrees of freedom, we estimate a model for total crime that focuses on age and age squared, along with the decomposition analysis for unemployment, marriage, and military service.[8] We centered age at the mean of the valid observation periods, with the result that the intercept refers to the log event rate of offending at age 24, and the linear age effect refers to the average rate of change in crime over observations.

The age results in Table 9.3 show a declining crime trend in the twenties and early thirties, with significant negative coefficients for age and age squared, respectively. To our mind the rather more remarkable and surprising results concern the time-varying covariates—all three within-individual change factors are significant. We expected one or two to survive a competitive analysis with respect to change over time, but clearly all three factors matter. Controlling for age and between-individual differences in propensity, Table 9.3 indicates that the Glueck men were less likely to commit crime (while free on the street) when they were in states of military service, marriage, *and* employment. Moreover, average differences in marriage and unemployment between men make a difference, but not military service. What this tells us is that the military association is strictly time varying, whereas the unemployment and marriage patterns hold both

Table 9.3 Hierarchical overdispersed Poisson model of total crime counts: 52 follow-up men and change from ages 17 to 32 ($N = 694$ complete observations)

| | Total crime | |
|---|---|---|
| | Coeff. (se) | $t$-ratio |
| Intercept | −7.256 | −22.577** |
| | (.3214) | |
| Within-individual | | |
| Age | −.0356 | −2.019* |
| | (.0176) | |
| Age$^2$ | −.0096 | −2.797** |
| | (.0034) | |
| Marriage | −.4110 | −3.183** |
| | (.1291) | |
| Military | −1.102 | −2.968** |
| | (.3712) | |
| Unemployment | .7224 | 5.125** |
| | (.1410) | |
| Between-individual | | |
| Marriage | −.9224 | −3.678** |
| | (.2508) | |
| Military | −.0003 | −.205 |
| | (.0016) | |
| Unemployment | 3.526 | 9.844** |
| | (.3582) | |
| Variance components | | |
| Between-individual | .3290** | |
| Within-individual | 1.179 | |
| Age slope | .0084** | |

* $p < .05$.    ** $p < .01$.

within and across persons. Consistent with our theoretical expectations and narrative analysis, then, life events are systematically related to crime in a truly dynamic fashion.

We now turn to a replication in Table 9.4 on the full delinquent group of 500 men, ages 17–32, where we have considerably more power. With the added cases at the person level we can control for more factors, and in addition, we were better able to estimate crime-specific models. Model 1 begins, as in Table 9.2, with alcohol/drug offenses as the outcome of interest. We see that the average rate of change in crime is negative from ages 17 to 32, and that this rate has a negative curvature (note quadratic term). Once again there is

**Table 9.4** Hierarchical overdispersed Poisson models of alcohol/drug crime and predatory crime (violent/property): Delinquent group sample ($N = 419$) and change from ages 17 to 32 ($N = 5{,}116$ complete observations)

| | Alcohol/drug crime | | Predatory crime | | | |
| | Model 1 | | Model 2 | | Model 3 | |
| | Coeff. (se) | t-ratio | Coeff. (se) | t-ratio | Coeff. (se) | t-ratio |
|---|---|---|---|---|---|---|
| Intercept | −10.130 | −17.093** | −9.112 | −21.480** | −9.125 | −21.545** |
| | (.5926) | | (.4242) | | (.4235) | |
| Within-individual | | | | | | |
| Age | −.0310 | −2.918** | −.1245 | −14.126** | −.1250 | −14.007** |
| | (.0106) | | (.0088) | | (.0089) | |
| Age$^2$ | −.0054 | −2.695** | .0025 | 1.404 | .0030 | 1.679 |
| | (.0020) | | (.0018) | | (.0018) | |
| Marriage | −.3124 | −3.054** | −.1959 | −2.654** | −.1936 | −2.650** |
| | (.1023) | | (.0738) | | (.0730) | |
| Military | −.8663 | −5.691** | −.5121 | −4.447** | −.5057 | −4.389** |
| | (.1522) | | (.1152) | | (.1152) | |
| Unemployment | .3375 | 3.733** | 1.096 | 12.808** | 1.083 | 12.711** |
| | (.0904) | | (.0856) | | (.0852) | |
| Alcohol/drugs | | | | | .1362 | 4.155** |
| | | | | | (.0328) | |

| | (1) | | (2) | | (3) | |
|---|---|---|---|---|---|---|
| Between-individual | | | | | | |
| Marriage | −.4228 | −1.517 | −.8892 | −5.176** | −.8888 | −5.162** |
| | (.2787) | | (.1718) | | (.1722) | |
| Military | −.0259 | −.089 | −.9834 | −2.117* | −.9854 | −2.111* |
| | (.2918) | | (.4646) | | (.4668) | |
| Unemployment | 1.759 | 6.373** | 3.545 | 22.417** | 3.547 | 21.807** |
| | (.2761) | | (.1581) | | (.1626) | |
| Unofficial delinquency | .0990 | 7.122** | −.0065 | −.506 | −.0072 | −.571 |
| | (.0139) | | (.0128) | | (.0127) | |
| IQ | .0048 | .822 | .0059 | 1.392 | .0061 | 1.426 |
| | (.0058) | | (.0042) | | (.0042) | |
| Childhood risk | .0421 | .239 | .1717 | 1.512 | .1691 | 1.491 |
| | (.1763) | | (.1135) | | (.1134) | |
| Alcohol/drugs | | | | | .0095 | .077 |
| | | | | | (.1226) | |
| Variance components | | | | | | |
| Between-individual | 2.213** | | .7170** | | .7236** | |
| Within-individual | .4305 | | 1.083 | | 1.072 | |
| Age slope | .0491** | | .0133* | | .0140** | |

* $p < .05$.  ** $p < .01$.

significant heterogeneity in the linear age slope, disconfirming a simple age invariance model at the individual level. In Model 2 the linear rate of change in predatory offending is also negative, but this time there is no further punch added by the quadratic age function $(p > .10)$.

After accounting for the direct effects of age, we consider next the three time-varying covariates. As for the 52 men in our follow-up (Table 9.3), states of marriage, employment, and military service are independently associated with lower event-rates of offending over time in the full delinquent group sample, whether alcohol/drug related or predatory (Models 1 and 2). The magnitudes of association are impressive. For our main indicator, being married is associated with an estimated reduction in offending of 27 and 18 percent for alcohol-related and predatory crimes, respectively, controlling for person-level differences in marriage and other traits. The estimated effect size for military service is larger for both crime types (approximately 40 and 58 percent reductions for predatory and alcohol/drugs, respectively). The magnitude of association for unemployment is also larger than marriage. However, we urge caution in interpreting the magnitude of the unemployment coefficient, because some of the association with crime may be spuriously due to incarceration. Although the number of days free is controlled in the exposure model, in the Gluecks' original coding scheme men who were incarcerated more than four months were sometimes considered to be unemployed. We reran the analysis selecting only observations where the men were free at least eight months as a check, and obtained similar results. Still, unlike military service and marriage where the coding was independent of incarceration, the unemployment results need to be interpreted with more caution.[9]

As in Table 9.2, Model 3 enters alcohol/drugs to predict propensity differences and within-individual changes in predatory crime. In the full delinquent group, it turns out that during periods when men are presumably engaged in excessive drinking, their event rates of predatory offending are significantly enhanced. This finding is consistent with Horney, Osgood, and Marshall (1995). Yet propensity (between-individual) differences in drinking are not linked to predatory crime (bottom panel of Table 9.4). Note also that stable differences during adulthood in marriage and military service are unrelated to propensity differences in alcohol/drug offenses (Model 1).

The main result for our purposes, however, is that controlling for simultaneous alcohol/drug offending does not in any meaningful way change the interpretation of the estimated effects of marriage, military service, or unemployment. In fact, comparing Models 2 and 3, which predict predatory crimes, the coefficients for these three predictors at both the within and the between-individual levels are invariant to the introduction of alcohol/drug offending.[10] Table 9.4 further suggests that exogenous (relative to age 17) child and adolescent factors are generally weak predictors of later between-person variations in propensity. Indeed, measured IQ and the childhood risk indicator are unrelated to both types of offenses, and the frequency of juvenile delinquency predicts early adult differences only in alcohol/drug offending.[11]

As a final test, we examined another set of models that took into account overall criminal propensity as estimated by a lagged version of the total number of crimes committed by each man. Specifically, we re-estimated Table 9.4 by replacing concurrent drinking with the total offense rate in the observation year prior to the measurement of the dependent variable and values of marriage. This procedure is a very conservative test since prior marriage transitions could have influenced prior crime. Nonetheless, the results of this test were very robust despite the expected high levels of stability for crime-related offenses across time—the $t$-ratios for the within-individual association of lagged crime with concurrent predatory offending and drinking/drug offenses were 4.86 and 4.99, respectively (both $p < .01$). Yet the within-individual marriage pattern maintained its presence, with a coefficient of $-.32$ for predatory offending ($t$-ratio $= -4.76$) and $-.29$ for drinking ($t$-ratio $= -2.88$). Even the between-individual marriage association remained significantly negative controlling for propensity differences in prior crime. Comparing these results with Table 9.4, we thus conclude that the estimated effects of marriage on predatory offending and drinking/drug offenses are not explained away by prior between-individual propensities to crime and prior within-individual changes in crime.

### Summary and Convergence

The findings from this chapter contribute the final pieces to the picture that has emerged in an interactive fashion over the course of analysis throughout this book. First, we have demonstrated the enormous variability over time in criminal offending and major life events among a group of boys chosen for their persistent delinquent activity. The vast majority of men experienced changes in marriage, military service, and unemployment states, and even for predatory crime, more than 50 percent of the variation in our follow-up group was within rather than between individuals. Second, the general pattern of age and desistance is strong—the average rate of change in crime and its curvature are both negative for total crime and alcohol/drug offenses. Third, we discovered significant individual heterogeneity in the rate of desistance as indicated by formal tests for variance in the age-crime slope. So while the direct effects of age are clearly evident, there is considerable variance in desistance rates as high-rate active delinquents age over the life course.

Most important from our perspective, changes in the event rate of crime, controlling for age, are systematically related to adult transitions to marriage, unemployment, and military service. Our inferences are strongest for marriage, where we have person-period observations from 17 to 70: when in states of marriage (but also military service and employment), men are less likely to be criminal (see also Farrington et al. 1986; Horney, Osgood, and Marshall 1995; Farrington and West 1995). The strength of our hierarchical analytic approach was that it separated within-person variability and simultaneously modeled between-person influences of life-course transitions. Although both were significant, the results for within-individual "turning points" are of particular interest. Namely, when deviations from a person's overall propensity to be married were examined over time, the major results demonstrated that offending was lower when men were married. We estimated the marriage effect to be as large as a 40 percent reduction in the rate of criminal offending associated with a within-person state of being married. This finding was not explained away by age effects, overall propensity to be married, criminal propensity as reflected in prior total offending, concurrent drinking/drug offending (for predatory crimes), or exogenously defined childhood and adolescent risk factors—all of which we controlled.

At first glance it may appear that the findings on marriage are inconsistent with our earlier theoretical emphasis and empirical findings on the quality or strength of social bonds, such as marital attachment, rather than the event of marriage itself (see Sampson and Laub 1993;

Laub, Nagin, and Sampson 1998). Unfortunately, because of data limitations we cannot directly model yearly changes in social bonds such as marital attachment and job stability from ages 17 to 70. On the other hand, one needs first to enter the state of marriage to experience marital attachment, and one cannot have job stability without a job. In the Glueck data, in fact, marital attachment from ages 25 to 32 is highly correlated with the lifetime proportion of years the men were married ($r = .71, p < .01$), giving support to the idea that the investment quality of good marriages grows stronger over time. Job stability is also substantially negatively associated with the mean proportion of years unemployed during the age period 17–32 ($r = -.70, p < .01$). We thus believe our present focus on time-varying transitions in marriage, employment, and military service over the full life course makes both theoretical and empirical sense.

None of this denies the enduring legacy of high-risk childhoods. Although one may quarrel with some of the specifics, our thirteen-item risk scale from Chapter 5 incorporates most if not all the major risk factors identified in the literature and proves to be predictive of future offending at the group level. On average, high-risk children are more likely to offend in the latter years than those defined by low childhood risk. Yet individual predictions into adulthood remain poor, and childhood risk fails to explain trajectory patterns and differential rates of desistance.

These results undermine the common wisdom emanating from the selection-bias view of the world, where the life-course correlates of crime are seen as inauthentic. If adult life changes are mere stand-ins for other factors, they would not survive rigorous within-individual analysis where each person serves as his or her own control for time-stable factors. The data suggest that, if anything, the opposite is true. Our hierarchical analysis of change indicates that more frequently than not, it is the dynamic prediction of within-individual change where the life-course events are most salient. Consistent with Farrington (1988) and Horney, Osgood, and Marshall (1995) but taking a longer view of the life course, we find that even when delinquent men predisposed to crime in their early years experience states of marriage, military service, and employment, they are less likely to commit crime. This does not mean such effects are lasting, or that selection bias plays no role. Rather it means that, as Chapters 6–8 indicate, situational and structural life circumstances simultaneously shape human behavior.

Overall, then, our final quantitative analyses have converged to validate the importance of proximate adult social processes, especially marriage but also employment and military service, that are systematically associated with less crime across the adult years, just as they have converged to show how childhood risk factors are consequential not only in childhood but spanning into adulthood as well. It would appear that child and adult factors are continually and interactively at play in a complex process that winds through time along a number of pathways. Despite the complexity, however, in the end the qualitative and quantitative analyses agree more than they disagree on the fundamental pathways to eventual desistance from crime.

# CHAPTER TEN

# Rethinking Lives in and out of Crime

Both science and autobiography affirm that a capacity for change is as essential to human development as it is to the evolution of new species. The events of the opening years do start an infant down a particular path, but it is a path with an extraordinarily large number of intersections.

—JEROME KAGAN (1998)

The events that go wrong in our lives do not forever damn us.

—GEORGE E. VAILLANT AND CAROLINE VAILLANT (1981)

We return to the lives of Arthur and Michael, whom we introduced in Chapter 1. Despite remarkably similar beginnings, Arthur and Michael constructed radically different adult lives. Recall that at age 65 Arthur was in poor health and living alone on social security. He smoked four to five packs of cigarettes a day and was taking Paxil for stress. Married and divorced twice, Arthur was a self-described loner. Somewhat pathetically, he told us, "I live alone. I'm happier that way. If I want to get laid, I get a broad for $15." Besides soliciting prostitutes, Arthur had been extensively involved in a variety of crimes as an adult and was no stranger to prison and jail. Given his lack of meaningful connections to people and institutions, Arthur's prospects for change, even in old age, appear to be grim.

In contrast, Michael's adult life was a story of success. He was a decorated war veteran and had recently become a homeowner. Happily married for forty years and a grandfather six times over, Michael has a close relationship with his wife and their five adult children. Although he officially retired at age 63, he still moonlights as a security guard. Living off pensions, social security payments, and income from his wife's job and his part-time work, Michael has not missed a mortgage payment in the seven years since he purchased his house. He suffered some health problems once he hit the age of 60, but his response was to stop drinking and take his medication on a regular basis. Perhaps most important for this book, Michael clearly desisted from criminal behavior as an adult. Although we have recognized the complexity of turning points and their interpretation throughout our analysis, his explanation was a simple but powerful one—"Well, you can say that the Army changed me."

A dominant theme in our culture is that divergent adult outcomes are the result of varying childhood experiences. Strong versions of the notion that "wounded inner childhoods" explain adult experiences are more popular than ever (see, for example, Merkin 2002). It is interesting to speculate on why notions of childhood determinism have such appeal in our society (see Kagan 1998, 83–150; Bruer 1999). We believe that cultural beliefs about the childhood-adult connection are in part distorted by dominant methodological approaches. If we start with adult offenders, the childhood origins of crime and antisocial behavior become evident and relatively straightforward. The simple "bad boys–bad men" connection seems to fit quite well. If we begin with children, however, and follow their paths to adulthood, we find considerable heterogeneity in adult outcomes. Some antisocial children do become involved in delinquency as adolescents and then they graduate to adult offending; yet other children and adolescents cease all offending by adulthood. Retrospective data tend to confuse and simplify cause and effect for both laypersons and scholars alike. Although maddeningly difficult to carry out, only prospective longitudinal data—studying lives going forward—can sort out causal ordering and shed light on how complex processes emerge over time (Vaillant 1995; 2002, 29–33). As George Vaillant pointed out with regard to retrospective narratives, "It is all too common for caterpillars to become butterflies and then to maintain that in their youth they were little butterflies" (2002, 30).

## Advances in the Study of Whole Lives

Like following life thro' creatures you dissect,
You lose it in the moment you detect.

—ALEXANDER POPE (1993 [1733])

Drawing on what is arguably the longest study of criminal behavior in the world, we have sought to understand the lives of Arthur and Michael and others like them. Our approach contrasts with that of many

social scientists, especially criminologists, who have sought to identify and isolate distinctive "effects" due to individual traits, family,
school, peer group, and neighborhood. The problem with this latter
approach is that it has "led to an overly simplified view of the relations of parts to wholes and of causes to effects" (Lewontin 2000,
72). As noted by John Modell (1994), we were guilty of this as well
in *Crime in the Making* (1993). The problem, according to Richard
Lewontin, an evolutionary biologist, is that the organism is the nexus
of a very large number of weakly determining forces (2000, 76) and
"much of the uncertainty of evolution arises from the existence of
multiple possible pathways even when external conditions are fixed"
(2000, 88). In other words, when thinking about a phenomenon like
crime, there is a multiplicity of causal chains and pathways, all of
which have a weak individual influence (Lewontin 2000, 94; Rutter
1988; Rutter, Giller, and Hagell 1998).

Of course, the challenge is to find a middle ground between a naive
reductionism and a wholism that does not allow for any precise explanation. We believe we have done so by capitalizing on a wide range
of both quantitative and qualitative data and by taking seriously the
life-history narratives provided by the men themselves. We have
worked throughout to integrate quantitative and qualitative data,
weaving back and forth between rigorous analysis of both within-individual longitudinal records and narrative accounts. Systematic integration such as this is paid lip service by many social scientists but is
rarely carried out, especially in an interactional sequence that allows
one data source to challenge and inform the other. With our extensive
and varied forms of data gathered for a large number of serious criminal offenders across the full life course, we believe we are well positioned to address the major challenges to our previous work on
behavioral change and stability over time, as well as to answer unre-
solved questions. In so doing, we hope to move criminological theory
and policy forward in new and productive ways. In our view, criminology seems to be falling into a simplistic debate between "kinds of
people" versus "kinds of contexts" arguments, although doing so in a
sophisticated and technically complex manner. Both arguments fail to
take seriously the idea of behavioral change across the life course.

One of the advantages of employing life-history narratives is their
ability to uncover new ideas and challenge conventional wisdom. We
are struck by the surprises in our data, surprises that challenge not

only the prevailing wisdom in criminology but also some of the themes in our prior work, *Crime in the Making*. A prominent example is findings that challenge the structural determinism of turning points in the life course. We now turn to these new themes and articulate in more detail our revised theory of crime, which recognizes the importance of human agency and choice as embedded in social structures. We also summarize our revised conception of the mechanisms that underlie persistent offending and desistance from crime.

## Desistance by Default

Such a theory might start with the observation that the commitment made without realization that it is being made—what might be termed the "commitment by default"—arises through a series of acts no one of which is crucial but which, taken together, constitute for the actor a series of side bets of such magnitude that he finds himself unwilling to lose them.

—HOWARD S. BECKER (1960)

The process of desistance is complex and occurs for all types of offenders (for example, serious and nonserious, violent and nonviolent) at different ages over the life course. Although there are multiple pathways to desistance, our data indicate that desistance is facilitated by self-described "turning points"—changes in situational and structural life circumstances like a good marriage or a stable job—in combination with individual actions (that is, personal agency). Although age is clearly important in understanding desistance, a focus on age and age alone obfuscates understanding the life course of crime. From our perspective, desistance is best viewed as a process realized over time, not a single event.

Our stance on the desistance process contrasts with emerging theories of desistance that emphasize cognitive transformations or identity shifts as necessary for desistance to occur (see Giordano, Cernkovich, and Rudolph 2002; Maruna 2001). We believe that most offenders desist in response to structural turning points that serve as the catalyst for long-term behavioral change. The image of "desistance by default" best fits the desistance process we found in our data. Desistance for our subjects was not necessarily a conscious or deliberate process, but rather the consequence of what Howard Becker calls "side bets" (1960, 38). Many men made a commitment to go straight without even realizing it. Before they knew it, they had invested so much in a marriage or a job that they did not want to risk losing their investment (H. Becker 1960, 1964; see also Matsueda and Heimer 1997, 171). In other words, "habits provide an anchor by strengthening the forces making for persistence in behavior" (G. Becker and Murphy 2000, 152). We agree that the offenders' own perspectives and words need to be brought into the understanding of desistance, and we believe we have done so. However, offenders can and do desist without a conscious decision to "make good" (compare Maruna 2001), and offenders can and do desist without a "cognitive transformation" (compare Giordano, Cernkovich, and Rudolph 2002).

Some of the men we studied, of course, did want to make good, and they in fact desisted from crime. Consider, for example, Richard and his wife, who have taken in foster children who were wards of the state for many years. Our main point is that many of the desisters did not seek to make good—they simply desisted with little if any cognitive reflection on the matter. "Redemption scripts" (Maruna 2001) were also noticeably absent in most of the life-history narratives. The majority of men we interviewed desisted from crime largely because they were able to capitalize on key structural and situational circumstances. They often selected these structural and situational circumstances (for example, they decided to get married, get that job, hang out with those friends), but these institutions and relationships in turn influenced the men as well (see also G. Becker and Murphy 2000). Thus the developmental phase of cognitive transformation or making good is not a necessary pathway to desistance.

### (De)Connectivity and Marginality

> The lyricism of marginality may find inspiration in the image of the "outlaw," the great social nomad, who prowls on the confines of a docile, frightened order.
>
> —MICHEL FOUCAULT (1995 [1975])

Men who desisted from crime were embedded in structured routines, socially bonded to wives, children, and significant others, drew on resources and social support from their relationships, and were virtually and directly supervised and monitored. In other words, structures, situations, and persons offered nurturing and informal social control that facilitated the process of desistance from crime. Even the most hardened offender is not a persistent offender in the true sense of the term and, as we have observed in our long-term follow-up study, virtually all offenders eventually desist albeit at different rates and ages.

The key question is, What is it about "persistent" offenders that distinguishes them from other offenders? In our view, more than being identified by a single trait like poor verbal intelligence or low self-control or even a series of static traits, the persistent offender, to the extent the term has meaning, seems devoid of linking structures at each phase of the life course, especially involving relationships that can provide nurturing, social support, and informal social control. Generally, the persistent offenders we interviewed experienced residential instability, marital instability, job instability, failure in school and the military, and relatively long periods of incarceration. Except when in prison or jail, they were "social nomads," to use Foucault's term (1995 [1975]). In contrast to the men who desisted from crime, the life of the persistent offender was marked by marginality and a lack of structure that led to even more situations conducive to crime. For those without permanent addresses, steady jobs, spouses, children, and other rooted forms of life, crime and deviance is an unsurprising result—even for those possessing so-called prosocial traits. As a consequence of chaotic and unstructured routines, one has increased contact with those individuals who are similarly situated—in this case, similarly unattached and free from nurturing, social capital or support, and informal social control. Thus while group offending may well decline with age (Warr 2002, 130), we find in our narrative data that the influence of deviant peers and criminal networks is particularly salient in the lives of persistent offenders.

### Will: The Power of Human Agency

> Will is the conscious foreshadowing of specific intention capable of being acted on or not. It is a sense of option that must be rendered in context.
>
> —DAVID MATZA (1969)

For a number of our formerly delinquent men, personal agency looms large in the processes of persistence and desistance from crime. Our narratives showed that some men who persisted in crime consciously chose to continue involvement in crime and did not apologize or make excuses for their criminal behavior (see also Katz 1988). Many men who desisted from crime similarly displayed a variety of voluntaristic actions that facilitated the process of desistance. In our life-history narratives, one thus sees strong evidence for both will/human agency and "commitment by default" (H. Becker 1960), often in the same man's life. In other words, there is no escaping the tension surrounding conscious action and unconscious action generated by default.

The net result is that our work offers a dual critique of social science and popular thinking about crime over the life course. Many developmental criminologists believe that childhood and adolescent risk characteristics are all that really matter, but our work shows otherwise. Not to be overlooked and equally important is our critique of structuralist approaches in criminology that contend that location in the social structure, namely poverty and social class, are all that really matter. The men we studied were active participants in constructing their lives, a finding that challenges more deterministic theories like Moffitt's (1993), derived from developmental psychology, as well as theories like Merton's (1938), Cohen's (1955), Cloward and Ohlin's (1960), and Wilson's (1987), derived from sociology.

In our view, both objective and subjective factors are implicated in the processes by which some offenders commit crime at a higher rate and for a longer period of time than other offenders (see also Giordano, Cernkovich, and Rudolph 2002; Maruna 2001; Shover 1996). The linked ideas of "contingencies" and "intercontingencies" are useful in this discussion (see H. Becker 1998, 28–35). Events and their resulting actions are contingent upon other events and their accompanying actions. Intercontingencies are events and actions that are dependent upon events and actions by other people. Thus a quality marriage may be a turning point for some men because of the event itself, their subjective state, and the behavior of others around them as well as the subsequent events that result because of the fact that they are now married.

Perhaps the concept that best captures this theoretical idea is "situated choice." Our interest is the interaction between life-course transitions, macro-level events, situational context, and individual will. Moreover, we recognize that both the social environment and the individual are influenced by the interaction of structure and choice. This view of individual choice extends well beyond selection effects—

structures are determined by individual choices, and in turn structures constrain, modify, and limit individual choices. In other words, choices are always embedded in social structures. Following Gary Becker and Kevin Murphy (2000), we believe that the interaction of choice and structure produces behavior that cannot be predicted from a focus on one or the other. From our perspective, it is particularly important to reconcile the idea of choice or will with a structuralist notion of turning points (Abbott 1997, 96–97). Indeed, as Abbott has written, "A major turning point has the potential to open a system the way a key has the potential to open a lock . . . action is necessary to complete the turning" (1997, 102). In this instance, action is both thought and behavior, and thus individual action needs to align with the social structure in order to produce behavioral change and to maintain change (or stability?) over the life course. As noted above, this process of change reflects the continuous interplay between purposeful action and default "side bets" (H. Becker 1960) that accumulate over time.

## Who Cares about Boston Boys Born in the 1920s?

Perhaps you ask, "Are these lives from a previous generation relevant to us today?"

—JOHN CLAUSEN (1993)

We have argued that the effects of historical context cannot be ignored in any study of offending patterns over time. This raises the question—is our work merely a historical document or does it speak to the issues of the day? In other words, who cares about Boston boys born in the 1920s if one is interested in understanding and doing something about antisocial behavior and crime in the new millennium? To push the deconstruction argument a bit further, why should we be concerned about a study of all boys in the first place? Along similar lines, why should we be concerned about white boys? Paul Tracy and Kimberly Kempf-Leonard, for example, summarily dismissed the findings in *Crime in the Making* because they were drawn from an "all-white, all-male sample" and offered "only a distorted perception of the reality of crime" (1996, 62–63).

From our perspective, the context of criminal opportunities and the ways in which antisocial tendencies are manifested needs to be recognized in any discussion of offending patterns over time. Moreover, we believe that the patterns of persistence in and desistance from crime that we have uncovered are more general than specific with respect to place, historical time, gender, and race (see also Laub and Sampson 2001, 2002).

Let's take the example of marriage, the most consistent factor to emerge on the basis of both the qualitative narratives and the longitudinal analysis of within-individual change (where each man acted as his own control for stable traits). Why is marriage important in the process of desistance? From our data, it appears that at least five dimensions of marriage affect desistance, and none of them to our knowledge are limited to a particular historical period or demographic subgroup. First, marriage offers the potential resources of another person (social support and capital). Presumably, as marriage continues, these investments grow over time and get stronger. Second, marriage contains an element of direct social control. Spouses often monitor and supervise their mates regarding a variety of behaviors, including crime and deviance. The strategies adopted by spouses vary from "zero tolerance" to "management and containment," but the intent is the same—informal social control. Third, marriage means a change in routines and lifestyle activities, namely, new friends, new family, and new time obligations. Previous routines may no longer be possible because of competing demands and obligations. Fourth, marriage often means a residential change, which can affect routine activities and in turn influence both opportunities and barriers to crime. Fifth, marriage may lead to children, who can not only change one's worldview but dramatically alter routine activities. This view is readily accepted in the popular culture. Consider a recent statement by the actor Nicolas Cage: "Before I was the anarchist setting off fireworks. Once I had my son, instead of big explosions, I looked for stability in my life" (Hawkes 2002, 4).

We are witnessing a revival of interest in the causal effects of marriage, and there is serious discussion and debate regarding the larger role of marriage in society (see Amato and Booth 1997; Waite and Gallagher 2000; Wilson 2002). We do not take a normative stance on marriage, but considering the present climate our findings on the importance of marriage seem relevant. We see our work as central to the debate about how within-individual behavior changes or remains stable over time as individuals connect or disconnect across a variety of institutional domains (for example, marriage, work, the military). Indeed, these were the central questions pursued here by both the qualitative and the quantitative analysis. In any case, as Waite and Gallagher (2000) summarize, most people marry and most who divorce get married again, so the idea that marriage is not relevant to the study of crime is indefensible.

The apparently strong effects of marriage on health are particularly suggestive: if marriage can influence or regulate physiological responses (Kiecolt-Glaser and Newton 2001; Mazur and Michalek 1998), it is possible to conceive of behavioral responses to marriage. To be sure, in this book we have studied the connection of marriage to criminal deviance among men. It is not obvious that women reap the same benefit, although in the case of health the evidence suggests, contrary to prevailing wisdom, that the net gains are positive for all participants (Waite 1995; Waite and Gallagher 2000, 47–64; Kiecolt-Glaser and Newton 2001).

With respect to persistence in crime, consider next the role of addiction and substance abuse. Drawing on a large body of empirical literature, Michael Rutter and his colleagues have concluded, "Antisocial behavior at an earlier age increases the risk of alcohol or drug problems at a later age and vice versa" (1998, 152). Whether involving alcohol or other drugs, substance abuse is an important component in the maintenance of crime over the life course. Moreover, since most of the Glueck men who were substance abusers abused alcohol, it is worthwhile to point out that "alcohol is a more important risk factor for antisocial behavior than are other drugs (because it is more frequently taken in excess)" (Rutter et al. 1998, 154). As revealed in the life-history narratives, drug and alcohol abuse sustains crime in part because of the negative consequences and social difficulties caused by heavy drinking and drug use in the domains of work, family, and the military. Like our findings on marriage, our findings on the role of substance abuse in sustaining criminal behavior over time are not isolated. The Glueck men do not have to have used crack cocaine in order to be relevant to current criminological thinking.

Critics whose gaze is limited to the present thus suffer in the end from a lack of scientific sense. Because our focus is on within-individual patterns of stability and change, we must rely on longitudinal data that other investigators began collecting many years ago in order to empirically study various life adaptations over the long-term (see also

Vaillant 2002). There is no other way to proceed—the study of crime cannot sit still while the principal investigators of today's ongoing longitudinal studies collect data. To be sure, we look forward to learning more about trajectories of adult crime and their linkage to childhood behavior in such studies (for example, the Pittsburgh Youth Study; Rochester Youth Development Study; Dunedin cohort study; Project on Human Development in Chicago Neighborhoods) when those subjects turn age 70 in the year 2045 and well beyond. But of course by then those data too will be criticized as old.

## Implications for Developmental Criminology

Development (*svillupo* in Italian, *desarrollo* in Spanish, *Entwicklung* in German) is literally an unfolding or unrolling of something that is already present and in some way preformed.

—RICHARD LEWONTIN (2000)

If one defines development as life-history change, then developmental criminology should focus on changes in the development of crime and antisocial behavior over time. Relying on what Michael Tonry and David Farrington (1995) refer to as the central insight from Shakespeare—that the child is father to the man (see Caspi 2000)—researchers have addressed how developmental processes are linked to the onset, continuation, and cessation of criminal and antisocial behavior. Much has been learned and developmental criminology is now ascendant. One of the most popular and compelling theories of crime in the developmental camp is Terrie Moffitt's dual taxonomy theory of offending.

In our view, the character of "development" in developmental criminology is a key theoretical issue. Lewontin has stated that "the term *development* is a metaphor that carries with it a prior commitment to the nature of the process" (2000, 5). Using the analogy of a photographic image, Lewontin argues that the way the term "development" is used is a process that makes the latent image apparent. This seems to be what developmental criminological theory is all about. For example, in Moffitt's theory of crime, the environment offers a "set of enabling conditions" that allow individual traits to - express themselves. Although reciprocal interactions with the environment are allowed, life-course-persistent offenders and adolescence-limited offenders follow a preprogrammed line of development—an unwinding, an unfolding, or an unrolling of what is fundamentally "already there." The view of development as a predetermined unfolding is linked to a typological understanding of the world—different internal programs will have different outcomes for individuals of a different type. Lewontin writes, "If the development of an individual is the unfolding of a genetic program immanent in the fertilized egg, then variations in the outcome of development must be consequences of variations in that program" (2000, 17).

Debates about development in the social sciences are not new (see, for example, the exchange between Dannefer (1984) and Baltes and Nesselroade (1984)). As noted, some developmentalists recognize social interactions, but in the end they embrace a between-individual focus that emphasizes the primacy of early childhood attributes that are presumed to be stable. We view the life course as something altogether different. Furthermore, we see development as it is typically defined and emphasized in the literature as not necessarily pertinent to the study of situated human behavior. In our theory of crime, development is better conceived as the constant interaction between individuals and their environment, coupled with the factor of chance or "random developmental noise" (Lewontin 2000, 35–36). Recognizing developmental noise implies that "the organism is determined neither by its genes nor by its environment nor even by interaction between them, but bears a significant mark of random processes" (2000, 38).

From this view it makes sense that we uncovered enormous heterogeneity in criminal offending over the life course. Some offenders start early and stop; others start early and continue for long periods of time. A sizable portion of the offending population displays a zigzag pattern of offending over long time periods. Most important, long-term patterns of offending cannot be explained by individual differences (for example, low verbal IQ), childhood characteristics (for example, early onset of misbehavior), or adolescent characteristics (for example, chronic juvenile offending). In our conception of development, then, the sum of the parts includes individual differences, environmental differences, social interactions, and random, chance events. All of this leads to considerable "noisy, unpredictable development." Coupled with the analyses presented throughout this book, this description captures well the life-course reality of much crime.

## On the Dangers of Offender Typologies

The price of metaphor is eternal vigilance.

—ALEXANDER ROSENBLUETH AND NORBERT WEINER (1951),
AS QUOTED IN LEWONTIN (2000)

The typological idea is a fairly simple and straightforward one that has superficial plausibility, but it is also an idea whose time has probably gone.

—DON GIBBONS (1985)

Richard Lewontin has cautioned that while metaphors are important in intellectual debates, there is a significant danger of confusing the metaphor with the thing of real interest (2000, 4). The discipline of criminology would do well to heed this warning, for if the trend toward reifying offender groups as distinct rather than approximations or heuristic devices continues, we may well miss indications that statistically constructed groups or types do not, in fact, exist. In other words, despite appropriate cautions and caveats, research questions and research designs run a considerable risk of reinforcing the "metaphorical imagery."

Typological configurations pose a related but perhaps more vexing risk. Despite early warnings by Don Gibbons in the 1980s, the popularity of typological approaches to crime has, if anything, increased in recent years. In our view, the problems with typological approaches are many and far reaching. In a general sense, typologies are related to the larger issue of development as a packaged unfolding, as discussed above. But in other ways, the issue of typologies in criminological theory and research is distinct and different from the larger issue of development. One fundamental problem is that most typological approaches in criminology are atheoretical and post hoc. After the fact, it appears possible to find groups in any data set, many of which cannot be replicated or validated with independent data.

The underlying question is whether delinquency and crime are homogeneous or a unidimensional phenomenon. As Travis Hirschi pointed out more than thirty years ago, "the problem with the typological approach is that it begs the question of causal homogeneity by focusing exclusively on the question of behavioral homogeneity" (1969, 53). As we witnessed in our long-term follow-up data, it is more likely that offender groupings follow a fairly continuous distribution across variables. The key finding from our analyses is that the process of desistance follows a remarkably similar path for all offenders, albeit at different rates. Moreover, we could find no credible evidence that this finding is an artifact of our data source.

The notion of offender typologies is also inextricably linked to interventions. The fundamental idea is that different interventions are needed for different types of offenders (see Gibbons 1985). One result of this intellectual approach is the development of specialized study groups and the emergence of the risk-factor paradigm. For instance, in 1995 the U.S. Office of Juvenile Justice and Delinquency Prevention convened a study group on serious and violent juvenile offenders (Loeber and Farrington 1998). The unexamined assumption was that serious and violent juvenile offenders are distinct and different from nonserious and nonviolent juvenile offenders in ways other than what their outcomes indicate. A few years later, a second study group was formed on child delinquents (Loeber and Farrington 2000). The underlying assumption of this study group is that early offenders are different from later offenders. The next study group will no doubt focus on yet another offender category or offense type.

An obvious problem is that there is little consistent empirical support in decades of criminological research for the idea of offense specialization and differential causal forces (Wolfgang, Figlio, and Sellin 1972; Wolfgang, Thornberry, and Figlio 1987; Gottfredson and Hirschi 1990; Piquero, Farrington, and Blumstein 2003). Moreover, depending upon the data source (official versus self-report), offender types are at best a loose reflection of reality and do not capture the complexity of offending over the life course. When one considers long-term follow-up data, offender typologies become even murkier and difficult to justify on empirical grounds. Indeed we designed our follow-up study to capture a typology of adult offending, only to question it as the complexity of the men's lives became apparent. Finally, the success of specialized, targeted interventions focusing on offender types such as life-course-persistent offenders has not been demonstrated; this approach may lead to grandiose proclamations like those seen in the National Summit on Violence pamphlet (1999) that far exceed the state of scientific knowledge in the field of criminology.

By raising critical questions about typological approaches, we are not arguing that groups or grouping techniques have no place in criminology. As discussed in earlier chapters, groups serve many useful purposes, and methods such as trajectory group analysis (Nagin and Land 1993) are innovative in recent criminology. Nevertheless, serious problems arise when groups are defined atheoretically and reified as substantively real without prospective or external validation. Despite the appeal of groups for simplifying a messy reality, we believe that criminologists may be better served by attending to individual trajectories of crime. Understanding general causal pathways to crime at all points in the life course is the research question that criminology might profitably begin to address.

## Reconsidering the Risk-Factor Paradigm

> Certainly the art of constructing [prediction] instruments for use at an early age is in a somewhat parlous state.
>
> —DAVID J. BORDUA (1961b)

The conference "Delinquents under 10: Targeting the Young Offender" was held in Minneapolis in 1999. As the name indicates, the risk-factor and prediction paradigm has again taken hold of criminology, especially for those interested in crime prevention and crime control policies (for an excellent overview of this approach, see Farrington 2000). Investigators know what the risk factors are; however, what we don't know very well is which kids will do what and when. In other words, as David Bordua observed more than forty years ago, our ability to predict behavior prospectively over the long term continues to be weak at best.

An analogy may be appropriate here. In an article in *Science,* Robert Geller and his colleagues have concluded that earthquakes cannot be predicted. They write:

> Whether any particular small earthquake grows into a large earthquake depends on a myriad of fine details of physical conditions throughout a large volume, not just in the immediate vicinity of the fault. This highly sensitive nonlinear dependence of earthquake rupture on unknown initial conditions severely limits predictability. The prediction of individual large earthquakes would require the unlikely capability of knowing all of these details with greater accuracy. Furthermore, no quantitative theory for analyzing these data to issue predictions exists at present. Thus, the consensus . . . was that individual earthquakes are probably inherently unpredictable. (Geller et al. 1997, 1616)

What is needed, Geller and his colleagues conclude, are "observable and identifiable precursors that would allow alarms to be issued with high reliability and accuracy" (1997, 1616).

In the field of criminology do such precursors in fact exist? Yes and no. The yes refers once again to the fact that adult criminals seem always to possess early childhood risks (Robins 1966, 1978), a sturdy finding in criminology. The no refers to the prospective reality. There is a lengthy history of prediction research in criminology showing that childhood variables are quite modest prognostic devices, going forward in time. Known as the false positive problem, prediction scales often result in the substantial overprediction of future criminality (Loeber and Stouthamer-Loeber 1987; Farrington and Tarling 1985). Likewise, prediction attempts often fail to identify accurately those who will become criminal even though past behavior suggests otherwise (false negatives). In one of the best studies that illustrates the problem, Jennifer White and her colleagues (1990, 521) document that "early antisocial behavior is the best predictor of later antisocial behavior." This study examined behavior from age 3 to age 15. Nevertheless, their data clearly show the limitations of relying only on childhood information to understand behavior over time. As White et al. (1990, 521) argue, a high false positive rate precludes the use of early antisocial behavior alone as a predictor of later crime. They go on to note the general inaccuracy of specific predictions and describe how the heterogeneous nature of delinquency in later adolescence (and by implication, adulthood) thwarts accurate prediction. White's findings complement our own. Using data from ages 7 to 70 we have illustrated the inherent difficulties in predicting crime prospectively over the life course. This long history of problems in predicting crime and delinquency has been a core criticism of the Gluecks' research program dating back to the 1950s and 1960s (Sampson and Laub 1993; Laub and Sampson 1991).

## Incarceration and Offender Reentry

> The most terrible moment in the life of an offender is not that in which the prison door closes upon him, but that in which it opens to permit his return to the world.
>
> —FREDERICK HOWARD WINES (1919)

The study of criminal recidivism after prisoner release has a venerable tradition in criminology and has produced some of the field's most important works (for example, Glaser 1969), but what to do about offender "reentry" after incarceration remains a major policy issue. This concern is being driven by the number of ex-prisoners returning home (roughly 1,600 a day) and by the unexamined belief that the needs of ex-offenders are different today than in eras gone by (see Travis, Solomon, and Waul 2001; compare Glaser 1969).

One of the more troubling findings from our analysis of the Gluecks' data concerns the possible counterproductive effects of punitive sanctions, such as incarceration, when considered in the long run of individual lives. Our analyses over the years have found that employment is directly influenced by criminal sanctions—incarceration as a juvenile and as a young adult had a negative effect on later job stability, which in turn was negatively related to continued involvement in crime over the life course (Sampson and Laub 1993; Laub and Sampson 1995). Notwithstanding positive assessments of juvenile incarceration in the narratives of some men who desisted, the view of incarceration, especially long-term incarceration, was overwhelmingly negative among those men who persisted in crime over the life course. From these findings as well as other evidence on the consequences of imprisonment (see Fagan and Freeman 1999; Hagan 1993; Western 2002), the idea of cumulative disadvantage seems germane. Cumulative disadvantage posits that arrest and especially incarceration may spark failure in school, unemployment, and weak community bonds, in turn increasing adult crime (Sampson and Laub 1997; Thornberry 1987; Thornberry and Krohn 2001).

This line of inquiry in life-course criminology appears directly relevant to policies based on deterrence and other forms of punitive intervention as well as to efforts addressing prisoner reentry. We need to take into account the potential negative effects of sanctioning in forestalling desistance, along with factors that facilitate offender reintegration. What is needed is a mechanism or, better yet, a series of mechanisms to bring offenders back into the institutional fabric of society. The critical question that should be on the table, then, is how does society facilitate reconnections that are so essential to the process of desistance from crime?

"Well sir, I guess there's just a meanness in this world," sings Bruce Springsteen (1982). Our data also reveal the inherent complexities and difficult challenges facing offenders in their reentry efforts. Behavioral change is complicated, varied, and seemingly impossible to predict. We studied men who were arrested in every decade of their life, some of whom committed murder, child rape, and armed robbery well into adulthood with no regrets whatsoever. Their crimes, attitudes, and lifestyles confirmed for us what James Q. Wilson noted decades ago: "Wicked people exist" (1975, 260). Or as Jack Katz (1988) observed, many offenders are deeply and possibly forever attracted to the seductions of what we might call "doing harm." In confronting the pathos and destruction of such men, we were struck by the Pollyannaish quality of much criminological talk about reintegration. Nevertheless, although warm and cuddly prisoner reentry options seem ill suited for such hardened men, we do not wish to use this fact to attack all rehabilitation efforts and crime prevention programs, as Wilson did. We believe these initiatives are essential and well justified from a scientific standpoint (Cullen and Gendreau 2000; Sherman et al. 1997). Moreover, we see these initiatives as important components of a fair, just, and humane society. Our point is a cautionary one to those who have embraced "offender reentry" as the answer to the crime problem, especially the idea that we merely need to help offenders "make good." The road is long, the participants often unwilling, and our state of knowledge quite limited.

## Conclusion

Whereas in *Crime in the Making* we saw informal social control as the primary explanation of crime and desistance over the life course, here we offer a more nuanced perspective. As David Matza said almost forty years ago, the missing element in traditional social control theory is human agency (1964, 183); motivation has always been its weakest link. Moreover, as we argued in the past, traditional social control theory suffers from other problems: it is narrowly portrayed as a static, cross-sectional theory that ignores the dynamic, longitudinal aspects of informal social control and support; the theory neglects the role of social structure in the social bonding process; and the theory fails to appreciate the feedback effects of crime and incarceration on social bonds as an important part of the causal story. And though beyond the scope of this book, traditional social control cannot easily explain (or possibly even comprehend) crime that results when individuals are socially bonded and tightly connected to strong subcultures or higher-echelon segments of society. Events such as the Enron and WorldCom scandals, alleged insider trading by Martha Stewart, terrorism here and abroad, and sex abuse by priests in the Catholic Church should cause even the most ardent supporter of traditional social control theory some discomfort and consternation.

Although we do not abandon control theory, we see other concepts as equally relevant for understanding persistent offending and desistance from crime over the life course. As we discussed in Chapter 3, these concepts include personal agency and situated choice, routine activities, aging, macro-level historical events, and local culture and community context. We have thereby offered an expanded vision of our age-graded theory of informal social control presented in *Crime in the Making* and our other writings over the last decade. Interestingly, as much as our earlier theory was linked to our methodological and analytical approach (for example, regression models focusing on holding individual differences constant to see the effects of turning points), our revised theory here is also linked to our method and analytical strategy (for example, life-history narratives derived from the men themselves integrated with quantitative longitudinal data reconstructed from the Glueck archive supplemented by our own follow-up study at age 70). This merging of quantitative and qualitative data allowed us to gain insight into the life course of crime that would not have been possible using traditional approaches. Within-individual hierarchical models and trajectory analyses turned out to sit rather well with in-depth narratives and qualitative analysis, at least for the purposes of better understanding lives through time. Integrative and emergent findings pushed us to expand our theory of informal social control to include, among others, the idea of situated choice as central to an understanding of crime from childhood through old age. As the Glueck men near the end of their lives, the complexities and possibilities of such choices become ever more apparent and, inevitably, ever more consequential.

*Notes*

*References*

*Index*

# NOTES

## 1. Diverging Pathways of Troubled Boys

1. In our life-course theory of crime, the existence of multiple pathways to crime or desistance from crime does not necessarily mean that each pathway has a distinct causal process or applies only to a particular group of offenders. On the contrary, there can be many roads to desistance (for example, marriage, work, religion), but each road can still share enough with other roads to be considered part of a general process or common theoretical concept.

2. This is not to say that there are only three. Throughout this book we address many of the challenges to our work. Other major challenges have been dealt with elsewhere (especially Sampson and Laub 1993, 1995; Laub, Nagin, and Sampson 1998), particularly those offered by Gottfredson and Hirschi (1990) and Wilson and Herrnstein (1985). These authors offer a single-pathway explanation and contend that crime can be explained by a "population heterogeneity" model, either due to variation in self-control, as suggested by Gottfredson and Hirschi, or variation in constitutional and/or personality differences, as suggested by Wilson and Herrnstein. This view emphasizes continuity in behavior and rejects the idea that meaningful change occurs over the life course that cannot be explained by either childhood factors or aging. This important issue was a major focus of *Crime in the Making,* and we do not revisit the debate in this book. The differences and similarities between Gottfredson and Hirschi and Sampson and Laub are also well articulated in a published exchange in *Studies on Crime and Crime Prevention.* See Hirschi and Gottfredson (1995) and Sampson and Laub (1995) for details regarding their respective positions on the issue of continuity and change in

criminal behavior over the life course. See Cohen and Vila (1996) for an independent adjudication of this debate.

3. Daniel Nagin and his colleagues have built on this kind of thinking to identify several kinds of offending trajectories (see, for example, Nagin, Farrington, and Moffitt 1995). Whether there are two groups, four groups, or six groups is not relevant here. What is at stake is whether there are distinct causal pathways for some offenders or whether all offending trajectories can be explained by the same general tendencies, as we have argued (Sampson and Laub 1993).

4. These designations are placed in quotes because using them in effect reifies groups, and the very language seems to imply different causal processes are at work in each designation or grouping. Whether this is the case or not is one of the motivating questions for this book. As will be discussed below, we use categorizations such as these as a way of organizing our data and for heuristic purposes. At this point, we merely note that groupings like these are potentially problematic.

## 2. Persistence or Desistance?

1. Although we seek to paint a fairly broad theoretical picture here, our research base is considerably more detailed. For a more traditional review of the literature on desistance from crime and other problem behavior, see our in-depth treatment in Laub and Sampson (2001).

2. Extant theories that have employed the idea of state dependence predict, all else equal, that crime will generate more crime, thus leading to continuity in offending over time. For example, labeling theory (Lemert 1972), social learning theory (Akers 1998), general strain theory (Agnew 1992), interactional theory (Thornberry 1987), and even our theory of cumulative disadvantage and stability of delinquency (Sampson and Laub 1997) all seem to predict escalating crime.

3. Like Shover, Maruna (2001) has focused on subjective orientations in the desistance process in an effort to understand how desistance works. Maruna contends that maturation occurs independent of age and leads to subjective changes that are essential to sustain desistance from crime. Simply put, people who are going straight undergo a change in personality and self-concept. Thus phrases like a "new person" or a "new outlook on life" apply to those who desist from crime. Using data from life-history narratives for 55 men and 10 women drawn from a snowball sampling frame, Maruna found reformed offenders were more other-centered and found fulfillment in generative behaviors; felt a greater control over their destiny and took responsibility for shaping their future; and saw a "silver lining" in the negative situation resulting from crime and found meaning and purpose in life. As Maruna (2001) has pointed out, this pattern fits the essential elements of the "pro-

totypical reform story," and this reform tale may be an important part of the desistance process (see also Maruna 1997).

4. Two recent theories of desistance draw on the symbolic interactionist perspective in an effort to better understand the processes of persistence in and desistance from crime. For example, Matsueda and Heimer (1997) focus on role taking, role commitments, and role transitions, emphasizing the meaning of life-course transitions to the individuals involved and interactions within immediate situations. Giordano, Cernkovich, and Rudolph (2002) develop a theory of "cognitive transformation," which emphasizes an individual's openness to change, exposure and receptivity to "hooks" for change, identity transformation, and changes in the meaning and desirability of deviance. We see these theoretical approaches as largely compatible with our revised life-course theory of informal social control and crime developed in the next chapter.

5. The life-course perspective can also be distinguished from the criminal career model. We regard the life-course perspective as broader in scope and driven by theoretical rather than by policy concerns. In contrast, the criminal career model is largely atheoretical and more concerned with developing policy about "career criminals" than theory about "criminal careers."

6. This view is consistent with recent research in the health area. For instance, Lamont and his colleagues (2000) found that adult lifestyle and biological risk markers measured in adulthood explained more variance in cardiovascular disease risk than the direct and indirect contributions of early childhood experiences.

## 3. Explaining the Life Course of Crime

1. Maruna writes, "By 'making good,' not only is the desisting ex-offender 'changed,' but he or she is reconstituted" (2001, 10). On the basis of our life-history interviews with men who desisted from serious, persistent offending, we believe that this idea may be no more than psychological new-age optimism. The idea of reconstitution implies a different person, as does the idea of the "ex-offender." We see this as a case of the "group mentality" being applied within the lives of the same person. In our theory, there is no need to "make good" if situations and structures engender a commitment to desist from crime. Indeed, for many of our men, their identity reflection changed not a whit, and in fact for many offenders the capacity for self-reflection was painfully absent. Criminological theories must allow for behavioral change absent identity reconstruction, whatever the latter might mean. We return to this issue in Chapter 10.

2. At this point we make no claim about the beneficial effect of marriage for women, although there well may be such an effect (see Giordano, Cernkovich, and Rudolph, 2002). It is not inconsistent, for example, that marriage

could hurt women even as at the same time it benefits their male partners. We return to this vexing dilemma in the concluding chapter.

3. According to Waite (1995), the prime difference between cohabitation and marriage concerns time horizons and commitment. In addition, couples exhibit a sense of responsibility toward each other in marriages that is not evident in cohabitation.

4. One former delinquent we call Leon talked about his surprise at the extent of segregation by race in the service. Growing up in a racially and ethnically diverse Boston neighborhood, Leon said that it never occurred to him that segregation existed. In his own words, this experience in the service demonstrated how "incredibly naive [he] was at twenty-odd years of age." For more from Leon's life history, see Chapter 6.

5. In the Gluecks' research design all delinquent youths were incarcerated, so there is no variation in the prevalence of institutionalization that can influence later development. There is, however, considerable variation among the delinquents in the time they served, not only in adolescence but in adulthood as well. For example, the average time served during the juvenile period (up to age 17 in Massachusetts) was 553 days (about eighteen months), though some individuals served about four months while others were incarcerated up to seven years. To assess the relevance of incarceration we calculated the actual number of days (not sentence length) each subject spent in a custodial institution as a juvenile (<17) and at ages 17–25 and 25–32. For the 52 men we interviewed, we calculated the number of days served from age 32 to age 70. See data on these men in Chapters 6, 7, and 8.

6. In point of fact, the original title of Travis Hirschi's dissertation was "Crime as Infraction" (Laub 2002, 105). Perhaps wisely (in retrospect), he later changed it to "Causes of Delinquency." The work went on to become a modern classic of criminology.

7. The men who desisted from crime expressed attitudes toward violence that were similar to those depicted by the persistent offenders (see Chapters 6 and 7). We contend that the differences in behavior lie in the structure of the men's lives and how they are managed by outsiders (for example, wives, in-laws, bosses), which in turn influences their rates of offending.

### 4. Finding the Men

1. Twenty-five subjects had died during the Gluecks' original follow-up study up to age 32, and these cases were not included in our records search. Also, although the Gluecks collected data for 438 subjects who could be found and cooperated at all three waves, we used as our base for the criminal record searches all known living subjects ($N = 475$).

2. Violent offenses primarily included homicide, assault, rape, and robbery. Property crimes primarily included burglary, larceny, auto theft, fraud, and

vandalism. Alcohol and drug offenses included drunkenness, operating under the influence, and narcotics (both selling and possession). The other category included a wide range of offenses such as conspiracy to commit theft, impersonation of a police officer, disorderly conduct, vagrancy, gambling, traffic offenses such as speeding, lewdness, offenses against the family (for example, nonsupport), resisting arrest, and hunting near a dwelling.

3. We thank Winnie Reed of the National Institute of Justice for her help in securing these data.

4. The problems regarding data on dispositions from FBI, state, and local rap sheets have been extensively discussed in the literature (see Geerken 1994; Belair 1985; Weisburd and Waring 2001). Thus, like other researchers, we focus on arrests.

5. We thank George Vaillant for his assistance in gaining access to these records.

6. For example, we were not able to interview any offenders who had a violent arrest as a juvenile and in later adulthood (32 to 70), but not between ages 17–32. There were only two cases in this group—one was dead and the other did not respond to our request for an interview.

7. Given the long retrospective window in our life-history calendar, we developed a series of "memory markers" to help the subjects place events in time. Some of these markers were universal (for example, the year of the assassination of President John F. Kennedy) while others were specific to locale of the study (for example, the digging of the tunnel connecting the city of Boston to Logan airport). One of the more unusual yet quite helpful memory markers were the years of World Series appearances by the Boston Red Sox, which occurred in nearly each decade of our follow-up study—1967, 1975, and 1986.

8. One question continually asked of qualitative researchers is, Are there enough cases to make any concrete statements? The question of sample size is an important issue for both qualitative and quantitative research. Unfortunately, there is no clear answer to the question of "how many observations are enough" (King, Keohane, and Verba 1994, 213–217). Given the questions posed here and the variability in the dependent variable we obtained through our sampling design, we believe 52 life-history narratives are sufficient. Moreover, as discussed in Chapter 9, when we examine changes in life circumstances and changes in crime for these 52 men from age 17 to 70, we increase the number of observations to almost 2,500.

9. Much to our surprise, the FBI rap sheets often did not include the social security number of the subject. We had anticipated that this would be an excellent source for gaining social security numbers for many of the men. We were wrong.

10. For an interesting discussion of the methods used in tracing and securing cooperation of subjects in the Cambridge Study in Delinquent Development, see Farrington, Gallagher, et al. (1990).

11. Extensive analyses of these lost cases reveal nothing unusual about them, and it is assumed that their exclusion does not affect the results (see also Sampson and Laub 1993, 55–59).

12. We interviewed 40 men face to face (77 percent) and 12 men by telephone (23 percent). Of the face-to-face interviews, 24 (60 percent) took place at the man's home.

### 5. Long-Term Trajectories of Crime

1. Rolf Loeber and his colleagues have developed a risk-factor paradigm that focuses on three different pathways to problem behavior and delinquency. The three pathways include an overt pathway, an authority conflict pathway, and a covert pathway (Loeber and Hay 1997, 385). This multiple-risk/pathway scheme is highly reminiscent of the research strategy and crime prevention recommendations of Sheldon and Eleanor Glueck (see Laub and Sampson 1991).

2. For those readers who think we overstate this concern, consider the announcement of the National Summit on Violence throughout the Lifespan (1999). One of the goals of this conference was to "view advanced working programs which may be applied in communities, at each critical juncture throughout the lifespan, for the 'Lifetime Persistent' and 'Adolescent Limited' Violent Offender" (1999, 2). Other pronouncements included: "The latest generation of research has revealed that one of the only effective opportunities to prevent Lifetime Persistent offending may be within the first three years of life" and that "although Violent Juveniles perpetrate an average of 100 crimes a year, nearly 80% end their criminal careers at the age of 21, with or without intervention, hence 'Adolescence Limited' " (1999, 5, 9). It is rare to witness such certainty in social science research.

3. See Chapter 4, note 2, for a detailed description of the individual offenses under each crime type. Note also that this analysis is restricted to 480 of the original 500 delinquents. As described in Chapter 4, 20 cases were lost in the early 1970s during the archiving process and thus have missing data from ages 7 to 32.

4. The high rate of offending through the middle adult years is central to the validity of our assessment of Moffitt's (1993) perspective, which emphasizes the heterotypic continuity of offending. For example, she argues that life-course persistents who steal and fight as adolescents will as adults segue into other patterns of antisocial activity, such as drug abuse, alcoholism, domestic violence, and theft from employers. Although our data may not capture all of these behaviors, it is clear that a substantial portion of the Glueck men committed a wide variety of antisocial acts (for example, driving while intoxicated, failing to pay child support) well into their forties. If life-course-persistent offenders exist, we should be able to find them in our data.

5. We explored numerous alternative conceptualizations of childhood and adolescent risk and behavior (for example, parental criminality and alcohol abuse, parental mental disturbance, the number of grades repeated, and personality variables such as stubbornness). These analyses showed the same pattern, that is, we did not see any indication that stable, individual characteristics can account for variation in offending in later life conditioned on adolescent delinquency.

6. Because the exact cause of death can be ascertained from the death record, it is possible to investigate the timing of death in relation to the frequency and type of criminal offending (for example, violent versus property) over the life course. In a comparative study of mortality in the Glueck delinquent and nondelinquent samples, Laub and Vaillant (2000) found that delinquents were more likely to die earlier in the life course and were more likely to die as the result of homicide, accidents, and poor self-care than their nondelinquent counterparts. Laub and Vaillant also found that childhood characteristics were not helpful in predicting death. Proximal unhealthy behaviors such as alcohol abuse were more important than childhood and adolescent variables like education, dysfunctional upbringing, and adolescent delinquency.

7. The models presented here were estimated using the SAS-based TRAJ procedure (Jones, Nagin, and Roeder 2001). The trajectory method estimates these model parameters using maximum likelihood for a fixed number of groups. The optimal number of groups is assessed using the Bayesian Information Criterion (BIC), which can inform the selection of the best model for comparison of both nested and unnested models (see D'Unger et al. 1998; Nagin 1999). The BIC is estimated using the following equation,

$$BIC = -2\log(L) + \log(n)*k,$$

where $L$ is the maximum likelihood, $n$ is the sample size, and $k$ is the number of model parameters. Although the Bayesian Information Criterion has been emphasized as the criteria to assess the optimal number of groups, the model selection process is often more complex. As Nagin and Land point out in their original article, the groupings "may be seen as only an approximation of a postulated underlying continuous dimension of hidden heterogeneity in offending propensity" (1993, 357). Since these groupings are abstractions or approximations and not a true reflection of reality, researchers tend to use the BIC as one criterion for choosing the number of groups, but not the sole criterion. For instance, Brame, Nagin, and Tremblay find a six-group model to be the optimal model based on the BIC for their childhood aggression analysis and yet they "describe the four-group model because the results from this more parsimonious solution are qualitatively similar" (2001, 506). In the majority of the estimated models in this analysis, the BIC is used to select the optimal model.

8. As outlined in Nagin (1999), we can also estimate each individual's probabil-

ity of membership in the offender groups. This posterior probability is determined using the equation

$$\hat{P}(j|Y_i) = \frac{\hat{P}(Y_i|j)\hat{\pi}_j}{\sum_j \hat{P}(Y_i|j)\hat{\pi}_j},$$

where $\hat{P}(Y_i|j)$ is the estimated probability of observing the actual offending behavior $Y_i$ conditional on membership in group $j$ for person $i$, and $\hat{\pi}_j$ is the estimated proportion of the population in group $j$. On the basis of these probabilities, each individual is assigned to the group displaying the largest group assignment probability. In other words, individuals are assigned to the group to which they are most likely to belong on the basis of their ex-post offending patterns. According to Nagin, these posterior probabilities "are among the most useful products of the group-based modeling approach" (1999, 149).

9. The mean group posterior probabilities for this analysis range from .87 to .99, which are clearly high.

10. The mean group assignment probabilities range from .86 to .99 for property crime, .72 to .93 for violent crime, and .85 to .99 for alcohol and drug crime.

11. For an interesting analysis of variations in trajectory groupings based on varying lengths of follow-up, incarceration, and mortality, see Eggleston, Laub, and Sampson (2004).

12. In order to assess whether the trajectory method adequately captured heterogeneity, we ran random effects models within each trajectory grouping. One important feature of the random effects model is that it estimates the correlation between the error terms over time (rho). This correlation is the proportion of the joint variation in the error that is attributable to the time-stable individual-specific component. This correlation will be close to zero if the population of interest represents a homogenous population (Nagin and Paternoster 1991). We found that for total crime as well as crime-specific trajectories, rho was at or near zero for almost every trajectory group. The largest rho was .23 for the high-rate chronic group for alcohol/drug crime.

13. The group comparisons were assessed with an ANOVA test. If the $F$ test was significant, we conducted a post hoc test to determine which group means were statistically different from one another. In some cases the mean differences appear to be large but they are not statistically significant, whereas in other cases small mean differences are significant. These occurrences arise because of the different metrics and standard errors for the risk factors.

14. Even if we limit the analysis to offenders with an arrest in every single decade of their lives—a reasonable definition of active offenders—the age-crime curve holds (data not shown).

15. Again, see Loeber and Farrington (1998) and the pamphlet from the National Summit on Violence throughout the Lifespan (1999).

16. For excellent reviews of general versus developmental and static versus dynamic criminological theories, see Paternoster et al. (1997, 232–240) and Cohen and Vila (1996).

### 6. Why Some Offenders Stop

1. Compared with the persistent offenders discussed in the next chapter (see Table 7.2), the men who desisted from crime had remarkably similar IQ scores and total report scores for "unofficial delinquency." Total reports of unofficial delinquency combine self-, parent, and teacher reports of delinquency and other misconduct into one summary measure (for more details, see Sampson and Laub 1993, 50–53). Our measure of adolescent competence captures the idea of planfulness, conscientiousness, ambitions and attitudes toward school, and school performance (see Laub and Sampson 1998 for more details).

2. Interestingly, for men who were not married and still lived at home, mothers continued to exert direct social control. For example, one subject was asked if he ever had to miss any days from work because of hangovers. He responded, "No, no. My mother wouldn't let me. She'd be yelling at me the next morning. Oh, no, no, no. I'd pay to get out of the house." This same man said that his mother would say, "You gotta stop [drinking]. Stay home [instead of going to bars]." This man surmised that he "smartened up on account of his mother."

3. Kenaszchuk (1996) found that men who desisted from crime as a result of a good marriage displayed an increased commitment to achieving economic security for their families. Thus marriage brought into focus the importance of work as a means to a successful union. This confirms the idea raised above that stable work is important in sustaining the desistance process.

4. The Gavin House is a well-known community-based program in South Boston for the treatment of alcoholics.

5. Even though these subjects came from disadvantaged neighborhoods and were delinquent in their youth, many were quite successful as adults. One man told us that he had made "more than $90,000 a year since 1950." As evidence of the attraction of deviance and illicit action even among desisters, this same man won $80,000 playing pool. He celebrated by taking his wife to Italy to see relatives.

6. Adler (1992) notes a parallel in her study of ex-drug dealers. She writes, "Although these individuals may be too old to keep up with their former drug-using pace or to return to the fast life, many still enjoy a touch of hedonism. In an era when most middle-aged people are former marijuana smokers, party drinkers, and general revelers, these ex-drug traffickers still like to have their adventures. It remains a part of their life-style and new identity, carried over from earlier times" (1992, 125).

### 7. Why Some Offenders Persist

1. We remind the reader that our measure of delinquency combines self-, parent, and teacher reports of delinquency and other antisocial behaviors into one summary score (see Sampson and Laub 1993, 50–53). It is our best measure of "unofficial" delinquency in childhood and adolescence.
2. One can speculate that the obsession with cars for Billy's generation has been replaced by a fascination with guns for today's teenagers.
3. In Cohen and Taylor's classic study of long-term imprisonment, inmates mark the passage of time in two ways—mind-building (reading or studying) or body-building (usually weightlifting)—"in order to protect themselves from the terror of the misty abyss" (1972, 95).
4. In order to protect Billy's confidentiality, we cannot discuss the details of these legal cases here.
5. Billy did go to school while in federal prison and learned soldering. He worked in a cable shop in prison and earned 11 cents an hour. But apart from the money, Billy achieved recognition for his work because he would work more hours than he had to. "I would go in for 4 o'clock count and have my supper and then go back to work. Until it got dark and I would do all these extra things and help out the other people." He received four incentive awards for his work there. Billy worked hard in federal prison because he wanted to keep busy. He told us that he had to go to school for a long time for this job. It was difficult, but he did it. Billy obtained a job in prison in the clean room of the electric cable factory doing special work for the armed forces. He did that particular type of work because he became a good solderer. But after he got out of prison he couldn't find any place to work at that kind of job. The benefits of this job were temporary and only in the prison context.
6. As far as we can tell, this statement is not true. Billy told us on another occasion that he had a serious fight in prison in which he hit an inmate with a chair. Another time Billy recounted that he was approached by three teenagers who demanded his wallet. He told them, "If you want my wallet, you will have to kill me." Although age 68 at the time, he was fully prepared to use violence in this instance. Thus, for Billy, violence is to be used in situations when one is confronted by a threatening force.
7. Although Billy was arrested for bank robbery at age 59, he contends that he was not involved in this particular crime. According to Billy, it is the only time in his career that he did not plead guilty, because he did not commit the crime. Despite his plea of innocence and various legal challenges, Billy was convicted and sentenced to federal prison. He maintains to this day that he was falsely accused by the brother of one of his co-defendants. The brother was facing a long sentence for dealing drugs in a school zone, and he offered "information" about the bank robbery to avoid prison. This information implicated Billy and two others in the crime.

8. As a reminder of the ambiguities inherent in official criminal histories, Billy claimed that a charge of breaking and entering on his record was the result of a plea bargain. "When I went to court the prosecutor said 'you had to plead guilty to this as well as this.' And I would agree because they wanted to give me like five years. And I thought perhaps they were going to give me like twenty. So for the five years I would tell them anything. If that was what they wanted that's what I would tell them."

9. The issue of fraudulent enlistment is complicated. One of the men who desisted from crime during much of his later adult life was a career military man. After our interview, the man we call Ron wrote to us because he had "left out some facts that should be covered to give a true picture of [his] young life." Ron said that after Lyman reform school he was "assigned" to Deer Island (a jail for the city of Boston). When he was released, he went back to his old gang. His brother gave him a watch that had been stolen. The police "caught" him and confiscated the watch. The next day Ron went to the Marine recruiter and enlisted under his cousin's name. He served several years, including a period during the Korean War when he was awarded the Purple Heart and decorated for bravery. After the war, Ron "declared" himself a "Fraud Enlistee." At the time, he was a staff sergeant. He asked to be allowed to remain in the Marine Corps and to change his name to his real one. His request was approved and he remained in the service for fifteen more years.

10. Charlie went on to say that years ago if you were a burglar you would never have carried a weapon, not even a knife. It was an unwritten rule. Many of the persistent offenders referred to a "criminal code of honor" regarding acceptable criminal customs and suitable victims. Nicky, in reference to the code of honor, said, "It was screwy, but it existed." For example, Jimmy told us that in certain neighborhoods like South Boston crimes like rape or handbag snatching did not occur because you never knew who might be related to the victim. This reflects a sense of community whereby all members of a neighborhood and their extended family were protected. At the same time, it would be misleading to think these men did not use violence or would not use their guns if needed. For example, Buddy told us, "Well, . . . if I had a problem, with a gun available, I'd go back and get it and go looking for people that I had a problem with or get some kind of a weapon."

11. However, it may be worthwhile to note the following passage from Frankie's age 25 interview—the subject is "quite bitter over the workings of the police and the parole system in Massachusetts—claims that all authorities are 'down on him.' He could not get a driver's license in Mass, for example, because of his record and the cops were out to get him."

12. Virtually all of the persistent offenders who were alcoholics dismissed Alcoholics Anonymous as an effective treatment strategy. The viewpoint of Frankie is illustrative—"I went to AA for twenty-something years and still drank. Everybody that goes to AA drinks soon as they come out."

13. The negative views surrounding juvenile reform schools are not confined strictly to persistent offenders. Similar themes emerge in some of the narratives of men who desisted from crime in adulthood as well as those who exhibited intermittent offending over the life course. Recall, however, that one unexpected finding was that the reform school experience was perceived as a positive turning point for some desisters (see Chapter 6).

14. What is strikingly evident is the lack of deterrent or rehabilitative effects of incarceration. One can argue that incapacitative effects were also not fully realized, because many of the persistent offenders continued to commit crimes while in prison. This is not to say that the persistent offenders we interviewed liked doing time—clearly they did not. If anything, long periods of confinement (or multiple incarcerations) seem to have created an institutional dependency that hampered their ability to quit committing crimes or made them even more defiant of authority. More than forty years ago, Sykes (1958) raised the question whether prisons added to the deterioration of prisoners rather than steering them away from crime. The narrative data from the persistent offenders in our long-term follow-up study indicates that the answer is yes.

## 8. Zigzag Criminal Careers

1. The concept of intermittency raises a number of questions about the nature of criminal careers and the natural history of offending. After all, to a large extent all offending is intermittent (or impermanent). Even persistent offenders spend most of their waking hours crime-free, and according to our data all offenders eventually desist from crime.

2. We learned that former residents of the West End have powerful resentment toward the government. There is a strong sense that the government in collusion with real estate developers joined together to destroy a viable, tight-knit neighborhood, when it was demolished as part of a major urban renewal project in the 1950s (Gans 1962). The language and emotions that this topic generated were among the most intense expressed in our interviews. "Well-educated crooks—outsiders—who came in and took away our home" captures the conventional wisdom of the Glueck men on this topic.

3. These facts serve to underscore that criminal charges may be ambiguous with respect to the underlying purpose or motivation of the crime. Another man, Mickey, recounted that while he was in New York, he met a friend in a building near Wall Street. His friend told him to "wait here. I'll be right back." This occurred around 3:00 P.M. on a Saturday afternoon. Both of them had been drinking. Mickey fell asleep while he was waiting for his friend to return. At 6:00 P.M. Mickey tried to get out of the building and in so doing he set off the alarm system. He was arrested for breaking and entering. There is considerable ambiguity in our narratives on domestic situations as well regarding nonsupport, domestic violence, and neglect of children.

4. Like many of the men we interviewed, Mickey did not go to Alcoholics Anonymous to help him stop drinking. When asked if he went to AA, Mickey responded, "No. I went to AA once and I got laid, relayed, and parlayed. And everybody was offered drinks in this place. So what happened was . . . we'd take a trip up to New Hampshire and I was buying a half a gallon of scotch every couple of weeks. And this went on for about three or four years. And then I got a half a gallon of scotch and I put it in the cabinet and there was a half a gallon there—I hadn't had a drink in probably two months. So it was around Christmas time. I put ribbons on it and gave it away. I gave up drinking just like that. Just walked away from it." The men we interviewed for the most part stopped drinking "cold turkey" without the benefit of AA or any other form of treatment. Of course, there are exceptions; see narratives from Patrick and Sean above.

5. To further illustrate the messy lives that some of the Glueck men led, consider Sean's response to our question on how many children he had with his wife. He replied he was not sure. They had four children, but he was not sure he was the father of any of them except the first one. He told us that his wife and his brother had an affair while he was in jail. His wife was in and out of the state mental hospital because she was always cutting herself, among other things. When Sean went to jail, "I remember saying to my brother when I was going to jail—'Go and take care of [name].' He had never met her, and I said, 'Go and make sure she has whatever she needs and look over her, and watch over her for me.' Bad mistake, bad mistake." Not only are the lives of offenders messy, but the messiness extends across generations as well. We were constantly struck by the amount of problems the Glueck men's offspring have.

6. Some of the rationalizations may be because the consequences of engaging in criminal lifestyles were less serious in the World War II era. Almost all of the men noted a strong period effect regarding guns, drugs, and gangs. When asked if he ever owned a gun, Donald replied, "I had guns. Yeah, I had a gun. You know, for my own use, in the house in case somebody come and broke in my house. [But] I never carried it." Donald went on to tell us that gun availability was not a concern because "you could get any gun you want." When asked the difference between violence now and violence when he was growing up, Donald responded, "I figure on account of dope. I think it's on account of dope what some of this crime is for. People are carrying guns." Donald speculated that if he carried a gun, he "would have used it maybe . . . See, I was a cocky kid at that time and I might have used it. That's the difference." All of his fights involved fists, no weapons. "Now they use baseball bats or guns or knives. Years ago you didn't use anything, you used your hands." Donald's wife interjected, "If somebody was down and you kicked them, you were a dirty fighter." Donald was in a gang, and there were gang fights about strangely familiar issues like territorial disputes. "Yeah, we were in a gang," Donald said, but he emphatically stated that gangs in his day "all fought with

hands." In any discussion of offending patterns over time, the immediate context of opportunities available to the subject and how manifestations of antisocial tendencies are realized thus need to be recognized.

### 9. Modeling Change in Crime

1. On the basis of marriage dates from the life-history calendars and the Glueck archives up to age 32, we coded whether each man was married (1 = yes, 0 = no) during each year from age 17 to 70.

2. This model is similar to the negative binomial model with unobserved hetero-geneity often used in the criminal career literature. The difference is that we do not impose any distributional assumptions (for example, gamma distrib-uted) on the extra-Poisson variance parameter. Although there are a number of options, we use the HLM5 software of Raudenbush et al. (2000) to esti-mate population-average model parameters with robust standard errors. To be consistent with the logic and technical requirements of the Poisson model with variable exposure (Raudenbush et al. 2000, 148–150), we selected all observations (96 percent of the total) where men were free on the street at least one day in the year of observation. In other words, we required that the street exposure time be greater than 0 days in any one year. As noted, the overwhelming majority of observations met this requirement and thus con-tributed to the analysis. We experimented with less satisfying models where these observations were included and exposure time was ignored. The results were nonetheless generally similar and robust in overall patterns.

3. There is little precedent for fitting age parameters from 17 out to 70, al-though we do have our analysis in Chapter 5 as a guide. We experimented with age, age squared, and age cubed in the same models, but generally age cubed was not significant and adding it did not change the variance compo-nents. Because the high correlation between age and age cubed ($r = .92$) also proved to be a problem when estimating individual coefficients when both were in the model, we focus in this chapter on the orthogonal quadratic model, which fits the data well. In Chapter 5 we were interested in displaying the overall age curve from 7 to 70, and so including all three parameters served a different purpose. Interestingly, however, when all three age parame-ters were estimated, the patterns for our key between- and within-individual factors remained the same. The main results were thus quite robust to vary-ing age specifications.

4. Technically, the parameters of major interest for us are the average within-in-dividual estimates derived from the between-person model. For example, the average time-varying effect of marriage in the level 1 model, $\beta_{3,i}$, is captured in the between-person model by the term $\gamma_{3,0}$ (see Horney, Osgood, and Mar-shall 1995, 661, for further discussion). We should note also that of the men who married, all had done so by the age of 43—the average age we use to

center the analysis—providing additional substantive justification for our age specification and centering scheme (see Raudenbush and Bryk 2002, 182).

5. As expected, the data are consistent with an over- (or extra-) dispersed Poisson model, yielding an estimate of $\sigma^2$ of more than 1.5 (see Raudenbush et al. 2000, 160). We should also note that with the large number of yearly observations and reasonable sample size of men even in the follow-up, our estimates of reliability in the level 2 models are also adequate for both crime and life-course predictors. For example, the estimated reliability for measuring between-individual differences in total crime, $\beta_{0,i}$, is a considerable .82. As Raudenbush and Bryk (2002, 49–50) note, person-level reliability is generally a function of (1) the sample size ($n$) of time points ($t$) for each man, $i$, and (2) the proportion of the total variance that is between men ($\tau_{00}$) relative to the amount that is over time ($\sigma^2$). Even individual differences in the linear age effect are modestly reliable in our data, at .48. The reliability for marriage is estimated to be .93 for ages 17–70. Unemployment and military service yield person-level reliabilities of .81 and .76, respectively, for ages 17–32 in the full delinquent sample.

6. As noted above, violence is extremely rare in any given person-year, and so not surprisingly the reliability for violence is the only one of all crimes below .50 (.44). We also had difficulty getting models of violence to converge, and the pattern of results was inconsistent across specifications. As in Figure 9.2, we therefore combined violence with property crime to estimate the number of predatory offenses. The reliability of predatory crime is considerably higher than violence alone (.72), and the percentage of variation that lies within persons is 58. The between-person reliability for alcohol/drug offenses is very similar to predatory crime (.73). Analysis of property crime generated very similar results for our key factors.

7. For exploratory purposes, we estimated a model where age, drinking/drug arrests, and the individual risk factors in Table 9.2 were used to predict the log-odds of marriage. We found that substance abuse was negatively associated with the probability of marriage in any given year, making the resilience of the marriage effect on crime in Model 3 all the more impressive.

8. As before, we experimented with adding age cubed but found similar results. Generally the linear and quadratic age models proved to be a better fit to the data.

9. For several reasons, we do not believe that this caution affects our earlier work linking juvenile incarceration to weakened job stability in adulthood (see Sampson and Laub 1993, 163–168; Laub and Sampson 1995). First, the measurement of juvenile incarceration was not in any way confounded with unemployment in the Gluecks' coding scheme. Second, our measure of job stability in *Crime in the Making* included work habits and stability of most recent employment regardless of incarceration.

10. Interestingly, a similar inference is obtained if we simultaneously control for

predatory offending when estimating drinking-related offenses. We entered both the within-individual count of predatory crimes (person-centered) and the between-individual mean of predatory offenses in Model 1 of Tables 9.2 and 9.4. Despite this strict control for predatory offending over time and between individuals, the key results held up. For example, the within-individual marriage estimates were $-.44$ ($p < .01$) and $-.28$ ($p < .01$) in Tables 9.2 and 9.4, respectively.

11. We examined a number of additional specifications for the effects of age on crime in Tables 9.1 to 9.4. In one set of models we freed the variance component for the quadratic age effect. The variance component for age squared was either not significant or not estimable, and in no case did the results materially change for other coefficients. In another set of models we entered the exogenously defined childhood and adolescent risk factors as predictors of the rate of change in adulthood—a cross-level age interaction. For the full delinquent-group models (ages 17–32 in Table 9.4), the interactions were insignificant across the board and the residual variance component for the linear age effect remained significant. For the follow-up men (Table 9.3) and especially for ages 17–70 (Tables 9.1 to 9.2), the results were inconsistent, and again in no case did the interactions significantly reduce the heterogeneity in the average rate of change. Some individual coefficients were significant, however; for example, those in the high childhood risk category exhibited a higher average rate of decline in crime than did those with low risk. Still, the estimates for marriage, employment, and military service, both within and between individuals, were very similar in these models. Overall, then, the results in Tables 9.1 to 9.4 are robust to a number of different age-interactions and specifications of how age influences crime.

# REFERENCES

Abbott, Andrew. 1997. "On the Concept of Turning Point." *Comparative Social Research* 16: 85–105.

Adler, Patricia A. 1992. "The 'Post' Phase of Deviant Careers: Reintegrating Drug Traffickers." *Deviant Behavior* 13: 103–126.

Agnew, Robert. 1992. "Foundation for a General Strain Theory of Crime and Delinquency." *Criminology* 30: 47–87.

Akers, Ronald L. 1990. "Rational Choice, Deterrence, and Social Learning Theory in Criminology: The Path Not Taken." *Journal of Criminal Law and Criminology* 81: 653–676.

——— 1998. *Social Learning and Social Structure: A General Theory of Crime and Deviance.* Boston: Northeastern University Press.

Amato, Paul R., and Alan Booth. 1997. *A Generation at Risk: Growing Up in an Era of Family Upheaval.* Cambridge, Mass.: Harvard University Press.

*American Heritage Dictionary, Second College Edition.* 1982. Boston: Houghton Mifflin Company.

Andrews, D. A., and James Bonta. 1994. *The Psychology of Criminal Conduct.* Cincinnati: Anderson.

Baltes, Paul, and John Nesselroade. 1984. "Paradigm Lost and Paradigm Regained: Critique of Dannefer's Portrayal of Life-Span Developmental Psychology." *American Sociological Review* 49: 841–847.

Barnett, Arnold, Alfred Blumstein, and David P. Farrington. 1989. "A Prospective Test of a Criminal Career Model." *Criminology* 27: 373–388.

Baskin, Deborah R., and Ira B. Sommers. 1998. *Casualties of Community Disorder: Women's Careers in Violent Crime.* Boulder, Colo.: Westview Press.

Becker, Gary S., and Kevin M. Murphy. 2000. *Social Economics: Market Behavior in a Social Environment.* Cambridge, Mass.: Belknap Press of Harvard University Press.

Becker, Howard S. 1960. "Notes on the Concept of Commitment." *American Journal of Sociology* 66: 32–40.

—— 1964. "Personal Change in Adult Life." *Sociometry* 27: 40–53.

—— 1966. "Introduction." Pp. v–xviii in *The Jack-Roller: A Delinquent Boy's Own Story,* by Clifford R. Shaw. Chicago: University of Chicago Press.

—— 1996. "The Epistemology of Qualitative Research." Pp. 53–71 in *Ethnography and Human Development: Context and Meaning in Social Inquiry,* ed. Richard Jessor, Anne Colby, and Richard A. Shweder. Chicago: University of Chicago Press.

—— 1998. *Tricks of the Trade: How to Think about Your Research While You're Doing It.* Chicago: University of Chicago Press.

Belair, Robert R. 1985. *Data Quality of Criminal History Records.* Washington, D.C.: U.S. Department of Justice.

Bennett, James. 1981. *Oral History and Delinquency: The Rhetoric of Criminology.* Chicago: University of Chicago Press.

Bennett, William J., John J. DiIulio, Jr., and John P. Walters. 1996. *Body Count: Moral Poverty and How to Win America's War against Crime and Drugs.* New York: Simon and Schuster.

Birkbeck, Christopher, and Gary LaFree. 1993. "The Situational Analysis of Crime and Deviance." *Annual Review of Sociology* 19: 113–137.

Black, Donald. 1983. "Crime as Social Control." *American Sociological Review* 48: 34–45.

Blau, Peter M. 1977. *Inequality and Heterogeneity: A Primitive Theory of Social Structure.* New York: Free Press.

Block, Jack. 1971. *Lives through Time.* Berkeley: Bancroft Books.

Blumberg, Abraham S. 1967. *Criminal Justice.* Chicago: Quadrangle Books.

Blumstein, Alfred, and Jacqueline Cohen. 1979. "Estimation of Individual Crime Rates from Arrest Records." *Journal of Criminal Law and Criminology* 70: 561–585.

Blumstein, Alfred, Jacqueline Cohen, and David P. Farrington. 1988a. "Criminal Career Research: Its Value for Criminology." *Criminology* 26: 1–35.

—— 1988b. "Longitudinal and Criminal Career Research: Further Clarifications." *Criminology* 26: 57–74.

Blumstein, Alfred, Jacqueline Cohen, Jeffrey Roth, and Christy Visher, eds. 1986. *Criminal Careers and Career Criminals.* Washington, D.C.: National Academy Press.

Bonta, James. 1996. "Risk-Needs Assessment and Treatment." Pp. 18–32 in *Choosing Correctional Options That Work: Defining the Demand and Evaluating the Supply,* ed. Alan T. Harland. Thousand Oaks, Calif.: Sage Publications.

Bordua, David J. 1961a. "Delinquent Subcultures: Sociological Interpretations of Gang Delinquency." *Annals of the American Academy of Political and Social Science* 338: 119–136.

—— 1961b. *Prediction and Selection of Delinquents.* Washington, D.C.: U.S. Department of Health, Education, and Welfare.

Brame, Bobby, Daniel S. Nagin, and Richard E. Tremblay. 2001. "Developmental Trajectories of Physical Aggression from School Entry to Late Adolescence." *Journal of Child Psychology and Psychiatry* 42: 503–512.

Briar, Scott, and Irving Piliavin. 1965. "Delinquency, Situational Inducements, and Commitment to Conformity." *Social Problems* 13: 35–45.

Brotz, Howard, and Everett Wilson. 1946. "Characteristics of Military Society." *American Journal of Sociology* 51: 371–375.

Browning, Harley L., Sally C. Lopreato, and Dudley L. Poston, Jr. 1973. "Income and Veteran Status: Variations among Mexican Americans, Blacks, and Anglos." *American Sociological Review* 38: 74–85.

Bruer, John T. 1999. *The Myth of the First Three Years: A New Understanding of Early Brain Development and Lifelong Learning.* New York: Free Press.

Burgess, Ernest W. 1931. "Discussion." Pp. 235–254 in *The Natural History of a Delinquent Career,* by Clifford R. Shaw. Chicago: University of Chicago Press.

Bushway, Shawn D., Alex R. Piquero, Lisa M. Broidy, Elizabeth Cauffman, and Paul Mazerolle. 2001. "An Empirical Framework for Studying Desistance as a Process." *Criminology* 39: 491–515.

Butterfield, Fox. 1995. *All God's Children: The Bosket Family and the American Tradition of Violence.* New York: Knopf.

Call, Vaughn R. A., Luther B. Otto, and Kenneth I. Spenner. 1982. *Tracking Respondents: A Multi-Method Approach.* Lexington, Mass.: Lexington Books.

Capaldi, Deborah M., and Gerald R. Patterson. 1996. "Can Violent Offenders Be Distinguished from Frequent Offenders: Prediction from Childhood to Adolescence." *Journal of Research in Crime and Delinquency* 33: 206–231.

Carr, Deborah, Carol D. Ryff, Burton Singer, and William J. Magee. 1995. "Bringing the 'Life' Back into Life Course Research: A 'Person-Centered' Approach to Studying the Life Course." Paper presented at the annual meeting of the American Sociological Association, Washington, D.C.

Caspi, Avshalom. 1987. "Personality in the Life Course." *Journal of Personality and Social Psychology* 53: 1203–1213.

——— 2000. "The Child Is Father of the Man: Personality Continuities from Childhood to Adulthood." *Journal of Personality and Social Psychology* 78: 158–172.

Caspi, Avshalom, Daryl J. Bem, and Glen H. Elder, Jr. 1989. "Continuities and Consequences of Interactional Styles across the Life Course." *Journal of Personality* 57: 375–406.

Caspi, Avshalom, and Terrie E. Moffitt. 1993. "When Do Individual Differences Matter? A Paradoxical Theory of Personality Coherence." *Psychological Inquiry* 4: 247–271.

——— 1995. "The Continuity of Maladaptive Behavior: From Description to Understanding in the Study of Antisocial Behavior." Pp. 472–511 in *Developmental Psychopathology,* vol. 2: *Risk, Disorder, and Adaptation,* ed. Dante Cicchetti and Donald J. Cohen. New York: Wiley.

Caspi, Avshalom, Terrie E. Moffitt, Phil A. Silva, Magda Stouthamer-Loeber,

Robert F. Krueger, and Pamela S. Schmutte. 1994. "Are Some People Crime-Prone? Replications of the Personality-Crime Relationship across Countries, Genders, Races, and Methods." *Criminology* 32: 163–195.

Chaiken, Jan M., and Marcia R. Chaiken. 1982. *Varieties of Criminal Behavior: Summary and Policy Implications.* Report to the National Institute of Justice. Santa Monica, Calif.: Rand Corporation.

Chung, Ick-Joong, Karl G. Hill, J. David Hawkins, Lewayne D. Gilchrist, and Daniel S. Nagin. 2002. "Childhood Predictors of Offense Trajectories." *Journal of Research in Crime and Delinquency* 39: 60–90.

Clarke, Ronald V., and Derek B. Cornish. 1985. "Modeling Offenders' Decisions: A Framework for Research and Policy." Pp. 147–185 in *Crime and Justice: An Annual Review of the Research,* vol. 6, ed. Michael Tonry and Norval Morris. Chicago: University of Chicago Press.

Clausen, John A. 1993. *American Lives: Looking Back at the Children of the Great Depression.* New York: Free Press.

——— 1998. "Life Reviews and Life Stories." Pp. 189–212 in *Methods of Life Course Research: Qualitative and Quantitative Approaches,* ed. Janet Z. Giele and Glen H. Elder, Jr. Thousand Oaks, Calif.: Sage Publications.

Clinard, Marshall B., and Richard Quinney. 1973. *Criminal Behavior Systems: A Typology.* 2nd ed. New York: Holt, Rinehart and Winston.

Cline, Hugh F. 1980. "Criminal Behavior over the Life Span." Pp. 641–674 in *Constancy and Change in Human Development,* ed. Orville G. Brim, Jr., and Jerome Kagan. Cambridge, Mass.: Harvard University Press.

Cloward, Richard A., and Lloyd E. Ohlin. 1960. *Delinquency and Opportunity: A Theory of Delinquent Gangs.* Glencoe, Ill.: Free Press.

Cohen, Albert K. 1955. *Delinquent Boys: The Culture of the Gang.* Glencoe, Ill.: Free Press.

Cohen, Lawrence E., and Marcus Felson. 1979. "Social Change and Crime Rate Trends: A Routine Activity Approach." *American Sociological Review* 44: 588–608.

Cohen, Lawrence E., and Bryan J. Vila. 1996. "Self-Control and Social Control: An Exposition of the Gottfredson-Hirschi/Sampson-Laub Debate." *Studies on Crime and Crime Prevention* 5: 125–150.

Cohen, Stanley, and Laurie Taylor. 1972. *Psychological Survival: The Experience of Long-Term Imprisonment.* New York: Pantheon Books.

Cohler, Bertram J. 1982. "Personal Narrative and Life Course." Pp. 205–241 in *Life Span Development and Behavior,* vol. 4, ed. Paul B. Baltes and Orville G. Brim, Jr. New York: Academic Press.

Coie, John D., and Kenneth A. Dodge. 1998. "Aggression and Antisocial Behavior." Pp. 779–862 in *Handbook of Child Psychology,* vol. 3: *Social, Emotional, and Personality Development,* 5th ed., ed. William Damon and Nancy Eisenberg. New York: Wiley.

Coie, John, Robert Terry, Kari Lenox, and John Lochman. 1995. "Childhood Peer Rejection and Aggression as Predictors of Stable Patterns of Adolescent Disorder." *Development and Psychopathology* 7: 697–713.

Cook, Philip J., Mark H. Moore, and Anthony A. Braga. 2002. "Gun Control." Pp. 291–329 in *Crime: Public Policies for Crime Control,* ed. James Q. Wilson and Joan Petersilia. Oakland, Calif.: Institute for Contemporary Studies.

Cornish, Derek B., and Ronald V. Clarke. 1986. *The Reasoning Criminal: Rational Choice Perspectives on Offending.* New York: Springer-Verlag.

Cromwell, Paul F., James N. Olson, and D'Aunn Wester Avary. 1991. *Breaking and Entering: An Ethnographic Analysis of Burglary.* Newbury Park, Calif.: Sage Publications.

Cullen, Francis T. 1994. "Social Support as an Organizing Concept for Criminology: Presidential Address to the Academy of Criminal Justice Sciences." *Justice Quarterly* 11: 527–559.

———— 1996. Personal communication. May 25.

Cullen, Francis T., and Paul Gendreau. 2000. "Assessing Correctional Rehabilitation: Policy, Practice, and Prospects." Pp. 109–175 in *Criminal Justice 2000,* vol. 3: *Policies, Processes, and Decisions of the Criminal Justice System,* ed. Julie Horney. Washington, D.C.: U.S. Department of Justice.

Cusson, Maurice, and Pierre Pinsonneault. 1986. "The Decision to Give up Crime." Pp. 72–82 in *The Reasoning Criminal: Rational Choice Perspectives on Offending,* ed. Derek B. Cornish and Ronald V. Clarke. New York: Springer-Verlag.

Cutright, Phillips. 1974. "The Civilian Earnings of White and Black Draftees and Nonveterans." *American Sociological Review* 39: 317–327.

Dannefer, Dale. 1984. "Adult Development and Social Theory: A Paradigmatic Reappraisal." *American Sociological Review* 49: 100–116.

Denzin, Norman K. 1989. *Interpretive Interactionism.* Newbury Park, Calif.: Sage Publications.

Devlin, Mark. 1985. *Stubborn Child.* New York: Atheneum.

D'Unger, Amy V., Kenneth C. Land, Patricia L. McCall, and Daniel S. Nagin. 1998. "How Many Latent Classes of Delinquent/Criminal Careers? Results from Mixed Poisson Regression Analyses." *American Journal of Sociology* 103: 1593–1630.

Eggleston, Elaine P., and John H. Laub. 2002. "The Onset of Adult Offending: A Neglected Dimension of the Criminal Career." *Journal of Criminal Justice* 30: 603–622.

Eggleston, Elaine P., John H. Laub, and Robert J. Sampson. 2004. "Methodological Sensitivities to Latent Class Analysis of Long-Term Criminal Trajectories." *Journal of Quantitative Criminology* 20.

Elder, Glen H., Jr. 1986. "Military Times and Turning Points in Men's Lives." *Developmental Psychology* 22: 233–245.

———— 1998. "The Life Course as Developmental Theory." *Child Development* 69: 1–12.

Elder, Glen H., Jr., and Tamara K. Hareven. 1993. "Rising above Life's Disadvantage: From the Great Depression to War." Pp. 47–72 in *Children in Time and Place: Developmental and Historical Insights,* ed. Glen H. Elder, Jr., John Modell, and Ross D. Parke. Cambridge: Cambridge University Press.

Elder, Glen H., Jr., John Modell, and Ross D. Parke, eds. 1993. *Children in Time and Place: Developmental and Historical Insights.* Cambridge: Cambridge University Press.

Elliott, Delbert S., David Huizinga, and Scott Menard. 1989. *Multiple Problem Youth: Delinquency, Substance Use, and Mental Health Problems.* New York: Springer-Verlag.

Emirbayer, Mustafa. 1997. "Manifesto for a Relational Sociology." *American Journal of Sociology* 103: 281–317.

Emirbayer, Mustafa, and Ann Mische. 1998. "What Is Agency?" *American Journal of Sociology* 103: 962–1023.

Fagan, Jeffrey, and Richard B. Freeman. 1999. "Crime and Work." Pp. 225–290 in *Crime and Justice: A Review of Research,* vol. 25, ed. Michael Tonry. Chicago: University of Chicago Press.

Farrington, David P. 1986. "Age and Crime." Pp. 189–250 in *Crime and Justice: An Annual Review of Research,* vol. 7, ed. Michael Tonry and Norval Morris. Chicago: University of Chicago Press.

——— 1988. "Studying Changes within Individuals: The Causes of Offending." Pp. 158–183 in *Studies of Psychosocial Risk: The Power of Longitudinal Data,* ed. Michael Rutter. Cambridge: Cambridge University Press.

——— 1991. "Childhood Aggression and Adult Violence: Early Precursors and Later Life Outcomes." Pp. 5–29 in *The Development and Treatment of Childhood Aggression,* ed. Debra J. Pepler and Kenneth H. Rubin. Hillsdale, N.J.: Lawrence Erlbaum.

——— 1992. "Explaining the Beginning, Progress, and Ending of Antisocial Behavior from Birth to Adulthood." Pp. 253–286 in *Facts, Frameworks, and Forecasts,* ed. Joan McCord. New Brunswick, N.J.: Transaction Books.

——— 2000. "Explaining and Preventing Crime: The Globalization of Knowledge—The American Society of Criminology 1999 Presidential Address." *Criminology* 38: 1–24.

——— 2002. "Key Results from the First Forty Years of the Cambridge Study in Delinquent Development." Pp. 137–183 in *Taking Stock of Delinquency: An Overview of Findings from Contemporary Longitudinal Studies,* ed. Terry Thornberry and Marvin D. Krohn. New York: Kluwer/Plenum.

Farrington, David P., Bernard Gallagher, Lynda Morley, Raymond J. St. Ledger, and Donald J. West. 1986. "Unemployment, School Leaving, and Crime." *British Journal of Criminology* 26: 335–356.

——— 1990. "Minimizing Attrition in Longitudinal Research: Methods of Tracing and Securing Cooperation in a 24-Year Follow-Up Study." Pp. 122–147 in *Data Quality in Longitudinal Research,* ed. David Magnusson and Lars R. Bergman. Cambridge: Cambridge University Press.

Farrington, David P., Rolf Loeber, Delbert S. Elliott, J. David Hawkins, Denise B. Kandel, Malcolm W. Klein, Joan McCord, David C. Rowe, and Richard E. Tremblay. 1990. "Advancing Knowledge about the Onset of Delinquency and Crime." Pp. 283–342 in *Advances in Clinical Child Psychology*, vol. 13, ed. Benjamin B. Lahey and Alan E. Kazdin. New York: Plenum.

Farrington, David P., and Roger Tarling, eds. 1985. *Prediction in Criminology*. Albany, N.Y.: State University of New York Press.

Farrington, David P., and Donald J. West. 1995. "Effects of Marriage, Separation, and Children on Offending by Adult Males." Pp. 249–281 in *Current Perspectives on Aging and the Life Cycle*, vol. 4: *Delinquency and Disrepute in the Life Course*, ed. Zena Smith Blau and John Hagan. Greenwich, Conn.: JAI Press.

Fisher, Edwin B., Jr., Edward Lichtenstein, Debra Haire-Joshu, Glen D. Morgan, and Heather R. Rehberg. 1993. "Methods, Successes, and Failures of Smoking Cessation Programs." *Annual Review of Medicine* 44: 481–513.

Foucault, Michel. 1995 [1975]. *Discipline and Punish: The Birth of the Prison*. 2nd Vintage Books ed. New York: Vintage Books.

Freedman, Deborah, Arland Thornton, Donald Camburn, Duane Alwin, and Linda Young-DeMarco. 1988. "The Life History Calendar: A Technique for Collecting Retrospective Data." *Sociological Methodology* 18: 37–68.

Freeman, Richard B. 1991. *Crime and the Employment of Disadvantaged Youths*. Cambridge, Mass.: National Bureau of Economic Research.

Gans, Herbert. 1962. *The Urban Villagers: Group and Class in the Life of Italian-Americans*. New York: Free Press of Glencoe.

Gartner, Rosemary, and Irving Piliavin. 1988. "The Aging Offender and the Aged Offender." Pp. 287–315 in *Life-Span Development and Behavior*, vol. 9, ed. Paul B. Baltes, David L. Featherman, and Richard M. Lerner. Hillside, N.J.: Lawrence Erlbaum Associates.

Geerken, Michael R. 1994. "Rap Sheets in Criminological Research: Considerations and Caveats." *Journal of Quantitative Criminology* 10: 3–21.

Geller, Robert J., David D. Jackson, Yan Y. Kagan, and Francesco Mulargia. 1997. "Earthquakes Cannot Be Predicted." *Science* 275: 1616–17.

Gendreau, Paul, Francis T. Cullen, and James Bonta. 1994. "Intensive Rehabilitation Supervision: The Next Generation in Community Corrections?" *Federal Probation* 58: 72–78.

Gibbons, Don C. 1985. "The Assumption of the Efficacy of Middle-Range Explanation: Typologies." Pp. 151–174 in *Theoretical Methods in Criminology*, ed. Robert F. Meier. Beverly Hills, Calif.: Sage Publications.

Giordano, Peggy C., Stephen A. Cernkovich, and Jennifer L. Rudolph. 2002. "Gender, Crime, and Desistance: Toward a Theory of Cognitive Transformation." *American Journal of Sociology* 107: 990–1064.

Glaser, Daniel. 1969. *The Effectiveness of a Prison and Parole System*. Abridged ed. Indianapolis: Bobbs-Merrill.

Glueck, Sheldon, and Eleanor Glueck. 1930. *500 Criminal Careers*. New York: A. A. Knopf.

——— 1940. *Juvenile Delinquents Grown Up*. New York: Commonwealth Fund.

—— 1943. *Criminal Careers in Retrospect.* New York: Commonwealth Fund.

—— 1945. *After-Conduct of Discharged Offenders.* London: Macmillan.

—— 1950. *Unraveling Juvenile Delinquency.* New York: Commonwealth Fund.

—— 1968. *Delinquents and Nondelinquents in Perspective.* Cambridge, Mass.: Harvard University Press.

—— 1974. *Of Delinquency and Crime: A Panorama of Years of Search and Research.* Springfield, Ill.: Charles C. Thomas.

Goodman, Paul. 1956. *Growing Up Absurd.* New York: Random House.

Gottfredson, Michael R., and Travis Hirschi. 1986. "The True Value of Lambda Would Appear to Be Zero: An Essay on Career Criminals, Criminal Careers, Selective Incapacitation, Cohort Studies, and Related Topics." *Criminology* 24: 213–234.

—— 1988. "Science, Public Policy, and the Career Paradigm." *Criminology* 26: 37–55.

—— 1990. *A General Theory of Crime.* Stanford, Calif.: Stanford University Press.

Gove, Walter R. 1985. "The Effect of Age and Gender on Deviant Behavior: A Biopsychosocial Perspective." Pp. 115–144 in *Gender and the Life Course,* ed. Alice S. Rossi. New York: Aldine Publishing Co.

Gove, Walter R., Michael Hughes, and Michael Geerken. 1985. "Are Uniform Crime Reports a Valid Indicator of the Index Crimes? An Affirmative Answer with Minor Qualifications." *Criminology* 23: 451–501.

Graham, John, and Benjamin Bowling. 1995. *Young People and Crime.* Research Study 145. London: Home Office.

Greenwood, Peter W. 1982. *Selective Incapacitation.* Report to the National Institute of Justice. Santa Monica, Calif.: Rand Corporation.

Hagan, John. 1993. "The Social Embeddedness of Crime and Unemployment." *Criminology* 31: 465–491.

Hagan, John, and Bill McCarthy. 1997. *Mean Streets: Youth Crime and Homelessness.* Cambridge: Cambridge University Press.

Hawkes, Ellen. 2002. "An Interview with Nicolas Cage." *Washington Post Parade Magazine,* June 9.

Hawkins, J. David, Todd I. Herrenkohl, David P. Farrington, Devon Brewer, Richard F. Catalano, Tracy W. Harachi, and Lynn Cothern. 2000. *Predictors of Youth Violence.* Washington, D.C.: U.S. Department of Justice.

Henry, Bill, Terrie E. Moffitt, Avshalom Caspi, John Langley, and Phil A. Silva. 1994. "On the 'Remembrance of Things Past': A Longitudinal Evaluation of the Retrospective Method." *Psychological Assessment* 6: 92–101.

Hill, Thomas W. 1971. "From Hell-Raiser to Family Man." Pp. 186–200 in *Conformity and Conflict: Readings in Cultural Anthropology,* ed. James P. Spradley and David W. McCurdy. Boston: Little, Brown and Co.

Hindelang, Michael J., Michael R. Gottfredson, and James Garofalo. 1978. *Vic-*

*tims of Personal Crime: An Empirical Foundation for a Theory of Personal Victimization.* Cambridge, Mass.: Ballinger Publishing Company.

Hirschi, Travis. 1969. *Causes of Delinquency.* Berkeley: University of California Press.

Hirschi, Travis, and Michael R. Gottfredson. 1983. "Age and the Explanation of Crime." *American Journal of Sociology* 89: 552–584.

—— 1995. "Control Theory and the Life-Course Perspective." *Studies on Crime and Crime Prevention* 4: 131–142.

Hoffman, Peter B., and James L. Beck. 1984. "Burnout—Age at Release from Prison and Recidivism." *Journal of Criminal Justice* 12: 617–623.

Horney, Julie, D. Wayne Osgood, and Ineke Haen Marshall. 1995. "Criminal Careers in the Short-Term: Intra-Individual Variability in Crime and Its Relation to Local Life Circumstances." *American Sociological Review* 60: 655–673.

Horney, Julie, Jennifer (Johnson) Roberts, and Kimberly D. Hassell. 2000. "The Social Control Function of Intimate Partners: Attachment or Monitoring?" Paper presented at the annual meeting of the American Society of Criminology, San Francisco, Calif.

Jack-Roller, The, and Jon Snodgrass. 1982. *The Jack-Roller at Seventy: A Fifty-Year Follow-Up.* Lexington, Mass.: Lexington Books.

Janowitz, Morris. 1972. "Characteristics of the Military Environment." Pp. 166–173 in *The Military and American Society: Essays and Readings,* ed. Stephen E. Ambrose and James A. Barber, Jr. New York: Free Press.

Janson, Carl-Gunnar. 1990. "Retrospective Data, Undesirable Behavior, and the Longitudinal Perspective." Pp. 100–121 in *Data Quality in Longitudinal Research,* ed. David Magnusson and Lars R. Bergman. Cambridge: Cambridge University Press.

Johnson, David R., and Alan Booth. 1998. "Marital Quality: A Product of the Dyadic Environment or Individual Factors?" *Social Forces* 76: 883–904.

Jones, Bobby L., Daniel S. Nagin, and Kathryn Roeder. 2001. "A SAS Procedure Based on Mixture Models for Estimating Developmental Trajectories." *Sociological Methods & Research* 29: 374–393.

Kagan, Jerome. 1998. *Three Seductive Ideas.* Cambridge, Mass.: Harvard University Press.

Katz, Jack. 1988. *Seductions of Crime.* New York: Basic Books.

Kenaszchuk, Chris. 1996. "Things Ain't What They Used to Be: A Qualitative Analysis of Marriage and Desistance from Crime, circa 1950." M.A. thesis. Northeastern University Graduate School of Criminal Justice. Boston.

Kiecolt-Glaser, Janice K., and Tamara L. Newton. 2001. "Marriage and Health: His and Hers." *Psychological Bulletin* 127: 472–503.

King, Gary, Robert O. Keohane, and Sidney Verba. 1994. *Designing Social Inquiry: Scientific Inference in Qualitative Research.* Princeton, N.J.: Princeton University Press.

Kohli, Martin. 1986. "The World We Forgot: A Historical Review of the Life Course." Pp. 271–303 in *Later Life: The Social Psychology of Aging*, ed. Victor W. Marshall. Beverly Hills, Calif.: Sage Publications.

LaFree, Gary. 1998. *Losing Legitimacy: Street Crime and the Decline of Social Institutions in America*. Boulder, Colo.: Westview Press.

Lamont, Douglas, Louise Parker, Martin White, Nigel Unwin, Stuart M. A. Bennett, Melanie Cohen, David Richardson, Heather O. Dickinson, Ashley Adamson, K. G. M. M. Alberti, and Alan W. Craft. 2000. "Risk of Cardiovascular Disease Measured by Carotid Intima-Media Thickness at Age 49–51: Lifecourse Study." *British Medical Journal* 320: 273–278.

Lattimore, Pamela K., Richard L. Linster, and John M. MacDonald. 1997. "Risk of Death among Serious Young Offenders." *Journal of Research in Crime and Delinquency* 34: 187–209.

Laub, John H. 2002. "Introduction: The Life and Work of Travis Hirschi." Pp. xi–xlix in *The Craft of Criminology: Selected Papers by Travis Hirschi*. New Brunswick, N.J.: Transaction Books.

Laub, John H., Daniel S. Nagin, and Robert J. Sampson. 1998. "Trajectories of Change in Criminal Offending: Good Marriages and the Desistance Process." *American Sociological Review* 63: 225–238.

Laub, John H., and Robert J. Sampson. 1991. "The Sutherland-Glueck Debate: On the Sociology of Criminological Knowledge." *American Journal of Sociology* 96: 1402–1440.

——— 1993. "Turning Points in the Life Course: Why Change Matters to the Study of Crime." *Criminology* 31: 301–325.

——— 1995. "Crime and Context in the Lives of 1,000 Boston Men, circa 1925–1955." Pp. 119–139 in *Current Perspectives on Aging and the Life Cycle*, vol. 4: *Delinquency and Disrepute in the Life Course*, ed. Zena Smith Blau and John Hagan. Greenwich, Conn.: JAI Press.

——— 1998. "The Long-Term Reach of Adolescent Competence: Socioeconomic Achievement in the Lives of Disadvantaged Men." Pp. 89–112 in *Competence and Character through Life*, ed. Anne Colby, Jacquelyn James, and Daniel Hart. Chicago: University of Chicago Press.

——— 2001. "Understanding Desistance from Crime." Pp. 1–69 in *Crime and Justice: A Review of Research*, vol. 28, ed. Michael Tonry. Chicago: University of Chicago Press.

——— 2002. "Sheldon and Eleanor Glueck's Unraveling Juvenile Delinquency Study: The Lives of 1,000 Boston Men in the Twentieth Century." Pp. 87–115 in *Looking at Lives: American Longitudinal Studies of the Twentieth Century*, ed. Erin Phelps, Frank F. Furstenberg, Jr., and Anne Colby. New York: Russell Sage Foundation.

Laub, John H., and George E. Vaillant. 2000. "Delinquency and Mortality: A 50-year Follow-up Study of 1,000 Delinquent and Nondelinquent Boys." *American Journal of Psychiatry* 157: 96–102.

Laufer, Robert S., and M. S. Gallops. 1985. "Life-Course Effects of Vietnam

Combat and Abusive Violence: Marital Patterns." *Journal of Marriage and the Family* 47: 839–853.

Lauritsen, Janet L., Robert J. Sampson, and John H. Laub. 1991. "The Link between Offending and Victimization among Adolescents." *Criminology* 29: 265–292.

LeBlanc, Marc, and Rolf Loeber. 1993. "Precursors, Causes, and the Development of Criminal Offending." Pp. 233–263 in *Precursors and Causes in Development and Psychopathology,* ed. Dale F. Hay and Adrian Angold. New York: John Wiley.

Leibrich, Julie. 1996. "The Role of Shame in Going Straight: A Study of Former Offenders." Pp. 283–302 in *Restorative Justice: International Perspectives,* ed. Burt Galaway and Joe Hudson. Monsey, N.Y.: Criminal Justice Press.

Lemert, Edwin M. 1972. *Human Deviance, Social Problems, and Social Control.* 2nd ed. Englewood Cliffs, N.J.: Prentice-Hall.

Lewontin, Richard. 2000. *The Triple Helix: Gene, Organism, and Environment.* Cambridge, Mass.: Harvard University Press.

Loeber, Rolf, and David P. Farrington, eds. 1998. *Serious and Violent Juvenile Offenders: Risk Factors and Successful Interventions.* Thousand Oaks, Calif.: Sage Publications.

——— 2000. "Young Children Who Commit Crime: Epidemiology, Developmental Origins, Risk Factors, Early Interventions, and Policy Implications." *Development and Psychopathology* 12: 737–762.

Loeber, Rolf, and Dale Hay. 1997. "Key Issues in the Development of Aggression and Violence from Childhood to Early Adulthood." *Annual Review of Psychology* 48: 371–410.

Loeber, Rolf, and Marc LeBlanc. 1990. "Toward a Developmental Criminology." Pp. 375–473 in *Crime and Justice: A Review of Research,* vol. 12, ed. Michael Tonry and Norval Morris. Chicago: University of Chicago Press.

Loeber, Rolf, and Magda Stouthamer-Loeber. 1987. "Prediction." Pp. 325–382 in *Handbook of Juvenile Delinquency,* ed. Herbert C. Quay. New York: John Wiley & Sons.

Lofland, John. 1969. *Deviance and Identity.* Englewood Cliffs, N.J.: Prentice-Hall.

Lombroso, Cesare. 1912. *Crime, Its Causes and Remedies.* Boston: Little, Brown and Co.

Luckenbill, David F. 1977. "Criminal Homicide as a Situated Transaction." *Social Problems* 25: 176–186.

MacDonald, Michael Patrick. 1999. *All Souls: A Family Story from Southie.* Boston: Beacon Press.

Maruna, Shadd. 1997. "Going Straight: Desistance from Crime and Life Narratives of Reform." Pp. 59–93 in *The Narrative Study of Lives,* vol. 5, ed. Amia Lieblich and Ruthellen Josselson. Thousand Oaks, Calif.: Sage Publications.

——— 2001. *Making Good: How Ex-Convicts Reform and Rebuild Their Lives.* Washington, D.C.: American Psychological Association Books.

Mason, William M., George Y. Wong, and Barbara Entwisle. 1983. "Contextual Analysis through the Multilevel Linear Model." *Sociological Methodology* 14: 72–103.

Matsueda, Ross L., and Karen Heimer. 1997. "A Symbolic Interactionist Theory of Role-Transitions, Role-Commitments, and Delinquency." Pp. 163–213 in *Developmental Theories of Crime and Delinquency,* ed. Terence Thornberry. New Brunswick, N.J.: Transaction Publishers.

Mattick, Hans W. 1960. "Parolees in the Army during World War II." *Federal Probation* 24: 49–55.

Matza, David. 1964. *Delinquency and Drift.* New York: Wiley.

—— 1969. *Becoming Deviant.* Englewood Cliffs, N.J.: Prentice-Hall.

Maughan, Barbara, and Michael Rutter. 1998. "Continuities and Discontinuities in Antisocial Behavior from Childhood to Adult Life." Pp. 1–47 in *Advances in Clinical Child Psychology,* vol. 20, ed. Thomas H. Ollendick and Ronald J. Prinz. New York: Plenum Press.

Mazur, Allan, and Joel Michalek. 1998. "Marriage, Divorce, and Male Testosterone." *Social Forces* 77: 315–330.

McAdams, Dan P., and Ed de St. Aubin. 1992. "A Theory of Generativity and Its Assessment through Self-Report, Behavioral Acts, and Narrative Themes in Autobiography." *Journal of Personality and Social Psychology* 62: 1003–1015.

McCord, Joan. 1979. "Some Child-Rearing Antecedents of Criminal Behavior in Adult Men." *Journal of Personality and Social Psychology* 37: 1477–86.

—— 1980. "Patterns of Deviance." Pp. 157–165 in *Human Functioning in Longitudinal Perspective: Studies of Normal and Psychopathic Populations,* ed. Saul B. Sells, Rick Crandall, Merrill Roff, John S. Strauss, and William Pollin. Baltimore: Williams & Wilkins.

McCord, Joan, and Margaret E. Ensminger. 1997. "Multiple Risks and Comorbidity in an African-American Population." *Criminal Behaviour and Mental Health* 7: 339–352.

McCord, William, and Joan McCord. 1953. "Two Approaches to the Cure of Delinquents." *Journal of Criminal Law, Criminology, and Police Science* 44: 442–467.

Merkin, Daphne. 2002. "The Truth Will Set You Free: The Wounded Inner Child in Everyone." Review of *The Truth Will Set You Free: Overcoming Emotional Blindness and Finding Your True Adult Self,* by Alice Miller. *New York Times,* January 27.

Merton, Robert K. 1938. "Social Structure and Anomie." *American Sociological Review* 3: 672–682.

Miller, Jerome G. 1991. *Last One over the Wall: The Massachusetts Experiment in Closing Reform Schools.* Columbus: Ohio State University Press.

Mishler, Elliott G. 1996. "Missing Persons: Recovering Developmental Stories/Histories." Pp. 73–99 in *Ethnography and Human Development: Context and Meaning in Social Inquiry,* ed. Richard Jessor, Anne Colby, and Richard A. Shweder. Chicago: University of Chicago Press.

Modell, John. 1989. *Into One's Own: From Youth to Adulthood in the United States, 1920–1975.* Berkeley: University of California Press.

——— 1994. Book review of *Crime in the Making: Pathways and Turning Points through Life. American Journal of Sociology* 99: 1389–91.

Moffitt, Terrie E. 1993. "Adolescence-Limited and Life-Course-Persistent Antisocial Behavior: A Developmental Taxonomy." *Psychological Review* 100: 674–701.

——— 1994. "Natural Histories of Delinquency." Pp. 3–61 in *Cross-National Longitudinal Research on Human Development and Criminal Behavior,* ed. Elmar G. M. Weitekamp and Hans-Jurgen Kerner. Dordrecht: Kluwer Academic.

Mulvey, Edward P., and Mark Aber. 1988. "Growing out of Delinquency: Development and Desistance." Pp. 99–116 in *The Abandonment of Delinquent Behavior: Promoting the Turnaround,* ed. Richard L. Jenkins and Waln K. Brown. New York: Praeger Publishers.

Mulvey, Edward P., and John F. LaRosa. 1986. "Delinquency Cessation and Adolescent Development: Preliminary Data." *American Journal of Orthopsychiatry* 56: 212–224.

Nagin, Daniel S. 1999. "Analyzing Developmental Trajectories: A Semi-Parametric, Group-Based Approach." *Psychological Methods* 4: 139–157.

Nagin, Daniel S., David P. Farrington, and Terrie E. Moffitt. 1995. "Life-Course Trajectories of Different Types of Offenders." *Criminology* 33: 111–139.

Nagin, Daniel S., and Kenneth C. Land. 1993. "Age, Criminal Careers, and Population Heterogeneity: Specification and Estimation of a Nonparametric, Mixed Poisson Model." *Criminology* 31: 327–362.

Nagin, Daniel S., and Raymond Paternoster. 1991. "On the Relationship of Past to Future Participation in Delinquency." *Criminology* 29: 163–189.

——— 1994. "Personal Capital and Social Control: The Deterrence Implications of a Theory of Individual Differences in Criminal Offending." *Criminology* 32: 581–606.

——— 2000. "Population Heterogeneity and State Dependence: State of the Evidence and Directions for Future Research." *Journal of Quantitative Criminology* 16: 117–144.

Nagin, Daniel S., and Joel Waldfogel. 1995. "The Effects of Criminality and Conviction on the Labor Market Status of Young British Offenders." *International Review of Law and Economics* 15: 109–126.

National Center for Health Statistics. 1990. *National Death Index User's Manual.* Hyattsville, Md.: U.S. Department of Health and Human Services.

National Summit on Violence throughout the Lifespan. 1999. Conference Pamphlet from the Colorado Violence Prevention Center, Denver.

Ohlin, Lloyd E., Robert B. Coates, and Alden D. Miller. 1974. "Radical Correctional Reform: A Case Study of the Massachusetts Youth Correctional System." *Harvard Educational Review* 44: 74–111.

Osgood, D. Wayne, and Hyunkee Lee. 1993. "Leisure Activities, Age, and Adult Roles across the Lifespan." *Society and Leisure* 16: 181–208.

Osgood, D. Wayne, and David C. Rowe. 1994. "Bridging Criminal Careers, Theory, and Policy through Latent Variable Models of Individual Offending." *Criminology* 32: 517–554.

Osgood, D. Wayne, Janet K. Wilson, Patrick M. O'Malley, Jerald G. Bachman, and Lloyd D. Johnston. 1996. "Routine Activities and Individual Deviant Behavior." *American Sociological Review* 61: 635–655.

Paternoster, Raymond. 1989. "Decisions to Participate in and Desist from Four Types of Common Delinquency: Deterrence and the Rational Choice Perspective." *Law and Society Review* 23: 7–40.

Paternoster, Raymond, and Robert Brame. 1997. "Multiple Routes to Delinquency? A Test of Developmental and General Theories of Crime." *Criminology* 35: 49–84.

Paternoster, Raymond, Charles W. Dean, Alex Piquero, Paul Mazerolle, and Robert Brame. 1997. "Generality, Continuity, and Change in Offending." *Journal of Quantitative Criminology* 13: 231–266.

Patterson, Gerald R. 1982. *Coercive Family Process.* Eugene, Ore.: Castalia Publishing Co.

Patterson, Gerald R., L. Crosby, and S. Vuchinich. 1992. "Predicting Risk for Early Police Arrest." *Journal of Quantitative Criminology* 8: 335–355.

Patterson, Gerald R., and Karen Yoerger. 1993. "Developmental Models for Delinquent Behavior." Pp. 140–172 in *Mental Disorder and Crime,* ed. Sheilagh Hodgins. Newbury Park, Calif.: Sage Publications.

Pattillo-McCoy, Mary. 1999. *Black Picket Fences: Privilege and Peril among the Black Middle Class.* Chicago: University of Chicago Press.

Pavalko, Eliza K., and Glen H. Elder, Jr. 1990. "World War II and Divorce: A Life-Course Perspective." *American Journal of Sociology* 95: 1213–34.

Piquero, Alex R. 2000. "Frequency, Specialization, and Violence in Offending Careers." *Journal of Research in Crime and Delinquency* 37: 392–418.

Piquero, Alex R., Alfred Blumstein, Robert Brame, Rudy Haapanen, Edward P. Mulvey, and Daniel S. Nagin. 2001. "Assessing the Impact of Exposure Time and Incapacitation on Longitudinal Trajectories of Criminal Offending." *Journal of Adolescent Research* 16: 54–74.

Piquero, Alex R., David P. Farrington, and Alfred Blumstein. 2003. "The Criminal Career Paradigm: Background and Recent Developments." Pp. 137–183 in *Crime and Justice: A Review of Research,* vol. 30, ed. Michael Tonry. Chicago: University of Chicago Press.

Pope, Alexander. 1993 [1733]. "Epistle I: To Sir Richard Temple, Lord Viscount Cobham." Pp. 15–36 in *Epistles to Several Persons (Moral Essays),* ed. F. W. Bateson. London: Routledge.

Raudenbush, Stephen W., and Anthony S. Bryk. 2002. *Hierarchical Linear*

*Models: Applications and Data Analysis Methods.* 2nd ed. Thousand Oaks, Calif.: Sage.

Raudenbush, Stephen W., Anthony S. Bryk, Yuk Fai Cheong, and Richard Congdon. 2000. *HLM 5: Hierarchical Linear and Nonlinear Modeling.* Lincolnwood, Ill.: Scientific Software International.

Reiss, Albert J., Jr. 1989. "Ending Criminal Careers." Prepared for the Final Report of the "Desistance/Persistence Working Group" of the Program on Human Development and Criminal Behavior. MacArthur Foundation and National Institute of Justice.

Robins, Lee N. 1966. *Deviant Children Grown Up.* Baltimore: Williams & Wilkins.

—— 1978. "Sturdy Childhood Predictors of Adult Antisocial Behavior: Replications from Longitudinal Studies." *Psychological Medicine* 8: 611–622.

Roebuck, Julian B. 1966. *Criminal Typology.* Springfield, Ill.: Charles C. Thomas.

Rutter, Michael. 1988. "Longitudinal Data in the Study of Causal Processes: Some Uses and Some Pitfalls." Pp. 1–28 in *Studies of Psychosocial Risk: The Power of Longitudinal Data,* ed. Michael Rutter. Cambridge: Cambridge University Press.

—— 1996. "Transitions and Turning Points in Developmental Psychopathology: As Applied to the Age Span between Childhood and Mid-Adulthood." *International Journal of Behavioral Development* 19: 603–626.

Rutter, Michael, Henri Giller, and Ann Hagell. 1998. *Antisocial Behavior by Young People.* Cambridge: Cambridge University Press.

Sampson, Robert J. 1986. "Effects of Socioeconomic Context on Official Reaction to Juvenile Delinquency." *American Sociological Review* 51: 876–885.

Sampson, Robert J., and Dawn Jeglum Bartusch. 1998. "Legal Cynicism and (Subcultural?) Tolerance of Deviance: The Neighborhood Context of Racial Differences." *Law and Society Review* 32: 777–804.

Sampson, Robert J., and John H. Laub. 1993. *Crime in the Making: Pathways and Turning Points through Life.* Cambridge, Mass.: Harvard University Press.

—— 1995. "Understanding Variability in Lives through Time: Contributions of Life-Course Criminology." *Studies on Crime and Crime Prevention* 4: 143–158.

—— 1996. "Socioeconomic Achievement in the Life Course of Disadvantaged Men: Military Service as a Turning Point, circa 1940–1965." *American Sociological Review* 61: 347–367.

—— 1997. "A Life-Course Theory of Cumulative Disadvantage and the Stability of Delinquency." Pp. 133–161 in *Developmental Theories of Crime and Delinquency,* ed. Terence P. Thornberry. New Brunswick, N.J.: Transaction Publishers.

Scott, Jacqueline, and Duane Alwin. 1998. "Retrospective versus Prospective Measurement of Life Histories in Longitudinal Research." Pp. 98–127 in *Methods of Life Course Research: Qualitative and Quantitative Approaches,* ed. Janet Z. Giele and Glen H. Elder, Jr. Thousand Oaks, Calif.: Sage Publications.

Scott, Marvin B., and Stanford M. Lyman. 1968. "Accounts." *American Sociological Review* 33: 46–62.

Shaw, Clifford R. 1930. *The Jack-Roller: A Delinquent Boy's Own Story.* Chicago: University of Chicago Press.

Shaw, Clifford R., and Henry McKay. 1942. *Juvenile Delinquency and Urban Areas.* Chicago: University of Chicago Press.

Sherman, Lawrence W. 1993. "Defiance, Deterrence, and Irrelevance: A Theory of the Criminal Sanction." *Journal of Research in Crime and Delinquency* 30: 445–473.

Sherman, Lawrence W., Denise Gottfredson, Doris MacKenzie, John Eck, Peter Reuter, and Shawn Bushway. 1997. *Preventing Crime: What Works, What Doesn't, What's Promising.* Washington, D.C.: U.S. Department of Justice.

Short, James F., Jr., and Fred L. Strodtbeck. 1965. *Group Process and Gang Delinquency.* Chicago: University of Chicago Press.

Shover, Neal. 1985. *Aging Criminals.* Beverly Hills, Calif.: Sage Publications.

―――― 1996. *Great Pretenders: Pursuits and Careers of Persistent Thieves.* Boulder, Colo.: Westview Press.

Shover, Neal, and Carol Y. Thompson. 1992. "Age, Differential Expectations, and Crime Desistance." *Criminology* 30: 89–104.

Singer, Burton, Carol D. Ryff, Deborah Carr, and William J. Magee. 1998. "Linking Life Histories and Mental Health: A Person-Centered Strategy." *Sociological Methodology* 28: 1–51.

Smelser, Neil J. 1998. "The Rational and the Ambivalent in the Social Sciences." *American Sociological Review* 63: 1–15.

Springsteen, Bruce. 1982. "Nebraska." New York: Columbia.

Stall, Robb, and Patrick Biernacki. 1986. "Spontaneous Remission from the Problematic Use of Substances: An Inductive Model Derived from a Comparative Analysis of the Alcohol, Opiate, Tobacco, and Food/Obesity Literatures." *International Journal of the Addictions* 21: 1–23.

Stattin, Hakan, and David Magnusson. 1991. "Stability and Change in Criminal Behavior up to Age 30." *British Journal of Criminology* 31: 327–346.

Steffensmeier, Darrell J., Emilie Andersen Allan, Miles D. Harer, and Cathy Streifel. 1989. "Age and the Distribution of Crime." *American Journal of Sociology* 94: 803–831.

Straus, Robert. 1974. *Escape from Custody: A Study of Alcoholism and Institutional Dependency as Reflected in the Life Record of a Homeless Man.* New York: Harper & Row.

Sullivan, Mercer L. 1989. *"Getting Paid": Youth Crime and Work in the Inner City.* Ithaca, N.Y.: Cornell University Press.

Sutherland, Edwin H. 1947. *Principles of Criminology.* 4th ed. Chicago: J. B. Lippincott Co.

Sykes, Gresham M. 1958. *The Society of Captives: A Study of Maximum Security Prison.* Princeton, N.J.: Princeton University Press.

Sykes, Gresham M., and David Matza. 1957. "Techniques of Neutralization: A Theory of Delinquency." *American Sociological Review* 22: 664–670.

Thornberry, Terence P. 1987. "Toward an Interactional Theory of Delinquency." *Criminology* 25: 863–891.

Thornberry, Terence P., and Marvin D. Krohn. 2001. "The Development of Delinquency: An Interactional Perspective." Pp. 289–305 in *Handbook of Youth and Justice,* ed. Susan O. White. New York: Plenum.

Tittle, Charles R. 1995. *Control Balance: Toward a General Theory of Deviance.* Boulder, Colo.: Westview Press.

Toby, Jackson. 1957. "Social Disorganization and Stake in Conformity: Complementary Factors in the Predatory Behavior of Hoodlums." *Journal of Criminal Law, Criminology, and Police Science* 48: 12–17.

Tonry, Michael, and David P. Farrington. 1995. "Strategic Approaches to Crime Prevention." Pp. 1–20 in *Building a Safer Society: Strategic Approaches to Crime Prevention,* ed. Michael Tonry and David P. Farrington. Chicago: University of Chicago Press.

Tracy, Paul E., and Kimberly Kempf-Leonard. 1996. *Continuity and Discontinuity in Criminal Careers.* New York: Plenum Press.

Tracy, Paul E., Marvin E. Wolfgang, and Robert M. Figlio. 1985. *Delinquency in Two Birth Cohorts: Executive Summary.* Washington, D.C.: U.S. Department of Justice.

Travis, Jeremy, Amy L. Solomon, and Michelle Waul. 2001. *From Prison to Home: The Dimensions and Consequences of Prisoner Reentry.* Washington, D.C.: Urban Institute.

Tyler, Tom R. 1990. *Why People Obey the Law.* New Haven, Conn.: Yale University Press.

Uggen, Christopher. 2000. "Work as a Turning Point in the Life Course of Criminals: A Duration Model of Age, Employment, and Recidivism." *American Sociological Review* 65: 529–546.

Uggen, Christopher, and Irving Piliavin. 1998. "Asymmetrical Causation and Criminal Desistance." *Journal of Criminal Law and Criminology* 88: 1399–1422.

Umberson, Debra. 1992. "Gender, Marital Status, and the Social Control of Health Behavior." *Social Science and Medicine* 34: 907–917.

Vaillant, George E. 1977. *Adaptation to Life.* Boston: Little, Brown and Co.

—— 1983. *The Natural History of Alcoholism.* Cambridge, Mass.: Harvard University Press.

—— 1988. "What Can Long-term Follow-up Teach Us about Relapse and Prevention of Relapse in Addiction?" *British Journal of Addiction* 83: 1147–57.

—— 1995. *The Natural History of Alcoholism Revisited.* Cambridge, Mass.: Harvard University Press.

——— 2002. *Aging Well: Surprising Guideposts to a Happier Life from the Landmark Harvard Study of Adult Development*. Boston: Little, Brown and Co.

Vaillant, George E., and Eva S. Milofsky. 1982. "Natural History of Male Alcoholism: IV. Paths to Recovery." *Archives of General Psychiatry* 39: 127–133.

Vaillant, George E., and Caroline O. Vaillant. 1981. "Natural History of Male Psychological Health: X. Work as a Predictor of Positive Mental Health." *American Journal of Psychiatry* 138: 1433–40.

Vaughan, Diane. 1986. *Uncoupling: Turning Points in Intimate Relationships*. New York: Oxford University Press.

Waite, Linda J. 1995. "Does Marriage Matter?" *Demography* 32: 483–507.

Waite, Linda J., and Maggie Gallagher. 2000. *The Case for Marriage: Why Married People Are Happier, Healthier, and Better Off Financially*. New York: Doubleday.

Warr, Mark. 1993. "Age, Peers, and Delinquency." *Criminology* 31: 17–40.

——— 1998. "Life-Course Transitions and Desistance from Crime." *Criminology* 36: 183–216.

——— 2002. *Companions in Crime: The Social Aspects of Criminal Conduct*. Cambridge: Cambridge University Press.

Weisburd, David, and Elin Waring. 2001. *White-Collar Crime and Criminal Careers*. Cambridge: Cambridge University Press.

Weitekamp, Elmar G. M., and Hans-Jurgen Kerner. 1994. "Epilogue: Workshop and Plenary Discussions, and Future Directions." Pp. 439–449 in *Cross-National Longitudinal Research on Human Development and Criminal Behavior,* ed. Elmar G. M. Weitekamp and Hans-Jurgen Kerner. Dordrecht: Kluwer Academic Publishers.

Western, Bruce. 2002. "The Impact of Incarceration on Wage Mobility and Inequality." *American Sociological Review* 67: 526–546.

Western, Bruce, and Katherine Beckett. 1999. "How Unregulated Is the U.S. Labor Market? The Penal System as a Labor Market Institution." *American Journal of Sociology* 104: 1030–60.

White, Harrison C. 1970. *Chains of Opportunity: System Models of Mobility in Organizations*. Cambridge, Mass.: Harvard University Press.

White, Jennifer L., Terrie E. Moffitt, Felton Earls, Lee N. Robins, Phil A. Silva. 1990. "How Early Can We Tell? Predictors of Childhood Conduct Disorder and Adolescent Delinquency." *Criminology* 28: 507–533.

Whyte, William Foote. 1993. *Street Corner Society: The Social Structure of an Italian Slum*. 4th ed. Chicago: University of Chicago Press.

Widom, Cathy Spatz. 1989. "Child Abuse, Neglect, and Violent Criminal Behavior." *Criminology* 27: 251–271.

Willis, Paul E. 1977. *Learning to Labour: How Working Class Kids Get Working Class Jobs*. Farnborough, England: Saxon House.

Wilson, James Q. 1975. *Thinking about Crime*. New York: Basic Books.

——— 2002. *The Marriage Problem: How Our Culture Has Weakened Families.* New York: Harper Collins.

Wilson, James Q., and Richard J. Herrnstein. 1985. *Crime and Human Nature.* New York: Simon and Schuster.

Wilson, William Julius. 1987. *The Truly Disadvantaged: The Inner City, the Underclass, and Public Policy.* Chicago: University of Chicago Press.

——— 1996. *When Work Disappears: The World of the New Urban Poor.* New York: Alfred A. Knopf.

Wines, Frederick Howard. 1919. *Punishment and Reformation: A Study of the Penitentiary System.* New ed., rev. and enl. by Winthrop D. Lane. New York: Thomas Y. Crowell Company.

Wolfgang, Marvin, Robert Figlio, and Thorsten Sellin. 1972. *Delinquency in a Birth Cohort.* Chicago: University of Chicago Press.

Wolfgang, Marvin E., Terence P. Thornberry, and Robert Figlio, eds. 1987. *From Boy to Man, from Delinquency to Crime.* Chicago: University of Chicago Press.

Wright, Richard T., and Scott H. Decker. 1994. *Burglars on the Job: Streetlife and Residential Break-ins.* Boston: Northeastern University Press.

——— 1997. *Armed Robbers in Action: Stickups and Street Culture.* Boston: Northeastern University Press.

# INDEX

Abbott, A., 39, 282
Adolescence-limited offenders, 7, 29–30
Adolescent competence, 305n1
Age: age-crime debate, 16–17, 19–20, 81, 82; relationship to crime, 82, 85–91, 104–107, 110, 256–258, 259, 262, 266, 267–270, 272, 312n11
Age-graded theory. *See* Informal social control
Aging: accounts of desistance, 26–28; decision calculus, 28, 31, 190–191, 228–229; theory of informal social control, 39, 145, 272, 293
Akers, R., 32
Alcohol abuse: persistent offending, 56, 166–167, 171, 186–188, 284; zigzag offending, 205–209, 220–221, 232, 238–240, 241–243; relationship to predatory crime, 263, 270–271
Alcoholics Anonymous, 139, 140, 142, 187–188, 239, 242–243, 309n4
Ambivalence, 147, 190
Asymmetrical causation, 18
Attraction of crime, 38, 54, 164–165, 182

Becker, H., 147, 149, 196, 278–279, 281
Beckett, K., 51
Between-individual change, 252–253; marriage, 259–262, 266–267; childhood predictors, 262, 263, 271, 273; military ser-

vice, 262, 266–267; employment, 262, 266–267; by crime type, 262–266, 267–271; alcohol/drugs, 263, 270–271. *See also* Within-individual change
Black, D., 55
Blumstein, A., 16, 82
Booth, A., 45
Bordua, D., 165, 289
Bryk, A., 253–254, 311n5
Butterfield, F., 165

Caspi, A., 145
Cernkovich, S., 149, 279, 299n4
Childhood risk: risk factors, 4; measure, 92–94; trajectories of crime, 94–96, 98–100, 101–103, 107–110, 111–112; interaction with family risk, 97–98; between-individual change, 262, 263, 271, 273
Child sexual abuse, 213–216
Chronic juvenile offending: measure, 96–97; relationship to crime, 96–97, 107–110
Chronic offenders. *See* High-rate offenders
Clarke, R., 30–31
Class and ethnic conflict, 185–186, 219, 244
Clausen, J., 67, 282
Cline, H., 15, 16–17
Cognitive transformation, 28, 29, 278–279, 299n4

Cold Case Squad, Boston Police. *See* Follow-up study methodology
Cornish, D., 30–31
Crime: definition of, 18; perceptions of, 56, 58–59, 213, 216, 243, 249
*Crime in the Making,* 5–8, 39, 46; revisions of, 9, 35, 40–41, 53–57. *See also Unraveling Juvenile Delinquency*
Criminal careers: long-term studies of, 14–17, 83–84; limitations of current research, 17, 81; predictors of desistance, 17–18; conceptualization of, 36–37; policy implications, 84–85; critique of, 110–113. *See also* Age; Developmental criminology
Criminal propensity, 23
Criminal records search. *See* Follow-up study methodology
Criminal sanctions. *See* Incarceration; Reform school
Cullen, F., 45
Cumulative continuity, 51. *See also* Cumulative disadvantage
Cumulative disadvantage, 291. *See also* Cumulative continuity
Cusson, M., 31

Dannefer, D., 28, 33, 34
Death records search. *See* Follow-up study methodology
Defiance of authority, 38, 54; persistent offending, 165–166, 182–186, 235–236; sense of injustice, 184–186, 219, 308n2; class and ethnic conflict, 185–186, 219, 244
Delinquent peers, 32–33, 38, 42, 135, 145–146, 156, 164
*Delinquents and Nondelinquents in Perspective.* See *Unraveling Juvenile Delinquency*
Denzin, N., 39
Desistance: predictors of, 17–18; measurement of, 19–21; compared with termination, 21–22; as a gradual process, 22, 41–42, 137–138, 225; theoretical frameworks of, 26–35; theory of informal social control, 37–41, 53–57, 276–282; human agency, 38, 54–55, 125, 141–143, 146, 280–282; historical context, 38, 56–57, 132, 143–144; situational context, 38–39, 55–56, 279–280; marriage,

41–44, 118–123, 134–138, 145–147, 148–149, 259–262, 263–266, 266–267, 270–271, 272–274; residential change, 43, 126, 135, 141; employment, 46–47, 129, 138–139, 145–147, 266–267, 270–271, 272, 273; military service, 48–51, 123–126, 127–128, 130, 131–134, 142, 145–146, 148–149, 266–267, 270–271, 272, 273; reform school, 51–53, 122–123, 125, 126–129, 129–131; as a general process, 94–98, 105–107, 110, 128–129, 148–149, 287–288; by injury or death, 139; Alcoholics Anonymous, 139–140, 142; mentors, 141; by default, 147, 278–279, 281; compared with drug and alcohol abstinence, 148; by crime type, 262–266, 267–271. *See also* Incarceration; Mortality
Desisters: selection, 115; criminal history, 115; social history, 118, 131, 134, 138. *See also* Life-history narratives; Trajectories of crime
Developmental accounts of desistance, 28–30; compared with life-course accounts, 33–34
Developmental criminology: typologies, 82–85; critique of, 110–113; implications for, 285–289. *See also* Developmental accounts of desistance; Typologies
Developmental taxonomies. *See* Typologies
Deviance, 18
Differential association theory. *See* Delinquent peers; Social learning accounts of desistance
Domestic violence, 180, 212–213, 236, 243
Drugs, 57, 284. *See also* Alcohol abuse

Elder, G., 33, 50
Emirbayer, M., 54, 146
Employment: theory of informal social control, 46–47; persistent offending, 46–47, 51, 159, 174; desistance, 46–47, 129, 138–139, 145–147, 262, 266–267, 270–271, 272, 273; routine activities, 47, 138; identity transformation, 47, 138, 139; selection effect, 47–48; zigzag offending, 223, 225

Family risk: risk factors, 97; measure, 98; interaction with childhood risk, 98; relationship to crime, 98–100, 103, 107–110

Farrington, D., 15–16, 18, 84–85, 148, 288
FBI rap sheets. *See* Follow-up study methodology
Figlio, R., 15, 16, 83–84
Firearms. *See* Guns
Follow-up study methodology, 9–10; goals and obstacles, 61–63; criminal records search, 63–65; death records search, 65–66; classification trajectories, 66–67; life-history interviews, 66–70, 115; locating and selecting subjects for interviews, 70–75, 79–80. *See also* Life-history narratives; *Unraveling Juvenile Delinquency*
Formal social control. *See* Incarceration; Reform school
Foucault, M., 279, 280

Gallagher, M., 44, 284
Gans, H., 146, 308n2
Geller, R., 289–290
Generativity, 126, 144, 192
Gibbons, D., 83, 287, 288
G.I. Bill. *See* Military service
Giordano, P., 149, 279, 299n4
Glaser, D., 36, 38
Glueck, S., and Glueck, E., 5, 8, 14, 26–27, 61–62, 75–79, 83, 113
Goodman, P., 47
Gottfredson, M., 16, 21, 23, 27–28, 44, 81, 85, 112, 248, 255, 297n2
Gove, W., 29
Groups. *See* Developmental accounts of desistance; Developmental criminology; Typologies
Guns, 163, 180–181, 192, 233–234, 306n2, 309n6

Heimer, K., 195, 299n4
Herrnstein, R., 297n2
Heterotypic continuity, 302n4
Hierarchical linear modeling, 253–256; reliability of measures, 311nn5,6
High-rate offenders, 18, 83–85. *See also* Criminal careers; Life-course-persistent offenders
Hirschi, T., 16, 21, 23, 27–28, 44, 81, 85, 112, 248, 255, 287, 297n2, 300n6
Historical context, 38, 56–57, 59, 132, 143–145, 192, 238–239, 282–285, 306n2, 309n6
Horney, J., 42, 44, 263

Human agency: theory of informal social control, 38, 54–55, 58, 280–282, 293; desistance, 125, 141–143, 146; persistent offending, 162–164, 179–182, 195; zig-zag offending, 221–222, 225–226, 227–228
Human subjects review board, 62, 74. *See also* Follow-up methodology

Identity transformation, 146, 147, 149, 299n1; marriage, 43, 135; employment, 47, 138, 139; military service, 50
Incarceration: cumulative disadvantage, 51, 291; theory of informal social control, 51–53; trajectories of, 101–102, relationship to desistance measurement, 101–103, 111; persistent offending, 167–169, 188–190; acts of violence, 188–190; desistance, 190–191; offender reentry, 290–292. *See also* Reform school
Informal social control: age-graded theory of, 35, 37–41, 53–57, 279–280, 292–293; marriage, 41–44; employment, 46–47; military service, 50. See also *Crime in the Making*
Institutional dependency, 169, 190, 308n14
Intermittency: alcohol abuse, 205–209, 220–221, 232, 239–240, 241–243; perceptions of violence, 213, 216, 243, 249; reform school, 218–219, 229, 230–232, 237, 245; turning points, 219–220, 224–225, 230, 249; human agency, 221–222, 225–226, 227–228; marriage, 223, 224–225, 226–228, 245–246; employment, 223, 225; military service, 229, 245; local culture, 232, 237, 238, 240; situational context, 232–234; historical context, 238–239. *See also* Intermittent offenders; Late desisters; Late onset of violence offenders
Intermittent offenders: selection, 196–198; social histories, 198, 239; criminal histories, 198, 242. *See also* Intermittency; Life-history narratives; Trajectories of crime
IQ, 92, 262, 263, 271

Job stability. *See* Employment
Johnson, D., 45
Justice system. *See* Incarceration; Reform school

Katz, J., 54, 165, 182
Kempf-Leonard, K., 15, 282
Kenaszchuk, C., 135, 305n3
Knifing-off phenomenon, 49–50, 145, 148
Kohli, M., 54

Land, K., 103–104, 289
LaRosa, J., 28
Late desisters: selection, 196–198; criminal histories, 198; social histories, 198. *See also* Intermittency; Life-history narratives; Trajectories of crime
Latent class models. *See* Semiparametric group-based approach
Late onset of violence offenders: selection, 196–198; criminal histories, 198, 209, 211; social histories, 198, 205, 209, 220. *See also* Intermittency; Life-history narratives; Trajectories of crime
Legal cynicism, 184–186, 219. *See also* Defiance of authority
Legitimacy, 53
Leibrich, J., 31
Lewontin, R., 33, 34, 277, 285–286, 287
Life-course-persistent offenders, 7, 29–30, 84; identifying, 91–110, 110–113, 193–194. *See also* Typologies
Life-course theory: overview, 5–6, 33; compared with developmental theory, 33–34; accounts of desistance, 33–35
Life-history calendar, 67–69, 251–252
Life-history method. *See* Follow-up study methodology
Life-history narratives, 9–10; rationale for, 57–59, 277–278; strategy and background, 66–70, 115. *See also* Desisters; Intermittent offenders; Late desisters; Late onset of violence offenders; Persistent offenders
Loeber, R., 7, 84–85, 288, 302n1
Lyman School for Boys. *See* Reform school

Marital attachment. *See* Marriage
Marriage: theory of informal social control, 41–46; delinquent peers, 42, 135, 146; routine activities, 42–43, 135; identity transformation, 43, 135; selection effect, 44–46; gender, 45–46, 284, 299n2; desistance, 118–123, 134–138, 145–147, 148–149, 259–262, 263–266, 266–267, 270–271, 272–274, 283–284; persistent offending, 159, 174, 177, 178–179; zig-

zag offending, 223, 224–225, 226–228, 245–246; health, 284
Marshall, I., 42
Maruna, S., 19, 29, 40, 149, 279, 298n3, 299n1
Matsueda, R., 195, 299n4
Mattick, H., 49
Maturation. *See* Aging
Matza, D., 36, 54, 145, 164, 179, 184–185, 280, 292
McCord, J., 14–15
Mentors, 141
Methodology. *See* Follow-up methodology
Military service: theory of informal social control, 48–51; routine activities, 50; identity transformation, 50; G.I. Bill, 50, 57, 127–128, 133–134; consequences of combat, 50–51, 229, 241; desistance, 120, 123–126, 127–128, 130, 131–134, 142, 145–146, 148–149, 262, 266–267, 270–271, 272, 273; similarity to reform school, 125, 130–131; persistent offending, 160, 174, 178; fraudulent enlistment, 173; zigzag offending, 229, 245. *See also* Knifing-off phenomenon
Miller, J., 52–53
Modell, J., 7–8, 57
Moffitt, T., 7, 29–30, 81, 84, 85, 97–98, 111, 113, 145, 193–194, 285–286, 302n4
Moral beliefs, 31
Mortality, 20, 100–101, 111, 303n6. *See also* Follow-up study methodology
Mulvey, E., 28

Nagin, D., 7, 24–25, 41–42, 44, 81, 103–104, 289, 298n3
National Death Index. *See* Follow-up study methodology

Offender reentry. *See* Incarceration
Offenders. *See* Adolescence-limited offenders; Desisters; Intermittent offenders; Late desisters; Late onset of violence offenders; Life-course-persistent offenders; Persistent offenders
Official criminal records, 63–65; limitations of, 65, 216, 247–248, 307n8. *See also* Follow-up study methodology
Ontogenetic accounts of desistance. *See* Aging; Developmental accounts of desistance

Organized crime, 181, 237–238, 243
Osgood, W., 42

Parenthood, 43, 135, 228–229, 283. *See also* Marriage
Paternoster, R., 24–25, 31, 41–42, 81, 112
Patterson, G., 7
Pattillo-McCoy, M., 238
Peers. *See* Delinquent peers
Persistent offenders: selection, 150–151; criminal history, 150–151, 173, 179; social history, 150–151, 173; lifestyles of, 172–174; eventual desistance, 176–179. *See also* Life-history narratives; Trajectories of crime
Persistent offending: measurement of, 18–19; explanations of, 24–25; theory of informal social control, 37–57, 193–195; attraction of crime, 38, 54, 164–165, 182; defiance of authority, 38, 54, 165–166, 182–186; employment, 51, 159, 174; cumulative disadvantage, 51, 291; reform school/prison, 51–53, 160, 167–169, 174, 178, 188–190; human agency, 54–55, 162–164, 179–182, 195; situational context, 55–56; alcohol abuse, 56, 166–167, 171, 186–188, 284; historical context, 56–57, 192; marriage, 159, 174, 177, 178–179; military service, 160, 174, 178; lack of positive turning points, 160–161, 174–176; long-term consequences of, 169–172, 190–191; redemption, 171–172, 192; fear of punishment, 181–182, 191
Person-based approach. *See* Life-history narratives
Pinsonneault, P., 31
Piquero, A., 101
Population heterogeneity, 24–25, 33–35, 277–278
Prediction, 289–290. *See also* Risk-factor paradigm
Prison. *See* Incarceration
Propensity. *See* Criminal propensity

Racism, 217–218. *See also* Class and ethnic conflict
Rational choice accounts of desistance, 30–32
Raudenbush, S., 253–254, 311n5
Reform school: desistance, 51–53, 122–123, 125, 126–129, 129–131; description, 52; abuse, 52–53, 130–131, 189–190, 218, 230–231; similarity to military service, 125, 130–131; persistent offending, 160, 174, 178, 189–190; zigzag offending, 218–219, 229, 230–232, 237, 245
Reiss, A., 20, 100
Religion, 139, 246
Residential change, 43, 126, 135, 141
Risk-factor paradigm, 84–85, 111, 288, 289–290
Risk factors. *See* Childhood risk; Family risk
Robins, L., 15, 16
Routine activities: theory of informal social control, 38–39, 55–56; marriage, 42–43, 135; employment, 47, 138; military service, 50. *See also* Situational context
Rudolph, J., 149, 279, 299n4
Rutter, M., 17–18, 40, 284

Sample description. *See* Age; Follow-up methodology
Sellin, T., 15, 16, 83–84
Semiparametric group-based approach, 7, 103–104, 112–113, 303nn7,8, 304n12
Shame, 31
Sherman, L., 165
Shirley Industrial School for Boys. *See* Reform school
Shover, N., 28, 31, 42–43, 46, 58, 59, 167
Situated choice. *See* Human agency
Situational context, 38, 55–56, 58, 232–235, 279–280. *See also* Routine activities
Social capital. *See* Informal social control
Social control theory, critique of, 292–293
Social learning accounts of desistance, 32–33
Social support. *See* Informal social control
Specialization, 37, 179, 288
Spontaneous remission, 20, 27
State dependence, 24–25, 33–35, 277–278
Subjective contingencies, 28–29, 146, 281
Superpredators. *See* High-rate offenders
Sykes, G., 164, 167, 184–185, 189, 308n14
Symbolic interactionist perspective, 195, 299n4

Techniques of neutralization, 164, 184–185, 190
Termination of offending. *See* Desistance

Thornberry, T., 15
Timing of life events, 125–126, 176, 225
Tracing and finding subjects. *See* Follow-up study methodology
Tracy, P., 15, 282
Trajectories of crime, 4, 9; classification of the sample, 66–67; by childhood risk, 94–96, 98–100, 101–103; by chronic juvenile offending, 96–97; by family risk, 98–100, 103; latent class analysis, 104–107. *See also* Age; Follow-up study methodology
Turning points: definitions of, 39–41, 58; residential change, 43, 126, 135, 141; Alcoholics Anonymous, 139–140, 142, 239; mentors, 141; lack of positive, 160–161, 174–176, 219–220; among desisting persistent offenders, 176–179; structural determinism of, 278, 282. *See also* Employment; Incarceration; Informal social control; Marriage; Military service
Typologies: history and background, 82–85; policy implications, 84–85, 113, 288; test of, 91–110; critique of, 110–113, 197, 247–249, 287–289

Uggen, C., 48
Umberson, D., 43
Unemployment. *See* Employment

Unofficial delinquency, 262, 271, 305n1
*Unraveling Juvenile Delinquency,* 5, 8, 14, 52, 61–62, 75–79, 82, 113

Vaillant, G., 47, 137, 148, 167, 241, 276, 303n6
Vaughan, D., 22

Waite, L., 44, 284, 300n3
Warr, M., 32–33, 38
Western, B., 51, 291
White, J., 290
Willis, P., 165
Wilson, J. Q., 292, 297n2
Wilson, W. J., 47
Within-individual change, 251–252, 256–257; age, 259, 262, 266, 267–270, 272, 312n11; marriage, 259–262, 263–266, 266–267, 270–271, 272–274; by crime type, 262–266, 267–271; alcohol/drugs, 263, 270–271; employment, 266–267, 270–271, 272, 273; military service, 266–267, 270–271, 272, 273. *See also* Between-individual change
Wolfgang, M., 15, 16, 83–84
Work. *See* Employment

Zigzag criminal careers. *See* Intermittency